# THE CAMBRIDGE COMPANION TO SHAKESPEARE AND WAR

Written by a team of leading international scholars, *The Cambridge Companion to Shakespeare and War* illuminates the ways Shakespeare's works provide a rich and imaginative resource for thinking about the topic of war. Contributors explore the multiplicity of conflicting perspectives his dramas offer: war depicted from chivalric, masculine, nationalistic, and imperial perspectives; war depicted as a source of great excitement and as a theater of honor; war depicted from realistic or skeptical perspectives that expose the butchery, suffering, illness, famine, degradation, and havoc it causes. The essays in this volume examine the representations and rhetoric of war throughout Shakespeare's plays, as well as the modern history of the war plays on stage, in film, and in propaganda. This book offers fresh perspectives on Shakespeare's multifaceted representations of the complexities of early modern warfare, while at the same time illuminating why his perspectives on war and its consequences continue to matter now and in the future.

DAVID LOEWENSTEIN is Edwin Erle Sparks Professor of English and the Humanities at the Pennsylvania State University – University Park. His publications include *Milton and the Drama of History: Historical Vision, Iconoclasm, and the Literary Imagination* (1990); *Representing Revolution in Milton and His Contemporaries: Religion, Politics, and Polemics in Radical Puritanism* (2001; winner of the James Holly Hanford Award for Distinguished Book); *The Cambridge History of Early Modern English Literature* (2002; coeditor); *The Complete Works of Gerrard Winstanley* (2009; coeditor); *Treacherous Faith: The Specter of Heresy in Early Modern English Literature and Culture* (2013); and *Shakespeare and Early Modern Religion* (2015; coedited with Michael Witmore). He is an honored scholar of the Milton Society of America and the recipient of a Guggenheim Fellowship.

PAUL STEVENS is Professor and former Canada Research Chair in Early Modern Literature and Culture at the University of Toronto. A Fellow of the Royal Society of Canada, his publications include *Imagination and the Presence of Shakespeare in Paradise Lost* (1985); *Discontinuities: New Essays on Renaissance Literature and Criticism* (1998; coedited with Viviana Comensoli); and *Early Modern Nationalism and Milton's England* (2008; coedited with David Loewenstein), which won the 2009 Irene Samuel Memorial Prize. He has twice won the James Holly Hanford Award for Most Distinguished Essay. A former visiting fellow at All Souls College, Oxford, he has served as President of the Milton Society of America and is the recipient of a Guggenheim Fellowship.

T0373881

# THE CAMBRIDGE
# COMPANION TO
# SHAKESPEARE
# AND WAR

EDITED BY
## DAVID LOEWENSTEIN
*Pennsylvania State University, University Park*

## PAUL STEVENS
*University of Toronto*

CAMBRIDGE
UNIVERSITY PRESS

# CAMBRIDGE
## UNIVERSITY PRESS

University Printing House, Cambridge CB2 8BS, United Kingdom

One Liberty Plaza, 20th Floor, New York, NY 10006, USA

477 Williamstown Road, Port Melbourne, VIC 3207, Australia

314–321, 3rd Floor, Plot 3, Splendor Forum, Jasola District Centre,
New Delhi – 110025, India

103 Penang Road, #05–06/07, Visioncrest Commercial, Singapore 238467

Cambridge University Press is part of the University of Cambridge.

It furthers the University's mission by disseminating knowledge in the pursuit of
education, learning, and research at the highest international levels of excellence.

www.cambridge.org
Information on this title: www.cambridge.org/9781316510971
DOI: 10.1017/9781316998106

First published 2021

Printed in the United Kingdom by TJ Books Limited, Padstow Cornwall

A catalogue record for this publication is available from the British Library.

*Library of Congress Cataloging-in-Publication Data*
NAMES: Stevens, Paul, 1946– editor. | Loewenstein, David, editor.
TITLE: The Cambridge companion to Shakespeare and war / edited by David Loewenstein,
Paul Stevens.
DESCRIPTION: Cambridge ; New York, NY : Cambridge University Press, 2021. |
Includes bibliographical references and index.
IDENTIFIERS: LCCN 2021006964 (print) | LCCN 2021006965 (ebook) | ISBN 9781316510971
(hardback) | ISBN 9781108464963 (paperback) | ISBN 9781316998106 (epub)
SUBJECTS: LCSH: Shakespeare, William, 1564-1616–Criticism and interpretation. |
War in literature.
CLASSIFICATION: LCC PR3069.W37 C36 2021 (print) | LCC PR3069.W37 (ebook) |
DDC 822.3/3–dc23
LC record available at https://lccn.loc.gov/2021006964
LC ebook record available at https://lccn.loc.gov/2021006965

ISBN 978-1-316-51097-1 Hardback
ISBN 978-1-108-46496-3 Paperback

In memory of David Bevington

CONTENTS

CONTENTS

# FIGURES

# CONTRIBUTORS

CATHERINE M. S. ALEXANDER
Shakespeare Institute, University of Birmingham

DAVID BEVINGTON
The University of Chicago

PAUL E. J. HAMMER
University of Colorado, Boulder

MICHAEL HATTAWAY
NYU London

DAVID SCOTT KASTAN
Yale University

MAGGIE KILGOUR
McGill University

LYNNE MAGNUSSON
University of Toronto

WILLY MALEY
University of Glasgow

CLAIRE MCEACHERN
University of California, Los Angeles

GAIL KERN PASTER
Folger Shakespeare Library

FRANZISKA QUABECK
University of Münster

DAVID SCHALKWYK
Queen Mary University of London

GREG SEMENZA
University of Connecticut

PAUL STEVENS
University of Toronto

GARRETT A. SULLIVAN JR.
Pennsylvania State University-University Park

# PREFACE

The topic of *The Cambridge Companion to Shakespeare and War* could not be more timely. War remains a staple of our morning papers and nightly news. As many commentators have pointed out, the refusal of history to come to an end with the fall of the Soviet Union and war to disappear after all the suffering of the twentieth century has given Shakespeare's insight into the intractability of war renewed relevance. While the memory of two world wars, the Cold War, and the savagery of innumerable postcolonial wars from Vietnam to Afghanistan lives on, both the conventional and new asymmetrical wars of the last two decades have given Shakespeare's perspectives on war a new urgency. Such is Shakespeare's cultural authority that even as war has radically changed since his time, his representation of it continues to attract attention and stimulate intellectual reflection. The most remarkable feature of Shakespeare on war is not, however, any one overarching theory or moral lesson but the multiplicity of conflicting perspectives his dramas offer: war depicted from chivalric, masculine, nationalistic, and imperial perspectives; war depicted as an exciting sport in which to kill; war depicted as a theater of honor; war depicted from realistic or more skeptical perspectives that expose the butchery, suffering, illness, famine, degradation, and havoc it causes. For some, this indeterminacy and the possibilities it presents is a measure of Shakespeare's abiding value; for others, it is a cause for concern.

In his thoughtful review of Paola Pugliatti's *Shakespeare and the Just War Tradition* (*English Historical Review*, August 2012), the late C. S. L. Davies gives this last point some focus. He suggests the degree to which Shakespeare fails to provide any kind of coherent guide to the ethics of war even as he understood the phenomenon in his time: "I would argue that Shakespeare accepts war as an inescapable fact of life," says Davies, "on which he comments in various ways but does not try to push a particular line. He can point up the horrors of war, especially for non-participating civilians, or assert that peace is fatal to morality ... [he] can subscribe to or sneer at the cult of military honour, and in the case of Hotspur, do both at once" (977). He can make all kinds of fine moral and legal distinctions but his "seeing and not resolving different viewpoints," says Davies, "is ultimately unsettling." For example, we might note that satires on the "cormorant" nature of war like *Troilus and Cressida* often seem neutralized by the aestheticizing fantasies and sheer excitement of war conveyed in *Henry V* or *Coriolanus*. While in *Henry V*, the ethical worries and troubling questions raised by Williams often seem eclipsed by the spectacular triumphs of the English at Agincourt, in the much later play *Coriolanus*, the ancient hero's unrestrained ferocity is metamorphosed into something rich and strange, choreographed into a terrifying symmetry of violence: "from face to foot / He was a thing of blood whose every motion / Was timed with dying cries" (2.2.105–7). It is precisely this relativism or moral ambivalence that is at the heart of Tolstoy's disdain for Shakespeare in *What Is Art?* and, even more pointedly, in his 1906 *Critical Essay on Shakespeare* (New York: Funk & Wagnalls). Because Tolstoy feels that there is no overriding moral vision in Shakespeare, whether he is representing war or anything else, he considers the effect of Shakespeare's art baleful: the reader, says Tolstoy, "ceases to distinguish directly and clearly what is artistic from an artificial imitation of art" (123). But, above all, having assimilated Shakespeare's amoral view of life, the reader "loses the capacity of distinguishing good from evil." The power of Shakespeare's irrepressible indeterminacy, exacerbated by the almost limitless possibilities of theatrical performance, is such, so Tolstoy feels, that we lose our moral compass.

The obvious response to this sense of confusion, we might argue, is that Shakespeare's works are not "Drama" as Tolstoy idealizes it but popular plays written for the commercial theater, often occasional and discrete, dramas necessarily oppositional, conflicted, and multivoiced. Indeed, one of the many reasons why Shakespeare continues to matter is that he offers such a remarkably rich and varied resource through which to comprehend the phenomenon of war. But we might also argue that there is something of great constancy or coherence in the plays' enduring struggle to bring the phenomenon of war within the remit of human understanding. Because war seems like "an inescapable fact of life" doesn't mean that it cannot be interrogated, essayed, represented, and re-presented. In Shakespeare's open-ended, Montaigne-like curiosity, and specifically in his struggle to understand war, it is difficult not to feel the intellectual force of early modern Europe's *studia humanitatis*, both in that movement's relentless drive for human agency and in the concomitant skepticism it produces. What we aim to do in this volume, then, is give our readers a comprehensive, if not uncritical, overview of Shakespeare's struggle to understand and represent war in all its multifaceted dimensions – but also in all its assurance and self-reflective skepticism.

Our overview embraces all of Shakespeare's plays but most importantly the fifteen or so centrally concerned with war and politics and the four great tragedies. We focus first on two critically important historical contexts. While Paul Hammer (Chapter 1) describes how the impact of England's response to the sixteenth-century revolution in European warfare influences Shakespeare's morally ambiguous portrayal of war, Franziska Quabeck (Chapter 2) shows how the playwright both accepts the premises and imaginatively complicates the parameters of traditional just war theory. In Chapters 3 and 4, we turn to the types of war Shakespeare represents. While the late David Bevington (Chapter 3) focuses on the significant presence of civil and dynastic conflict and war in Shakespeare's plays, Claire McEachern (Chapter 4) shows how plays representing foreign wars – "foreign quarrels" (2 *Henry IV*, 4.3.343) routinely associated with the emerging nation-state – are closely interconnected with the English history play and its representations of civil discord. We then look at Shakespeare's creative reworking of his sources with Maggie Kilgour (Chapter 5) analyzing his indebtedness to the classical world of war and David Kastan (Chapter 6) his critical reading of the record of warfare in Holinshed's English *Chronicles*. Chapters 7 and 8 examine gender issues in relation to war. Gail Paster examines masculinity, specifically the significance of Shakespeare instrumentalizing martial anger, and David Schalkwyk contemplates more generally the sexuality of war, specifically the complex relationship between *eros* and violence (a topic likewise examined in Kilgour's chapter [Chapter 5]). In Chapters 9–12, contributors consider the language and mediums of representation, with Lynne Magnusson (Chapter 9) discussing Shakespeare's war rhetoric, "words of war," and diplomacy in the plays, Michael Hattaway (Chapter 10) examining the modern history of staging the war plays, and Gregory Semenza (Chapter 11) writing about the ingenuity deployed in filming Shakespeare's battle scenes and the fresh perspectives generated by representing them in film. This group closes with Garrett Sullivan (Chapter 12) analyzing the propaganda uses of Shakespeare in World War II Britain, most importantly how they are inflected through cinema as well as such neglected media as radio. Chapters 13–15 offer three detailed readings of specific plays about war. While Paul Stevens (Chapter 13) analyzes religion and aestheticizing pleasures of political theology in *Henry V*, Willy Maley (Chapter 14) explicates the relationship between *Macbeth* and post–traumatic stress disorder both in Shakespeare's time and our own. The final chapter by Catherine Alexander (Chapter 15) offers *Coriolanus* as complex anatomy of war, seeking to understand why the play resonates so much in the present.

We hope that this book will illuminate Shakespeare's multifaceted representations of the complexities and dynamics of early modern warfare, while at the same time illuminating why his perspectives on war and its consequences continue to matter now and in the future.

# ACKNOWLEDGMENTS

We are deeply grateful to Sarah Stanton and Emily Hockley, our editors at Cambridge University Press, for all of their valuable advice as this project has developed. Sarah Stanton warmly encouraged the project from its inception by recognizing that the topic of Shakespeare and war was a timely one for a *Cambridge Companion to Shakespeare*. Emily Hockley has helped us in numerous ways, including in our efforts to shape this volume so that it appeals to a broad readership. At the University of Toronto, Julia Boyd has served as an exemplary research assistant as we prepared the final manuscript for press. She prepared the index with the help of Lauren Cenci at Penn State-University Park. Mattison Schuknecht has helped to make sure all quotations from Shakespeare's works cited in the book are consistent with the third edition of *The Norton Shakespeare*, general editor Stephen Greenblatt (New York and London: W. W. Norton, 2016).

As we were working on the final stages of this volume, we lost one of its most distinguished contributors and one of the world's leading Shakespeareans: David Bevington. Besides being a great scholar and critic, he was a most generous colleague; as Ben Jonson said of Shakespeare, we might say of David Bevington: "He was, indeed, honest, and of an open and free nature." Although we are deeply saddened by his loss, we are also very grateful to have his contribution on civil and dynastic wars in Shakespeare. This volume is dedicated to his memory.

# I

PAUL E. J. HAMMER

# Beyond Shallow and Silence

## War in the Age of Shakespeare

In *2 Henry IV*, Shakespeare famously satirizes the recruitment of soldiers for war in a scene involving Justices Shallow and Silence. These two gentlemen, supposedly justices of the peace (JPs) in Gloucestershire, have summoned a handful of local men for military service selection by Sir John Falstaff and his corporal, Bardolph: Ralph Moldy, Simon Shadow, Thomas Wart, Francis Feeble, and Peter Bullcalf. As the names suggest, this is a richly comedic scene. The garrulous Justice Robert Shallow – unchallenged by his kinsman, the aptly named Justice Silence – cannot even count beyond the number of fingers on one hand. Instead of the "half a dozen sufficient men" requested by Falstaff (3.2.87), Shallow and Silence have mustered only five men for the selection. Nevertheless, Shallow insists "here is two more called than your number" (3.2.170) and repeatedly states that Falstaff can reject two men and still meet the quota of four recruits. When Falstaff and Bardolph accept bribes from Moldy and Bullcalf to release them, the levy ultimately produces only three men for the army – and patently the least physically impressive specimens. Falstaff's bombastic justification for his choices only seems to confirm the incompetence and unfairness of the process. When Falstaff finally assures Justice Shallow that "these fellows will do well" (3.2.258), the comedy of the scene suggests the exact opposite is true.

Although supposedly portraying the raising of soldiers to fight for Henry IV against domestic rebels in 1405, the recruitment scene in *2 Henry IV* reflects the practices of Shakespeare's own day, not those of Lancastrian England. Scholars have long recognized this fact, and the comic bumbling of Justices Shallow and Silence has frequently been cited to characterize the military capacity of Elizabethan England as equally amateurish and corrupt. There is a grain of truth in this view. Historical parallels can be found for all of the comedic features of Falstaff's perverse recruitment process, including incompetent local officials, bribery for exemption from service, and unfortunate misfits being forced off to war. Shakespeare's contemporaries also apparently recognized the realities that inspired the scene and enjoyed the

I

joke. Writing at the start of James I's reign in England, Sir Charles Percy teased a correspondent that an extended spell of "contrie businesse" in Gloucestershire would make him "so dull that I shall bee taken for Justice Silence or Justice Shallow." Percy asked his friend to send him reports of news from London. Such reports "will not exempt mee from the opinion of a Justice Shallow at London, yet I will assure you thee [they] will make mee passe for a very sufficient gentleman in Gloceshshire."[1]

Despite the farcical proceedings portrayed through Justices Shallow and Silence, war became an increasingly real and intrusive presence in the lives of Shakespeare and his contemporaries. Directly or indirectly, fighting or pre-paring for war – and, above all, paying for these things – touched the lives of virtually everyone in Elizabethan England and Wales on a regular basis. Over the course of Elizabeth I's long reign, the nature of war itself also changed, reflecting broader changes in military technology, battlefield tactics, and bureaucratic and financial developments. Together, these changes drove a "renaissance" or "revolution" in European war-fighting during the sixteenth century and set the scene for further escalation in the seventeenth century.[2]

When Elizabeth I came to the throne in 1558, England's military capacity seemed alarmingly weak. Although Henry VIII had succeeded in wresting the port of Boulogne from France (at terrible cost) in 1544, Edward VI's government signed it away in the wake of Protector Somerset's disastrous attempt to occupy parts of Scotland, which left England militarily and financially crippled. French troops were also now stationed on its northern land border. In 1557, Mary I's desperation to salvage her marriage to Philip of Spain thrust England into a new war with France. English troops figured prominently in the great French defeat at St. Quentin, but only a few months later French forces captured Calais, eliminating England's last-remaining prize from the Hundred Years' War. Mary's government proved humiliat-ingly unable to defend or recover the town. The loss of Calais on New Year's Day, 1558 not only demoralized England but transformed its strategic outlook. For more than 200 years, Calais and its surrounding fortresses had served as both the front line of defense against France and a key base for attacking it. Now England had lost its last Continental toehold. Henceforth, the front line would be the Channel or, worse, the harbors and beaches of England itself.[3]

Elizabeth's England joined the general peace embodied in the 1559 Treaty of Cambrai but that peace seemed alarmingly tenuous. France remained hostile, serious tensions soon arose with Spain, and Elizabeth's reinstatement of Protestantism in her realm opened the way for new threats fueled by religious zeal. Elizabeth and her advisers frantically sought to rebuild

England's shattered military power. Arms and armor were secretly imported from Germany and the Low Countries to restock the realm's empty arsenals, breaching an imperial ban on arms exports. Elizabeth also sought to support her coreligionists, but avoid open war, by providing aid to Scottish (and later to French and Dutch) Protestants in forms that offered her plausible deniability. Money was sent in the form of foreign coins. English officers supposedly went to join Protestant rebellions abroad merely on their own individual initiative, as did the growing numbers of volunteer soldiers who served under them. Elizabeth feigned an inability to prevent private gentlemen from raising such forces and leading them abroad, even though royal officials actively facilitated their movement. By the 1580s, the stream of English Protestant adventurers had swelled to become an army of several thousand volunteers fighting in the Low Countries. Elizabeth also provided logistical and financial support for French and Dutch Protestants within England itself. When Elizabeth launched an overt military intervention in Scotland in 1560, the costly failures of English troops at the siege of Leith made the venture a close-run thing. Ultimately, France withdrew its troops and Scotland underwent a Calvinist revolution. This opened the way for a new amity between England and Scotland, winding down centuries of bitter conflict. However, things might have ended very differently if France had not been distracted by its own religious strife at home. A subsequent official English occupation of the French port of Le Havre (Newhaven to the Elizabethans) in 1562–63 resulted in a crushing defeat. To make matters worse, the surviving English troops spread an outbreak of plague. Perhaps 20,000 died in London alone. After this humiliation, Elizabeth avoided official military action on the Continent until she was finally forced to cast aside all pretense in 1585.[4]

The Elizabethan rebuilding of England's military defenses stepped up dramatically in the 1570s. To counter the growing threat of Spain – and especially the powerful army that it established in Flanders in 1567 – England adopted what would today be called an "offset strategy" by investing heavily in rebuilding and expanding the queen's fleet of warships. Geoffrey Parker has called this "the *Dreadnought* revolution of Tudor England."[5] The queen's new (or rebuilt) warships reflected lessons learned by English privateers such as John Hawkins and Francis Drake, whose attacks on Spanish ships and settlements in the New World in the 1560s and 1570s did much to fuel the hostility of Spain. Beginning with the *Dreadnought* in 1573, English galleons were constructed to a "race-built" design that reduced top-weight, increased maneuverability, and, above all, allowed them to be armed with large batteries of heavy cannon. Unlike earlier warships, which carried a motley assortment of guns and were designed for grappling and boarding enemy vessels, the new English ships were intended to pound and sink their targets from a distance. These galleons were arguably the highest tech weapons of the day. By the 1580s, Elizabeth had the most powerful navy in Europe and her naval commanders (especially Drake) were increasingly confident in their ability to defeat any fleet mustered by Spain. Indeed, if the winds had blown the right way, the famous showdown against Spain's *Gran Armada* in 1588 would have been fought off the Spanish coast, not within sight of the cliffs of Dover.[6]

In the wake of its famous victory in 1588, England launched a succession of counter-armadas of its own against Spain. An expedition to Portugal in 1589, which almost rivaled Spain's force of the previous year in size, proved just as disastrous as its Spanish counterpart. More successful was a 1596 expedition that resulted in the brief occupation of the key Spanish port of Cádiz. The departure of such large fleets must have been as spectacular as the image conjured up by the Chorus at the start of act 3 of *Henry V*:

> Oh, do but think
> You stand upon the rivage and behold
> A city on th'inconstant billows dancing,
> For so appears this fleet majestical.   (3.0.13–16)

Nevertheless, despite the dramatic paintwork and bristling firepower of Elizabeth's warships, the limitations of sixteenth-century technology meant that naval operations were always vulnerable to storms and shipborne disease. During the years of open war against Spain after 1585, ambitious plans for English fleets to blockade the Spanish coast, intercept Spanish treasure fleets in the Azores, or seize key Spanish bases in the New World all consistently failed to deliver on the grand promises of the commanders who promoted them. Even the famous victory at Cádiz proved short-lived and provoked yet another failed Spanish attempt to invade England. Indeed, the resurgence of Spanish naval power in the 1590s meant that England endured new failed armadas in 1596 and 1597, as well as a costly false alarm (the "Invisible Armada") in 1599. Although Elizabeth relied upon her fleet as the realm's first line of defense, the queen ultimately became almost as frustrated as Philip of Spain with the results of costly long-range naval operations.[7] Royal officials, however, from the Lord Admiral down, continued to make a financial killing from the huge private industry of legalized piracy – privateering – which brought huge quantities of money and exotic goods into England.[8]

In contrast to its years of steady investment in the royal fleet, the efforts of Elizabeth's government to modernize the realm's land defenses, which also stepped up in the 1570s, proved slow, difficult, and incomplete. Armies in

Tudor England were traditionally constructed from the private retinues of aristocrats, bishops, and courtiers, or from the county militias. The only standing forces in England paid for by the crown itself were garrisons at some royal fortresses (the largest being at Berwick on the Scottish border), the royal guard, and the elite courtly band of Gentlemen Pensioners. Unlike royal warships, which the queen herself owned and maintained, the majority of land power was controlled by the gentlemen who governed the counties and the merchant councils that oversaw the realm's leading towns and cities. Modernizing such a plethora of land forces therefore depended upon inspiring or cajoling the local political elites into action and requiring them to spend their own money (and that of their neighbors and tenants) on equipping and supplying their militias – and to continue doing so, year after year. This was a monumental task which the Privy Council pursued on behalf of the queen over the course of several decades.

Older histories, taking their cue from the characters of Justices Shallow and Silence, tend to portray this effort in a rather negative light. Based upon such judgments, it has been suggested that England's militias would have had little chance of defeating a Spanish landing if an armada had succeeded in evading or defeating the English fleet.[9] However, recent studies have advanced a more positive assessment.[10] To be sure, the state of county militias was variable and the readiness of individual counties waxed and waned over time but the broader picture suggests remarkable improvements in England's ability to mobilize defensive land forces quickly and effectively by the late 1580s. This was an extraordinary, but underappreciated, administrative and political achievement. Yet, like the consistently heavy spending on the navy, the constant pressure on counties to train and equip their militias ultimately proved impossible to sustain once the war with Spain wound down after Elizabeth's death in 1603.[11] When England returned to war again under Charles I in the 1620s, his efforts were not only burdened with expectations inflated by nostalgic recollections of Elizabeth's reign but also crippled by two decades of underinvestment after the queen's death.

One of the prime drivers for modernizing the county militias was a desire to retire England's traditional infantry weapons, the longbow and the bill, and to replace them with the pike and the arquebus (called the caliver in England), and its heavier cousin, the musket. Although the longbow had been central to a tactical system that gave England remarkable military success since the early 1300s, it seemed increasingly outdated by Elizabeth's reign. This decline of the longbow in Shakespeare's time is evident in the recruitment scene in 2 *Henry IV*. Although any English army in 1405 would have contained many archers, the only mention of the longbow here is that "old Double," who "drew a good bow" and "shot a fine shot," is reported dead, even though Justice Shallow immediately forgets this fact (3.2.37–41). Pointedly, none of the potential recruits for Falstaff are bowmen. Critics have suggested that Shakespeare's conspicuous down-playing of the longbow in his plays – even in *Henry V*, which celebrates the victory at Agincourt, which was only won because of the longbow – may reflect a conscious rejection of the militarist nostalgia evoked in works such as Holinshed's *Chronicles*.[12]

Whether or not Shakespeare intended some kind of implied criticism of jingoist histories of England's glorious military past, the recruitment scene in 2 *Henry IV* can be seen as simply reflecting the military reality of Shakespeare's own time. When questioned by Shallow, Falstaff justifies his unimpressive selection of recruits by dismissing the need for tall and strong men: "Care I for the limb, the thews, the stature, bulk, and big assemblance of a man? ... Oh, give me the spare men, and spare me the great ones!" (3.2.233–43). According to Falstaff, what mattered was "spirit" and even men such as "ragged" Thomas Wart could "manage" a caliver – a weapon that did not exist in 1405 but was mandated for widespread use in Elizabeth's reign. While comically expressed, Falstaff's boasting about his expertise in choosing men for war touched upon histor-ical reality. In skilled hands, a Tudor warbow was a formidable weapon.[13] Justice Shallow claims that "old Double" had been able to hit a bullseye at 240 yards and could still hit a larger target 40 or 50 yards beyond that (3.2.42–45). Judging by the longbows and skeletons of archers recovered from Henry VIII's warship *Mary Rose*, which sank in 1545, such claims may not have been fanciful. Tudor warbows had an immense draw-weight and the physical strength needed to use them effectively is evident in the size and distinctive skeletal deformation of the archers' remains. Nevertheless, battlefield reports suggest that the longbow's military effect-iveness was patently declining by the 1540s. Despite shooting farther and much faster than any gun, the crucial weakness of the weapon was its utter dependence upon the health and long years of training of individual archers. Men who could shoot a great warbow were always in limited supply, even before the physical impact of an extended campaign took its toll. This meant that there was a hard limit to the number of bowmen England could muster and serious losses in their ranks could not easily be replaced. By contrast, raw recruits could rapidly be trained to use guns or pikes, dramatically expanding the pool of militarily useful manpower. Beginning in the sixteenth century, European armies therefore began to expand as mass-produced weapons were issued to mass-produced soldiers and the immediate limits on army size instead became money, logistics, and governmental administration.

Elizabeth's government soon recognized that reequipping all of England's county militias was impossible. Beginning in the early 1570s, the Privy Council therefore required counties to select a proportion of their men – supposedly the best men – and to equip only them with modern weapons. Crucially, these forces were expected to receive (relatively) regular training: initially, ten days a year, spread over three brief camps. The cost of the new weapons, the wages of the soldiers and their officers during training camps, and the gunpowder that was expended in target practice were to be borne by the county community itself. This smaller, modernized version of the county militias became known as the trained bands. Compelling the county communities to act on this plan and make their trained bands into militarily useful fighting forces was a slow and painful process, especially in inland counties such as Gloucestershire that seemed reassuringly distant from any immediate threat. Progress was driven by endless hectoring letters from the Council to local JPs and charted in a sea of paperwork, often returned by county officials in maddeningly variable and incomplete form. In 1577, for example, there were officially 9,821 able men in the county of Gloucestershire, of whom 2,485 were described as "hable men selected," but only 1,139 of them were "hable men furnished." Most of the latter were still armed with longbows and bills. A mere eighty-three men were described as equipped with calivers or handguns.[14] As Patricia Cahill has noted, the Elizabethan regime's remorseless gathering of detailed information on the military resources of the counties is evident even in the bumbling of Justices Shallow and Silence.[15] Shallow uses a muster roll ("Where's the roll?" he asks three times [3.2.90]) to check off the potential draftees by name. After Shadow, Wart, and Feeble were "pricked" for service, their names would also have been listed in a formal indenture that placed them under the authority of Falstaff as a legally deputed recruiting officer of the crown.

Muster rolls, and the numerical summaries based upon them that were certified to the Privy Council, show that most other counties (and especially the City of London) were far better equipped than backward Gloucestershire. Even so, serious progress in military preparedness was most evident after England finally entered into open war with Spain in 1585, when Elizabeth sent English troops to avert a Dutch defeat in the Low Countries. Experienced captains, many of whom had previously served as mercenaries in the Low Countries, were appointed to every county as muster-masters to oversee the preparation of the trained bands. Perhaps even more important was the appointment of lord lieutenants for each county. Typically a nobleman, the lord lieutenant was deputed to oversee all aspects of military administration for his county and to lead its combined trained bands in times of war. Many of the lord lieutenants appointed in 1585–86 were also members of the

Privy Council, which gave the Council a very direct connection to the military preparedness and internal security of key counties across the realm.[16] As reports of Spanish preparations for an invasion of England grew after 1586, the Council consistently stepped up the pressure on counties to strengthen their trained bands. The city of Gloucester, which was jurisdictionally distinct from the county, finally set up its own trained band in 1586, when 300 men were chosen and "dyverse tymes trained." In 1587, the city spent £37 on powder for training. In 1588, the city's expenditure on powder grew to a hefty £112.[17] During the same period, the county of Gloucestershire certified that 11,700 "hable men" remained outside the trained bands. The latter now comprised 3,000 men (actually 3,020), in 12-foot bands, with 1,140 men armed with calivers, 300 men armed with muskets, and 600 with pikes. However, 485 men were still armed with longbows and 495 with bills. There were also two horse companies, comprising 160 light horsemen (armed with swords and pistols) and forty heavy lancers.[18]

In many counties, the creation of the trained bands saw jockeying among local gentlemen – especially JPs of the sort represented by Shallow and Silence – to ensure that they would command men drawn from their own "country." The smaller forces and regular training raised the stakes for these gentlemen, who felt their local eminence required them to hold a captaincy in the trained bands. Since many gentlemen were inexperienced in war, and particularly in the deployment of guns and pikes, the late sixteenth and early seventeenth century saw a mini boom in military manuals aimed at gentleman officers.[19] The local politics of military command were further complicated by the Council's appointment of the muster-masters, many of whom were outsiders to the county community and were insistent that their own military expertise should be treated with deference by local gentlemen, even by those of more illustrious lineage. That the county was required to pay the hefty salary of these outsiders added salt to the wounded pride of many county elites. The Council was regularly forced to intervene and settle disputes.

Despite such problems, the system of trained bands proved surprisingly efficient in most counties during the great armada crisis of 1588 and in the 1590s. In Devon, training in the spring of 1598 was carefully spread over eighteen days at eleven different locations to minimize the time soldiers spent away from home. When the false alarm of the "Invisible Armada" occurred in August 1599, the county mobilized its trained bands ahead of schedule and held them ready for action even as the summer harvest remained ungathered. The cost was a massive £300 a day. By the time the false alarm was over, Devon had allegedly spent more than £10,000 from local funds – an eye-watering amount.[20] During the same false alarm, Cambridgeshire was able to have 500 foot soldiers and fifty cavalries on the road to London within two days of the Council's order for mobilization. The county authorities there also raised £620 to cover the cost of the effort.[21] Such examples show how quickly the trained bands could respond in a crisis. However, the very heavy costs associated with the training, equipment, and extended mobilizations of these forces also demonstrate how burdensome the system could be on the queen's subjects. It should be noted that the many collections of money for the trained bands and other local military expenses were in addition to the regular national taxes authorized by Parliament.

The creation of the trained bands in the 1570s also had major implications for the campaigns that England fought in Ireland and on the Continent in the final three decades of Elizabeth's reign. The manpower and equipment of the trained bands were explicitly reserved for home defense. This meant that troops for service overseas had to be raised by other means and from other sources of manpower. Although some men volunteered for military service abroad, the basic model of recruitment followed that shown with Shallow, Silence, and Falstaff in 2 *Henry IV*. When fresh troops were needed, the Privy Council allocated specific numbers to individual counties, where local JPs were responsible for mustering suitable men, from whom the required number would be conscripted ("pressed") by deputy lieutenants or other local officials. The men would be given uniforms and arms (although policy on the latter sometimes varied) and entrusted to a local gentleman or (more commonly) a captain nominated by the Council, who would "conduct" them to their designated port of embarkation. The county would subsequently be reimbursed at the Exchequer in Westminster for the cost of equipping and marching the men to their rendezvous according to a standard rate ("coat and conduct money"). For example, in June 1598, the Privy Council ordered the Earl of Pembroke, Lord President of Wales, to raise 1,200 men for service in Ireland. Pembroke, in turn, sent orders to his deputy lieutenants in each Welsh county, specifying the numbers they were required to meet. The target for Caernarvonshire was set at 100 men. On July 4, the deputy lieutenants there wrote to JPs in the county requiring that they "geve openn soomones and proclamacion" in "all churches, markettes and places of assemblie within your jurisdiction" for all men aged between sixteen and seventy to assemble at Caernarvon by 9 a.m. on July 12 "to bee vewed, mustered and sett forth for this her Majeste's service as apperteineth."[22] The JPs were also expected to raise money locally to pay for the levy. Indeed, between March 1599 and December 1602, Caernarvonshire received eleven separate demands for soldiers to serve in Ireland. In all, these levies involved dispatching 420 men out of the county and cost its inhabitants £1,607.[23] During the same period, the City of London was required to provide 2,675 men for Ireland, 4,800 men for the defense of Ostend, twelve ships, and two oared galleys, at a combined cost of at least £19,857.[24]

The comedic recruitment process dramatized in *2 Henry IV* was thus a procedure that would have been extremely familiar to Shakespeare and his audience. Indeed, Shakespeare had also alluded to the very same procedure in *1 Henry IV*, when Falstaff boasted to the audience that

> I have misused the King's press damnably. I have got in exchange of a hundred
> and fifty soldiers, three hundred and odd pounds. I press me none but good
> householders, yeoman's sons; inquire me out contracted bachelors, such as had
> been asked twice on the banns, such a commodity of warm slaves as had lief
> hear the devil as a drum, such as fear the report of a caliver worse than a struck
> fowl or a hurt wild duck.... And such have I to fill up the rooms of them as
> have bought out their services that you would think that I had a hundred and
> fifty tattered prodigals lately come from swine-keeping, from eating draff
> and husks. (4.2.12–32)

Some of the humor of the recruitment scene in *2 Henry IV* was therefore that it directly presented a kind of *reductio ad absurdum* of Falstaff's admitted abuse of "the King's press" in the previous *Henry IV* play. Nevertheless, there is an oddity about these evocations of military recruitment. In both plays, the purpose of raising soldiers was to defeat domestic rebellions but they both portray an Elizabethan mechanism for raising men specifically for service overseas. In Shakespeare's time, a domestic rebellion would instead be countered by calling upon the private retinues of peers, courtiers, and senior clergy or by mobilizing the trained bands of counties adjacent to the rebellion.

Shakespeare presumably satirized the "press" in the *Henry IV* plays, despite their focus on domestic wars, because this was an all-too-regular feature of late-Elizabethan life and because abuses of the procedure offered rich comic potential. However, in addition to its potential for corruption, the compulsory levying of men for service abroad from among the "able men" who were excluded from the trained bands raised political and legal concerns. Indeed, the process was arguably illegal. This concern began to surface in the mid-1590s. In Caernarvonshire, JPs refused to proceed with a levy in March 1596, "though for the furtheraunce of her Majestie's service," because the order seemed to lack proper authority.[25] Even more dramatic was Sir John Smythe's tirade at a muster of the Essex trained bands at Colchester in June 1596. Smythe proclaimed that "there are traitors aboute the Court, and the Lord Treasurer is a traitor, yea, a traitor of traitors." He claimed that 9,000 men had been "consumed ... foolishly" in foreign wars and "that there are as many menn slayne and lyeng upon heapes about the

Court in Grenewich as menne might goe over the shoes in bloode." Smythe also told the assembled bands that it was "unlawfull for her Majestie to sende any of her subjects to serve in warre out of the land" and pointedly promised a "reformation" for "the common people [who] have bene long oppressed and used as bondmen 30 yeares." Attorney General Coke was clear that this performance was both "treason at the common law" and punishable under the 1571 Treasons Act but Lord Treasurer Burghley ultimately insisted that the affair should not be publicized by a trial and that Smythe's excuse of speaking in "doot dronkennes without any intent" should be accepted.[26]

Smythe's extraordinary outburst in 1596 reflected the heavy toll that years of war had taken on Elizabeth's realm. Not only were the counties repeatedly forced to raise men and money, but many of those who were pressed for service abroad failed to return. In *1 Henry IV*, Falstaff claimed that his "ragamuffins" were so "peppered" in battle that "there's not three of my hundred and fifty left alive" (5.3.35–36). Substantial numbers of men also returned home physically maimed or permanently weakened by the many illnesses that flourished in war zones. In 1593, Parliament passed "An acte for the relief of souldiours [and mariners]" that set up a nationwide system of weekly rates, charged upon every parish, for the support of those who had "adventured their lyves and loste their lymmes or disabled their bodies . . . in the defence and service of her Majestie and the state."[27] By the mid-1590s, when the realm suffered the worst succession of harvest failures of the century, things had become even worse. In 1595, London was roiled by riots on Tower Hill, which provoked the imposition of martial law. In 1596, soaring grain prices prompted an abortive popular rising in Oxfordshire, which the Privy Council punished as overt treason.[28] Smythe's offense, however, was even more striking because he was accompanied at the musters by Thomas Seymour, a son of the Earl of Hertford who had a potential claim on the throne. At the time, Hertford and his sons had only recently been released after a period of detention following another scandal. In late 1595, it was discovered that the lieutenant of the Tower of London had been stockpiling arms and supplies in the Tower in anticipation of a Seymour succession after the queen's death, which the lieutenant had believed to be imminent. Remarkably, like Smythe (but unlike the commoners in Oxfordshire), the lieutenant avoided trial and execution for treason.[29]

The continual grind of England's wars at sea, in the Low Countries, in France, and in Ireland perhaps created a need for a national hero figure. This was a role that an elderly female sovereign like Elizabeth I could not play. In the 1590s, this function was eagerly (and very consciously) performed by Robert Devereux, second Earl of Essex.[30] In 1586, Essex was knighted after the battle at Zutphen in which Sir Philip Sidney was mortally wounded. Sidney, a cousin by marriage, bequeathed Essex one of his two best swords and the earl subsequently married Sidney's widow. In 1589, Essex stole away from court to join the failed expedition to Portugal, ultimately breaking "his launce, with terror and renowne," against the gates of Lisbon.[31] In 1591–92, Essex led an English army to besiege Rouen, a city that was powerfully evocative of the Hundred Years' War. Essex's fame peaked after the great English victory at Cádiz in 1596, although credit for the victory subsequently became a bone of bitter contention between Essex, Sir Walter Ralegh, and the Lord Admiral. Essex was thwarted in his effort to publish a "True relacion" of the victory in 1596, but succeeded in claiming the lion's share of credit by circulating manuscript accounts of the action and proliferating portraits of himself featuring a spade-shaped beard, which became the virtual "face of Cadiz."[32]

Essex was such a towering political and cultural presence in the last decade of Elizabeth's reign, and had such a variety of direct and indirect connections to the London stage, that he inevitably left many traces in the plays of Shakespeare and his contemporaries.[33] Jonathan Bate has even asked if Shakespeare was himself "an Essex man." Peter Lake is not willing to go quite so far, but Essex features prominently in his recent book, *How Shakespeare Put Politics on the Stage: Power and Succession in the History Plays* (2016). In Lake's analysis, Shakespeare's *Henry VI* plays seem to refract aspects of Essex's Normandy campaign (140–47). As is well known, even stronger echoes of Essex and his martial reputation can be seen in *Henry V*. Famously, the Chorus before act 5 seems to allude directly to Essex and his triumphal departure to confront the rebel Irish confederacy of Hugh O'Neill, Earl of Tyrone, on March 27, 1599 (5.0.22–34), when thousands of Londoners accompanied Essex as far as Highgate, "as thoughe the Godde of the yerthe had ben new come emongst us."[34] Elsewhere in the play, the departure of Henry V's fleet for France is described like that of Essex's fleets in 1596 and 1597, while the famous battle cry of Henry V at the siege of Harfleur ("Cry 'God for Harry! England and Saint George!'" [3.1.34]) seems to echo Essex's conspicuous use of the flag of St. George at Cádiz.[35] Henry V's strict insistence that his men would not plunder the French populace (and the fatal price that Bardolph pays for robbing a church) seems to parallel reports of Essex's behavior after the fall of Cádiz. The character of Fluellen has also often been seen as being modeled on Essex's old comrade in arms, Sir Roger Williams. If so, Shakespeare very deliberately inverted Williams's well-known advocacy for military modernization – which Essex also espoused – in favor of a comic conservatism and pedantry.[36]

Essex was especially active in the 1590s in trying to ameliorate the failings of the English system of pressing men for service abroad. Local cost cutting and a desire to rid the community of financial burdens meant that new drafts of men for overseas wars were often poorly equipped and filled with men swept out of local gaols. As Falstaff boasted in *1 Henry IV*, "no eye hath seen such scarecrows ... there's not a shirt and a half in all my company.... But that's all one; they'll find linen enough on every hedge" (4.2.34–35, 38–39, 42–43). The Privy Council repeatedly scolded county officials for such failings. Essex sought to preempt these problems by personally writing dozens of letters to local officials urging their "carefullnes" and "good endevours" in choosing suitable soldiers and equipping them properly: "and what yow shall doe, the rather at my request, I will recken for an argument of your love and requite yow by all the freindly offices that I can."[37] Essex also sought to stiffen his armies by adopting the latest Dutch practice of grouping them into smaller companies, thereby increasing tactical flexibility and boosting the proportion of officers. He also encouraged very large numbers of gentlemen volunteers to join his expeditions. John Donne was among the hundreds of gentleman "voluntaries" who joined Essex's great naval expeditions in 1596 and 1597, while John Harington accompanied Essex's army to Ireland in 1599. Such men were expected to encourage the common soldiers by their presence and add esprit to the army as a whole. Indeed, these men were so important to the fighting power of Elizabethan armies that Essex was forced to resort to desperate measures to stop them heading home from Ireland in 1599, even knighting them by the score.[38]

Essex's 1599 failure in Ireland, and the subsequent political disgrace that eventually resulted in his arrest and execution on charges of treason in February 1601, signaled the final phase of war in Elizabeth's reign. In Ireland, under Lord Mountjoy, and in the Low Countries (especially in the long bloody siege of Ostend, the "new Troy"), England now waged ruthless wars of attrition – "this cormorant war," as it is termed in *Troilus and Cressida* (2.2.6).[39] With Essex dead, "Great England's glory and the world's wide wonder," as Spenser had praised the earl in 1596, had been reduced to patently false hopes in "promised glory" and an ignoble pursuit of "the wide world's revenue" (2.2.204–6).[40]

The war in Ireland proved especially difficult and stretched England's resources of men and money in the last years of Elizabeth's reign almost to the breaking point. Like modern wars in Afghanistan, local knowledge and an emphasis on mobility allowed the native Irish to set the terms for most engagements, artfully using bogs, trenches, and woods to hinder English columns and peppering them with fire from calivers. On occasions when the English troops could bring their armor, cannon, and cumbersome muskets to bear, the Irish simply slipped away.[41] Beginning in 1600, Lord Mountjoy began to turn the tide by fighting the sort of sustained attritional war that Essex had sought to avoid. However, the decisive moment came when a Spanish army finally landed in the British Isles, at the southern Irish port of Kinsale, in September 1601. English forces promptly trapped the Spanish and began an epic winter siege, which forced Tyrone into an equally extraordinary march south to rescue his allies. At last, Tyrone was forced to fight on Mountjoy's terms. On December 24, the Irish army was caught in the open near Kinsale and destroyed by the English cavalry.[42] After this disaster, Tyrone's Irish allies began to peel away and submit to Elizabeth's authority. Even so, Elizabeth's Privy Council had to force an unwilling queen to offer Tyrone very generous terms to finally end the war in Ireland in March 1603.

As is well known, Shakespeare relied heavily upon Holinshed's *Chronicles* as a source for his English history plays. However, Shakespeare portrayed war in a very different and more morally ambiguous way than the authors of the *Chronicles*. The patriotic treatment of war (and the longbow) in Holinshed in the 1570s and 1580s was driven partly by a desire to mobilize the realm against the looming Spanish threat and to revive confidence in English arms after the demoralizing failures of the 1550s and 1560s.[43] Many of Shakespeare's plays, by contrast, were written while enduring the strains of wartime, with its repeated threats of Spanish invasion and seemingly endless demands for money and men. Even the charismatic Essex – the Elizabethan Achilles – was finally consumed by the war, trapped by his enemies and metaphorically "dragged through the shameful field" like Hector in *Troilus and Cressida* (5.11.5).[44] When James VI of Scotland succeeded to Elizabeth's throne, the long conflict between England and Spain effectively subsided, except for the continuing bloody siege of Ostend. However, even when the fighting was over, the wounds remained. When Mountjoy and the newly pardoned Tyrone traveled back to England to meet James in May 1603, "no respect to him [Mountjoy] could containe many weomen in those parts, who had lost husbands and children in the Irish warres, from flinging durt and stones at the earle as he passed, and from reviling him with bitter words."[45] Like the character of Thersites in *Troilus and Cressida*, these women saw past the professions of aristocratic honor and martial glory and felt compelled to resort to "spiteful execrations" to express the reality of wars that had cost them so dearly (2.3.6).

### Further Reading

Fissel, Mark Charles. *English Warfare, 1511–1642*, London, Routledge, 2001.
Gadja, Alexandra. "Debating War and Peace in Late Elizabethan England," *Historical Journal*, 52 (2000), pp. 851–78.

Hammer, Paul E. J. *Elizabeth's Wars: War, Government and Society in Tudor England, 1544–1604*, Basingstoke, Palgrave Macmillan, 2003.

*The Polarisation of Elizabethan Politics: The Political Career of Robert Devereux, 2nd Earl of Essex, 1585–1597*, Cambridge, Cambridge University Press, 1999.

Lawrence, David R. *The Complete Soldier: Military Books and Military Culture in Early Stuart England, 1603–1645*, Leiden, Brill, 2009.

Nolan, John S. *Sir John Norreys and the Elizabethan Military World*, Exeter, Exeter University Press, 1997.

Rapple, Rory. *Martial Power and Elizabethan Political Culture: Military Men in England and Ireland, 1558–1594*, Cambridge, Cambridge University Press, 2009.

Schwoerer, Lois G. *Gun Culture in Early Modern England*, Charlottesville, University of Virginia Press, 2016.

Smuts, Malcolm. "Organized Violence in the Elizabethan Monarchical Republic," *History*, 99 (2014), pp. 418–43.

Trim, D. J. B. "The Context of War and Violence in Sixteenth-Century English Society," *Journal of Early Modern History*, 3 (1999), pp. 233–55.

Younger, Neil. *War and Politics in the Elizabethan Counties*, Manchester, Manchester University Press, 2012.

## NOTES

1 Sir Charles Percy to "Mr. Carlington," December 27, [no year stated], SP 12/275/146, fo. 240r, The National Archives (formerly Public Record Office), Kew (hereafter TNA). Although the letter has commonly been assigned to 1600, this date is clearly incorrect. Here and below, abbreviations in quotations from manuscript sources are silently expanded and capitalization is modernized.

2 Paul E. J. Hammer (ed.), *Warfare in Early Modern Europe, 1450–1660* (Aldershot: Ashgate, 2007), pp. xi–xxxix; *Elizabeth's Wars: War, Government and Society in Tudor England, 1544–1604* (Basingstoke: Palgrave Macmillan, 2003); and John S. Nolan, "The Militarization of the Elizabethan State," *Journal of Military History*, 58 (1994), pp. 391–420.

3 Hammer, *Elizabeth's Wars*, pp. 9–53.

4 D. J. B. Trim, "The 'Secret War' of Elizabeth I: England and the Huguenots during the Early Wars of Religion, 1562–77," *Proceedings of the Huguenot Society*, 27 (1999), pp. 189–99; and "Fighting 'Jacob's Wars': The Employment of English and Welsh Mercenaries in the European Wars of Religion; France and the Netherlands, 1562–1610," unpublished PhD thesis, King's College, London (2002).

5 Geoffrey Parker, "The *Dreadnought* Revolution of Tudor England," *Mariner's Mirror*, 82 (1996), pp. 269–300; and N. A. M. Rodger, *The Safeguard of the Sea: A Naval History of Britain, 660–1649* (London: HarperCollins, 1997), vol. 1, pp. 204–21.

6 Hammer, *Elizabeth's Wars*, pp. 147–48.

7 R. B. Wernham, "Amphibious Operations and the Elizabethan Assault on the Spanish Atlantic Economy," in D. J. B. Trim and Mark Charles Fissel (eds.), *Amphibious Warfare 1000–1700: Commerce, State Formation and European Expansion* (Leiden: Brill, 2006), pp. 181–215.

8  Kenneth R. Andrews, *Elizabethan Privateering: English Privateering during the Spanish War, 1585–1603* (Cambridge: Cambridge University Press, 1964); and Mark G. Hanna, *Pirate Nests and the Rise of the British Empire, 1570–1740* (Chapel Hill: University of North Carolina Press, 2015), pp. 21–57.

9  Geoffrey Parker, "If the Armada Had Landed," *History*, 61 (1976), pp. 358–68.

10 Neil Younger, *War and Politics in the Elizabethan Counties* (Manchester: Manchester University Press, 2012).

11 Nolan, "The Militarization of the Elizabethan State"; Hammer, *Elizabeth's Wars*, pp. 236–64.

12 Evelyn Tribble, "Where Are the Archers in Shakespeare?," *English Literary History*, 82 (2015), pp. 789–814.

13 Matthew Strickland and Robert Hardy, *The Great Warbow: From Hastings to the Mary Rose* (Stroud: Sutton Publishing, 2005).

14 SP 12/119/22, fo. 48r, TNA.

15 Patricia A. Cahill, *Unto the Breach: Martial Formations, Historical Trauma and the Early Modern Stage* (Oxford: Oxford University Press, 2008), pp. 86–88.

16 Neil Younger, "Securing the Monarchical Republic: The Remaking of the Lord Lieutenancies in 1585," *Historical Research*, 84 (2010), pp. 249–65.

17 Younger, *War and Politics*, pp. 108, 112.

18 SP 12/205/32, fo. 58r; and SP 12/209/1, fo. 2r, TNA.

19 David R. Lawrence, *The Complete Soldier: Military Books and Military Culture in Early Stuart England, 1603–1645* (Leiden: Brill, 2009).

20 Ian David Cooper, "Networks, News and Communication: Political Elites and Community Relations in Elizabethan Devon, 1588–1603," unpublished PhD thesis, Plymouth University (2012), pp. 117, 130.

21 Hammer, *Elizabeth's Wars*, p. 256.

22 J. R. Dasent et al. (eds.), *Acts of the Privy Council of England* (APC), new series, 46 vols. (London: HMSO, 1890–1964), vol. XXVIII, pp. 525–27; and MS 464E/199, National Library of Wales (NLW).

23 Clenennau letters and papers, app. 1, no. 109, NLW.

24 Calculated from Ian Archer, "Gazzeteer of Military Levies from the City of London, 1509–1603," hosted by the Oxford University Research Archive: https://ora.ox.ac.uk/objects/uuid:adb577fc-6ffb-440b-9dd9-7c5c39a4a64c.

25 Clenennau letters and papers, no. 107, NLW.

26 SP 12/259/57, fo. 136r–v; SP 12/259/59, fo. 139r; and SP 12/263/59, fo. 79r–v, TNA.

27 35 Elizabeth c. 4: *The Statutes of the Realm*, vol. IV, pt. 2 (London, 1819), pp. 847–49.

28 John Stow, *The Annales of England* [...] *untill This Present Yeere, 1601* (London, 1601), pp. 1279–81; and John Walter, "A 'Rising of the People'? The Oxfordshire Rising of 1596," *Past and Present*, 107 (1985), pp. 90–143.

29 Roger B. Manning, "The Prosecution of Sir Michael Blount, Lieutenant of the Tower of London, 1595," *Bulletin of the Institute of Historical Research*, 57 (1984), pp. 216–24.

30 Paul E. J. Hammer, *The Polarisation of Elizabethan Politics: The Political Career of Robert Devereux, 2nd Earl of Essex, 1585–1597* (Cambridge: Cambridge University Press, 1999); "The Smiling Crocodile: The Earl of Essex and Late-Elizabethan 'Popularity,'" in Steve Pincus and Peter Lake (eds.), *The "Public*

*Sphere" in Early Modern England* (Manchester: Manchester University Press, 2007), pp. 95–115; "'Base Rogues' and 'Gentlemen of Quality': The Earl of Essex's Irish Knights and Royal Displeasure in 1599," in Brendan Kane and Valerie McGowan-Doyle (eds.), *Elizabeth I and Ireland* (Cambridge: Cambridge University Press, 2014), pp. 184–208; "Myth-Making: Politics, Propaganda and the Capture of Cadiz in 1596," *Historical Journal*, 40 (1997), pp. 621–42; Alexandra Gajda, *The Earl of Essex and Late Elizabethan Political Culture* (Oxford: Oxford University Press, 2012); and Roy Strong, "Faces of a Favourite: Robert Devereux, 2nd Earl of Essex and the Uses of Portraiture," *British Art Journal*, 5 (2004), pp. 80–90.

31  George Peele, *An Eglogue Gratulatorie. Entituled to the Right Honorable and Renowmed Shepheard of Albion's Arcadia: Robert Earle of Essex and Ewe* (London, 1589), sig. B1v.

32  Hammer, "Myth-Making"; Strong, "Faces of a Favourite."

33  Paul E. J. Hammer, "Shakespeare's *Richard II*, the Play of 7 February 1601, and the Essex Rising," *Shakespeare Quarterly*, 59 (2008), pp. 1–35; Jonathan Bate, "Was Shakespeare an Essex Man?," *Proceedings of the British Academy*, 162 (2009), pp. 1–28; and Peter Lake, *How Shakespeare Put Politics on the Stage: Power and Succession in the History Plays* (New Haven: Yale University Press, 2016).

34  MS 40, fo. 89r, Longleat House, Thynne.

35  Julian S. Corbett (ed.), "Relation of the Voyage to Cadiz, 1596, by Sir William Slyngisbie," in John Knox Laughton (ed.), *The Naval Miscellany*, vol. xx of the Publications of the Navy Records Society (London: Navy Records Society, 1902), p. 63.

36  D. J. B. Trim, "Williams, Sir Roger (1539/40–1595)," in *Oxford Dictionary of National Biography* (Oxford: Oxford University Press, 2004).

37  MS 9051E/169, NLW; and Neil Younger, "The Practice and Politics of Troop-Raising: Robert Devereux, Second Earl of Essex, and the Elizabethan Regime," *English Historical Review*, 127 (2012), pp. 566–91.

38  Hammer, "'Base Rogues.'"

39  James O'Neill, "A Kingdom Near Lost: English Military Recovery in Ireland, 1600–1603," *British Journal for Military History*, 3 (2016), pp. 26–47; *The Nine Years' War, 1593–1603* (Dublin: Four Courts Press, 2017); and Edward Belleroche, "The Siege of Ostend or the New Troy, 1601–1604," *Proceedings of the Huguenot Society of London*, 3 (1888–1891), pp. 427–539.

40  Edmund Spenser, *Prothalamion* (1596), in William A. Oram et al. (eds.), *The Yale Edition of the Shorter Poems of Edmund Spenser* (New Haven: Yale University Press, 1989), p. 768, l. 146.

41  O'Neill, *Nine Years' War*, p. 100.

42  Hiram Morgan (ed.), *The Battle of Kinsale* (Bray, Co. Wicklow: Wordwell, 2004); John J. Silke, *Kinsale: Spanish Intervention in Ireland at the End of the Elizabethan Wars* (Dublin: Four Courts Press, 2000); and Des Ekin, *The Last Armada: Queen Elizabeth, Juan del Aguila and Hugh O'Neill; the Story of the 100-Day Spanish Invasion* (New York: Pegasus, 2016).

43  Paul E. J. Hammer, "War," in Paulina Kewes, Ian W. Archer, and Felicity Heal (eds.), *The Oxford Handbook of Holinshed's "Chronicles"* (Oxford: Oxford University Press, 2013), pp. 443–58.

44 John Channing Briggs, "Chapman's *Seaven Bookes of the Iliades*: Mirror for Essex," *Studies in English Literature, 1500–1900*, 21 (1981), pp. 59–73; and Paul E. J. Hammer, "The Earl of Essex," in Malcolm Smuts (ed.), *The Oxford Handbook of the Age of Shakespeare* (Oxford: Oxford University Press, 2016), pp. 37–50, 48–50.

45 Fynes Moryson, *An Itinerary Containing His Ten Yeeres Travell* [...], 4 vols. (Glasgow: James MacLehose and Sons, 1908), vol. III, p. 336.

# 2

FRANZISKA QUABECK

# Just War Theory and Shakespeare

## Theories of War

It is difficult to theorize war. War seems to many too disastrous to deserve a theory about its paradigms. Moreover, a theory of war may seem as if it consolidated the phenomenon. If we consider war's premises from a theoretical perspective, so many have argued, we signal a certain tolerance for its existence. Theoretical approaches to war that do not condemn it altogether often seem to imply an inadvertent justification in their premises. This is why theoretical considerations of war run the risk of offending sensibilities. However, the many theoretical approaches to war that do exist prove how many people have felt inclined to conceptualize it beyond practical or military concerns, and this tradition is much older than one might think. In fact, debates about war ensued in antiquity and since their very beginning, they have circled around three major questions: Do we always have to prevent war by any means? Or is war a condition that is uncontrollable and exempt from our sphere of morality? If not, can war ever be justified? The three approaches that have developed out of these questions are commonly termed, respectively, pacifism, realism, and just war theory. We can see discussions of each of them in Shakespeare's plays.

Pacifists argue that war can never be permissible. There are two modes of reasoning: either one can argue that violence against human beings is generally prohibited, which includes war a fortiori, or one can argue that the atrocities that result from war can never be in proportion to the good it may bring. In any case, the pacifist argument against war is universal and even an unjust peace cannot constitute a legitimate cause for war.[1] In that sense, ethical considerations of war are void, since they would premise war's permissibility, which pacifism rules out explicitly. The other theoretical approach to war sees no possibility of an ethical evaluation of war either, but for very different reasons. An ancient Latin proverb states "*inter arma silent leges*": in times of war, the law is silent. This traditional view of war is often referred to as realism or militarism and sometimes as bellicism. It constitutes the very opposite of pacifism, for it postulates that war is first of all inevitable and secondly segregated from our moral universe: "War is a world apart, where life itself is at stake, where human nature is reduced to its elemental forms, where self-interest and necessity prevail."[2] In other words, war is hell, as General Sherman put it, and therefore exempt from moral judgment. The argument suggests that war puts human nature under such duress that war and ethics do not mix. Therefore, we cannot hold human action in war to the standards of common morality in peacetime.

Pacifism and realism are mutually exclusive theoretical approaches to war. While the first holds all wars in condemnation, the latter claims that condemnation is no valid principle in or about war. Yet, they have a basic premise in common: "Realism and ... pacifism agree that there is no moral distinction to be made between just and unjust wars; none is prohibited or all are prohibited."[3] For this reason, just war theory is often regarded as a middle ground between the two, for it concedes that there may be just wars. The argument is that war is part of our moral universe and therefore people acting in war are morally responsible. The theory holds that war may be permissible under certain circumstances, but this can only be the case when a certain number of moral premises are fulfilled: "Just war theory gives content to the idea of an ethics of war, and so it allows an engagement with ethics by those wielding political and military power."[4] In contrast to pacifism and realism, just war theory allows us to make distinctions between right and wrong, just and unjust actions in war, and it enables us to hold responsible those who enter into the condition of war. This is not a modern phenomenon: the theory of just war derives from antiquity and saw its most complex theoretical development in the Middle Ages. Most scholars regard St. Augustine of Hippo (354–430) as the "father" of just war theory.[5] Augustine regarded war as inevitable, "for peace is an uncertain good, since we cannot see into the hearts of those with whom we wish to maintain that peace."[6] However, the only just objective of war is peace: "Wars ... are conducted with the intention of peace."[7] Augustine's political thought in general and his deliberations on the justice of war in particular are not always concise, but his arguments laid the groundwork for just war theory as it holds to this very day. Augustine had already formulated that war may only be waged with the right intention. This intention must be the preservation or reestablishment of peace; only this can constitute a just cause. While Augustine's thoughts therefore seem inaugural of the just war tradition, it was St. Thomas Aquinas (1225–74) who first conceptualized those thoughts into a coherent framework of just war principles.

According to Aquinas, wars are just when those who wage war can fulfill three principles: legitimate authority, just cause, and right intention. First, Aquinas established that only those might go to war who hold the political office and therefore the right to do so: "For it does not pertain to a private person to declare war, because he can prosecute his rights at the tribunal of his superior."[8] Second, he emphasized the just cause, "that is, those against whom war is to be waged must deserve to have war waged against them because of some wrongdoing." Third, those who go to war must only do so with the right intention: "they should intend either to promote a good cause or avert an evil.... For it can happen that even if war is declared by a legitimate authority and for a just cause, that war may be rendered unlawful by a wicked intent."[9] Aquinas's development of Augustine's initial ideas in the form of these three prerequisites for a just war have been central to just war theory ever since. While the face of warfare has changed considerably since the Middle Ages, these fundamental ethical principles of the just war tradition have not. However, the catalog of premises for just wars has grown considerably since then and especially since the revival of just war theory in the twentieth century.

While the theory of just war has an ancient origin, academic debates on the subject only rekindled after a long hiatus through the 1977 publication of Michael Walzer's *Just and Unjust Wars: A Moral Argument with Historical Illustrations*. The events and wars of the twentieth century had shown the gruesome reality of war and academic debates were largely pacifist in nature for decades. Therefore, it seemed surprising that one would return to the just war tradition with its seeming affirmation of war and its consequences. However, as Walzer has argued since his seminal book, just war theory should not be considered an affirmation of war: "Just war theory is not an apology for any particular war, and it is not a renunciation of war itself. It is designed to sustain a constant scrutiny and immanent critique."[10] Many political and philosophical theorists have contributed to this scrutiny for the past forty years and while there are several points they disagree on, they have come up with a catalog of principles for a just war that builds on and expands Aquinas's initial first principles: "For a war to be just, it must (1) have a *just cause*; (2) be declared by a *legitimate authority*; (3) be fought with a *rightful intention*; (4) show *proportionality* in the balance between the good and harm it does; (5) be a *last resort*; and (6) have a *reasonable chance of success*."[11] All of these are so-called *ad bellum* principles, that is, principles that determine the *jus ad bellum*, the justice *of* war. These principles have to be distinguished from *jus in bello* principles, which determine justice *in* wars, that is, the justice or injustice of human action in battle. According to Walzer, these are two distinct moral spheres: "The two sorts of judgment are logically independent. It is perfectly possible for a just war to be fought unjustly and for an unjust war to be fought in strict accordance with the rules."[12] Thus, just war theory has established that if all of these principles are fulfilled, a war may be necessary and just.

### Views of War in the Renaissance

We can trace the development of just war theory from Augustine and Aquinas to the Spanish scholasticism of Vitoria and Suarez and to the political theories of Kant and Hegel, but Elizabethan England saw no notable theorist in this tradition. It is commonly agreed upon that the principles of just war as argued by Aquinas were long established by the Elizabethan age, but it seems that both realism/militarism and pacifism were more dominant political theories at the time. This might have been due to the wide reception of the writings of Niccolò Machiavelli and his introduction of *realpolitik* on the one hand, and on the other, the many humanists, most notably Erasmus, who began to argue convincingly and sustainably for pacifism. Both writers, who were well received in Elizabethan England, did not foreground theoretical considerations of war, but rather emphasized the necessities of good political governance. The mirrors for princes, a distinct genre of political writings, were immensely popular at the time both in England and on the Continent – Machiavelli's *The Prince* (1513, pub. 1532) and Erasmus's *The Education of a Christian Prince* (1516) were both influential in Renaissance political thought, although they could hardly be more contrary.

Both Machiavelli and Erasmus concern themselves primarily with the strategies of gaining and/or holding sovereignty, and war is only a secondary, but immanent, concern. However, their advice for their (fictional) princes is completely different, since Machiavelli argues like a realist and Erasmus like a pacifist. According to Machiavelli, war is inevitable and in the prince's interest to maintain political power; according to Erasmus, the prince has to avoid war at all costs. Erasmus's pacifism does not rule out the possibility of war altogether, but he places the emphasis on the fact that the costs of war will not be proportional to the good it can achieve:

> There is scarcely any peace so unjust, but it is preferable on the whole, to the justest war. Sit down, before you draw the sword, weigh every article, omit none, and compute the expence of blood as well as treasure which war requires, and the evils which it of necessity brings with it; and then see at the bottom of the account whether, after the greatest success, there is likely to be a balance in your favour.[13]

Erasmus implies that the costs of war can never be justified, which is why war can almost never be just. This is why he advises the "wise prince" never to undertake foreign wars to preserve the peace within his own realm, but instead that "he must strive to his utmost for this end: that the devices of war may never be needed."[14] However, if the prince finds himself in a dilemma that requires war, which "cannot by any means be avoided," he is morally obliged to wage war "with the least possible harm" and "to end it as quickly as possible."[15] (Erasmus is unclear on what he might consider a just war, but he repeatedly alludes to the fact that he finds its existence very doubtful: "I am not sure that any of the kind could be found."[16]) Thus, the only definition of a just war he gives is a definition *ex negativo*: "wars not caused by ambition, anger, arrogance, lust, or greed." This definition also implies a central argument in his advice for a Christian prince, who should keep himself occupied, "so that he will never feel the need, bored by inactivity, to seek war."[17] Thus, Erasmus argues against the common Elizabethan guideline that waging war abroad will secure peace at home. Machiavelli, on the other hand, does consider war the appropriate means to demonstrate power both within and outside the prince's realm. His "might makes right" premise allows the prince to maintain sovereignty by forcefully acquiring power and violently executing it. In his theory, war is politics by other means: "A ruler, then, should have no other objective and no other concern, nor occupy himself with anything else except war and its methods and practices, for this pertains only to those who rule. And it is of such efficacy that it not only maintains hereditary rulers in power but very often enables men of private status to become rulers."[18] In this theory, war functions as a tool to preserve a single person's power. The prince is allowed all immoral means at his disposal and war is one of the most effective ones. Machiavelli does not consider the ethics of cause and costs or authority and intention. In fact, a prince or ruler "cannot always act in ways that are considered good," but is forced to act "treacherously, ruthlessly or inhumanely."[19]

This *realpolitik* has become a familiar concept in political thought and Machiavelli's dark power politics has influenced European cultural history since the publication of *The Prince*. The Elizabethan age and the Elizabethan stage especially took the theory on quickly, the latter with an astute eye for its dramatic potential, as we can see in both Marlowe and Shakespeare. However, the question of whether Erasmus's humanist pacifism or Machiavelli's militarist *realpolitik* had a more profound impact on the Elizabethans' attitude toward war has remained more or less unresolved. Voices from both sides are clearly audible in Elizabethan cultural history and many critics and historians have tried to argue for a dominance of either. An overview of statements about the Elizabethan attitude toward war offers quite disparate voices. Some critics have claimed that war constituted no pressing reality for the Elizabethans: "Tudor England had been able to regard war as a distant activity which she could join or abandon as she chose."[20] Others have argued that the rise of humanism lent a distinctly pacifist moment to the age as emerging thinkers such as Erasmus "ushered in not only humanism" but also "the formation of a group that might be called a 'peace movement.'"[21] In direct contrast, earlier critics had claimed that "on no social or intellectual level is there to be found impressive argumentation for peace."[22] At the other end of the scale, more recent studies have emphasized a distinct "Tudor pro-war polemic" that specifically "sustained attack on any remaining vestiges of Christian pacifism."[23] However, J. R. Hale, one of the leading historians on war in England, has countered such an impression of a militarist Elizabethan age. He has frequently argued that there was a clear understanding of war as inevitable, but not desired:

> All agreed that the motive of war must be just, that it should only be waged at the command of a sovereign superior, and that the means used, and the nature of the peace-settlement, should be as moderate as possible. All, moreover, agreed that war was a continuation of justice by other means and should only be undertaken when all possibilities of peaceful arbitration had been exhausted.[24]

Considering these inconsistencies in scholarly arguments about theoretical Elizabethan perspectives on war, all that is certain is that the three theories of war – pacifism, realism, and just war theory – were duly established by or even before the beginning of Shakespeare's dramatic career.

## Shakespeare's Theories of War

There were notable pacifist voices in Elizabethan England and there were notable militarist voices in Elizabethan England. It should not come as a surprise, therefore, that there are pacifist and militarist voices in Shakespeare. In fact, Shakespeare seems to have felt the influence of both movements and of the writings of Erasmus and Machiavelli in particular. Accordingly, the history of the reception of Shakespeare's theory of war is as disparate as the reception of the Elizabethan theorists in general. When Shakespeare scholars rediscovered the subject of war in Shakespeare's plays toward the end of the twentieth century, they also felt inclined to settle for an interpretation in favor of either pacifism or militarism, and the plays provided them with multiple voices on either side to manifest their arguments. In the first book-length study on the subject, Paul Jorgensen argued that Shakespeare's plays are overwhelmingly militarist and that pacifism per se "is espoused by not a single admirable character in Shakespeare."[25] Others have argued with a specific focus on the author and have emphasized Shakespeare's own "peaceful attitude."[26] Thus, Theodor Meron has claimed, "Shakespeare was certainly not a warmonger," since his plays are "replete with references to the brutality, bloodiness, and horrors of war."[27] Steven Marx has argued that Shakespeare changed his mind halfway through his dramatic career, dispensing with the militarism of the early history plays in favor of pacifism from *Troilus and Cressida* onwards, thus turning "from a partisan of war to a partisan of peace," until the last plays "function as propaganda for peace."[28] Thus, for most of the second half of the twentieth century, Shakespeare criticism was stuck between pacifism and realism/militarism as the two horns of this dilemma, although Norman Rabkin had already argued in his famous analysis of *Henry V* in 1977 that Shakespeare deliberately includes both theories in equal measure. Rabkin claimed that any decision for either horn of the dilemma in the case of *Henry V* would mean that we "exclude too much to hold it."[29] Rabkin assumed that Shakespeare's "habitual recognition of the irreducible complexity of things" had led him to a "point of crisis" and that the play showed "a spiritual struggle" at its heart.[30] As a result, Shakespeare's ambiguity has become a critical commonplace, but this has also led critics to conclude the opposite: "*no* 'view' on war emerges from the evenhandedness with which he has his characters express sentiments appropriate to their roles."[31]

At the beginning of the twenty-first century, critics turned away from the question of Shakespeare's personal point of view and began to focus on the justice of Shakespeare's wars, which shows in their use of the terminology of just war theory. This is most notable in several analyses of *Richard III* and *Henry V*, two plays that are very rich in their considerations of the justice of war and the justice in war. In 2000, for instance, John Mark Mattox published an article on *Henry V* in which he argued that the protagonist was a model of the just warrior in keeping with the just war tradition. He emphasized the "keen awareness" of the playwright "concerning the theory of just war" and he argued that Shakespeare established Henry's compliance with the just war tradition.[32] Shortly afterwards, Nicholas Grene published his analysis of the history plays and found an increasing emphasis on the justice of wars throughout the early plays. He showed that Shakespeare's depiction of the Wars of the Roses revealed "the equivalence between the two sides was a measure of their equal lack of moral justification."[33] The Battle of Bosworth constitutes the "climax and closure for the whole play series," because it is the just war that can end civil strife: "the momentum is built up to ensure that, when an armed counterforce appears under the command of Richmond, it is to be welcomed as the just war to end the cycle of violence." In the same year, Michael Hattaway stated, "the Battle of Bosworth in *Richard III* may be the only example of a just war in the canon,"[34] and a year later R. A. Foakes pointed out, "Shakespeare seems especially interested in ... the emerging question whether there can be a just war."[35] In his full-length study of war and Shakespeare, Simon Barker also emphasized *Richard III*'s engagement in an "abstract discourse of the just war" and considered Richmond's rhetoric before the Battle of Bosworth "a sanitised and lukewarm version of the just war ethic, set against the emerging 'realism' of the theorists."[36] The emergence of just war terminology in Shakespeare criticism is not coincidental. A chronological reading of his plays reveals that Shakespeare's theory of war grows increasingly more refined and turns toward the discourse of the just war tradition. In his early plays, Shakespeare pits pacifism against realism and emerges at the end of the first tetralogy with a theory of the just war that continues to shape his dramatization of war for the rest of his career.

## Jus ad Bellum in Shakespeare

Since the rediscovery of the early history plays, there has been general agreement that Shakespeare already explores many of his major themes here and gives them increasing complexity until he has "all the tools of his profession well in hand" by the end of *Richard III*.[37] This is also true for Shakespeare's theory of war. There are pacifist and realist/militarist voices in the early history plays, but by the end of the play series, Shakespeare establishes the theory of the just war. Shakespeare's Henry VI is a classic Christian pacifist. In keeping with the tradition, he repeatedly argues, "I always thought / It was both impious and unnatural / That such immanity and bloody strife / Should reign among professors of one faith" (*1 Henry VI*, 5.1.11–14). Henry's speeches on the value of peace not only echo Erasmus's pacifist writings but also refer directly to the Bible: "For blessed are the peacemakers on earth" (*2 Henry VI*, 2.1.34). Unfortunately, his pacifism renders Henry politically incapable and his passivity in the civil war makes him culpable for lives lost: "Weep, wretched man; I'll aid thee tear for tear, / And let our hearts and eyes, like civil war, / Be blind with tears and break o'ercharged with grief" (*3 Henry VI*, 2.5.76–78). In the realist Machiavellian world of the early history plays, Henry's pacifism is sadly misplaced and Shakespeare never returns to arguments against war that are politically ineffective.

In these early plays, Shakespeare increases the pathos of Henry's pacifism by pitting him against dominant characters like York and Richard of Gloucester, who are prototypical Machiavels. Their strategies are inextricably intertwined with the incapability to care about the losses their wars cause. York boasts, "I will stir up in England some black storm / Shall blow ten thousand souls to heaven or to hell" (2 *Henry VI*, 3.1.349–50). Richard of Gloucester similarly praises his own readiness for ruthlessness when he decides to "set the murderous machiavel to school" (3 *Henry VI*, 3.2.193). Throughout the whole play series, there is only one law: "Away with scrupulous wit; Now arms must rule" (3 *Henry VI*, 4.8.61). All nobles act to their advantage and do not consider the costs of their actions in the true spirit of "might makes right" policy: "By words or blows here let us win our right" (3 *Henry VI*, 1.1.37). The tone is militarist, the action unscrupulous. The chaos that results demonstrates that out of the two possible strategies, pacifism or militarism, neither promises long-lasting success, let alone perpetual peace. From these early history plays onwards, characters repeatedly try to make claims for the justice of their causes, although this is merely in name. Warwick's claim in 3 *Henry VI*, "York in justice puts his armour on" (2.2.130) remains both uncontested and unconvincing. In these plays, war is truly hell and there is no justice on either side, no matter all protestations to the contrary. This is evident in a metonymical stage tableau that captures the injustice of civil war. When a nameless father discovers that he has killed his own son in the war, he implicitly draws attention to the principles of just war theory: "I'll bear thee hence, and let them fight that will, / For I have murdered where I should not kill" (3 *Henry VI*, 2.5.121–22). His choice of words is telling: the injustice of the war turns his action into murder. He does no longer kill lawfully as a soldier. This civil war is so unjust that it implicates even those typically freed from responsibility for it.

It is evident that references to just and unjust causes and intentions increase in number, but the Battle of Bosworth is the first just war in Shakespeare's plays. He dramatizes this war as just without historical or dramatic necessity, since Richard's deposition needs no further justification, and he uses an extraordinarily long harangue in order to do so. While his argumentation leaves no doubt of Richard's tyranny, however, it also establishes Aquinas's three principles for a just war: legitimate authority, just cause, and right intention. Richmond establishes himself as the legitimate authority, since he deposes a usurper "made precious by the foil / Of England's chair where he is falsely set" (*Richard III*, 5.3.248–49). His cause is just, since he attempts to avert an evil in the form of Richard, who was "raised in blood" and is "in blood established" (5.3.245). Lastly, Richmond promises to establish peace, thereby demonstrating his right intention: "if I thrive, the gain of my attempt, / The least of you shall share his part thereof" (5.3.265–66). In addition to the three initial principles of *jus ad bellum*, Richmond's argument also turns his "good cause" (238) into a war of defense: "If you do fight against your country's foes, / Your country's fat shall pay your pains the hire" (255–56). Thus, in keeping with Aquinas's principle that a war is only just if it tries to avert an evil or bring forth a good, Richmond promotes his aggression as the just war that will establish perpetual peace in England. The speech is long and tedious, much less attractive than Richard's own call to arms, and in dramatic terms not even necessary: the tragic genre requires Richard's deposition and death, Richmond's character has no need to demonstrate the justice of his cause. Yet, Shakespeare goes to great lengths to include the necessary precepts of just war theory in this speech and this constitutes the first climax of just war theory in the plays.

The second tetralogy shows a more refined awareness of the justice and injustice of causes. Although it depicts a civil war, Shakespeare does not return to the hyperbolic militarism of the early plays. Both sides continue to argue the justice of their causes, but they begin to take different aspects of justice into account. Henry IV argues for the protection of peace like his dramatic predecessor, Henry VI, and uses his Machiavellian talents to depose Richard peacefully, so that *Richard II* stands out from the history plays for its notable lack of war. Henry's reluctance to go to war is consistent with his characterization in both parts on his reign, in which he frequently uses parleys to prevent open battle: "You have deceived our trust, / And made us doff our easy robes of peace / To crush our old limbs in ungentle steel" (*1 Henry IV*, 5.1.11–13). The rebels, on the other hand, insist on their right intention – "the arms are fair / When the intent of bearing them is just" (5.2.87–88) – and for the first time in the chronology of the plays, the principle of proportionality occurs as a prerequisite for a just war: "I have in equal balance justly weighed / What wrongs our arms may do, what wrongs we suffer, / And find our griefs heavier than our offenses" (*2 Henry IV*, 4.1.67–69 [digital ed.]). Despite Shakespeare's indication that the rebellion against Henry is not justified, he still gives the rebels arguments for the justice of their claim. Unlike the militarist aggressors of the first tetralogy, the rebels act in perfect accordance with the rules of *jus ad bellum* here: they claim they have considered whether the cause and cost are in proportion and have found that the wrong that persists without war is greater than the wrong that war causes. The play further emphasizes the principles of just war theory through an implicit discussion of the logical independence of the justice of war and the justice in war at Galtres. When Prince John, another modified Machiavellian, defeats the rebels, he only manages to do so through an unjust confusion of *jus ad bellum* and *jus in bello*: promising the rebels protection in exchange for their surrender, he sentences them to death once they are disarmed. The very justified charge "Is this proceeding just and honorable?" is only met with a laconic "Is your assembly so?" (2 *Henry IV*, 4.1.277–78). Shakespeare makes use of the distinction between *jus ad bellum* and *jus in bello* here in order to indicate unjust conduct: John argues that the injustice of the rebel cause does not entitle them to just treatment, which goes against not only the precepts of just war theory, but against any sense of common decency.

Shakespeare's *Henry V* is the play that seems most deliberately engaged with arguments for and against the justice of wars and the play's scholarly reception is deserving of its very own chapter, as Paul Stevens shows in this volume (Chapter 13). I will therefore restrict my own discussion of the play to its extraordinary awareness of a number of just war principles, but I would like to make clear at the beginning that the play's treatment of the justice of and in wars is severely tainted by its protagonist's insincerity. Like Henry IV and Prince John, Henry V is also a talented Machiavellian schemer who is perfectly capable of putting on the right appearance for his purposes. Stephen Greenblatt called Henry V a "conniving hypocrite"[38] and most critics, including myself, agree with this interpretation. However, such a reading does not diminish the insight that the play constitutes an exploration of the principles of just war theory and places particular emphasis on the principle of proportionality. Like the archbishop in 2 *Henry IV*, King Henry also seems to consider the cause and costs of war very carefully:

> For God doth know how many now in health
> Shall drop their blood in approbation
> Of what your reverence shall incite us to.
> Therefore take heed how you impawn our person,
> How you awake our sleeping sword of war;
> We charge you in the name of God, take heed.
> For never two such kingdoms did contend
> Without much fall of blood, whose guiltless drops
> Are every one a woe, a sore complaint
> 'Gainst him whose wrongs gives edge unto the swords
> That makes such waste in brief mortality.   (*Henry V*, 1.2.18–28)

His speech juxtaposes the cause and the costs of war to emphasize that they must be at least in equal proportion. Otherwise, too many drops of blood will be shed without reason, and as the aggressor, Henry will be responsible for their deaths. The theme of responsibility occurs throughout the play and Henry is eager to relieve himself of the burden repeatedly, but he rightfully points out here that he would be responsible for the lives lost in battle, which makes it necessary that he fight a just war. Lives must not be lost in vain. It is only a just war, if it is necessary to wage it, so that soldiers know what they have to die for. If there is no such just cause, the guilt of wasting thousands of lives is insurmountable. This discussion of the principles of responsibility and proportionality recurs in Shakespeare's *Troilus and Cressida*, for here, the discussions take place after the fact, that is, after too many lives have already been wasted:

> She's bitter to her country. Hear me, Paris:
> For every false drop in her bawdy veins
> A Grecian's life has sunk; for every scruple
> Of her contaminated carrion weight
> A Trojan hath been slain. Since she could speak
> She hath not given so many good words breath
> As, for her, Greeks and Trojans suffered death.
>
> (*Troilus and Cressida*, 4.1.69–75)

If we can overlook the way Diomedes speaks about Helen, we notice that in this play both sides argue for the injustice of their cause due to its disproportionality, which adds to the cynical tone that makes *Troilus and Cressida* one of the most problematic problem plays. The play's depiction of war is less gruesome than Shakespeare's portrayal of the Wars of the Roses and yet it is possibly more disturbing. As ruthlessly as both parties treat each other in Shakespeare's early history plays, at least they repeatedly insist that they have good reason for doing so. In *Troilus and Cressida*, no one even pretends to believe in their cause for war. It seems that Shakespeare deliberately demystified the Trojan War to expose it as essentially unjust and disproportional.

## *Jus in Bello* in Shakespeare

Prince John's unjust treatment of the rebels at Galtres indicates that Shakespeare draws a clear line between the justice of war and the justice in war. Just war theorists have argued that the distinction is so important to make because it is perfectly possible that unjust warriors fight fairly or that just warriors fight unfairly. Shakespeare's Hector is a case in point: throughout the entire play, he seems to be the voice of justice, reason, and honor, only to pursue an unarmed soldier in the last act for nothing but material gain, which adds to the play's seeming disillusionment with traditional values. More importantly, however, the distinction between *ad bellum* and *in bello* is made with a focus on the question of responsibility. Soldiers are not supposed to be responsible for the war per se: they did not make the decision to go to war, "their war is not their crime."[39] Shakespeare seems to share the view, which becomes obvious when we return to *Henry V*, and it is noteworthy that neither Augustine nor Aquinas had made the point yet. The distinction of *ad bellum* and *in bello* is a vital principle of just war theory, but there is no evidence that this idea was already prevalent in Elizabethan times.

King Harry frequently finds himself confronted with responsibility for his actions and he always tries to relieve himself of it. He places responsibility for his war with France first on the clergy, then on the French dauphin, and ultimately on God. He blames the citizens of Harfleur for the harm they will receive from his hands if they do not surrender and he blames his soldiers for their wasted lives, although he is the one who wastes them. The pattern is too obvious for an audience to overlook and yet Shakespeare creates a scene dedicated to the subject that constitutes a remarkable deviation from his sources and the historical record. "Warlike" Harry is sidelined for a moment in favor of the perspective of his not-so-warlike soldiers: "We see yonder the beginning of the day, but I think we shall never see the end of it" (*Henry V*, 4.1.87–88). Hardly optimistic about their prospects to survive the upcoming battle as common soldiers, both Williams and Bates have death on their minds. They cannot help but wonder whether they will die in vain, so they raise the topic of the justice of Harry's cause in conversation with the king in disguise: "if the cause be not good, the King himself hath a heavy reckoning to make.... Now, if these men do not die well, it will be a black matter for the King that led them to it – who to disobey were against all proportion of subjection" (*Henry V*, 4.1.125–35, 136–39). Williams's statement is in perfect accordance with the principles of just war theory: if the cause is not just, the burden of wasted lives falls indeed upon the king. The soldiers themselves, however, are not guilty, as Bates insists: "we know enough if we know we are the King's subjects. If his cause be wrong, our obedience to the King wipes the crime of it out of us" (4.1.121–24). The unusual concern the whole play shows for the justice of Henry's cause is thus shared by these fictitious common soldiers, who have no place in a historical record and die nameless on the field of Agincourt.[40] Yet, the ethical evaluation they make of the war and the distinction of *jus ad bellum* and *jus in bello* is flawless. In keeping with his general character, Henry turns the argument on its head to relieve himself of the responsibility, but the important statement has been made very clear: his cause is unjust, so thousands of soldiers will die in vain.

This discussion between king and common soldiers demonstrates how far Shakespeare's theory of war has developed toward just war theory. Shakespeare's plays show an awareness of all three discourses, pacifism, militarism, and just war theory, but from *Richard III* onwards, just war theory gains priority over both pacifism and realism. Moreover, the plays include all of its central premises. The desire to restore the peace or avert an evil is the only just cause for war and the only identifiable just wars are Bosworth and Dunsinane. Shakespeare's characters argue on an increasingly complex theoretical level for and against the justice of their causes, their legitimate authority, and their right intentions. They consider the principles of proportionality and responsibility and common soldiers make a distinction between *jus ad bellum* and *jus in bello*. Thus, Shakespeare's theory of war is primarily concerned with the justice and injustice of wars, but this is not to say that his plays provide an implicit affirmation of war – quite the contrary. In fact, Shakespeare's dramatic engagement with just war theory reveals that, most of the time, a justification for war is hard to find.

*Further Reading*

Barker, Simon. *War and Nation in the Theatre of Shakespeare and His Contemporaries*, Edinburgh, Edinburgh University Press, 2007.

Foakes, R. A. *Shakespeare and Violence*, Cambridge, Cambridge University Press, 2003.

Goy-Blanquet, Dominique. *Shakespeare's Early History Plays: From Chronicle to Stage*, Oxford, Oxford University Press, 2003.

Greenblatt, Stephen. *Shakespearean Negotiations: The Circulation of Social Energy in Renaissance England*, Oxford, Clarendon Press, 1988.

Grene, Nicholas. *Shakespeare's Serial History Plays*, Cambridge, Cambridge University Press, 2002.

Hattaway, Michael (ed.). *The Cambridge Companion to Shakespeare's History Plays*, Cambridge, Cambridge University Press, 2002.

Leggatt, Alexander. *Shakespeare's Political Drama: The History Plays and the Roman Plays*, London, Routledge, 1988.

Pugliatti, Paola. *Shakespeare and the Just War Tradition*, Farnham, Ashgate, 2010.

Rackin, Phyllis. *Stages of History: Shakespeare's English Chronicles*, London, Routledge, 1990.

Walzer, Michael. *Just and Unjust Wars: A Moral Argument with Historical Illustrations*, 5th ed., New York, Basic Books, 2015.

## NOTES

1 Steven Lee, *Ethics and War: An Introduction* (Cambridge: Cambridge University Press, 2012), pp. 22–28.

2 Michael Walzer, *Just and Unjust Wars: A Moral Argument with Historical Illustrations*, 5th ed. (New York: Basic Books, 2015), p. 3; and *Arguing about War* (New Haven: Yale University Press, 2004), p. 22.

3 Lee, *Ethics and War*, p. 28.

4 Lee, *Ethics and War*, p. 29.

5 James Turner Johnson, *Ideology, Reason and the Limitation of War: Religious and Secular Concepts 1200–1740* (Princeton: Princeton University Press, 1975).

6 St. Augustine of Hippo, *The City of God against the Pagans*, ed. and trans. R. W. Dyson, Cambridge Texts in the History of Political Thought (Cambridge: Cambridge University Press, 1998), p. 925.
7 St. Augustine of Hippo, *The City of God*, p. 934.
8 St. Thomas Aquinas, *Political Writings*, ed. R. W. Dyson, Cambridge Texts in the History of Political Thought (Cambridge: Cambridge University Press, 2002), p. 240.
9 St. Thomas Aquinas, *Political Writings*, p. 241.
10 Walzer, *Arguing about War*, p. 22.
11 Lee, *Ethics and War*, p. 70.
12 Walzer, *Just and Unjust*, p. 21.
13 Desiderius Erasmus, "The Complaint of Peace," in David Kinsella and Craig L. Carr (eds.), *The Morality of War: A Reader* (London: Lynne Rienner Publishers, 2007), pp. 37–42, 40; and *The Education of a Christian Prince*, ed. Lisa Jardine, Cambridge Texts in the History of Political Thought (Cambridge: Cambridge University Press, 2017).
14 Erasmus, *Education*, p. 65.
15 Erasmus, *Education*, p. 103.
16 Erasmus, *Education*, p. 105.
17 Erasmus, *Education*, p. 101.
18 Niccolò Machiavelli, *The Prince*, ed. Quentin Skinner and Russell Price, Cambridge Texts in the History of Political Thought (Cambridge: Cambridge University Press, 2008), p. 52.
19 Machiavelli, *The Prince*, p. 62.
20 Corelli Barnett, *Britain and Her Army 1509–1970: A Military, Political and Social Survey* (London: Allen Lane, The Penguin Press, 1970), p. 24.
21 R. S. White, *Pacifism and English Literature: Minstrels of Peace* (Basingstoke: Palgrave Macmillan, 2008), p. 110.
22 Paul A. Jorgensen, "Theoretical Views of War in Elizabethan England," *Journal of the History of Ideas*, 13 (1952), pp. 469–81, 471; and *Shakespeare's Military World* (Berkeley: University of California Press, 1956).
23 Simon Barker, *War and Nation in the Theatre of Shakespeare and His Contemporaries* (Edinburgh: Edinburgh University Press, 2007), p. 109.
24 J. R. Hale, *Renaissance War Studies* (London: The Hambledon Press, 1983), p. 339.
25 Jorgensen, *Shakespeare's Military World*, p. 197.
26 Thomas Kullmann, "Shakespeare and Peace," in Ros King and Paul J. C. M. Franssen (eds.), *Shakespeare and War* (Basingstoke: Palgrave Macmillan, 2008), pp. 43–55, 46.
27 Theodor Meron, *Henry's Wars and Shakespeare's Laws: Perspectives on the Law of War in the Later Middle Ages* (Oxford: Clarendon Press, 1993), p. 36.
28 Steven Marx, "Shakespeare's Pacifism," *Renaissance Quarterly*, 45 (1992), pp. 49–95, 50.
29 Norman Rabkin, "Rabbits, Ducks and *Henry V*," *Shakespeare Quarterly*, 28 (1977), pp. 279–96, 294.
30 Rabkin, "Rabbits, Ducks and *Henry V*," p. 296.
31 J. R. Hale, "Shakespeare and Warfare," in John F. Andrews (ed.), *William Shakespeare: His World, His Works, His Influence*, 3 vols. (New York: Charles Scribner's Sons, 1985), vol. 1, pp. 85–98, 97 (my emphasis).

32 John Mark Mattox, "Henry V: Shakespeare's Just Warrior," *War, Literature and the Arts*, 12 (2000), pp. 30–53, 31. See also Meron, *Henry's Wars*; and Alexander Harrington, "War and William Shakespeare," *Dissent*, 50 (2003), pp. 104–7.

33 Nicholas Grene, *Shakespeare's Serial History Plays* (Cambridge: Cambridge University Press, 2002), p. 92.

34 Michael Hattaway, "The Shakespearean History Play," in Hattaway (ed.), *The Cambridge Companion to Shakespeare's History Plays* (Cambridge: Cambridge University Press, 2002), pp. 3–24, 14.

35 R. A. Foakes, *Shakespeare and Violence* (Cambridge: Cambridge University Press, 2003), p. 83.

36 Barker, *War and Nation*, p. 128.

37 Dominique Goy-Blanquet, *Shakespeare's Early History Plays: From Chronicle to Stage* (Oxford: Oxford University Press, 2003), p. 290.

38 Stephen Greenblatt, *Shakespearean Negotiations: The Circulation of Social Energy in Renaissance England* (Oxford: Clarendon Press, 1988), p. 41.

39 Walzer, *Just and Unjust*, p. 37.

40 Phyllis Rackin, *Stages of History: Shakespeare's English Chronicles* (London: Routledge, 1990), pp. 225–28.

# 3

DAVID BEVINGTON

# Shakespeare on Civil and Dynastic Wars

Civil and dynastic conflict was a hot topic in the 1590s. Spain's attempt to invade England with her Great Armada fleet in 1588 was freshly remembered. The English gratefully attributed their victory on that occasion to God, the weather, and the expert seamanship of Sir Francis Drake and other naval commanders. The Earl of Leicester then followed up on the armada triumph by helping the Protestant Dutch defend themselves against Philip II of Spain.

Accompanying disruptions on the civil front were no less threatening. Mary Queen of Scots abdicated the Scottish throne in 1567 after the sensational murders of her Catholic counselor David Rizzio and then the Earl of Darnley, Mary's husband, and her marriage to the Earl of Bothwell, with whom Mary was suspected of having connived in the murder of Darnley. Mary took refuge in England and remained there under house arrest until her execution in 1587. As granddaughter of Margaret Tudor (sister of Henry VIII) and James IV of Scotland, Mary Stuart was the direct heir to the Tudor throne if Queen Elizabeth should die without heirs. Mary's son by Lord Darnley, James, inherited her throne as James VI of Scotland when she abdicated. After her death in 1587, James was direct heir after Elizabeth to the English throne as well. Elizabeth, urged by her counselors to marry, was courted by the French duc d'Alençon and others, including the Earl of Leicester. She consented with great reluctance to the execution of Mary Stuart but did not marry or name a Protestant heir.

During her tempestuous life, Mary was inevitably the focus of several Catholic attempts to seat her on the English throne, including the notorious Babington conspiracy of 1586 to which Mary appears to have given her written consent. Catholic sentiment was still strong, especially in the north of England, where an armed insurrection known as the Northern Rebellion had been put down in 1569 only by determined military force. The leadership of this resistance movement included names like Northumberland (the Percy clan), Westmorland, and Norfolk that would play a prominent role, albeit with different holders of those noble titles, in Shakespeare's history plays. During the 1570s and 1580s, Jesuit clergymen were coming secretly from the Continent as part of a determined effort of the Catholic church to persuade wavering worshippers to return to the Catholic fold. A number of the clergymen who held sway as schoolmasters at the King Edward VI grammar school in Stratford-upon-Avon, where Shakespeare as a youth presumably studied, were Catholic. All through the 1580s, English authorities wondered anxiously whether English Catholics would rally to King Philip's invasion attempt of 1588. Philip and his generals assumed that they would. The English lords themselves, including the seventeenth Earl of Oxford, who had adopted the Catholic faith in 1576, were at considerable pains to reassure Elizabeth that they were politically loyal to her even if they chose to worship as Catholics. Sir Francis Walsingham, Elizabeth's spymaster, was continually busy keeping track of suspected or known dissidents. Arrests and interrogations were common.

Under these extraordinary circumstances, the newly born English history play took up religious and dynastic conflict as its most pressing topic. The most important writer of these plays by far was William Shakespeare, though Christopher Marlowe, Robert Greene, George Peele, Thomas Heywood, and others soon joined in. They had few dramatic precedents. An anonymous play of the late 1580s, *The Famous Victories of Henry V*, had introduced that prince to the stage, complete with his escapades in the company of a Falstaff-like roguish older man named Sir John Oldcastle, but that was a rare instance, and in any case was more interested in depicting Henry's wayward youth than in depicting dynastic conflict. To the significant extent to which Shakespeare's *Henry VI* plays in the years 1589 to 1592 were first in the attempt to grasp the momentous issue of England divided against herself in civil war, they are truly the originals of the English history play as it was to flourish on the London popular stage in the 1590s.

What in fact is an English history play? David Kastan has deftly shown us that the label does not really describe a literary or dramatic genre. From the Athenian fifth century BCE and Aristotle in the fourth century on down to the Renaissance, critics and theorists had categorized drama largely in terms of tragedy and comedy. Each had its characteristic structure and suitable types of characters, royal figures, and gods on the one hand and young lovers, tyrannical fathers, bawds, pimps, and such on the other. How could a play like *1 Henry VI* or *2 Henry IV* be described in these terms? An English history play turns out to be a drama, of serious and/or comic features, ending happily or unhappily as occasion demands. Its name bears no relation to generic form. An English history play is a play about English history.[1]

Yet to this neutral definition we can perhaps add this important qualifier: as invented and practiced by Shakespeare and then by Marlowe and others, the English history play was and is a dramatic study of civil conflict in England, with important ramifications for foreign involvement as well. Above all, its purpose is to explore the causes, the struggles, the personal motivations of the major participants, and the means by which civil conflict is intermittently brought under control. It is a story with implications about civil discord at all times and in all places, but its usual concern (excepting a few plays like Marlowe's *Edward II* and Shakespeare's *King John* and *Henry VIII*) is with English history of a very particular time, from the early years of the fifteenth century down to Henry Tudor's victory over Richard III at the Battle of Bosworth Field in 1485.

The English history play is thus a study of the anarchic period that led up to the commencement of the Tudor regime to which Shakespeare's spectators in the early 1590s were subjects. Under these circumstances, the English history play could serve the crucial role of analyzing and celebrating the coming to power of Elizabeth's grandfather Henry VII and by implication her own successful reign. The timeliness of this celebration was vividly underscored by the ongoing struggle in England between Catholicism and Protestantism and by the increasing awareness that Elizabeth would not bear children. What then would happen to England at her death?

*Henry VI, Part 1* is replete with military actions against the French, mainly at Orleans, Rouen, and Bordeaux. Historically, these events cover some thirty years in Edward Hall's *The Union of the Two Noble and Illustre Families of Lancastre and Yorke* and Holinshed's *Chronicles*, from the 1420s to the 1450s. Joan of Arc is champion of the French at Orleans and Rouen. The military scenes are lively and even amusing at times, with the dissipated French defenders of Orleans leaping "o'er the walls in their shirts" (2.1.38 SD). Scaling-ladders are employed by the attacking English to climb these same walls of the tiring-house.

Yet the point of the military action is mainly to demonstrate alarming disaffection at the English court. The funeral of Henry V, with which the play begins, gives way almost at once to recriminations. When the Bishop of Winchester credits "The church's prayers" with having added to England's prosperity during Henry V's short reign, the young King Henry VI's uncle and Protector, the Duke of Gloucester, is quick to denounce the bishop as one who is notorious for loving "the flesh" and his readiness to "prey" on his political enemies when he should be praying (1.1.32, 41, 43). Winchester is also a member of the royal family, as great-uncle of the king and illegitimate son of John of Gaunt, a circumstance that barred him from the royal succession but scarcely prevented him from meddling in factional politics.

Gloucester for his part is later accused by his foes of being henpecked by his proud wife, Eleanor Cobham, and aspiring to control of the realm.

The literary form of the play's opening scene is thus one of interrupted ceremony, as bad news continues to pour in from France as a consequence of mismanagement of the war by competing factions at home. "Guyenne, Champagne, Reims, Rouen, Orléans, / Paris, Gisors, Poitiers are all quite lost," a messenger reports, not through treachery "but want of men and money. / Amongst the soldiers this is mutterèd, / That here you maintain several factions, / And whilst a field should be dispatched and fought, / You are disputing of your generals" (1.1.60–61, 69–73). This complaint is reiterated throughout the play, down to the disgraceful betrayal of Lord Talbot at Bordeaux. Richard Plantagenet, Duke of York and Regent of France, laments the loss of "Maine, Blois, Poitiers, and Tours" owing, in his view, to the malfeasance of the Duke of Somerset in failing or refusing to send desperately needed reinforcements to Lord Talbot (4.3.45).

When we seek to know more as to what is motivating this disaffection, we realize with increasing clarity that the quarrel goes back to Henry Bolingbroke's seizure of power from his first cousin, Richard II, in 1399. The Duke of York in *1 Henry VI* is son of Richard Earl of Cambridge and grandson of Edward Duke of Aumerle, an avid supporter of Richard II (as dramatized later by Shakespeare in *Richard II*). York is himself the product of a canny marriage between the Earl of Cambridge and Anne Mortimer, a prominent member of the Mortimer clan who were chief supporters of Richard II and claimants to be Richard's true successors through their descent from Lionel Duke of Clarence, an elder brother of John of Gaunt, both of whom were sons of Edward III. York for his own part derives his heritage from Edmund of Langley, Duke of York in Richard II's time, another of Edward III's numerous sons. Richard of York is thus, as his name and title suggest, the scion of the Yorkist claim to the throne in the wake of Henry V's death in 1422. Somerset, meantime, is another Beaufort, like his brother the Bishop of Winchester. They are descended, albeit illegitimately and barred from royal succession, from John of Gaunt, Duke of Lancaster. They support the Lancastrian claim to the throne, with its insistence that Henry IV, son of John of Gaunt, became legal king when Richard II resigned his kingship. Hence Henry IV's son, Henry V, has inherited (as the Lancastrians view the matter) a true title as England's monarch. His young son Henry VI now deserves to be honored and obeyed as England's monarch, even though, having been born in 1421, he was crowned king at the tender age of less than one year old.

Factions emerge formally in a remarkable scene invented by Shakespeare to dramatize the beginning of the Wars of the Roses. We are to imagine a gathering of England's political elite in the garden of Temple Hall in London, a building of the Knights Templar in Shakespeare's time, now part of the Inns of Court, where lawyers resided. The participants, dividing into two groups, are debating the dynastic claims outlined here in the previous paragraph. Cannot Richard Plantagenet claim descent from Lionel Duke of Clarence, third son of Edward III? asks the Earl of Warwick in defending the Yorkist claim. Perhaps so, counters the Earl of Somerset on the Lancastrian side, but was not Richard's father the Earl of Cambridge arrested for treason during Henry V's reign, so that his heirs are "attainted," that is to say, convicted and condemned of a capital crime? (2.4.82–92). No, answers Plantagenet, "My father was attachèd, not attainted," that is to say, arrested but without a proper bill of attainder (96). As the quarrel mounts in intensity, the antagonists pluck roses from the garden in which they stand, white roses for the Yorkist claim and red roses for the Lancastrian. The battle lines are drawn. No such confrontation appears to have occurred historically, but in Shakespeare's history plays it gives fictional form to a dramatic sequence that is all about civil and dynastic war.

Richard Plantagenet, subsequently Duke of York, emerges not only as the standard-bearer for the Yorkist claim but as a man who is alarmingly not unlike his namesake and youngest son, Richard Duke of Gloucester, who was ultimately to become King Richard III. Both are charismatic, masterful in their use of rhetoric, devious, and insatiably ambitious. Most of all they embody the divisive spirit of ruthless competition for power that will lead to England's loss of France and to political paralysis at home. England turns out to be her own worst enemy.

Throughout, Shakespeare studiously refuses to take sides in the Wars of the Roses. Villainies abound on both sides. Self-interested opportunism is at fault in both camps. Richard of York's towering ambition is all the more deplorable because it is so characteristic of many of those whom Richard plans to subvert as well as those with whom he collaborates for his own purposes. To be sure, Shakespeare's treatment of the Jack Cade rebellion in 2 *Henry VI* is openly satirical. Cade promises his followers that "There shall be in England seven halfpenny loaves sold for a penny, the three-hooped-pot shall have ten hoops, and I will make it a felony to drink small beer." Dick, one of his men, proposes, "The first thing we do, let's kill all the lawyers" (4.2.61–71). What this demonstrates more than anything else, however, is that opportunistic aristocrats on both sides are all too ready to exploit popular unrest for their own demagogic purposes. Richard admits in soliloquy that, "for a minister of my intent," he has "seduced a head-strong Kentishman, / John Cade of Ashford, / To make commotion … Under the title of John Mortimer' (3.1.355–59). The chief blame lies with aristocratic feuding.

Women are at the center of England's civil and dynastic quarrels, no less than men. They are victims and unwitting prizes; they also connive at times for their own advantage. Joan of Arc is a Frenchwoman, to be sure, but the way she uses her sexuality to tempt susceptible men like the dauphin and escape being executed by pleading a (false) pregnancy is sadly like female behavior at the English court. Granted too, Margaret of Anjou is another Frenchwoman. The daughter of the penniless Duke of Anjou and titular king of Naples and Jerusalem, she inveigles the Earl of Suffolk into an affair (with his full-hearted cooperation) that proves lastingly disastrous for England's dynastic and political hopes. Suffolk's design is to present Margaret to the young King Henry VI as his royal bride. Although Henry has been offered a far more politically and dynastically advantageous marriage, to the daughter of the Earl of Armagnac, a man close to the Dauphin Charles, now king of France, in an alliance that would substantially further the cause of peaceful reconciliation between England and France (*1 Henry VI*, 5.1.17), young Henry allows himself to become infatuated with Suffolk's alluring descrip-tion of Margaret even though Henry has seen nothing of her yet except her picture. Never mind that she comes with no dower and no useful political connections. Never mind that Henry is wholly unaware of Suffolk's personal motivation in promoting the marriage, which is to have Margaret in England where Suffolk can secretly enjoy her as his mistress. Suffolk ends *1 Henry VI* on this distracting note of surrender to sexual desire at the expense of the public good: "Margaret shall now be queen and rule the King, / But I will rule both her, the King, and realm" (5.6.107–8). Surrender to a corrupting sexual passion is here closely tied to a predictably male obsession with political power. Passion overwhelms reason at every turn.

This unwise surrender to personal indulgence is anticipatory of other male-female relationships in the entire four-play cycle with which Shakespeare began his dramatizations of English history. With notable exceptions, like Lord Talbot's firm but courtly negotiations with the Countess of Auvergne in *1 Henry VI*, male surrender to desire almost invariably leads to disastrous results. The French dauphin surrenders control of his army to Joan La Pucelle. In *2 Henry VI*, the well-intended and courageous Duke of Gloucester, Henry's uncle and Protector, is struck down by his enemies through Gloucester's marriage to Eleanor Cobham, who traffics ambitiously with sorcerers, witches, conjurers, priests, and a spirit named Asnath. The scenes of conjuration provide a grimly comic aspect to what is at heart a dismal business.

More is to come. Soon after achieving the kingship in *3 Henry VI*, the Yorkist Edward IV bitterly disappoints his younger brothers, Richard of Gloucester and George, Duke of Clarence, by insisting on his right to marry the Lady Grey, penniless widow of a Lancastrian officer slain in the wars. She has nothing to bring to this union other than her pleas for help and her sexual body, which she prudently withholds until the marriage contract is assured. In this she is both a reincarnation of Margaret of Anjou as bride of Henry VI and an anticipation of Anne Boleyn in her maneuvers to be Henry VIII's wife and consort before consenting to share his bed. Edward IV's profitless marriage supplants an alliance that the Earl of Warwick has been promoting between King Edward and the Lady Bona, sister to the French King Lewis, which would benefit England's interests in much the same way that was offered earlier to King Henry VI by means of a marriage to the Earl of Armagnac's daughter. History has a way of repeating itself.

This Earl of Warwick, the great kingmaker of 3 *Henry VI*, is so vexed in *Richard III* by King Edward's self-indulgent marriage to the Lady Grey that he shifts his allegiance from the Yorkist to the Lancastrian faction. George, equally dismayed, also deserts the Yorkist cause. In doing so he perjures himself, and indeed perjury becomes a major motif of *Richard III*. It is a weakness that Richard of Gloucester knows how to manipulate in his victims as he works his way toward the throne. Clarence's perjured desertion of the Yorkist cause leaves him vulnerable to Richard's insinuations that Clarence cannot be permitted to live. Lord Hastings, when he is summarily arrested and sent to execution by Richard and his henchmen, realizes too late that he has perjured himself by his insincere swearing of friendship to the queen and her allies. "O Margaret, Margaret," he laments, "now thy heavy curse / Is lighted on poor Hastings' wretched head!" (3.4.97–98), since it is Margaret who has predicted how Hastings's perjury will exact a fatal penalty. The queen's kindred, Rivers and Grey, realize too late that they have brought down Margaret's heavy curse on themselves for their acquiescing in Richard's having stabbed her son, Prince Henry of Lancaster (3.3.15–17). The Duke of Buckingham, realizing too late that he cannot trust the professed friendship of King Richard, acknowledges that he deserves to die for having perjured himself in professing love for the queen and her kin: "Wrong hath but wrong, and blame the due of blame" (5.1.29).

Margaret looms large in 3 *Henry VI* as the overbearing wife who rules her meek husband in what Elizabethans widely regarded as an inversion of the marriage contract. Husbands should rule their wives, according to the sixteenth-century Church of England marriage service, where wives are bidden to obey their husbands whereas men are not similarly commanded to obey their wives. Margaret's taking charge of the Lancastrian army is an ominous replay of Joan of Arc's military role in *1 Henry VI*. Both are seen as gross inversions of emotion over reason.

In *Richard III* the fraught relationships of men and women are an unceasing source of discord with momentous dynastic consequences. Margaret, now a widow, becomes an embittered prophetess of the doom that will befall all those who have perjured themselves in civil conflict. King Edward's unwise marriage with the Lady Grey causes widespread disaffection not simply because of the lost opportunity for an advantageous match between Edward and the Lady Bona but because it places the Lady Grey, now Queen Elizabeth, in a position of being able to promote the interests of her ambitious kinsmen. Rivers, Grey, and Dorset are hated and despised by titled aristocrats like Lord Hastings and Buckingham as arrivistes eager to exploit to personal advantage their new and undeserved royal connection. Richard knows how to turn this hatred to his advantage by offering to assist Hastings in ending the threat posed by these poseurs, these new men. Indeed, Richard has no trouble arranging the summary arrest and execution of the queen's kindred. Hastings, delighted, takes this as a sign that Richard is a powerful ally to be trusted. Richard, in turn, quickly gets rid of Hastings once that man has shown an unwillingness to support Richard's claim to the throne. Hastings is vulnerable in pursuing what is by now a predictable weakness in men: his amorous desire for Jane Shore. But Jane Shore is, or has been, the mistress of King Edward IV. How could Hastings venture on so dangerous a prize? Well, *cherchez la femme*.

Are women also weak and easily corrupted? Richard certainly thinks so, as demonstrated in his courtship of the Lady Anne. Winning her as his bride would seem to be an impossible task, since he has personally killed her first husband, Edward the Lancastrian Prince of Wales, and Edward's father, Henry VI. Richard takes on that impossibility with gusto and boasts of it incredulously when he has succeeded: "Was ever woman in this humor wooed? / Was ever woman in this humor won?" (1.2.213–14). He has won her through flattery, insisting that only she can save the life of one who is so in love with her that he has done terrible things for the sake of having her. She soon realizes her mistake. Her perjury in deserting the memory of her slain husband and father-in-law deserves no less than shame and punishment. She has "proved the subject of my own soul's curse" (4.1.75).

Once he is king, Richard III trusts that he can use his rhetorical genius to persuade Queen Elizabeth, once the Lady Grey and now the dowager widow of Edward IV, to give her daughter Elizabeth in marriage to Richard. The seeming impossibility of succeeding in this courtship of his own niece does not deter him any more than it did with his courting of the Lady Anne. We can see at once the dynastic brilliance of Richard's scheme. Elizabeth of York, the sole Yorkist survivor along with Richard himself now that her two brothers, Edward V and Richard, have been smothered in the Tower, would bring to such a marriage the inheritance of the Yorkist claim to the throne. The Duke of Clarence is dead and so apparently are his children. That leaves no one in the Yorkist family tree who could challenge Richard dynastically. On the Lancastrian side, Henry VI and his son have died at the hands of Richard. The plan seems to be complete.

Does Richard succeed in persuading Queen Elizabeth to consent to his design? Richard certainly thinks so. "Relenting fool, and shallow changing woman!" he exults (4.4.347), as she leaves him, seemingly having promised to do as he wishes. But perhaps the play leaves the matter ambiguous as to whether she means to act accordingly or whether she misleads him, stalling for time.

Certain it is, at any rate, that once Richard III has been defeated in battle by Henry Tudor, Earl of Richmond, Queen Elizabeth is more than ready to see her daughter marry the new King Henry VII. This marriage is a dynastic triumph, and in ways that mirror Richard's dynastic plan but in a form that is more complete and much better aimed at reconciling the conflicts of the Wars of the Roses. Richard's plan, after all, would have succeeded solely in Yorkist terms. The new king's marriage unites the sole living claimant on the Yorkist side with Henry Tudor as claimant on the Lancastrian side. This is the sense in which *Richard III* concludes Shakespeare's first historical four-play series by fulfilling the promise of Edward Hall's title for his history of these wars: *The Union of the Two Noble and Illustre Families of Lancastre and Yorke.*

That chronicle, first published in 1548, was written to justify and glorify the Tudor monarchs by showing how their lineage had at last reconciled the warring factions of Lancaster and York. The justification was vitally necessary. Henry VIII was still alive until 1547, but physically weakened and dynastically immersed in controversy about royal succession and separation from the Catholic faith. Henry's sole son, Edward, born in 1537, was a lad of nine when he became king after his father's death. Would England face another crisis of a minority kingship as it had done in 1377 when Richard II became king at the age of ten, and then again when Henry VI, nearly aged one, became monarch in 1422? In both instances, powerful and ambitious uncles hovered about the throne, vying for authority and resorting at times to assassination (as of Thomas of Woodstock in 1397). The situation was no less ominous in the late 1540s and 1550s. Elizabethan audiences would remember that Edward Seymour, Duke of Somerset, brother-in-law of Henry VIII and uncle of the young king, was virtual ruler of England as Protector during the minority reign of Edward VI (1547–53), and that his joint regent, John Duke of Northumberland, had married his son Lord

Guildford Dudley to Lady Jane Grey, great-granddaughter of Henry VII through his youngest daughter Mary and first cousin once removed of Edward VI, who had been induced to name her as his successor to the throne as Edward VI lay dying in 1553. The proclamation of Lady Jane as queen had ended in failure after nine days on July 19, 1553. Her life was spared at first, but then, after the discovery of the so-called Wyatt's Rebellion aiming to disrupt Queen Mary's plan of marrying Philip I of Spain, Jane was executed in 1554 along with her husband and her father-in-law Northumberland. No less harrowing was the uncertain sequence of events that had led to the accession to the throne in 1558 of Elizabeth, daughter of Henry VIII and Anne Boleyn, determining as it did the return of England to Protestantism after the five years of Mary's Catholic reign.

Under these circumstances, we can easily understand why *Richard III* vilifies its titular figure and appears instead to endorse the Tudor claim to the English throne. The evenhandedness that has characterized Shakespeare's earlier appraisals of the warring factions in the Wars of the Roses is no longer dramatically appropriate. Henry Tudor's takeover of British rule in 1485 was a coup d'état, however much Queen Elizabeth I and her ministers may have wished to repudiate it as a precedent for regicide. Henry's dynastic lineage was absurd: his paternal grandfather, Owen Tudor, had married Katherine of Valois, Henry V's widow, whereas on the maternal side Henry Tudor was descended from the Beauforts, those illegitimate offspring of John of Gaunt and his mistress, Catherine Swynford, who had been specifically barred from the royal succession. Once Henry Tudor became Henry VII, he was as matter-of-fact in dealing with rival claimants (Lambert Simnel, crowned at Dublin as Edward VI in 1487, and Perkin Warbeck, executed in 1499 for having proclaimed himself King Richard IV) as was alleged to have been the practice of Richard III. Elizabethan audiences needed to be reassured that the Tudor dynasty had begun with divine sanction. The Earl of Richmond in *Richard III* is as God-fearing and upright a figure as could be wished. His marriage to Elizabeth of York, the surviving Yorkist heiress, is dynastically complete in a way that Richard's intended marriage to Elizabeth could never be.

The dynastic dilemma posed in *King John*, a play written perhaps in the interval of time between Shakespeare's two historical tetralogies (1594–96), bears a marked resemblance to the crises of the fifteenth century. Shakespeare shows no interest in Magna Carta. Instead, the play focuses on the way in which King John occupies the English throne by "strong possession" (1.1.39) after the death of his older brother, Richard I, in 1199. Even his mother, Queen Eleanor, questions the legitimacy of John's claim: "Your strong possession much more than your right" (40), she whispers to him when the French ambassador, Chatillon, presents John with King Philip of France's challenge to John "in right and true behalf / Of thy deceased brother Geoffrey's son, / Arthur Plantagenet" (7–9). Geoffrey had died by this time, in 1186, but his son and heir Arthur, born that same year, was still alive in 1199 at the age of thirteen. In Shakespeare's play, the widowed mother of this boy, Constance, ceaselessly reminds the king of the wrong he has done, even if Richard I had apparently named John his successor in his last will and testament. But could such a will disinherit Arthur? The venerated English tradition of inheritance by primogeniture ruled that property should descend to the eldest son, and, since Richard I had no male heirs of his own, it should pass to the next brother and to that brother's heirs.

Shakespeare is careful, as usual, not to endorse either side in this struggle for power. To be sure, audiences are bound to sympathize with young Arthur as the innocent victim. Yet the case is by no means clear that England would be better off by righting his claim to rule with the help of a French army. Philip Falconbridge, the bastard son of Richard I, is a key choric figure in arguing for "commodity," that is, the pragmatic notion that the muddled compromise of the present state of affairs is preferable to the uncertainties of radical change. The French are meddling in English affairs for their own purposes, seeking to rebuke King John for having stood out against the "see of Rome" (5.2.72). To some Protestants in Elizabethan England, John, however flawed as a monarch, was a precursor of the Reformation in his resistance to the papacy. King John's disaffected English nobles learn almost too late that the treacherous French, with whom they have allied themselves against the English throne, intend, once their military action has succeeded, to "recompense the pains you [the nobles] take / By cutting off your heads" (5.4.15–16). The Bastard ends the play with his patriotic prediction that "This England never did, nor never shall, / Lie at the proud foot of a conqueror / But when it first did help to wound itself" (5.7.112–14).

The reigns of Richard II and his first cousin and successor, Henry IV, to which Shakespeare turned in his second historical tetralogy in 1596 and the following years, saw the beginnings of the dynastic crisis that would erupt into the Wars of the Roses. Moving back in historical time, Shakespeare embraced the opportunity to study the genesis of civil discord. Richard II, young and unwise in the art of political leadership, alienates his powerful uncles Gaunt and York by his disregard for the rule of law and custom and appears to be guilty of having consented to the death of his youngest uncle, Thomas of Woodstock, Duke of Gloucester.

That ominous name, "Gloucester," illustrates how the repetition of aristocratic titles tells a woeful tale of civil conflict: Thomas of Woodstock's title of "Gloucester" is also the title bestowed on Henry VI's intrepid uncle Humphrey in 2 *Henry VI* and finally on Richard, Duke of Gloucester, son of the Yorkist leader the Duke of York and subsequently King Richard III. The same is true of "York" and "Lancaster" and a host of Christian names as well, especially "Richard," "Henry," and "Edward." Among the women, the title of "Queen" is frequently applied, along with the recurrent names "Anne," "Katherine," and "Elizabeth." Feuding reciprocity in these plays often demands a Yorkist Edward for a Lancastrian Edward, and so on in endless succession.

In *Richard II*, Henry IV's problems with his nobles continue the pattern found in *King John* and all the history plays from *1 Henry VI* to *Richard III*. Henry owes the success of his coup d'état in 1399 in good part to the support of the northern lords, especially the powerful Percy clan that includes the Duke of Northumberland, his feisty son Harry Percy, known as Hotspur, and Northumberland's younger brother, the Earl of Worcester, along with Lord Mortimer the Earl of March, who has married the daughter of the rebel Welshman Owain Glyndŵr. Hotspur has married Mortimer's sister Kate. The Percies, having rallied to the cause of Henry Bolingbroke in 1399 as the readiest means to curb Richard II's assaults on their liberties, and originally finding this Lancastrian lord to be compliant and gracious with them, obviously hope that the new king will allow them to practice justice and political rule in their own jurisdictions as they see fit. At the start of *1 Henry IV*, they are fighting Henry IV's wars against their traditional enemies the Scots in the north and the Welsh in the west. But when Henry IV gets tough with them about ransom of captured warriors, insisting on his rights as king of England, they are taken aback.

Is King Henry being unreasonable? The Percies certainly think so, Hotspur most outspokenly. Yet the intelligence Henry has been receiving is not reassuring about the barons' intents. What is he to make of the unsettling news that Mortimer, a claimant to the English throne, has married the daughter of the Welsh leader that Mortimer was supposed to be fighting in the west (1.3.83–85)? Has he not, by this act, "betrayed / The lives of those that he did lead to fight / Against that great magician, damned Glyndŵr" (81–83)? This is no small matter, since Mortimer, the Earl of March, is indeed the man who was "proclaimed / By Richard, that dead is, the next of blood" (144–45). Mortimer's claim to the English throne is vehemently maintained by those who insist that Richard II was illegally deposed. Of course, King Henry has no intention of ransoming "revolted Mortimer" (92), his chief rival to the English throne. Shakespeare simplifies genealogy here by conflating two Edmund Mortimers, one who was captured by Glyndŵr and married his daughter and one who as the fifth Earl of March was proclaimed heir presumptive by Richard II, with the result that the "Mortimer" of *1 Henry IV* is a genuine threat to the new Lancastrian king.

Shakespeare has also changed the name of Hotspur's wife from "Elizabeth" to "Kate." Historically, she was very much a member of the Percy clan, being the daughter of the third Earl of March, sister of the fourth Earl of March, and aunt of the fifth earl. The third earl's marriage to Philippa, daughter of Lionel, Duke of Clarence, provided a line of descent going back to Edward III, since the Duke of Clarence was older brother to John of Gaunt, Duke of Lancaster, and father of Henry IV, whose troubled reign began in 1399. By the rule of primogeniture, once Richard II had died without heirs, his father Edward the Black Prince having deceased before him in 1376, the line of descent would then go to Richard's oldest uncle. William of Hatfield, next in line, had died young. Clarence was next, as were his descendants, if the line could legitimately pass through his daughter Philippa.

The *Henry IV* plays end with the rejection of Falstaff and the triumphant coronation of Henry V, but in a way that is surprisingly like that of *King John*. In both situations the issue of succession is clouded by the phenomenon of coup d'état. Both end in compromise in the name of "commodity." Better this state of affairs, arguably, than continued civil unrest. That is very much the final position of Edmund Langley the Duke of York, younger brother of Gaunt and uncle of the new King Henry IV. York, in *Richard II*, first scolds his nephew Richard II by arguing that the taking away of property that Bolingbroke legally owns as Earl of Hereford is to "take from Time / His charters and his customary rights" (2.1.195–96). The issue is that serious. Having failed in this argument, York then tries to persuade Bolingbroke that by returning from exile to England with military force he is seriously in violation of the constitutional principles that England holds most dear. York is right on both counts: Richard II and Bolingbroke are both legally in the wrong. What to do? York finds that he has no realistic choice other than to go along with what has happened and cannot be stopped. It is the solution of the Bastard Falconbridge in *King John*, and as such it is inglorious. Yet it acknowledges the existential reality of what has occurred. Prince Hal's ultimate rejection of Falstaff is no less troublesome as an issue. Falstaff does embody the potentially anarchic impulses that have troubled all of Shakespeare's history plays up to this point, but he is also such a splendid comic commentator on the potential absurdity of war and dying and machismo that his absence leaves us with hard questions about the validity of "honor."

The very subject of Richard II's deposition and all that followed was an explosive topic in the late 1590s. Queen Elizabeth's government was quick to move against any version of the story that might seem to countenance the removal from office of an anointed monarch. When, on the eve of the ill-fated rebellion against Queen Elizabeth's government by the Earl of Essex in 1601, Shakespeare's company was commissioned by some of Essex's follow-ers to perform a play about Richard II, almost surely Shakespeare's version, the actors were severely interrogated. "I am Richard II. Know ye not that?" the Queen famously remarked to her archivist, William Lambarde, as they were reviewing some historical documents from Richard's reign.[2] Richard's deposition was such a sensitive matter that Shakespeare's dramatization of it in act 4, scene 1 had to be deleted from the first three quarto editions of *Richard II.*

*Henry V* opens with the young king being fully aware of the consequences of this "inconvenient" state of affairs. He faces opposition that bears the familiar face of support for the claim of Richard II's Yorkist descendants to the throne. One of the conspirators whom Henry arrests at Southampton, as the king is about to sail for France, is identified as "Cambridge" in the text (2.0, 2.2). He is never called anything else, but an astute observer in Shakespeare's audience might well realize that the man under arrest is Richard Earl of Cambridge, brother of the Duke of Aumerle, whose alle-giance to Richard II's cause was so troublesome to Aumerle's father, the Duke of York, who had sided with the new King Henry IV. This Earl of Cambridge had married Anne Mortimer, sister of the fifth Earl of March who claimed the title of Yorkist pretender to the throne. The son and heir of this marriage was Richard Plantagenet, Earl of Cambridge and Duke of York, the father of Edward IV, the Duke of Clarence, and Richard III. Shakespeare conceals all this information in *Henry V*, choosing instead to present "Cambridge" as a conspirator motivated like his fellows, Scrope and Grey, by a greedy and disloyal readiness to traffic with the perfidious French against King Henry.

One speech does briefly gesture toward truer historical circumstances when Cambridge says, "For me, the gold of France did not seduce, / Although I did admit it as a motive / The sooner to effect what I intended" (2.2.153–55). An alert spectator in Shakespeare's audience would have perceived that the intention of which Cambridge speaks was no less than the overthrow of what he regarded as the specious Lancastrian claim to the throne. Shakespeare does not allow this to be said in this play. The deletion makes for a heavily biased reinterpretation of history, no less so than Shakespeare's earlier portrayal of Richard III. George Bernard Shaw, from his own biased point of view, saw Henry V as a warmonger and Shakespeare's glorification of the king as arrant hyperbole.[3]

Still, an exploration of civil commotion as dramatized in Shakespeare's plays makes clear why he wished to satisfy his audiences' longing for an end to civil unrest. He does so in *Henry V*, even while frankly reminding his audience of what they knew all too well, that Henry V's triumph was to be short-lived. For all his greatness, Henry made the fearful mistake of dying young and leaving behind him as his male heir "Henry the Sixth, in infant bands crowned King ... Whose state so many had the managing / That they lost France and made his England bleed." This is, after all, a story "Which our stage has oft shown" (Epilogue, 8–13).

When Shakespeare turns to ancient Greek and Roman history, it is partly at least to show that these patterns of civil and dynastic violence are no less recurrent in classical civilization. Freed from the constraints of Christian providential interpretations of English history, a play like *Julius Caesar* (1599) dramatizes a political conflict in which simple clear answers are impossible to find. Many modern productions of this play, as for example in Chicago Shakespeare Theater's production of 2010 directed by Barbara Gaines, have seen an image of Mussolini's fascist Italy in the figure of Julius Caesar; the stage is festooned with fascist banners, and Caesar's soldiers and guards march in goose steps, while machine guns mow down innocent bystanders. The trouble with this kind of adaptation is that Brutus and Cassius are then cast into the role of freedom fighters, and this is a role that does not fit them. Shakespeare is fascinated instead with the way in which the conspirators are their own worst enemies. Their attempted revolution is defeated by reactionary forces all-too-ready to quell political unrest and destroy those very civil liberties for which Brutus and his fellow conspirators risk and then lose their lives.

*Troilus and Cressida* (c. 1601) adopts an evenhanded approach to a war that has yielded little more than stalemate and disaffection on both sides. The Trojans are no doubt more attractive than the Greeks; English history cast its lot historically on the Trojan side, based on a legendary tradition that England was founded by Aeneas's grandson Brutus. Yet morale is universally low. In both camps ironies of loyalty abound. The Greek Achilles is known to be in love with one of Priam's daughters, Polyxena (3.3.191–92). Paris wronged the Greeks by stealing Menelaus's wife Helen but did so in reprisal for "an old aunt whom the Greeks held captive" (2.2.77), namely Hesione, Priam's sister, who had been rescued from the wrath of Poseidon by Hercules and bestowed by him on the Greek Telamon, father of Ajax. The Trojan Hermione thus became the mother of the Greek Ajax. The Trojan Hector greets Ajax as "my father's sister's son, / A cousin-german to great Priam's seed," a circumstance that ought to be an "obligation of our blood" forbidding "A gory emulation twixt us twain" (4.5b.4–7), and yet there they are, about to engage in combat. Who started the war, anyway? Does it matter?

*Antony and Cleopatra* (1606–7) ultimately celebrates the greatness of the protagonists' love relationship as somehow rising above the trammels of their glamorous but reckless lives. The story, as taken from Plutarch, is one of constant political and military struggle. Antony freely admits that he has undone his own best interests, deserting a virtuous wife and his position as triumvir for a "trull" who, he fears, has "packed cards" with Octavius Caesar when Caesar has gained decisive military advantage in Egypt (3.6.97, 4.14.19). Caesar himself is a brilliant study in contradiction, as indeed he was generally regarded in the Renaissance: both a statesman with a clear-sighted vision of Roman greatness and a Machiavellian opportunist ready to take advantage of his partners or even his sister if need be for political advantage. He wins the day, no matter how fervently Cleopatra may insist that, by her suicide, she has found a way to "call great Caesar ass / Unpolicied" (5.2.303–4). *Coriolanus* (c. 1608) is no less mired in political impasse, in a world that seems to know no morality other than that of expediency.

Among the great Shakespearean tragedies, dynastic conflict is visibly present even if these plays are less interested in analyzing its causes and political consequences than in the sufferings and tribulations that afflict the protagonists. Hamlet does intensely resent the way in which his uncle has cut off Hamlet's right to inherit the throne of Denmark; although choice of monarch by "election" is allowed by custom, Hamlet has every reason to deplore how Claudius has "Popped in between th'election and my hopes" (5.2.65). Yet murder and incest are far more pressing issues. The play's political ending, with Fortinbras having achieved his ambition to become king of Denmark, seems an ironically matter-of-fact way to settle the old territorial dispute between Denmark and Norway. It is one that seems to confirm Horatio's stoic view of history as it has played itself out in *Hamlet* (c. 1600–1), a tale "Of carnal, bloody, and unnatural acts, / Of accidental judgments, casual slaughters, / Of deaths put on by cunning and for no cause, / And in this upshot purposes mistook / Fall'n on th'inventors' heads" (5.2.359–63). Such a reading of history is so wholly at variance with Hamlet's providential reading of his own destiny ("There is special providence in the fall of a sparrow" [5.2.191–92]) that we are left at the end with two incommensurate interpretations of Hamlet's tragedy and of political life in Denmark.

*King Lear* (c. 1605–6) begins with a dynastic struggle over the inheritance of Lear's kingdom. It ends with a political uncertainty that is devastatingly appropriate to the apocalyptic tragedy of Lear and Cordelia. Who is to reign? The Duke of Albany, the military victor, offers the crown jointly to Kent and Edgar, neither of whom has any vestige of dynastic authority. To be sure, almost no one else is still alive. Why Albany declines to name himself is unclear. Kent declines the offer, saying "My master calls me. I must not say no" (5.3.298), with the suggestion that Kent expects to die shortly. Edgar is left with the play's final speech, as though designating him monarch in the absence of any other candidate, but he himself says nothing to confirm that this is so. As in *Hamlet*, the ending seems incapable of providing closure for a tragedy in which political and social resolution, however desperately needed, eludes the grasp of those who are left to cope with a desolated reality.

The ending of *Macbeth* (c. 1606–7) does appear to offer reassurance of an end to dynastic strife. Macbeth pays for his crimes at the hands of his nemesis, Macduff, who thereupon offers the crown to Malcolm, oldest son of the murdered King Duncan. The "show of eight kings, and Banquo last" (4.1.110 SD) that Macbeth beholds on his final visit to the weird sisters is replete with comforting images of "two-fold balls and treble sceptres" (120) seeming to signify the double coronation of King James VI of Scotland and I of England along with his assumed title as king of Great Britain, France, and Ireland.

Yet this spectacle is conjured up by the weird sisters. Is destiny under their control? Shakespeare's chief source, Holinshed's *Chronicles*, is hardly reassuring on this score: the Macbeth who ruled in Scotland from 1040 to 1057 achieved the throne through assassination as part of a dynastic struggle between two clans. The Macbeth of Holinshed has good reason to be unhappy about Duncan's naming of Malcolm as Prince of Cumberland, since Scottish law specified that as long as such a son was still underage the crown should pass to "the next of blood unto him," namely, to Macbeth in this instance, since he was Duncan's cousin. Macbeth was slain in Holinshed's account by Malcolm, not Macduff. Not surprisingly, a number of modern productions of "the Scottish play" conjure up an ending in which political revolution is about to start up all over again; at the end of Roman Polanski's film version of 1971, for instance, Donaldbain searches ambitiously for the witches as a means of achieving the crown.

Civil and dynastic conflict is thus a huge and nearly constant presence in Shakespeare's plays. We see it even in what might be his first play, *The Comedy of Errors*. Its frame plot tells a sad tale of civil strife between Ephesus and Syracuse that threatens the life of old Egeon, father of the Antipholus twins. This frame story is Shakespeare's contribution to a plot chiefly derived from Plautus.

In what may well have been Shakespeare's formal farewell to the stage in *The Tempest* (c. 1611), the background Italian story is one of bitter and deadly rivalry between Milan and Naples. The play implies that life is like that in the fallen world from which Prospero and Miranda and the rest have come: brother turning against brother, tyrants seizing power and ruling by intimidation, and so on. We see the same pattern in *As You Like It*, in the "envious court" of Duke Frederick (2.1.4), in the hostile rivalry that characterizes Don John's uneasy relationship with his brother Don Pedro in *Much Ado About Nothing*, and in Cloten's resentment of his stepbrother Posthumus Leonatus in *Cymbeline*. *Henry VIII* (1613), written seemingly in collaboration with John Fletcher, offers a detailed analysis of the dynastic conflict that had led to Henry VIII's break with Rome in 1532–34. Lawrence Stone tells us that ruthless competitiveness was a general malaise of royal and aristocratic courts of the Renaissance.[4] We can say at least that civil and dynastic conflict serves Shakespeare brilliantly as essential to his craft as playwright.

*Further Reading*

Blanpied, John W. *Time and the Artist in Shakespeare's English Histories*, Newark, University of Delaware Press, 1983.

Cavanagh, Dermot, Stuart Hampton-Reeves, and Stephen Longstaffe (eds.). *Shakespeare's Histories and Counter-Histories*, Manchester, Manchester University Press, 2006.

Curry, Anne. *Henry V: From Playboy Prince to Warrior King*, London, Allen Lane, 2015.

Hattaway, Michael (ed.). *The Cambridge Companion to Shakespeare's History Plays*, Cambridge, Cambridge University Press, 2002.

Hodgdon, Barbara. *The End Crowns All: Closure and Contradiction in Shakespeare's History*, Princeton, Princeton University Press, 1991.

Howard, Jean E., and Phyllis Rackin. *Engendering a Nation: A Feminist Account of Shakespeare's English Histories*, London, Routledge, 1997.

Kastan, David Scott. *Shakespeare and the Shapes of Time*, Hanover, University Press of New England, 1982.

Leggatt, Alexander. *Shakespeare's Political Drama: The History Plays and the Roman Plays*, London, Routledge, 1988.

Patterson, Annabel. *Reading Shakespeare's Chronicles*, Chicago, University of Chicago Press, 1994.

Rackin, Phyllis. *Stages of History: Shakespeare's English Chronicles*, London, Routledge, 1990.

**NOTES**

1 David Scott Kastan, *Shakespeare and the Shapes of Time* (Hanover: University Press of New England, 1982).

2 Stephen Orgel, "I am Richard II," in Alessandra Patrina and Laura Tosi (eds.), *Representations of Elizabeth I in Early Modern Culture* (London: Palgrave MacMillan, 2011), pp. 11–43; and Jason Scott-Warren, "Was Elizabeth I Richard II? The Authenticity of Lambard's 'Conversation,'" *Review of English Studies*, 64 (2013), pp. 208–30.

3 George Bernard Shaw, review of *1 Henry IV*, Haymarket Theatre, April 8, 1896, in *Dramatic Opinions and Essays with an Apology*, 2 vols. (New York: Brentano's, 1906), vol. 1, pp. 421–31.

4 Lawrence Stone, *The Crisis of the Aristocracy, 1558–1641* (Oxford: Clarendon Press, 1965).

# 4

CLAIRE MCEACHERN

# Foreign War

In an age of nation-states, "foreign" war seems a relatively straightforward classification: a conflict between two or more state actors manifesting as a struggle over and in physical territory. The geographic divide may be attended or provoked by linguistic, ethnic, cultural, and political differences that allow characterization of the conflict by the parties concerned as a contest between homegrown "us" and an alien "them." When the grounds for such a characterization do not exist, they are often invented. Foreign war lacks the tragic affective load of internecine or "civil" war, can be cloaked with the moral righteousness of self-defense against the threat of an aggressor, or beg the justifications that attend being one. Whereas civil war speaks to divisions within a community, war with a foreign enemy can summon the sentimental appeal of a populace united against a common threat – even if the unity lasts only as long as the threat does. As Shakespeare's King Henry IV shrewdly advises his son Prince Hal, there is nothing quite like "foreign quarrels" with which to "busy giddy minds" (2 *Henry IV*, 4.3.342–43).

"This realm of England is an empire" declared Henry VIII in 1533, whose king "may yield justice and final determination to all manner of folk resident ... within this realm ... without restraint or provocation to any foreign princes or potentates of the world."[1] These words announced England's sovereignty and independence from papal dominion rather than a fellow state actor, but in the opposition between "folk resident" of a realm and "foreign princes or potentates" we can hear the conflict between native community and alien power that typically defines foreign war – and of course Protestant England's principal military antagonist throughout nearly half the long reign of Elizabeth I was the largest Catholic superpower in Europe, Spain. Early modern England had yet to complete the institutional and cultural transformations that would render it either a nation or a state in the modern sense of these terms – that is, a community identified with both place and state formation.[2] The military conflicts between geographically distant powers that Shakespeare dramatizes are primarily dynastic in nature, which is to say they concern the rival claims of feudal kings to territory. Yet these conflicts are frequently phrased by their participants as a struggle between native people and alien powers – or at least between English virtue and foreign decadence. In fact, insofar as the identities of nation or state as we will come to understand them can be heard in the plays, it may be chiefly in the military context.

Of course, not all of the plays that portray foreign war are concerned with England as a party to the conflict. Hamlet's Denmark is invaded by the Polish young Fortinbras; Othello leads Venetian forces against the Turk; the Roman plays canvas enemies of the republic or empire as the case warrants. Nor do all the plays in which England finds itself embattled by an alien state freight the conflict equally. In *King Lear*, for instance, we find ourselves siding with the French forces led by Cordelia in her quest to succor her father – or even forget that they *are* "alien" troops, our attention focused on the far more local power struggles of parents and children. As in *Hamlet*, the global conflict seems to be there only to remind us of how little it engages us in light of more individual struggles. In *Cymbeline*, likewise, Rome invades Britain via Wales, where the valiant lost princes Arviragus and Guiderius display both roughhewn bravery and tactical cunning in turning back an entire army by relying on their familiarity with the local terrain. But it is difficult to summon much indignation on behalf of the corrupt British court for which they fight. In *Coriolanus*, the choice of Romans or Volscians may feel as indifferent to us as it ultimately does to Coriolanus, who fights less for a mother country than a mother. Perversely, the play that most rouses a patriotic fervor in its simplest and most straightforward aspects – defensive, fierce, stalwart – may be *Macbeth*, where a courageous Scottish king fights off "English epicures" with much of the same energy and vocabulary that Jacobean Englishmen protested the prospect of union with their northern neighbor.

Such varied uses of the dramatic occasion of foreign war indicate Shakespeare's awareness of its multiple dramatic functions: mere backdrop or focal point, aggravating circumstance, or crucible of manly valor and self-sacrifice. In some plays war provides the central animating conflict, and the alliance of a community the heady stuff of a handfasted (if metaphorical) brotherhood; in others, it serves merely to make us realize our willingness to dismiss such abstractions as "country" or "sovereignty" in the face of the far more tangible – and sometimes more terrible – battles amongst family members or lovers. Or as Antony grandly puts it to Cleopatra, with words he will by the play's end be forced to make good on: "Let Rome in Tiber melt, and the wide arch / Of the ranged empire fall! Here is my space, / Kingdoms are clay.... The nobleness of life / Is to do thus, when such a mutual pair / And such a twain can do't" (*Antony and Cleopatra*, 1.1.34–39).

The magnanimous force of such a dismissal lies in the value we usually ascribe to kingdoms, and nowhere is English sovereignty more prioritized than in three of the English history plays: *1 Henry VI*, *King John*, and *Henry V*. England's wars with France provide the occasion for all three plays, all of which treat the tenuous hold of medieval English sovereigns upon their French possessions. To take them in historical rather than compositional or performance order, *King John* (c. 1595–96) concerns the conflict of the early thirteenth century in which the English crown lost the Duchy of Normandy; *Henry V* (1599) recounts the successful bid of the fourteenth-century English king to reestablish his claim (through conquest and then marriage) to the French throne; and *1 Henry VI* (c. 1591) portrays the wars of the first half of the fifteenth century during which King Henry VI gradually lost the ground secured by his father. However, as Henry V's triumph at the Battle of Agincourt is the subject of the last of these plays composed and staged, Shakespeare's original audiences would have concluded their decade-long experience of war in France on, as it were, a high note (were it not, of course, for the closing qualifications of the play's Epilogue, which reminds audiences that Henry VI "in infant bands crowned King / Of France and England ... Whose state so many had the managing / That they lost France and made his England bleed / Which oft our stage hath shown" [*Henry V*, Epilogue, 9–13]). Shakespeare's multiple visitations of the scenario of Anglo-French conflict come attended with persistent if evolving patterns whose repetition leads them to acquire the force of convention (and maybe even, by the writing of *Henry V*, a whiff of cliché).

One obvious place to begin in investigating the "foreign" face of war is with the way these plays collectively characterize the enemy's temperament and tactics. Shakespeare's Frenchmen collectively suffer from a habit of misplaced confidence compounded by a certain foppishness (notwithstanding that in both *1 Henry VI* and *King John* they are militarily successful). In *1 Henry VI*, these detriments are exacerbated by the dauphin's subjection to the wiles and arts of Joan La Pucelle (aka Joan of Arc), who is portrayed as part holy virgin, part witch. The play opens with the English musing as to whether the recent demise of the otherwise triumphant Henry V could have been due to "the subtle witted French / Conjurers and sorcerers, that, afraid of him / By magic verses ... contrived his end" (1.1.25–27). While this sorcery theory is mere speculation, the arrival of Joan and her prompt subjection of the slavish dauphin to her powers ("Bright star of Venus, fallen down on the earth, / How may I reverently worship thee enough?" [1.2.144–45]) casts a sinister shadow over the subsequent French military successes and underscores their unsavory dependence on a feminine false idol. The English, of course, rely on God alone: "Well, let them practice and converse with spirits. / God is our fortress, in whose conquering name / Let us resolve to scale their flinty bulwarks" (2.1.25–27). The latter piety does not, however, rob them of a certain pugnacity; in the words of the English hero Talbot: "Puzzel or *pucelle*, Dauphin or dogfish / Your hearts I'll stamp out with my horse's heels / And make a quagmire of your mingled brains" (1.5.85–87). It is not hard to imagine such a battle cry (with its dismissive piscatorial puns) meeting with enthusiasm on the part of the play's original audiences.

*Henry VI, Part 1* is now understood to be one of the plays in which Shakespeare collaborated with other writers (possibly Christopher Marlowe and/or George Peele). So the portrait of the French as "a fickle wavering nation" (4.1.138) all-too-ready in its arrogance to underestimate the enemy is something he either adopts or reprises in *Henry V*. Once again the dauphin is the locus of all things foolishly French; first a trifler with tennis balls (with which he mocks Henry V with the memory of his "wilder days" as Prince Hal) and then, on the night before the battle at Agincourt – whilst starving Englishmen shiver round their fires – recalling a sonnet he once wrote to his horse: "Nay, the man hath no wit that cannot from the rising of the lark to the lodging of the lamb vary deserved praise on my palfrey" (3.8.29–31). The latter scene reveals this fundamentally unserious leader of the French forces as an object of contempt even to his own compatriots: "He never did harm, that I heard of." "Nor will do none tomorrow. He will keep that good name still" (3.7.89–91). In *King John*, the figure of Austria clad in the erstwhile lion skin of Richard III also summons the stock dramatic type of the *miles glorioso* (or "braggart soldier"), more talk than action. While the French in *Henry V* receive no aid from supernatural powers (or pretenders thereto), and suffer defeat at Agincourt, their slaughter of the boys and the luggage in the latter battle – "expressly against the law of arms" (4.7.1–2), in Fluellen's expert determination – savors of a trademark resort to fighting dirty in lieu of manly fortitude.

This persistent characterization of the enemy as ineffective, indolent, and insensitive – "having all day caroused and banqueted" (*1 Henry VI*, 2.1.12) while the English shiver and starve – provides a foil to Shakespeare's recurrent emphasis on English stoicism and the refusal to turn and run even when prudence might normally dictate such a course of action. No doubt the fact that Elizabethan England considered its own chief antagonist to be the Roman papacy and its loyal state agents contributed to the sense we find in Shakespeare's plays that England is an underdog up against a baroque and meretricious enemy. English doughtiness is a theme that unites *1 Henry VI* and *Henry V*, Shakespeare's first and last engagements with English history of the fifteenth century. No matter how many times they encounter it, Shakespeare's arrogant Frenchmen are dumbfounded by the (under) dogged English will to prevail in the face of adversity. As Alençon grudgingly marvels in *1 Henry VI*, "Lean, raw-boned rascals! Who would e'er suppose they had such courage and audacity" (1.2.35–36)? By *Henry V*, it is *plus ça change*; on the eve of battle, the "confident and over-lusty French / Do the low-rated English play at [i.e., play for at] dice," while

> The poor condemnèd English,
> Like sacrifices, by their watchful fires
> Sit patiently and inly ruminate
> The morning's danger; and their gesture sad,
> Investing lank-lean cheeks and war-worn coats,
> Presenteth them unto the gazing moon
> So many horrid ghosts.　(4.0.18–28)

On the morrow, however, predictable as clockwork to seemingly all *but* the French, the ever-intrepid English prevail – again to Gallic chagrin: "Oh, perdurable shame! Let's stab ourselves! / Be these the wretches that we played at dice for?" (4.5.8–9). (It is interesting to speculate how Shakespeare's return to certain themes, characters, and dramatic situations in these plays may have intersected with the casting possibilities available to him and whether actors' reappearing from play to play in the guise of different historical iterations of the same political position might have reinforced thematic patterns. Whether or not there will always be an England in these plays, there is certainly always a dauphin.) This depiction of the English as stoic despite all privations and inferior numbers lends their cause an air of virtue even when they are – as is mostly the case in these plays – the interloping aggressors on territory that by Shakespeare's day was recognized as long since French.

　One of the ways Shakespeare emphasizes the overmatched (and hence more valiant) nature of the English warriors as opposed to an ostentatious and overweening French power is through his deployment of linguistic registers. A repeated device to this end is his lists of French territories, litanies of exotic possessions lost or won. In *1 Henry VI*, a messenger brings "sad tidings" in the first scene, with a roster whose verbal and geographical richness establishes the tragic magnificence of what has been ceded: "Guyenne, Champagne, Reims, Rouen, Orléans, / Paris, Gisors, Poitiers are all quite lost" (1.1.60–61). Later Richard Duke of York echoes the lament: "Maine, Blois, Poitiers, Tours are won away" (4.3.45), whereas

Talbot vaunts his clawed-back trophies in what has by act 4 become a kind of refrain: "Alençon, Orléans, Burgundy, / And ... the pride of Gallia" (4.6.14–15). In *Henry V*, the French king gilds his impressive forces with alliteration: "Therefore the Dukes of Berry and Bretagne, / Of Brabant and of Orléans, shall make forth" (2.4.4–5). In the wake of the battle, a similarly daunting series of mellifluous names serves to underscore the English triumph:

> Charles Delabreth, High Constable of France,
> Jacques of Chatillion, Admiral of France;
> The Master of the Crossbows, Lord Rambures;
> Great Master of France, the brave Sir Guichard Dauphin;
> John, Duke of Alençon; Anthony Duke of Brabant,
> The brother to the Duke of Burgundy; ...
> Grandpré and Roussi, Fauconbridge and Foix,
> Beaumont and Marle, Vaudemont and Lestrelles.
> Here was a royal fellowship of death!"    (4.8.86–95)

The English counterpoint to such an ornate registry, by contrast, is nearly monosyllabic, comparatively taciturn, and positively Saxon in its understatement: "Edward the Duke of York; the Earl of Suffolk, / Sir Richard Keighley; Davy Gam, esquire" (4.8.97–98). As in Henry V's wooing of Princess Katherine, the ostentatiously "plain" (albeit in the latter instance also garrulous) idiom of the English "soldier terms" stands in contrast to the elaborate polysyllabic French nomenclature, an aural version of the austerity that prevails on the battlefield.

The miraculous and providential aspects of the victory of the outmatched English forces at Agincourt would surely have resonated for Shakespeare's audience with the Elizabethan navy's own narrow escape from the Spanish Armada in 1588 (a defeat also suffered by the French King Philip in *King John*: "So by a roaring tempest on the flood, / A whole armada of convicted sail / Is scattered and disjoined from fellowship" [3.4.1–3]). Such an improbable victory was interpreted by contemporaries as a sign that England enjoyed divine favor and coincided with the beginning of a decade in which the English history play flourished on London stages. On the other hand, the incremental pattern of the English losses represented in these plays had culminated in the loss of Calais in the last year of Mary Tudor's reign in 1558 (a territory held by the English since 1347). Furthermore, the Spanish defeat in 1588 did not prevent Spain from fitting out two more fleets with intent to invade in 1596 and 1597, which meant that from the mid-1580s through the end of Elizabeth I's reign England was to some degree perpetually braced for invasion. Note, however, that an early modern understanding of war as the proper vocation of a successful king – unlike, say, "effeminate peace" – differs from any sense that foreign war should only be a tragic last resort and/or defensive necessity (*1 Henry VI*, 5.5.106). True, Henry V warns his ecclesiastical advisors to "take heed ... / How you awake our sleeping sword of war," reminding them that the "guiltless drops [of soldiers' blood] / Are ... a sore complaint / 'Gainst him whose wrongs gives edge unto the swords" (though he later denies, in debate with the common foot soldiers, any royal responsibility for the state of their souls) (*Henry V*, 1.2.21–22, 25–27). Nevertheless, one implication we might sense in Henry IV's statement about the need to "busy giddy minds / With foreign quarrels" is that in the military world Shakespeare portrays, the energies and activities of war are a cultural given; what lies at issue is simply what direction they are pointed in. (A royal statute of 1515, amending one from 1363 and renewed in 1633, mandated that every English village establish a municipal area for archery practice and that every household train male children over the age of seven in use of the bow.)[3] In *All's Well That Ends Well*, French noblemen head to the Italian wars less out of any political commitment than because the conflict provides a sort of pressure escape valve-*cum*-finishing school for a restive nobility: "it may well serve / A nursery to our gentry, who are sick / For breathing and exploit" (1.2.15–17). Given that in a feudal system subordinate power holders are necessarily (and literally) on edge, primed for battle, successful kingship consists in the ability to export war to foreign shores, the power to relocate "intestine shock / And furious close of civil butchery" to "broils ... in stronds afar remote," where "mutual well-beseeming ranks / March all one way and be no more opposed" (*1 Henry IV*, 1.1.12–15).

The David and Goliath paradigm (or, as per *1 Henry VI*, "Samsons and Goliases" [1.3.33]) is also present in *King John*, where the English forces contend not just with France but the perfidious power of the papacy, a circumstance that affords Shakespeare to write some highly anachronistic fighting words for his thirteenth-century English monarch: "no Italian priest / Shall tithe or toll in our dominions ... Yet I alone, alone do me oppose / Against the Pope and count his friends my foes" (3.1.79–97). In this anti-papist sentiment, if in no other evident capacity, Shakespeare's King John is a man ahead of his time. While confessional differences are not at issue in the pre-Reformation wars depicted in the history plays, and Shakespeare's anti-papist rhetoric is certainly milder than we find in many contemporary works, the sense we find in the plays that medieval England is an embattled and virtuous underdog up against a nefarious and despotic bully was surely informed by late sixteenth-century perceptions of the Reformation differences between Protestants and Catholics – not only Spanish Catholics, but the pope, whose "bull" (decree) of 1570 exculpated anyone (including her English subjects) who resisted Elizabeth's regime.

A corollary of this polarized manner of stereotyping the respective cultural characters of both parties to a battle is the manner in which Shakespeare represents battlefield tactics. The apparent vulnerability of the English forces and the way in which it leads the highly ornamental French to chronically underestimate them means that English successes are, on the one hand, providential, but also – absent military numbers – a result of their superior intellectual strength and battlefield smarts. In *1 Henry VI*, for instance, warfare is realized as a series of gullings in which the English persistently outmaneuver the French, in part by relying on the latter's arrogance. For instance, in 1.4, the French master gunner and a boy set a trap for Talbot and Salisbury, who then fall into it. Talbot surprises the smug French in return (2.1), but then is himself caught off guard by the Countess of Auvergne (2.3), whose own trap the audience has seen laid at the scene's outset. She had anticipated, due to "rumor of this dreadful knight" (2.3.7), a giant of a man, as prepossessing as his vaunted exploits. However, Talbot's anticlimactic physical presence (he is notoriously short, in a kind of epitome of English material insufficiency) nonplusses her, at which point Talbot calls in the reinforcements with which (as we also know) he was shrewd enough to have provided himself before walking into her trap. The tables are turned once again.

The entertainment value of this sequence results from the deployment of dramatic irony such that the audience is privy to scrappy and surprising English victories at the expense of complacent French dupes. A similar reliance on tactical acumen and dramatic irony governs Henry V's apprehension of the English traitors Scrope, Grey, and Cambridge at Southampton: first he solicits from them a severe punishment for a man "that railed against our person," then holds them to this same severity when charging them with treason; the audience is primed by a conversation at the beginning of the scene to anticipate his cleverness. The king's intellectual capacity is on display throughout the play, which is punctuated with ladlings of his "sweet and honeyed sentences" (*Henry V*, 1.1.50), by means of which rhetorical prowess he either rouses his own troops to heroic action or convinces the enemy to yield without bloodshed. Like Elizabeth I's rousing insistence at Tilbury on the eve of the armada that she possessed the "heart and stomach of a king" despite her otherwise unprepossessing female body, English soldiers in Shakespeare's plays repeatedly make up in heart and mind – and oratory – what they may lack in material substance.

Shakespeare's depiction of the English reliance on either strategic canniness or rhetorical power rather than superior numbers or arms also finesses the technical theatrical problem of credibly staging military battles with a handful of actors (battles whose historical counterparts were in fact sieges – not terribly prepossessing subjects for dramatic representation). Furthermore, it dovetails with the actual geographies of Elizabethan warfare. As in the theater, most English military activity took place "offstage," as it were – not only because the "theater" of English warfare in the fifteenth century had been French territory, but also because in Shakespeare's own day virtually all military actions occurred in locations other than on the principal British isle – in Ireland, the Low Countries, Cádiz, or at sea. The threat of Spanish invasion was chronic from the mid-1580s through the end of the century, incurring defensive preparations on the coasts, as well as high rates of taxation and episodes of conscription that would have been felt far from the coastal periphery. There was also the ever-present tandem fear of Catholic treachery from within – including the threat, until 1587, posed by the imprisoned Catholic Mary Queen of Scots as an example of an alternative royal confessional affiliation and a potential focus for insurrection. Nonetheless, the only instance of a foreign power achieving landfall on English soil occurred in 1595, with a Spanish raid on Cornish villages. Thus, for early modern England, the best defensive effort was primarily an offensive and preemptive one, a matter of fighting somewhere far away and overseas. In *Henry V*, the Chorus calls upon the audience to "make imaginary puissance" in order to extrapolate and infer the full panoply of a war from the relatively paltry gestures of theatrical illusion, but imagining a war taking place elsewhere by inferring its presence from rudimentary local signs and remnants was something English persons were also used to doing in real life (Prologue, 25). Indeed, the professional theater may have been as close as any English persons came to witnessing anything that even pretended to resemble warfare.

As this remote feature of Elizabethan warfare suggests, the early modern sense of cultural difference between the enemy and a distinct and insular "Englishness" was reinforced by an accident of geography that was frequently glossed as an instance of divine providence. Even though the medieval warfare depicted in the plays presumes that English territory extends across the channel, an emphasis on the island boundaries of Englishness is felt throughout the history plays. John of Gaunt's speech in *Richard II* is the most notorious and eloquent statement of the way in which the archipelago's natural situation serves in Shakespeare's plays as both defense of, and pretext for, a sense of communal integrity and independence based in natural isolation (a sense that has vigorously persisted into the current Brexit moment, and which continues to structure the national feelings of many a landlocked polity):

This other Eden, demi-paradise,
This fortress built by Nature for herself
Against infection and the hand of war,
This happy breed of men, this little world,
This precious stone set in the silver sea,
Which serves it in the office of a wall,
Or as a moat defensive to a house
Against the envy of less happier lands –
This blessèd plot, this earth, this realm, this England,
This nurse, this teeming womb of royal kings ...
This land of such dear souls, this dear, dear land,
Dear for her reputation through the world.    (2.1.42–58)

Strikingly, even paradoxically, the rhetoric here marries a celebration of the staunch defensive power of the island's geographic situation ("fortress," "wall," "moat defensive," "beats back the envious siege") with the diminutive, even unassuming register that describes the "little body with a mighty heart" mode of English soldiery on display elsewhere: "little world," "precious stone," "house," "plot," "earth," "land of dear souls" (*Henry V*, 2.0.17). The speech musters both the defensive sentiment of tender protectiveness on behalf of a vulnerable woman ("nurse," "teeming womb," "dear, dear land") and the xenophobic phallic aggression of military exploits: "royal kings, / Feared by their breed and famous by their birth, / Renownèd for their deeds as far from home – / For Christian service and true chivalry – / As is the sepulcher of stubborn Jewry" (*Richard II*, 2.1.51–55).

Gaunt's vision elides the fact that this "happy breed of men" had from time immemorial shared their "little world" – at times quite contentiously – with Welsh and Scottish co-occupants (not to mention Roman, Scandinavian, Germanic, or Norman invaders). In the *Henry IV* plays, for instance, the crown is beset by conflict on both Welsh and Scottish borders and then must repulse a challenge from the Earl of Mortimer, in pursuit of his own claim to the throne, who has allied himself with the "irregular and wild" Welshman he had been sent to subdue – an alliance that demonstrates that "foreign" is a political, not a geographical, condition (*1 Henry IV*, 1.1.40). So too Elizabethan England's imperial designs on Ireland and the New World belied the sense that England was content to confine Englishness to the island's shores. (In point of fact, despite the loss of Calais in 1558, English monarchs continued to "style" themselves as rulers of France until 1800 – well after the French themselves had dispatched the resident monarchy.) Furthermore, what strikes Gaunt in *Richard II* as a seamlessly bounded garden seems, to a less charitable Frenchman in *Henry V*, the "nook-shotten isle of Albion" (3.6.14). Not only is "foreign" in the eye of the beholder but so is the appearance of the land itself.

Nevertheless, dating from the loss of Calais, the southern coast, at least, could be imagined to echo the rhetorical ideal of an unbroken physical boundary to English identity. So too in the Ditchley portrait of Elizabeth I; the capacious hem of the monarch's dress quite literally skirts and shades the southern coast, making the equivalences between regal, national, and geographic chastity visible. (Elizabeth I's rhetoric on multiple public occasions, in which she professed herself married to or mother of her people as a means of demurral to the parliamentary urgings of marriage, mobilized a similar association between the monarch's virginity and her country's integrity.) The fact that foreign warfare in Shakespeare's English histories, as in Elizabethan England, principally takes place on foreign soil means that onstage challenges to the vaunted geographic membrane are scarce, but when the rare invasion does occur, the land itself seems to play a defensive role in repulsing alien invaders. In *King John*, for instance, while the dauphin does succeed in setting foot on English soil ("All Kent hath yielded; nothing there holds out / But Dover Castle" [5.1.30–31]), the bulk of his forces "are wrecked ... on Goodwin sands" (5.3.11). Unfortunately, however, the English forces under the Bastard suffer a similar repulse: "half my power this night, / Passing these flats, are taken by the tide – / These Lincoln Washes have devoured them" (5.6.39–41). As even one of England's enemies acknowledges, the land can succeed where politicians and armies fail: "that England hedged in with the main, / That water-wallèd bulwark, still secure / And confident from foreign purposes" (2.1.26–28).

As we can hear in Gaunt's speech in *Richard II*, gender identities figure prominently in Shakespeare's depictions of foreign war. Foreign warfare is an exceedingly and laudably masculine endeavor (as opposed to civil war, which is often depicted as a form of self-mutilation or an unfilial attack upon the mother country). As Parolles puts it in *All's Well That Ends Well*, "He wears his honor in a box unseen / That hugs his kicky-wicky here at home, / Spending his manly marrow in her arms, / Which should sustain the bound and high curvet / Of Mars's fiery steed" (2.3.266–70). This masculinity can be demonstrated negatively, by associating the enemy with the perverse participation of women in war – for instance, the dauphin's reliance on the "Amazon" Joan in *1 Henry VI* (1.2.104); or King Philip's on the influence of the formidable Constance in *King John*; or even the "beastly shameless transformation, / By those Welshwomen" in *1 Henry IV* (a reference to the alleged practice of female soldiers castrating enemy corpses and placing the severed genitals in the mouths of the mutilated bodies) (1.1.44–45). Just as pejoratively, Shakespeare characters describe the enemy with the more conventional feminine property of physical vulnerability, as when Henry V threatens the citizens of Harfleur with rape should they not open the city gates to him: "the fleshed soldier, rough and hard of heart, / In liberty of bloody hand shall range ... mowing like grass / Your fresh fair virgins and your flow'ring infants ... into the hand / Of hot and forcing violation" (*Henry V*, 3.3.11–21). Princess Katherine of France leavens this point in the following scene, when she asks to learn the English names for parts of her body, giggling at the way the terms for "foot" and "gown" sound like French profanities: "De foot *et* de count! *O Seigneur Dieu, ils sont les mots de son mauvais, corruptible, gros et impudique, pas pour les dames d'honneur d'user*" (3.4.47–49). The point, however, remains the same: female bodies are the ultimate battleground of foreign conquest.

Less crudely if no less phallocentrically, English men are (as in Gaunt's speech) the chivalric protectors of their mother country's virtue; or, like Talbot and his son, leagued in patrilineal fealty ("Oh, if you love my mother, / Dishonor not her honorable name / ... The world will say, 'He is not Talbot's blood, / That basely fled when noble Talbot stood'" [*1 Henry VI*, 4.5.13–18]); or, as in Henry V's call to arms, testament to generations of English warriors: "On, on you noblest English, / Whose blood is fet from fathers of war-proof ... / Dishonor not your mothers; now attest / That those whom you called fathers did beget you!" (*Henry V*, 3.1.17–21). England may be female in Shakespeare's plays – protected, vulnerable, fertile, nursing – but her warriors are male. Thus, the English invasion of France is at once sexual violation for the latter and testament to chastity (that is, honorable paternity) for the former.

In the prominence of this gendered vocabulary of antagonism and affiliation, Shakespeare mobilizes the Elizabethan idiom of the monarch as a "Virgin Queen," whereby national integrity is located in the monarch's physical inviolability. However, in depicting English victory over France as phallic aggression he may also be giving voice to what some historians have spoken of as a longing on the part of some Elizabethan policymakers for a more aggressive military policy, such as was imagined to have been the custom of former monarchs – in other words, the male ones.[4] Elizabeth I's notorious reluctance to engage English forces in foreign combat stood in stark contrast to her father's enthusiasm for it. Her avoidance of conflict likely had as much to do with the enormous debt with which Henry VIII's military exploits had encumbered her regime as it did with any trepidation inherent in the alleged timidity of her sex (unlike her monastery-funded father, she was acutely conscious of the risks to the crown posed by the heavy taxation and conscription required by war). There is nevertheless a strikingly nostalgic or recursive aspect to the masculinity of English warriors in Shakespeare's plays, as if *real* men were even in the past a thing of the past. The forces of Henry VI struggle to sustain the glorious achievements of Henry V or to imitate "that stout Pendragon" of Arthurian legend (*1 Henry VI*, 3.2.94). For his part, Henry V sets out to "invoke his warlike spirit" of his great-grandfather Edward III (*Henry V*, 1.2.104) and is welcomed as a "conquering Caesar"; the Chorus anticipates that the real-life Earl of Essex, at war in Ireland, will imitate this imitation of an imitation: "As, by a lower but a loving likelihood, / ... the General of our gracious Empress, / ... may, from Ireland coming, / Brin[g] rebellion broached on his sword" (5.0.29–32). The vigor of the Bastard in *King John* harks back to his valiant father Richard Coeur de Lion – "The very spirit of Plantagenet!" (1.1.167); Henry IV hopes to follow in the footsteps of the crusaders. Shakespeare imagines heroes from the past who themselves hope to emulate heroes from an even more remote past, and so on and so forth (or rather, so back). In *Henry V*, this mimetic desire allegedly infects even those without noble ancestors: "Now all the youth of England are on fire ... They sell the pasture now to buy the horse, / Following the mirror of all Christian kings / With wingèd heels, as English Mercuries" (2.0.1–7). Given that most of the engagements that Shakespeare dramatizes involve English losses, such glories as he summons necessarily come attended with the air of myth, of a once-upon-a-time when "England all Olivers and Rolands bred" (*1 Henry VI*, 1.2.30). Foreign war in these plays is thus as much an effort to recapture a faded English glory as French territory – to recover and reanimate former virile strengths from present ignominies. Or as the Bastard prays: "Saint George that swinged the dragon and e'er since / Sits on on 's horseback at mine hostess' door / Teach us some fence!" (*King John*, 2.1.288–90).

Thus much for the more jingoistic, saber-rattling, and/or idealized aspects of Shakespearean foreign wars. This being Shakespeare, however, these ways of sanctifying the English and demonizing their enemies coexist with many qualifications that cut against or demystify the celebrations of English valor (or, conversely, set them off all the more strongly by contrast). The most sobering check upon the feelings of national pride the plays summon – besides, of course, the largely losing record of the English forces – is their highly critical portrait of political conditions on the home front. Here we find no "keep calm and carry on" war effort, but infighting, bad kingship, and pervasive political instability. This element is especially prominent in *1 Henry VI*, where the internecine rumblings in England due to eventuate in the Wars of the Roses undermine the military effort in France. For instance, when Exeter asks the reason for an English loss, he hears the blunt answer

No treachery, but want of men and money.
Amongst the soldiers this is mutterèd:
That here you maintain several factions,
And whilst a field should be dispatched and fought,
You are disputing of your generals.
One would have ling'ring wars, with little cost;
Another would fly swift but wanteth wings;
A third thinks, without expense at all,
By guileful fair words peace may be obtained.
Awake, awake, English nobility!   (1.1.69–78)

As the play proceeds, the double-crossing *realpolitik* on the home front comes to rival and then eclipse the scenes of military valor abroad. So too in *Richard II*, the king's "Irish wars" are portrayed not as a cause for national unity but rather as a kind of expensive and exclusively monarchic indulgence (like expensive Italian fashion or parasitic friends) that not only lead to the shameful "leas[ing] out" of England, "Like to a tenement or pelting farm" in order to finance war but also prompt the king's unlawful incursion on baronial rights: "for these great affairs do ask some charge, / Towards our assistance we do seize to us / The plate, coin, revenues, and movables / Whereof our uncle Gaunt did stand possessed" (2.1.159–62). *Henry V* contains, in the speeches of the Chorus and the king, the most idealized visions of monarch and community of all the plays, but even there Shakespeare takes care to include a portrait of the backroom deals that take place between king and clergy that will allow the latter to escape fiscal pain in exchange for providing ideological sanction of the war and material contributions to the effort.

*King John* is Shakespeare's most scathing portrait of political disfunction in the history plays, where the true threat to English sovereignty and stability stems not from a foreign enemy but incompetence and incoherence at the highest reaches within the polity. The play begins with multiple contentions over what political legitimacy consists in, portrays the extraordinary spectacle of royalty being refused acknowledgment of its territorial claim to a city by that very city absent proof, and locates most of the political decision-making as well as moral agency in non-royal agents such as the citizen Hubert, the papal legate Pandulph, or the English Bastard Falconbridge. This is the only play that portrays the French as successfully invading England (indeed, to some local acclaim), but it also displays military glory as repeatedly short-sheeted by political maneuvering. The primary locus of patriotic sentiment and action in the play resides in the figure of the pugnacious Bastard. Although himself technically of gentle if illegitimate birth (he even claims at one point that the king's "royalty doth speak in me"

[5.2.129]), he functions as a chorus of semi-yeomanly critique with respect to the cynical maneuverings of the powerful – "Mad world, mad kings, mad composition!" (2.1.561) – as well as a (futile) cheering section for the enfeebled king: "Be stirring as the time, be fire with fire / Threaten the threatener, and outface the brow / Of bragging horror" (5.1.48–50). The Bastard's vigor and preference for the supposed clarity of "resolved and honorable war" over "base and vile-concluded peace" (2.1.586), so much in contrast to the deal-making bent of John's enervated royalty, recalls the revivifying baseborn energies and competencies of Joan La Pucelle in *1 Henry VI*, as well as the forthright ethics of the common soldier Williams in rebuking Henry V – "your majesty came not like yourself ... what your highness suffered under that shape, I beseech you take it for your own fault, and not mine" (*Henry V*, 4.8.46–50). Shakespeare also populates his civil war plays with some similarly disapproving invented lower-status characters (e.g., the gardener in *Richard II*), but this kind of bottom-up, more-Catholic-than-the-pope (as it were) brand of patriotism is unique to the context of Shakespeare's depictions of foreign war (contrast, for instance, the way in which in the "civil" war plays, the dissenting voices, like Falstaff's, tend to demystify war rather than glorify it). Nevertheless, while such commoners confronting their betters certainly instance dissent and critique of the conduct of the powerful, they are also all examples of the lower orders recognizing and supporting traditional English prerogatives (including the hierarchy that renders them commoners) when royalty fails to properly defend or uphold them. This rhetorical alliance of community and hierarchy was in fact a feature of the chief institution with any ambition to English homogeneity in the Elizabethan period: the church. In a state with no standing army, or consistent or comprehensive mechanisms of law enforcement or taxation, or methods of communication, and beset by linguistic and confessional and geographic variety, it was perhaps the *Book of Common Prayer* that best articulated the kind of culturally homogeneous nation that would become standard in subsequent ages: "where heretofore there hath been great diversity in saying and singing in churches within this realm," reads the preface, "now from henceforth all the realm shall have but one use." However, unlike modern nationhood, which tends to ally cultural homogeneity with democracy, Elizabethan expressions of community felt no contradiction between community and hierarchy: "to appease all such diversity" continues the preface, "all parties that so doubt, or diversely take anything shall away resort to the bishop of the diocese.... And if the bishop ... be in any doubt, then may he send thereof for the resolution unto the archbishop."[5]

One of the things foregrounded by the non-elite adherents of hegemony in the plays is the way in which, despite the centrality of a logic of opposition to an idea of Englishness – English vs. French, male vs. female, stoic vs. soft, etc. – Shakespeare portrays the conflicts as ultimately not between irreconcilably alien peoples but among aristocratic cousins who are just as ready to marry as to fight should it serve their mutual interests. As may be most on display in *King John*, parties who moments before may have been at each other's throats declaiming intransigent cultural differences can make common cause as convenience dictates, at which point the intransigent cultural differences melt away. (Even if the alliance means merely joining together to fight a common foe, as with the obstinate Harfleur in *King John*, or Islam in *Henry V*: "Shall not thou and I, between St. Denis and St. George, compound a boy, half French, half English, that shall go to Constantinople and take the Turk by the beard?" [5.2.193–95].) Opportunistic recombination is even the case when the conflict does not concern powers separated by an ocean, but takes place within English territory itself. In the *Henry IV* plays, for instance, the Welsh and Scottish antagonists of the crown are initially described as alien forces, but then ally with the English Earl of Mortimer in his challenge to Henry IV. This quicksilver conversion of "others" into allies (and sometimes back again) was also true of the shifting antagonisms that governed Elizabethan England. Catholics and Protestants, England and Spain (or France, or Scotland, etc.) were not categorical opponents, but situational ones (Ireland perhaps excepted). One conflict's enemy might be the next's confederate, making a sense of "the foreign" something that can be applied or suspended accordingly, geography notwithstanding.

The occasion-driven restlessness that characterizes the relations to foes also characterizes Shakespeare's depictions of English community, nowhere more so than in *Henry V*. While the earlier plays contain multiple perspectives upon English warfare voiced by different types of *characters* – the Bastard's idealized vision vs. the dispiriting conduct of King John; the Talbot's do-or-die kamikaze spirit vs. the squabbling bureaucrats at home – *Henry V* notoriously builds this anamorphic voicing into the very structure of the play, as well as into the person of the king.[6] The Chorus's idealized speeches about a harmonious English community alternate with scenes of the Eastcheap crew squabbling over Mistress Quickly; or the fractiousness of the ostensibly allied British captains Fluellen, Jamy, MacMorris, and Gower, united only in a commitment to jostling over their pecking order; or the cynicism of the English foot soldiers round their campfire. Henry himself, in the "St. Crispin's Day" speech, provides the most utopian vision of community – "We few, we happy few, we band of brothers – / For he today that fights with me / Shall be my brother. Be he ne'er so vile" (4.3.60–62) – but then, in the wake of the battle, proceeds to list the names of the English dead with a punctilious regard for rank – unless of course they have no rank, which is to say, to him, no name, let alone that of a brother: "none else of name, and of all other men, / But five-and-twenty" (4.8.99–100). In one scene the king threatens to rape and pillage, and in another he coolly sanctions the summary execution of his former tavern crony Bardolph for plundering a church (apparently having taken Henry at his word). The scene of Princess Katherine's language lesson transposes Henry's terms of rape into a comic key, just as her subsequent observation concerning Henry's attempt to occlude power relations in romantic language – "Is it possible dat I sould love de enemy of France?" – is turned by Henry into a winningly droll acknowledgment of ways in which soft and hard power conspire with each other:

> No; it is not possible you should love the enemy of France, Kate. But, in loving me you should love the friend of France. For I love France so well that I will not part with a village of it; I will have it all mine. And, Kate, when France is mine, and I am yours, then yours is France, and you are mine.     (5.2.163–67)

The song of English togetherness, then, much like French (or Welsh, or Scottish) foreignness, is something that can be turned on and off like a tap.

One of the things brought to the fore by Shakespeare's provision of such a variety of shifting perspectives is the way in which not only "foreign" but "community" itself is a function of an imaginative faculty summoned into action by oratory. As such, it can be deployed as – and where – occasion requires. The play that may make this most evident is *Macbeth*, which despite its luridly Scottish setting may be among Shakespeare's most English in the sense that it mobilizes and transposes the vocabularies and affective charges of English nationhood that had long been part of his repertoire.

In this effort Shakespeare was shadowed by James I, who at his accession to Elizabeth's throne in 1603 had moved swiftly to appropriate the idioms and figures of Englishness that had long served his predecessor and had also rung out on London stages. His new realm, James announced upon arriving in England, is

> *now* become like a little world within itself, being entrenched and fortified round about with a natural, and yet admirable strong pond or ditch, whereby all the former fond fears of this nation are quite cut off. . . . I am the husband and all the whole isle is my lawful wife; I am the head, and it is my body; I am the shepherd, and it is my flock.[7]

As we have seen, the trope of Britain as a world apart was a familiar one to English ears (not least from Shakespeare's plays). However, James made it sound as if the description required his own accession to make it true. Also, James's use of the imagery was subtly but crucially different from the Elizabethan invocations. That is, unlike Elizabeth (or Shakespeare), when describing the insular character of British geography, James sought not to emphasize the island's defensive virginal stance with respect to a tyrannical invading power, but rather his own powerful patriarchal embrace of territory previously subject (in his opinion) to the "fond fears" of internal dissension among neighboring peoples who mistakenly considered themselves to be at odds. In addition, what for Elizabeth I had been at least a superficial gesture of seemly feminine submission to the nation – "I have already joined myself in marriage to an husband, namely the Kingdom of England" – was for James a blunt patriarchal assertion of royal power over it: "What God hath conjoined, let no man separate: I am the husband, and all the whole Isle is my lawful wife."[8] Thus in James's speeches, the "sceptered isle" image that for Elizabethans expressed the barricaded purity of Englishness became, rather, a means to assail that integrity.

Perhaps not surprisingly, James's uses of the island and marriage tropes of national identity did not go over well with English audiences habituated to thinking of England in terms of insularity, or poised in a defensive crouch not only against Continental foes but "the weasel Scot" (*Henry V*, 1.2.170) and the "irregular and wild" Welsh. James's supporters insisted that the king's proposals – for instance, to change his kingdom's name in the royal style from the exclusive England to the more comprehensive Britain, his own title from "king" to "emperor," to naturalize the Scots, to suspend customs duties between northern and southern kingdoms – were simply a matter of common sense. Proponents of his plan emphasized the homogeneity of English and Scottish geography: "There be no mountains nor Races of hills, there be no Seas or great rivers, there is no diversity of tongue or language that hath invited or provoked this ancient separation or divorce."[9] However, some English ears heard in James's rhetoric not an offer of fatherly protection or harmony but a claustrophobic imposition of alien and even tyrannical ways that threatened to usurp ancient English traditions such as the common law and the constitutional prerogative ("the name of Emperor is impossible – No Kingdom can make their King an Emperor ... the name of King a sweet name – Plentitude of Power in it").[10] English objections to James's designs included plenty of anti-Scottish feeling directed at the alleged poverty and savagery of their northern neighbor in terms that sought to alienate what James would unify. Parliament members, for instance, rejected union with Scotland in the very terms the English had long used to repel the threat of Continental predators: "Italy is compared to a leg, Scotland to a louse"; "let us not adopt a younger brother, that he cousin the elder – Marry not a poor wife, to make her master." The island imagery that under Elizabeth had served to express a sense of insular integrity seamlessly bounded and united against foreign invasion was reimagined by some English voices as an internally varied geography where the "green and pleasant" south needed to defend itself from the alien Celtic "peripheries" contained within the island's coastal limit: "[Scotland] is full of Lakes and Loughs ... so that a map thereof looks like a pillory coat, bespattered all over with dirt and rotten eggs."[11] Underlying the invective was the truth that the mountainous geographies of the Celtic "peripheries" were more conducive to herding than husbandry than were the southeastern portions of the island, and hence there were real cultural differences between the different regions of the archipelago. England having so lately come to a language of unity on the grounds of homogeneity, the notion of unity-in-diversity was perhaps a bridge too far: "God hath made People apt for every Country; some for a cold climate, some for a hot climate, and the several countries he hath fitten for their several Natures and qualities ... a wise owner will not pull down the hedge quite ... If he do, the Cattle will rush in in Multitudes."[12]

In adopting and redirecting the established metaphors of insular Englishness in order to advocate *against* English insularity and *for* a composite Britishness, James I demonstrates what Shakespeare's plays about foreign war also record, which is the way in which the vocabularies of national feeling, no matter how allegedly indigenous to places or persons, are *vocabularies* – terms that can be appropriated and employed as occasion and intention demand, sometimes quite against the purposes of the previous instance. That is, nature doesn't make nations; words do. In *Macbeth*, Shakespeare explores the way in which a vocabulary of natural fact – "Birnam Wood" for instance, or "of woman born" – can mean different things in the mouth of a speaker versus the ear of a hearer. To King Duncan, for instance, "the air" of Macbeth's castle "nimbly and sweetly recommends itself / Unto our gentle senses" (1.6.1–3); to us, there be witches. Or, one person's green and pleasant "sceptered isle" is another's "nook-shotten isle."

Macbeth himself is a Janus-faced figure whose heroism depends on the political affiliations of the beholder. At times, he is someone to admire precisely on account of his patriotic zeal. We meet him as a valiant defender of Scottish sovereignty against the invading "kerns and galloglasses" (1.2.13) from the north, and, at the play's end, he fights off the "English epicures" from the south, engaged to his last breath in defending his country from foreign incursion. He asks the doctor if he might "cast / The water of my land, find her disease, / And purge it to a sound and pristine health" (5.3.50–52), with much the same uxorious tenderness that he extends to his own wife. But this very same ferocity on behalf of Scotland makes him a murderer of children, a captive to his wife and the riddles of witches, a ravening tyrannical monster who appears as "a tyrant" to his enemies and violates his mother country's body: "I think our country sinks beneath the yoke; / It weeps, it bleeds, and each new day a gash / Is added to her wounds" (4.3.39–40). The play ends with Malcolm proclaiming the anglicizing and domesticating of such Scottish ferocity: "My thanes and kinsmen, / Henceforth be earls, the first that Scotland / In such an honor named" (5.7.92–94). At stake in the difference between thanes and earls is how power is transferred: Scottish tanistry, unlike the English patrilineal power, conferred leadership on the grounds of ability, not biology.

On the face of it, the annexation and civilization of the allegedly savage and alien north is what James I claimed to be offering to his new English subjects, and we might well hear in the conversion of thanes to earls a composite Shakespearean nod to the pacific union proposals of the new monarch. (The savagery of their northern neighbors, especially when it came to deciding who a monarch should be, was in fact a slur deployed by some Englishmen in resistance to British union: "All evil from the north, saith proverb olde"; the Scots "have not suffered above two kinds to die in their beds, these two hundred years.")[13] However, insofar as the play cultivates sympathy for Macbeth, we are also poised to resist Malcom's renaming of thanes as earls. (Indeed, to some English ears, nothing rang more of Scottish tyranny than James's own proposals for union: "Popular opinions to be regarded. Kings have ever used to do it.")[14] The gloriousness of fighting to the death in the defense of one's country is something the play celebrates, which is why this savage Scot's death feels like a loss, rather than a triumph – even and maybe especially so to Jacobean English patriots eager to defend themselves against the very Scottish savagery they deplored in defense of their own national integrity. The way in which Scotland in this play stands as both self and other to England itself testifies to the way in which Shakespeare helped to shape the terms of foreign war for his culture and our own.

*Further Reading*

Baker, David J., and Willy Maley (eds.). *British Identities and English Renaissance Literature*, Cambridge, Cambridge University Press, 2011.
Barker, Simon. *War and Nation in the Theatre of Shakespeare and His Contemporaries*, Edinburgh, Edinburgh University Press, 2007.

Escobedo, Andrew. *Nationalism and Historical Loss in Renaissance England: Foxe, Dee, Spenser, Milton*, Ithaca, Cornell University Press, 2004.

Helgerson, Richard. *Forms of Nationhood: The Elizabethan Writing of England*, Chicago, University of Chicago Press, 1992.

Hammer, Paul E. J. *Elizabeth's Wars: War, Government and Society in Tudor England, 1544–1604*, Basingstoke, Palgrave Macmillan, 2003.

Hoenselaars, A. J. *Images of Englishmen and Foreigners in the Drama of Shakespeare and His Contemporaries: A Study of Stage Characters and National Identity in English Renaissance Drama, 1558–1642*, Rutherford, Fairleigh Dickenson Press, 1992.

Howard, Jean, and Phyllis Rackin. *Engendering A Nation: A Feminist Account of Shakespeare's English Histories*, London, Routledge, 1997.

Maley, Willy, and Andrew Murphy (eds.). *Shakespeare and Scotland*, Manchester, Manchester University Press, 2004.

McEachern, Claire. *The Poetics of English Nationhood, 1590–1612*, Cambridge, Cambridge University Press, 1996.

## NOTES

1 *Act in Restraint of Appeals of 1533* (24 Henry VIII c. 12), in Gerald Bray (ed.), *Documents of the English Reformation* (Minneapolis: Fortress Press, 1994), p. 78.
2 Benedict Anderson, *Imagined Communities: Reflections on the Origin and Spread of Nationalism*, rev. ed. (London: Verso, 2016).
3 Steven Gunn, "Archery Practice in Early Tudor England," *Past and Present*, 209 (2010), pp. 53–81, 54.
4 Paul E. J. Hammer, *Elizabeth's Wars: War, Government and Society in Tudor England, 1544–1604* (Basingstoke: Palgrave Macmillan, 2003), pp. 9–53.
5 *The Book of Common Prayer, 1559*, ed. John E. Booty (Charlottesville: University Press of Virginia, 1976), pp. 16–19.
6 Norman Rabkin, "Rabbits, Ducks and *Henry V*," *Shakespeare Quarterly*, 28 (1977), pp. 279–96.
7 King James I, "The King's Majesties Speech [...]," in Walter Scott (ed.), *The Somers Collection of Tracts: A Collection of Scarce and Valuable Tracts [...] Chiefly Such as Relate to the History and Constitution of These Kingdoms*, 13 vols. (London: T. Cadell et al., 1809), vol. II, pp. 59–69, 62.
8 William Camden, *The History of the Most Renowned and Victorious Princess Elizabeth, Late Queen of England*, ed. Wallace T. MacCaffrey (Chicago: University of Chicago Press, 1970), p. 29; and King James I, "King's Majesties Speech," 62.
9 Thomas Craig, *Scotland's Sovereignty Asserted* (London, 1605), sig. C5v.
10 *Journal of the House of Commons (CJ)* (London, 1803), vol. I (1547–1628), p. 184 (April 26, 1604).
11 *The Character of Scotland* (London, 1609), sig. A2r.
12 *CJ*, p. 334 (February 14, 1606).
13 *Northern Poems Congratulating the Kings Majesties Most Happy and Peaceable Entrance of the Crowne of England* (London, 1604), sig. A3r; and Scott (ed.), *Somers Tracts*, vol. II, p. 125.
14 *CJ*, p. 184 (April 26, 1604).

# 5

MAGGIE KILGOUR

# War and the Classical World

Readers who imagine Shakespeare as the quintessentially "English" writer have often cited Ben Jonson's observation that he had "small Latin and less Greek" as evidence that the genius did not need the classics for inspiration.[1] Yet in recent years scholars have shown how deeply classical works stimulated Shakespeare's imagination.[2] While it is true that his knowledge of Greek was slight, his education, like that of all Elizabethan schoolboys, was Latin-based, and he would have spent many hours translating Latin writers into English and back again, becoming familiar not with their words alone but also with their habits of thinking.[3] This education system reflected a deep-rooted assumption that classical works provided appropriate models for life in Renaissance England, a belief boosted further by the myth that the English were descended from Trojans. Elizabethan schoolboys were encouraged to emulate ancient authors and heroes. The effects of this curriculum were felt in many ways beyond the schoolroom. Like all educated Elizabethans, Shakespeare saw his own world through classical paradigms. Moreover, unlike writers such as Sir Philip Sidney and Ben Jonson, who fought in the Netherlands, John Donne, who fought at Cádiz, or Edmund Spenser, in Ireland, Shakespeare encountered war only through books. In this chapter I will show how the classics helped him develop the images of war and soldiering that he used in works based on classical subjects, as well as in the English histories and other plays. His treatments of classical subjects establish patterns of conflict between friends and foes, and even more often, between friends and within families, that Shakespeare shows are repeated throughout history. Shakespeare's knowledge of the place of war in the ancient world was thus central to his understanding of how that past permeated and informed his own present: in many ways, the legacy of the classical world was war.

## War in the Ancient World

In his reading of the classics generally, Shakespeare encountered a competitive world in which war was the driving principle of all existence; as Heraclitus said in a well-known tag, "War is the father of all and king of all."[4] In Aristotle's *Politics* 1253a, war is the natural expression of inherent hostility between men outside of society.[5] In the *Laws*, one of Plato's speakers could argue further that all men are "engaged in a continuous lifelong warfare against all cities whatsoever.... The peace of which most men talk is no more than a name; in real fact the normal attitude of a city to all other cities is one of undeclared warfare."[6] War shaped peace, as laws were instituted "with a view to war" (626a). To later readers, ancient Greece and Rome seemed in a constant state of war. Much of classical history, especially the works of Livy, Sallust, and Caesar that were staples in Elizabethan schools, focused on wars and especially the deeds and speeches of great leaders. The epic hero was above all a warrior, while for real leaders, war was the road to political power, honor, and fame. It made nations and heroes great. It was also seen as a way of uniting a nation and making it disciplined and strong. Peaceful countries in contrast seemed destined to become soft and fall apart, as some argued happened when an effete Greece fell to Rome and later a decadent Rome to the Goths; as Imogen claims in *Cymbeline*, "Plenty and peace breeds cowards" (3.6.21). War is the creative force that makes the world go round. In the bloodthirsty ancient world of *Coriolanus*, the servants of the Volscian warrior Aufidius therefore greet the return of war as a good thing for themselves and the world:

> SECOND SERVINGMAN: Why, then, we shall have a stirring world again. This peace is nothing but to rust iron, increase tailors, and breed ballad-makers.
>
> FIRST SERVINGMAN: Let me have war, say I. It exceeds peace as far as day does night. It's sprightly walking, audible, and full of vent. Peace is a very apoplexy, lethargy, mulled, deaf, sleepy, insensible, a getter of more bastard children than war's a destroyer of men.
>
> SECOND SERVINGMAN: 'Tis so, and as some wars in some sort may be said to be a ravisher, so it cannot be denied but peace is a great maker of cuckolds.
>
> FIRST SERVINGMAN: Ay, and it makes men hate one another.
>
> THIRD SERVINGMAN: Reason: because they then less need one another. The wars for my money. (4.5.218–31)

For many Renaissance writers and readers, classical stories of military prowess set the standards of heroism to be emulated. European rulers styled themselves new Alexanders, Augustuses, and Aeneases. The imitation of the classics even had an impact on actual warfare: *Henry V* satirizes a vogue for copying Roman military strategies in the classicizing Welshman Fluellen who praises "the disciplines of the pristine wars of the Romans" (3.3.25–26). The myth of England's descent from the Trojan Brutus/Brute encouraged the English to imagine themselves as a warrior race, shaped by the great struggle between Troy and Greece. Thomas Heywood could defend the theater on the grounds that staged representations of classical heroism would inspire new, English heroes: "To see a Hector all besmeared in blood, trampling upon the bulks of kings; a Troilus returning from the field in the sight of his father Priam ... to see a Pompey ride in triumph, then a Caesar conquer that Pompey; labouring Hannibal alive, hewing his passage through the Alps. . . . Oh these were sights to make an Alexander."[7] Ancient texts did not just represent heroes, they *made* them as well. As Alexander's success in conquest was often attributed to the fact that he always carried Homer with him into battle, Homer was also supposed to inspire English heroes. For Coleridge in the nineteenth century, the impact of the *Iliad* on English soldiers was still palpable: "to it perhaps the bravest of our soldiery might attribute their heroic deeds."[8] This emulation of past military heroism dominated the English attitude toward the classics until it was exploded in the trenches of the First World War.

Yet classical writers were also critical of war and concerned with the psychological and social effects of a militaristic ethos. While Homer celebrates warriors and delights in detailing gory deaths in battle, his Zeus says that the god of war Ares is he "whom most of all the Gods / Inhabiting the starry hill I hate; no periods / Being set to thy contentions, brawls, fights, and pitching fields."[9] In *Politics* 1253a, Aristotle also noted that love of war made men antisocial; war was destructive of the community that it was supposed to unite and protect. The doubleness of war was especially evident in Roman myth and culture. The Romans proudly traced their ancestry back to Mars, the Roman god of war, as proof of their bellicose nature as a people. The Roman Empire was built on the conquest of other countries. But from the first century BCE on, the empire was eaten away by war within, as Roman competitiveness and aggression turned inward into civil war. Roman myth had also said that Rome descended from Mars through his son, Romulus, the founder of the city, but also slayer of his twin brother Remus. Fratricide and civil war seemed built into the empire from the very beginning.

## Shakespeare's Classical Models

Shakespeare's plays depict a world in which war permeates every aspect of human life. It defines national identity: *Troilus and Cressida* (1601–2) and *Antony and Cleopatra* (1606–7) deal with the two momentous ancient wars that were seen as defining western civilization – battles between East and West, Troy and Greece, then Egypt and Rome, which together transferred power to the West and ultimately led to the establishment of the Roman Empire. As a dramatist, however, Shakespeare is most interested in the psychological impact of war on individual character. War shapes personal identity: appropriately named Martius, after the god of war, Coriolanus is renamed after the battle at Corioles, given "the whole name of the war" (2.1.125), as if the battle defined him. When he turns against the Rome that he feels has betrayed him, however, Coriolanus rejects this given name; tellingly, Aufidius repeatedly asks him "What's thy name?" (4.5.52–53, 56, 58, 61). Coriolanus has become "a kind of nothing, titleless" who has to fight against Rome to forge "himself a name o'th'fire / Of burning Rome" (5.1.13–15). War calls the hero's identity into question also in *Antony and Cleopatra* and *Troilus and Cressida*. The question of when Antony is "himself" is repeated throughout the play. Who is the real Antony, the Egyptian or the Roman, the lover or the warrior? The puzzle of Antony's particular identity is universalized in *Troilus and Cressida* to underlie a world in which the most common phrase is a version of "Who are you?" Identity confusion is increased by the theatricality of the play, evident in Achilles's and Patroclus's parodic "playing" of the other Greeks, and Ajax's aping of Achilles, which creates a literal theater of war. The practice of emulation that was central to theater and soldiery, as well as to Renaissance education, can make it hard to tell who anyone really is, or indeed to tell characters apart. War creates a situation in which people do not know each other. It further prevents them from knowing themselves; so Thersites claims that "Ajax goes up and down the field, asking for himself" (*Troilus and Cressida*, 3.3.244). Underneath the pun on jakes (toilet) lies a deeper truth: what the hero seeks in battle is himself.

The presence of the classics in Elizabethan education and culture means that it can be hard to pin down the precise classical sources of Shakespeare's works. At school, and through his culture in general, he would have been exposed to a wide range of Latin writers, many of whom he would have read only in selections. He would have picked up more knowledge of the classics through other works by later authors. He felt free to draw upon and mix sources, ancient and modern, foreign and native. It seems evident, however, that his understanding of war was influenced by two classical authors in particular: Plutarch and Virgil. In his representation of the psychology of soldiers, Shakespeare draws on Sir Thomas North's famous translation of Plutarch's *Lives* (1579, expanded in 1595 and again in 1603), with its intense and often dramatic character studies of great classical figures. Plutarch's study also pairs and compares Greek and Roman heroes, making classical history appear as a struggle between competing men. Like Plutarch, Shakespeare sees history as a series of rivalries between heroes whose relation combines opposition and likeness: Coriolanus vs. Aufidius, Caesar vs. Brutus, or most bluntly in *1 Henry IV*, "Harry to Harry" (4.1.121).

Yet for understanding the personal and social cost of war, Shakespeare is most indebted to Virgil, whom he would have first encountered at school. It is unlikely that he read Homer, except in translations; there are echoes of Chapman's Homer in that most epic of Shakespeare's English histories, *Henry V*, as well as in *Troilus and Cressida*.[10] For most Renaissance readers, Virgil and not Homer provided the model for the ideal epic; indeed, when Homer was read and translated it was usually through Virgil. For Shakespeare, the fall of Troy is the foundational and archetypal battle that sets the pattern for future conflicts; Lucrece and Hamlet refer to it to make sense of their own situations (*Hamlet*, 2.2.468–524; *Rape of Lucrece*, 1366–561). But Shakespeare's interpretation of that war is shaped by Virgil's very Roman, and therefore pro-Trojan, account in *Aeneid* 2, in which the Greeks win the war not through honorable fighting but through cheap subterfuge that preys on the honest Trojans' piety. In some places in which he retells Homer, Shakespeare's debt to Virgil is quite explicit. His version of the death of Hector, the climax of the *Iliad*, is ostentatiously revised through the *Aeneid*. According to Shakespeare, Hector is killed by the Greeks because he becomes briefly distracted by the fancy armor of a Greek whom he pursues and kills; disarmed, he is easily set upon by Achilles's Myrmidons. The episode is modeled on the death of Virgil's female warrior Camilla in *Aeneid* 11, which in Virgil shows the destruction of beauty in war. In Shakespeare, it further captures the Greeks' unscrupulous and unsporting brutality.

But what Shakespeare takes from Virgil above all is the consciousness of the impact of war. Virgil is interested in how war shapes both national and individual identity, not only for soldiers, but their wives, mothers, and fellow citizens. Written at the end of a period of civil war, Virgil's *Aeneid* traces the transformation of the Trojans, losers in the Trojan War, into the warlike winners, the Romans. Virgil thus makes Homeric epic a prequel to his own, and the story of Troy a stage in the founding of the Roman Empire. The Trojan prince Aeneas becomes a type for the Emperor Augustus who had brought the long years of civil war to an end. While celebrating the war in Italy on which Rome was founded, however, Virgil laments the cost of conflict, especially on families. His sympathies are with the losers: figures like the Trojan Queen Hecuba, the mourning wife and mother to whom Shakespeare also was repeatedly drawn. Defeated by the Greeks, she watches helplessly as Achilles's raging son, Pyrrhus, first kills her last remaining son and then impiously slays her husband Priam as he takes refuge at an altar. Shakespeare draws on this moving scene from *Aeneid* 2 in the First Player's speech in *Hamlet* 2.2.427–40, with which Hamlet deeply identifies.

In Virgil, however, it is not just the losers who suffer. Or rather, in war, everyone loses. So in *Aeneid* 11, Diomedes, one of Homer's keenest and most vicious fighters, denounces battle and laments the dismal fate of the Greeks who returned home, such as that of Agamemnon, murdered by his own wife. The knowledge that the winners are also destroyed by war troubles the end of the *Aeneid*, which concludes abruptly with the violent slaying in battle of Aeneas's enemy Turnus that leaves Aeneas the winner. But what has Aeneas won? Who has he become? What happens to the hero who must endlessly kill others? Virgil asks what it means to be a nation founded on killing and indeed fratricide.

## Of Arms and of Hands I

Like Virgil, Shakespeare is interested in how war shapes individual and national identity. Moreover, Shakespeare is interested in the legacy of *Virgil*'s vision of war. The influence of Virgil is an explicit theme in two of Shakespeare's earliest works on classical subjects, *Titus Andronicus* (c. 1589) and *The Rape of Lucrece* (1594). *Titus* takes place well after the time of Aeneas or even that of Augustus. Involving a conflict between Romans and Goths, it suggests vaguely the period before the collapse of the Roman Empire, when Rome was at war both abroad and at home, caught once more in a struggle between brothers as the conflict between Romulus and Remus is replayed in that between Saturninus and Bassianus. Other moments from the ancient past haunt the action. The situation generally evokes the archetypal war between the Greeks and the Trojans out of which Rome emerged: Titus has been gone for ten years (the length of the Trojan war) and compares himself to Priam in his loss of sons (1.1.82–84). The Andronici, however, seem to see themselves particularly through Virgil's story: Titus is "Andronicus, surnamèd Pius" (1.1.23), suggesting his kinship to Virgil's "pius Aeneas"; he named his daughter Lavinia, after Aeneas's future wife, and like her prototype, this Lavinia becomes the cause of a potential civil war. The word "arms," emphatically positioned at the ends of lines, serves as a kind of refrain in act 1, scene 1 (2, 30, 32, 41, 199), echoing Virgil's opening and its emphasis on Roman military power: "*Arma virumque cano*," of arms and the man I sing (*Aeneid*, 1.1). *Arma* literally means armor, but was used metonymically to mean war itself, as it is in Virgil. In the later epic tradition, moreover, the word *"arma"* becomes a metonym specifically for Virgilian epic. The opening scene of *Titus* thus thrusts us into a culture obsessed with emulating the heroic past, especially Virgil – one rather like Elizabethan England itself.

It is now, however, broadly assumed that this opening scene was written by George Peele, a writer greatly influenced by the classics. This might make it seem irrelevant to my discussion. We have little evidence for how Elizabethan collaboration in general worked, or of how closely coauthors worked together. But like Virgil himself, Peele seems to have inspired Shakespeare, who in the rest of the play picks up and explores further what it means to live in a Virgilian world. A central strategy here is literalization, which takes a rather grotesque form. When Shakespeare assumes control, Peele's opening play with the metonymic Virgilian "arms" unleashes a rather manic dismembering of real body parts that shows the severing of this body politic. The world and the bodies in it suddenly burst into isolated bits flying all over the place. The script becomes full of tongues, breasts, bosoms, heads, and especially *hands*, Shakespeare's cheeky and defiantly literal response to Peele's Virgilian and figurative *arms*. While in act 1, scene 1 the Andronici are "trained up in arms," Titus is "flourishing in arms," and his dead sons were "slain manfully in arms" (1.1.30, 41, 199), the subsequent acts show that their real *hands* get them into trouble. When Martius falls into Aaron's pit, he calls out to Quintus: "O brother, help me with thy fainting hand" (2.3.233), to which Quintus replies: "Reach me thy hand that I may help thee out" (237), and then asks for "Thy hand once more" (243) just before he is pulled in and joins his brother. Titus thus tells Lavinia that she is better off without her hands: " 'Tis well, Lavinia, that thou hast no hands, / For hands to do Rome service is but vain" (3.1.79–80). Poor mutilated Lavinia seems to set off the relentless play on hands, which begins with her rapists, who taunt her to "wash thy hands" and then chortle, "she hath no tongue to call, nor hands to wash" (2.4.6–7). Virgil's epic famously sings of "arms *and* the man": the grim joke in *Titus* is the detachment of arms, or at least hands, from the man – and indeed the woman.

Such relentlessly gruesome play on hands in *Titus* seems to be Shakespeare's answer to an idealization of war as abstracted *"arma"* or "arms." He shows how war tears individuals and societies apart. In *The Rape of Lucrece*, too, the violated Lucrece consoles herself by looking at an image of the Trojan War. The scene is based on *Aeneid* 1, in which Aeneas stares at an engraving of his own story in Carthage. In *Lucrece*, the warriors appear only as fragments, bits of bodies, parts gesturing toward wholes from which they seem irrevocably alienated:

> Here one man's hand leaned on another's head,
> His nose being shadowed by his neighbour's ear;
> . . .
> That for Achilles' image stood his spear,
> Gripped in an armèd hand; himself behind
> Was left unseen, save to the eye of mind:
>> A hand, a foot, a face, a leg, a head,
>> Stood for the whole to be imaginèd.
>>> (*Rape of Lucrece*, 1415–16, 1424–28)

*Lucrece* shows the events that lead to Brutus's expulsion of the Tarquins, the tyrannical kings who had ruled over Rome after Romulus, and to the creation of the Roman republic. The fragmentation here might suggest that Rome has become a decadent body politic that must be broken down to be made whole again. However, *Coriolanus* (1608) picks up the history of Rome shortly after Tarquin's expulsion, in which the young Coriolanus fought, to show a republic disintegrating from its very beginning. While the patrician senator Menenius tells the fable of the belly to insist on a holistic social order for the body politic (1.1.87–146), the play shows the members, here the different classes, at war with each other. Mars's city Rome is a world of arms indeed – but they happen to be cut off from and attacking the other parts of the body.

## Of Arms and of Hands II

The focus on hands in *Titus* has another function, however, that points to a different aspect of war. Although hands are associated with fighting, shaking or kissing hands is a means of uniting enemies and making peace. So Antony and Octavius make a temporary if ultimately disastrous peace (*Antony and Cleopatra*, 2.2.153–58), Aufidius welcomes Coriolanus into his camp (*Coriolanus*, 4.5.142–46), Marc Antony shakes bloody hands with each conspirator over Caesar's dead body (*Julius Caesar*, 3.1.185–91), and in *Troilus and Cressida* 4.5b, the Greeks and Trojans shake hands to make a temporary truce. Arms also are not just for fighting with, they are means of embracing others, as Nestor notes when greeting Troilus: "I would my arms could match thee in contention / As they contend with thee in courtesy" (89–90). Hands and arms divide people, but they can also unite them.

Joining hands is also of course a symbol of marriage (cf. *Troilus and Cressida*, 3.2.184–85 and *Antony and Cleopatra*, 2.2.153–60). Such hands and arms are connected to the erotic aspect of war expressed in the myth of the union of Aphrodite/Venus and Ares/Mars sung by the bard Demodocus in *Odyssey* 8. In the ancient world, love and war were seen as antithetical but fundamental principles associated with these two powerful deities: Aphrodite/Venus/love is the force that brings people together and Ares/Mars/war is the force that divides them. Homer's famous story suggests, however, that these two principles might be reconciled through marriage: love might soften war, while war could strengthen desire. The world is made through the struggle between these two principles and their ultimate resolution. But representations of the story in art and literature often suggest the dangers in this meeting of opposites. On the one hand, love may make the warrior effeminate and unwarlike by distracting him from his primary task. This view underlies medieval and Renaissance romance, in which scantily clad enchantresses often try to lure virtuous knights away from battle. So in *Antony and Cleopatra* the Romans believe Cleopatra has emasculated Antony. On the other hand, war may make love violent and aggressive – suggested in *The Rape of Lucrece*, in which Tarquin's act seems an inevitable extension of his behavior on the battlefield from which he has just come. There is a straight line from war to love and back again: as *Odyssey* 8 also makes clear, the Trojan War was fought for love.

The story of Mars and Venus had a particular significance for Romans, moreover, who traced their ancestry back not only to the god of war, father of Romulus, but also to the goddess of love and mother of Aeneas. There is of course much great Latin love poetry, especially that of Shakespeare's beloved Ovid, who cheekily presented the Romans not as warriors but as lovers. Given the enormous popularity of Ovid in the Renaissance, his presentation of the lover as a soldier who lays siege to his mistress, though not itself original, was extremely influential, and runs through Shakespeare's poetry as well as the plays. Virgil, however, sees love as a threat to social order and indeed individual sanity, a force deadlier than war itself. Homeric epic finds a central place for love: it is the cause of the Trojan War. In the *Iliad*, love is associated especially with the Trojans – not only the amorous Paris who stole Helen from her husband, but Hector who is represented as a loving husband and father and who in Shakespeare's *Troilus and Cressida* is literally disarmed by Helen (3.1.138–48). Love motivates the losers, who were also of course the ancestors of the Romans. Virgil's epic, however, excludes love: in order to become a victorious Roman, Aeneas must renounce *eros*, leaving behind first his wife and then his lover, Dido. Erotic desire has to be channeled into patriotism and, specifically, war itself, which offers the only true fulfillment of sexual desire, the ultimate sexual climax.

Love and war are continually intertwined in Shakespeare's works – comically, as in *A Midsummer Night's Dream*, in which Theseus wins his bride on the battlefield, and disastrously, as in *Othello*. The deadly eroticism of war is especially evident in the relation between Coriolanus and his future killer Aufidius, who welcomes him to his Volscian camp:

> I loved the maid I married; never man
> Sighed truer breath. But that I see thee here,
> Thou noble thing, more dances my rapt heart
> Than when I first my wedded mistress saw
> Bestride my threshold. Why, thou Mars, I tell thee,
> We have a power on foot, and I had purpose
> Once more to hew thy target from thy brawn,
> Or lose mine arm for't. Thou hast beat me out
> Twelve several times, and I have nightly since
> Dreamt of encounters 'twixt thyself and me –
> We have been down together in my sleep,
> Unbuckling helms, fisting each other's throat –
> And waked half dead with nothing.   (4.5.113–25)

While love and war seem opposites, they have similar effects. If war explodes bodily integrity, so does desire. When Troilus thinks of Cressida, he thinks of her in bits, lingering especially on her hand:

> Her eyes, her hair, her cheek, her gait, her voice;
> Handlest in thy discourse – oh, that her hand,
> In whose comparison all whites are ink
> Writing their own reproach, to whose soft seizure
> The cygnet's down is harsh, and spirit of sense
> Hard as the palm of plowman.   (1.1.51–56)

This kind of description, in which the lover catalogs the beloved's body bit by bit, is of course conventional in love poetry. But the term for it, "blazon," comes from war, specifically heraldry, referring to the heraldic description of a shield. The lover's arms and the soldier's arms are again conflated.[11] In Shakespeare's account, Lucrece's perception of the Greek and Trojan soldiers cited earlier mirrors her rapist Tarquin's view of her body in bed as a series of delicious but disjointed parts (starting again with her hand):

> Her lily hand her rosy cheek lies under,
> Coz'ning the pillow of a lawful kiss,
> Who therefore angry seems to part in sunder,
> Swelling on either side to want his bliss;
> Between whose hills her head entombèd is,
>> Where like a virtuous monument she lies
>> To be admired of lewd unhallowed eyes.

Without the bed her other fair hand was
On the green coverlet, whose perfect white
Showed like an April daisy on the grass,
With pearly sweat resembling dew of night.
Her eyes like marigolds had sheathed their light,
    And canopied in darkness sweetly lay
    Till they might open to adorn the day.

Her hair like golden threads played with her breath –
Oh, modest wantons, wanton modesty! –
Showing life's triumph in the map of death,
And death's dim look in life's mortality.
    As if beween them twain there were no strife,
    But that life lived in death, and death in life.

Her breasts like ivory globes circled with blue,
A pair of maiden worlds unconquerèd.
                          *(Rape of Lucrece*, 386–408)

As Nancy Vickers showed, the identity between the two kinds of blazons suggests how the female body is itself the territory over which war is waged. A similar parallel between conquest and courtship appears in *Henry V*. Before the Battle of Agincourt, Michael Williams observes the ruler's heavy responsibility for the deaths of his soldiers: "But if the cause be not good, the King himself hath a heavy reckoning to make when all those legs and arms and heads chopped off in a battle shall join together at the latter day and cry all, 'We died at such a place'" (4.1.125–28). As this suggests, the scattering of body parts in battle poses a logistical problem for the resurrection of the flesh at the Last Judgment. But this moment of theological angst looks back to the more playful dismembering in Katherine's English lesson when she tries to master the English words for body parts (one wonders what she expects to talk about with Hal). She too begins with the hand – "*Comment appelez-vous la main en anglais? / La main? Elle est appelée* de hand" (3.5.5–6) – and works through fingers, nails, through arms, "De arm" (19), elbow, to reach the neck and chin, before descending abruptly to the foot and gown/cown, leading to a dirty pun on *con*, which indeed is the aim of all such courtship by bits (1–55).

    The relation between the erotic and the military is especially complex in *Troilus and Cressida* and *Antony and Cleopatra*. Troy is fought over Helen, a situation doubled by Shakespeare in the battle between Troilus and Diomedes over Cressida. While, as I noted above, Shakespeare tells Homer's story of a war waged for love from a Virgilian perspective, he foregrounds the element of desire exiled by Virgil. Achilles's love of Polyxena prevents him from fighting, while Hector challenges the Greeks to a highly un-Homeric and even more un-Virgilian single combat over their respective mistresses (1.3.257–80). The play sets up a battle between different attitudes toward love, one that is not, however, a simple opposition. Shakespeare's Trojans, especially the idealistic and romantic Troilus, see love as valuable and worth fighting for. Yet the rape of Helen was not driven by romantic passion alone, but was a calculated retaliation for the Greeks' earlier kidnapping of Hesione (2.2.76–79). And while Troilus urges the Trojans to fight to retain Helen as a point of honor, he hands over his beloved Cressida without a struggle. In contrast, the Greeks are cynical about love, most notably the vicious Thersites who mocks the war, saying, "All the argument is a cuckold and a whore" (2.3.65). But we learn later (5.1.32–42) that Achilles cannot fight because of his love for the Trojan Polyxena, and the Greeks are in fact the ones who get the girls: Diomedes takes Cressida, and we know that eventually Helen will return to her husband. In *Antony and Cleopatra*, however, the conflict between love and war becomes starkly entrenched along national lines. The difference between Trojans and Greeks is replicated and deepened as the sensual world of Egypt, in which Antony loses himself in love, opposes the war-driven world of Rome, in which Antony's first wife is a soldier and the cold-blooded Octavius uses marriage for political purposes. Shakespeare's Romans are Virgilians who, remembering Dido, distrust passion, especially when it involves foreign females. The relation between Antony and Cleopatra suggests an alternative *Aeneid*, imagining what might have happened if Aeneas had stayed in Carthage and built an empire ruled not by a single man, but by a couple. But such a rewriting of Virgil turns out to be the fantasy of the loser; it is not possible in life, but only in death, and in the underworld in which Antony claims he and Cleopatra will be united:

> Where souls do couch on flowers; we'll hand in hand,
> And with our sprightly port make the ghosts gaze.
> Dido and her Aeneas shall want troops,
> And all the haunt be ours.   (4.14.51–54)

In history, the Virgilian pattern triumphs, and Octavius takes his place as a new Aeneas who destroys the possibility of romantic love.

## Wars Civil and Un-

According to Tacitus, Octavius gained power because he offered peace to a people drained by too many years of civil war. He replaced internal strife with a program of conquest by which he expanded the empire. This distinction between civil and foreign war was especially crucial in classical thought.

The Trojan War had been primarily a war between two separate nations, although Homer is extremely interested in the internal friction among the Greeks. In *Aeneid* 8, Venus gives her son Aeneas a shield engraved with figures telling the history of Rome up to Virgil's own present. At the very center is the image of the Battle of Actium in 31 BCE, in which Octavius secured power by defeating Antony and Cleopatra. Virgil presents it, moreover, not as simply a conflict between rival countries or even between West and East, but one between good and evil, order and chaos. The shield insists that at Actium antithetical cosmic forces and moral absolutes clashed over the fate of the universe.

Homer would never have considered the war between Trojans and Greeks in such black and white terms, and in this respect Shakespeare is more Homeric. But so in fact is Virgil, who knew that Actium was actually the last stage in a civil war, and a conflict between two Roman men, Octavius and Antony, vying for the empire. Shields protect soldiers: here that protection is also psychological, as Aeneas's shield gives the soldier an official image of a just war, a moral battle that enables him to fight wholeheartedly. Virgil's presentation of the actual war shows a much more complex and subjective struggle, however: in book 10, Venus presents the Trojans as persecuted peoples seeking their promised homeland, while Juno sees them as marauding invaders, disturbing a peaceful people. In battle, Aeneas fights tribes of Italians to whom he is related, and with whom he and the Trojans will mix to produce the Roman people. Rome is a city that under Octavius, now the emperor Augustus, aspired to include the entire world, as Romans punned on the Latin *urbs* (city) and *orbis* (world). When *urbs* becomes *orbis*, then foreign war is always really civil war.

Shakespeare's classical plays constantly return to the entanglement of domestic and foreign conflicts. The background of *Titus* is Rome against the Goths, but the real focus is the Romans turning on themselves. In *Coriolanus*, the war between the Romans and Volsces is a welcome but ineffectual distraction from the war intestine in the body politic. In *The Rape of Lucrece*, Tarquin comes straight from the siege of Ardea to begin the history of civil war that will continue to haunt Rome through *Julius Caesar*, in which a new Brutus dreams of restoring the republic. In *Troilus and Cressida*, as in Homer, much of the conflict is not between Trojans and Greeks, but among the Greeks themselves. The divisions between nations seem tenuous: Titus's son Lucius goes over to the Goths; Coriolanus joins his enemies; the Roman Antony becomes an Egyptian (while Cleopatra dies "after the high Roman fashion" [4.15.91]); Enobarbus deserts his leader. In *Troilus* especially, everyone seems to be switching sides: first, and fatally, Helen, the cause of the war, then Calchas, the cause of the play, and eventually his daughter Cressida and Antenor (who will be returned to the Trojans to betray them). Comically, Thersites leaves Ajax for Achilles. In the dramatic world of individual characters, as in the real world, the moral absolutes and national categories fixed by Virgil on Aeneas's shield will not stay put.

War's simultaneous reinforcement and erasure of national differences is part of the classical legacy in Shakespeare's English history plays, most notably the Virgilian *Henry V*. In the Renaissance as in the ancient world, it was generally assumed that foreign war could be an effective prophylactic against domestic strife. In *2 Henry IV*, therefore, the dying Henry IV, haunted by his own usurpation of the throne, tells his son to fight abroad in order to avoid civil war at home (4.3.341–44). Following this advice, Henry V wages war against the French, who see him as "Harry England" (*Henry V*, 3.6.48). But claiming his right by birth to the French throne, he insists that he is in fact waging a civil war, and the French are his rebellious subjects. His war with France is punctuated by scenes of internal unrest – the treachery of the three English lords, the rivalry between Nim and Pistol, and especially the conflict between the Irish MacMorris and the Welsh Fluellen, whose suggestion that the Irishman is not truly "English" twice prompts the outcry: "What ish my nation?" (3.3.61–63). It's a good question, central to an epic drama that acknowledges the heavy cost of victory for the victors and explores the impossibility of separating domestic from foreign strife.

## War and/in Peace

All classical war is inevitably civil war also because war abroad comes home with the hero. Greek tragedy is deeply concerned with the disasters that ensue when the warrior returns to the domestic world. Agamemnon and Hercules bring death back with them, both their own and those of others. Even in Homer, the returned Odysseus turns Ithaca into a slaughterhouse. While the soldier cannot fight all the time – and indeed most of Shakespeare's plays focus more on what the soldier does when he is *not* fighting – he also cannot simply turn off aggression and settle into a happy home life. The problem of domesticating the war veteran of which we are so conscious today is one with which Shakespeare would have been familiar both from Virgil's *Eclogues* (which begin with Augustus's confiscation of farms for retired soldiers) and from his own experience. What happens on the battlefield does not stay there, it leaks into every aspect of life, shaping the world of peace. In Shakespeare's classical plays, the real trouble begins when the actual fighting stops: when Titus has conquered enough Goths and comes home, when Tarquin leaves the siege of Ardea, when Coriolanus and

Caesar try the career move from general to politician, when Troilus and Antony disarm. While *Titus, Coriolanus, Julius Caesar,* and *Antony and Cleopatra* end with the establishment of peace, such peace is fragile, as we know the history that follows. In offering a resolution of war through a marriage that unites warring nations into a single family, *Henry V* recalls the Thirteenth Book of the *Aeneid,* written by the fourteenth-century Italian poet, Maffeo Vegio. While in Virgil, the *Aeneid* stops abruptly with the sudden and disturbingly brutal slaying of Turnus by Aeneas, Vegio tacks on a happy ending celebrating the marriage of Aeneas and Lavinia. In both *Henry V* and Vegio's sequel, however, we know that the respective heroes will not live long to enjoy peace; in England, of course, the aftermath of Henry's death is a return to civil war.

Heraclitus might suggest that this is inevitable because war is not just an activity, it is an eternal cosmic drive. The fact that we can use metaphors from battle to describe other activities, like loving, suggests that war is inherent in all human action. The world of the theater and the world of war are especially closely allied, not only by the metaphor of the "theater of war," as playwrights took war as their subject and were driven by fierce conflicts with rival authors and companies. The "War of the Theaters" is often seen as a subtext for *Troilus and Cressida.* Violence is an essential part of human nature, even, or perhaps especially, human creativity.

Yet it is equally possible and indeed attractive to argue that war is not natural at all but a cultural construct. In recent years, *Titus Andronicus* has often been read as a play that shows that the emulation of the classics, which Renaissance humanists believed would make men more civilized, in fact made them more barbaric.[12] It suggests that violence is instilled through the imitation of a violent tradition, the passing down of stories that glorify a barbaric heroism. The fault lies not in the stars, but in the schools.

If violence is simply learned, of course, then it can also be unlearned. Stories can be changed. Virgil himself had tantalizingly flirted with an alternative ending for both Aeneas's story and Roman history when he sent Aeneas to Carthage and Dido. As many recent critics have noted, Shakespeare's final play, *The Tempest,* offers a revision of the *Aeneid* in which war between brothers is ultimately renounced.[13] Prospero is an Aeneas who at the end refuses to take revenge and kill his enemy, and so breaks the violent cycle of history. Like Shakespeare's other late romances, the play offers the possibility of change and redemption. Yet it seems ingenuous to read *The Tempest* as Shakespeare's last word. For one thing, he did not know he would die in 1616. For another, it is not actually his last work. That honor goes to *The Two Noble Kinsmen,* cowritten with John Fletcher, which hurls us back into the classical world of war, and Thebes, the city of

Oedipus and his sons, a society identified with incest, parricide, fratricide, and civil war. Shakespeare's play shows Thebes easily defeated by Athens, suggesting the reassuring triumph of Athenian rationality over Theban barbarism. Although the two noble kinsmen are themselves Thebans, they denounce the corruption of their country. First seen trying to leave Thebes, they are drawn back only in its defense. At the very moment they swear their eternal friendship, however, they are made mortal enemies by sudden, violent love of the same woman. You can't take Thebes out of the Theban. Moreover, Athens is ruled by Theseus. As in *A Midsummer Night's Dream*, his marriage to the Amazon Hippolyta frames the action and suggests the end of the war between the sexes. As Shakespeare knew, however, the result of that marriage will be the son, Hippolytus, whose death Theseus causes. Athenian rationality does not destroy the violence of Thebes, it perpetuates it. From the perspective of *The Two Noble Kinsmen*, *The Tempest* looks like an author's fantasy of the power of revision. The end of all war appears as elusive to Shakespeare as it does to us today.

*Further Reading*

Bate, Jonathan. *How the Classics Made Shakespeare*, Princeton, Princeton University Press, 2019.

Burrow, Colin. *Shakespeare and Classical Antiquity*, Oxford, Oxford University Press, 2013.

Cantor, Paul A. *Shakespeare's Roman Trilogy: The Twilight of the Ancient World*, Chicago, University of Chicago Press, 2017.

James, Heather. *Shakespeare's Troy: Drama, Politics, and the Translation of Empire*, Cambridge, Cambridge University Press, 1997.

Kahn, Coppélia. *Roman Shakespeare: Warriors, Wounds, and Women*, New York, Routledge, 1997.

Martindale, Charles, and A. B. Taylor (eds.). *Shakespeare and the Classics*, Cambridge, Cambridge University Press, 2004.

Miola, Robert S. *Shakespeare's Rome*, Cambridge, Cambridge University Press, 1983.

Tudeau-Clayton, Margaret. *Jonson, Shakespeare and Early Modern Virgil*, Cambridge, Cambridge University Press, 1998.

## NOTES

1 Ben Jonson, "To the Memory of My Beloved, the Author, Master William Shakespeare, and What He Hath Left Us" (1623), l. 31.

2 Thomas Whitfield Baldwin, *William Shakespeare's Small Latine and Lesse Greeke*, 2 vols. (Urbana: University of Illinois Press, 1944); and more recently Colin Burrow, *Shakespeare and Classical Antiquity* (Oxford: Oxford University Press, 2013).

3 Peter Mack, *Elizabethan Rhetoric: Theory and Practice* (Cambridge: Cambridge University Press, 2002); and Burrow, *Shakespeare*.

4 Heraclitus, "[Fragments]," in S. Marc Cohen, Patricia Curd, and C. D. C. Reeve (eds.), *Readings in Ancient Greek Philosophy: From Thales to Aristotle*, 3rd ed. (Indianapolis: Hackett Publishing, 2005), 22B53.

5 Aristotle, *Politics*, in Jonathan Barnes (ed.), *The Complete Works of Aristotle: The Revised Oxford Translation*, Princeton/Bollingen Series 71, 2 vols. (Princeton: Princeton University Press, 1984), 1253a. All further citations are from this edition.

6 Plato, *Laws*, in Edith Hamilton and Huntington Cairns (eds.), *The Collected Dialogues of Plato*, trans. A. E. Taylor (New York: Bollingen Foundation; Pantheon Books, 1964), 625e–26a. All further citations are from this edition.

7 Thomas Heywood, *Apology for Actors* (London, 1612), sigs. B3v–B4r, cited in Burrow, *Shakespeare*, p. 240.

8 Samuel Taylor Coleridge, *Lectures 1808–1819: On Literature*, ed. R. A. Foakes, vol. v of *The Collected Works of Samuel Taylor Coleridge*, 2 vols. (Princeton: Princeton University Press, 1987), vol. I, p. 287.

9 Homer, *The Iliads of Homer: Prince of Poets, Never Before in Any Language Truly Translated, with a Comment on Some of His Chief Places* (1611), ed. Richard Hooper, trans. George Chapman (London: J. R. Smith, 1857), bk. 5, l. 884–86.

10 John H. Betts, "Classical Allusions in Shakespeare's *Henry V* with Special Reference to Virgil," *Greece and Rome*, 15 (1968), pp. 147–63; and Gary Taylor (ed.), *Henry V*, by William Shakespeare, The Oxford Shakespeare (Oxford: Oxford University Press, 2008).

11 Nancy Vickers, "'The Blazon of Sweet Beauty's Best': Shakespeare's Lucrece," in Patricia Parker and Geoffrey Hartman (eds.), *Shakespeare and the Question of Theory* (New York: Methuen, 1985), pp. 95–115; "'This Heraldry in Lucrece' Face,'" *Poetics Today*, 6 (1985), pp. 171–84; and Coppélia Kahn, *Roman Shakespeare: Warriors, Wounds, and Women* (New York: Routledge, 1997), pp. 56–57.

12 See Grace Starry West, "Going by the Book: Classical Allusions in Shakespeare's *Titus Andronicus*," *Studies in Philology*, 79 (1982), pp. 62–77.

13 Craig Kallendorf, *The Other Virgil: Pessimistic Readings of the "Aeneid" in Early Modern Culture* (Oxford: Oxford University Press, 2007), pp. 102–37.

# 6

## DAVID SCOTT KASTAN

# "The Question of These Wars"

### Shakespeare, Warfare, and the Chronicles

In Ben Jonson's *The Devil Is an Ass* (1616), the well-named Meercraft attempts to defraud Squire Fitzdottrel with a get-rich scheme involving the reclamation of swampland, promising him millions of pounds in profit and the inevitability of a title. Fitzdottrel is excited by the prospect, until Meercraft suggests that "Gloucester" might be the appropriate dukedom for him. Fitzdottrel immediately balks, revealing his impressive knowledge of English history:

> Thomas of Woodstock
> I'm sure was Duke, and he was made away
> At Calice, as Duke Humphrey was at Bury,
> And Richard the Third, you know what end he came to.

Meercraft is surprised that his gull is so "cunning i' the Chronicle," but Fitzdottrel admits to a different source for his historical information: "No, I confess I ha't from the playbooks, / And think they are more authentic."[1]

Fitzdottrel was not alone in thinking the playbooks were a reliable way to learn English history. In 1612, Thomas Heywood enthusiastically claimed that history plays have "instructed such as cannot read in the discovery of all our English Chronicles," and later Coleridge would famously report that the fourth Duke of Marlborough "was not ashamed to confess that his principle acquaintance with English history was derived" from Shakespeare's historical plays.[2] But the joke in *The Devil Is an Ass* is, of course, that Fitzdottrel has it backwards. The playbooks took their history from the chronicles, and primarily from the multivolume, collaborative project known then and now as Holinshed's *Chronicles*, although Raphael Holinshed was neither its originator nor its sole author, and indeed was dead well before the enlarged second edition of 1587 was even begun.[3]

There is, however, a sense in which Holinshed (although clearly it is more properly "Holinshed") arguably owes as much to Shakespeare as Shakespeare does to Holinshed. Holinshed matters to us mainly because

Shakespeare does. Without Shakespeare's dependence on the *Chronicles*, Holinshed would be a name of interest primarily to scholars of sixteenth-century historiography. And yet it must also be said that without Holinshed, Shakespeare's histories might possibly not have been written at all, and certainly would have been written differently. Whatever it is we think that Shakespeare is doing in the history plays can hardly be independent of what he found in his primary source, not least of which was a record of almost continuous warfare, both civil wars in England and foreign wars mostly with Scotland and France.

No doubt what Holinshed wrote was in large part the result of an English chronicle tradition extending back to William Caxton. Indeed, the publishing of history in England is virtually coextensive with the history of English publishing itself. Among the books printed by Caxton in the years immediately after he founded the first English press on Tothill Street in the shadow of Westminster Abbey in 1476 were two books of history writing: *The Chronicles of England* (1480), a translation of the *Brut*, an Anglo-French chronicle history of Britain beginning as its name suggests with its mythical founding by Brutus, a descendant of Aeneas, and continuing to the Battle of Halidon Hill in 1333; and a translation of Ranulph Higden's *Polychronicon* (1482), a universal history in seven books that begins with Adam and Eve and continues to 1358, with Caxton himself adding an eighth book in his printed edition extending the narrative to 1460. Caxton's versions of both the *Brut* and the *Polychronicon* went through multiple printed editions. By 1530, the *Brut*, which in its enlarged form had become known as "Caxton's Chronicles," had been published thirteen times, the *Polychronicon* six.

These two books set the pattern for much of what was to come in English history writing. The chronicles of the sixteenth century take their method and form from Caxton's publications. They arrange their material chronologically, usually dividing it by monarchical reign and subdividing it by calendar year, but with a capacious, opportunistic, and unsystematic sense of what should be included. The chronicles are all compilations, recycling materials, sometimes verbatim, from earlier chronicles, though each adds newly discovered information enlarging the history that was known, not least in a spirit of competition with its predecessors.[4] They collect and memorialize the significant events of the past, often with a surprisingly wide-angled social lens that could be (and often was) viewed as distracting from the high matters of church and state, but which might also serve as witness to "their natiue countries praise" and the "encouragement of theyr worthie countrie men," as Holinshed says in his preface.[5]

Holinshed's *Chronicles* were originally intended to be only a small portion of an ambitious but ultimately unsuccessful effort by Reyner Woolf to publish "an vniuersall Cosmographie of the whole worlde" (I, sig. ¶2$^r$). But even in its narrowed scope of the descriptions and histories of England, Scotland, and Ireland, it was still an enormous undertaking. Indeed, the first edition in 1577 was a book larger in size (measured by sheet count) than any book that had been to that time printed in England, larger even than the expanded edition of John Foxe's *Actes and Monuments*, published in 1570.[6]

What "caused the book to be so great," as Holinshed admitted, was that he was "loath to omit anything that might encreace the Readers knowledge." The British past was rendered monumentally, and although Holinshed expressed his wish that he "might have pleased all kindes of men," the size and cost of the volumes suggests a more restricted audience that was literate, relatively sophisticated, and reasonably prosperous (I, sig. ¶4$^r$). And yet it was a book generally admired and surprisingly popular (a second edition appeared within ten years), and neither its awkward size nor its daunting price, usually somewhere around a pound, proved off-putting for sales. It consistently found an audience, though sometimes only through cooperation and the existence of a secondhand book market, which allowed, for example, three men in 1654 to share a then-quite-old secondhand copy of the 1577 edition, paying seven shillings and sixpence for a book they would share, with the understanding that "the longest liver of the three" would eventually own it alone, and that his heirs should continue to enjoy it "for eivr" (sig. B2$^v$; Pratt and Kastan 42).

We know the names of these three men because they signed their agreement on the final page of book 1 of "The Historie of Ireland." Unsurprisingly, few other copies so accommodatingly reveal the names of their owners. There are signatures in some copies, and the title appears in a number of inventories. But if our sense of the "who" that owned Holinshed is necessarily limited, our sense of the "why" or "how" they read him is even more so. A few copies survive with marginalia, a few more with underlining or other noting marks, though none can be thought to be a "reading" of Holinshed; at most these copies attest to some usually unsystematic and mostly unsustained sets of personal interests. However unfashionable it may be to say so, with its embarrassing hint of bardolatry, arguably it is Shakespeare's use of Holinshed that should be considered the most substantial evidence we have of a contemporary reader's serious and sustained engagement with the *Chronicles*.

We don't know who owned the copy of Holinshed that Shakespeare read with such obvious care. (I have always been tempted by the idea that those large books, like Holinshed's *Chronicles* and Plutarch's *Lives*, in which Shakespeare regularly found the material on which he based his plays, might well have been owned by the theater company for consultation by him and the company's commissioned playwrights.) But we do know that Shakespeare, like other dramatists, found Holinshed to be an indispensable store of plots and characters for a burgeoning entertainment industry in constant need of what today we would call "content."

In 1617, the travel writer Fynes Moryson wrote that "The Citty of London alone hath foure or five Companyes of players with their peculiar Theaters Capable of [holding] many thousands, wherein they all play every day in the weeke but Sunday ... [and] there be, in my opinion, more Playes in London then in all the partes of the world I have seene."[7] Modern scholarship essentially confirms Moryson's report (adding that, in addition to Sundays, the theaters would have been closed for Lent).[8] While it is impossible to calculate with any certainty the number of London theater-goers, clearly thousands, more likely tens of thousands, went weekly to see plays in a city with a population of about two hundred thousand.

New content was therefore crucial for all of the companies, and history writing served as an obvious and convenient resource for the dramatists who provided it. By the time of the publication of Shakespeare's First Folio (1623), each of the twenty-four monarchs from William the Conqueror to Elizabeth had been represented in a play, and at least one play on an English historical subject had been published in twenty-five of the previous thirty years; and for most of these plays Holinshed served as the major source. Like other dramatists, Shakespeare turned to the *Chronicles*. He discovered in them not just plots for his plays, but also ideas about sovereignty and power, national identity, and the costs and conduct of warfare – a trio of concepts that has helped to make Shakespeare every age's "contemporary." And in Holinshed he also discovered that these were not three unconnected interests but ones that were crucially interrelated as ways of understanding the complex, tenuous, largely imagined unity that was England.

Warfare is of course threaded through the *Chronicles*, as unavoidable in the volumes as it seemed to be in the world Shakespeare lived in. During the span of Shakespeare's lifetime, 1564–1616, warfare was a continual concern and almost an uninterrupted reality.[9] English soldiers fought in the North, in Scotland, in the Netherlands, in Portugal, in France, and, seemingly always, in Ireland. There were English attacks on Cádiz in 1587 and again a decade later, and failed invasions from Spain in 1588, 1596, and 1597, as well as widespread anxiety all through 1599 about yet another armada that never materialized.

Trained bands and conscripted soldiers, estimated as involving perhaps as much as 15 percent of the male population of England, made the lived experience of warfare or the dread of it present all over the country.[10] Soldiers returning wounded from the wars, or worse, not returning, made every community aware of war's terrible consequences. The *Book of Common Prayer* petitions "Give us peace in our time, O Lord," as human effort was seemingly incapable of bringing it about.

War, then, was seemingly a constant of human life, and many urged the "collection and iudgement of the reports, historyes, & Chronicles written of warres" to prepare for it.[11] Written history, it was often argued, would provide the principles and precepts needed to discipline native English strength and will. In reality, however, the reading of history seems only to demonstrate the ubiquity of war and its uncertainties, rather than provide lessons that will let us avoid it or guarantee victory when we don't.

It was the military manuals, particularly in the 1590s, that were indeed concerned with weaponry, fortification, tactics, and the training of soldiers. They were designed to "teach them how to war" (*Henry V*, 3.1.25). The popular manuals enthusiastically promoted the development of a new military science, designed to revise or maybe replace "the disciplines of the pristine wars of the Romans" (3.3.25–26) for the experience of contemporary warfare.[12] The chroniclers didn't and certainly not Holinshed.

Though Holinshed writes of the various battles fought for control of the English throne between 1399 and 1486 (dramatized in the eight plays of the two so-called tetralogies), and of the larger international context in which these conflicts took place (the Hundred Years' War, 1337–1453), as well as later military action in the reigns of the Tudor monarchs (for example Henry VIII's wars with France in 1512–13, 1522–23, and 1544–46), there is little difference in the accounts. Warfare in Holinshed is more or less indistinguishable from century to century, a point visually reinforced by the recycling of woodcuts in the 1577 edition.

According to Victor Scholderer, only thirty-six blocks were used for the edition's 480 "warlike scenes."[13] A forced march is a forced march; a siege is a siege; a rout is a rout. Soldiers often wear armor that was then unknown and carry weapons not yet in use. The issue of anachronism is acknowledged, but it is buried deep in the text, indeed on its very last page.[14] The last note on the list of "faultes escaped" contains the admission:

> And where as in the pictures of battle, ther are in sundrie places gunnes before the invention of that kind of engine, whereby the reader may discerne some error, and desirous peradventure to know when they first came in use, he shal understand that we read not of any to be put in practice, till the year 1380, in the warres betwixt the Venetians and Genoways, at Chiozza. (II, sig. (¶ )2ᵛ)

For Holinshed, the historical fact about the introduction of guns is worth recording, however belatedly, but it does not affect "the pictures of battle" that are regularly marked by this sort of "error." An illustration in the account of Brute's arrival in Albion, "with a great traine of the posteritie of the dispersed Troianes" in "the 1127 [year] before Christ," shows soldiers firing muskets (I, sig. A2$^{r-v}$, sig. A7$^v$). The illustrated anachronisms in the *Chronicles*, however, do work in both directions, with other cuts showing weaponry long obsolete still being carried into the battles that are being recounted in the text. It is, of course, possible, maybe even likely, that foot soldiers would sometimes have carried out-of-date weapons, though the recycled illustrations are not trying to make that point.

The recycling is not making an historical point at all. It is a practical solution to the problem of cost. Only 211 (maybe 212) wood blocks are used for the almost 1,300 illustrations. Some could only be used once in the text, like the well-known image of Macbeth and Banquo meeting the weird sisters, but most of the blocks are unselfconsciously recycled multiple times throughout the edition (and some were even reused in other books, perhaps most interestingly a book on the Spanish conquest of Peru, printed in London four years after Holinshed's 1577 *Chronicles*, which uses a battle scene to illustrate Pizarro's attack on Cuzco in 1532 that had been used in Holinshed to depict the Irish invasion of Galloway in southwest Scotland in 870).[15] Similarly, portraits of kings reappear in the volume in the histories of later centuries, there given other names (like the cut of Paulus Suetonius, which is reused nine more times in the *Chronicles*); and woodcuts of military action recur again and again, speaking some truth about history that is deeper and darker than any of its supposed specificity. The cut of foot soldiers and horsemen attacking an enemy on sig. h2$^r$ appears thirty-five additional times in the volume. One of a rout, first appearing on sig. c2$^v$, is used twenty-nine times. An image of a cavalry charge used initially on sig. a6$^v$ recurs twenty-six times, while the illustration of a siege used first on d1$^r$ is just the first of its twenty-five appearances in the volume.[16]

It is possible Shakespeare never noticed the repetitions, or maybe he never even saw the volume. Scholars seem confident that Shakespeare primarily depended upon the 1587 edition of Holinshed, which had dispensed with the illustrations in favor of a longer text arranged in a more attractive layout (although it is hard to think he had never seen the "weird sisters" illustration).[17] But even at the level of description, warfare in Holinshed seems tediously repetitious, and the written accounts blur together, as the same aristocratic family names appear in actions across the centuries. There always seems to be a Northumberland unhappy with his king or a Scrope all-too-willing to betray him.

At its most uplifting, the history is designed to witness the "valiancie of the Englishmen," as a marginal note reminds us in the second year of the reign of Edward VI (1587, III, sig. 5D3$^v$). But at its least, what it provides is the dispiriting evidence of the seemingly inevitable recurrence of warfare in English history. That is what Shakespeare seems to have found in Holinshed, whether in the recycled illustrations of the first edition or the nearly indistinguishable actions and actors in the prose accounts of the second.

The plays suggest not so much Shakespeare's preoccupation with war as his mere recognition of its inescapability; that is, it wasn't so much a topic he sought as one he could not avoid. It isn't only the history plays in which soldiers and armies appear, but in the plays of every genre, not only in the plays set in England but in plays set wherever Shakespeare imagined them. In *Othello* war remains in the background, threatening somewhere off the coast of Cyprus; in *Henry V* it is arguably the real subject of the play, whether the action takes place in England or in France. The word "war" appears in thirty-three of his thirty-seven (or so) plays; and in one of the very few that it doesn't, *As You Like It*, "soldier" is recognized as one of the seven ages of man. Thirty-one other plays mention or explicitly call for "soldiers." Armies often pass silently over the stage, and battles are noisily fought, though usually off it.

In an obvious way, the wars Shakespeare found in Holinshed presented him with a practical staging problem. Sidney could satirize the drama played in the halls and inns of an earlier time when "two armies fly in, represented with four swords and bucklers, and then what heart will not receive it for a pitched field."[18] But the representation of battle was no easier for Shakespeare even with the most up-to-date resources of the theater available to him in the newly built Globe. The Chorus in *Henry V*, not entirely disingenuously, laments the fact that this play will "disgrace / ... / The name of Agincourt" with its dependence for its representation upon "four or five most vile and ragged foils / Right ill-disposed in brawl ridiculous" (4.0.49–52). No theater can do that much better.

Often the stage directions in the early texts are pragmatically unspecific about how many actors are needed for an army, agnostically specifying "with soldiers," whose exact number no doubt depended on what theater personnel was available to come onstage in any given performance. But in *1 Henry VI*, York enters with "many soldiers" (4.3.1 SD), and *2 Henry VI* makes even greater demands on the resources of the acting company: Cade enters "with infinite numbers" (4.2.30 SD) in support of his peasant rebellion.

In *Henry V*, the Battle of Agincourt, of course, is fought and won, but as none of it is enacted, there can be no "disgrace" to "The name of Agincourt." This is only one of the many times in the play that the Chorus promises something to the audience that is not delivered. The "brawl ridiculous" does not take place. It is easy to forget that the only required dramatized fighting in the so-called second tetralogy is at Shrewsbury in *1 Henry IV*. The single dramatized encounter in *Henry V* is Pistol's capture of Monsieur Le Fer in 4.4, threatening to cut the Frenchman's throat, but the surrender is accomplished by bluster alone.

What interests Shakespeare about war is not the drama of the battle-field. Holinshed had taught him that it is all the same, with its inevitable brutalities and dubious motivations – and taught him also that it is very hard to stage realistically. Shakespeare's interest is in the psychological and ethical issues that warfare raises, issues that Holinshed does not usually address directly but that he somehow exposes in what he says and doesn't say. Shakespeare reads him very carefully. Sometimes what Holinshed says is enough; sometimes not quite enough; and sometimes not at all.

In *Henry V*, after the battle at Agincourt has ended, Shakespeare's Henry reads the enumeration of French losses, of the

> ten thousand French
> That in the field lay slain. Of princes in this number
> And nobles bearing banners, there lie dead
> One hundred twenty-six. Added to these,
> Of knights, esquires, and gallant gentlemen,
> Eight thousand and four hundred, of the which
> Five hundred were but yesterday dubbed knights.  (4.8.74–80)

It is not some biographical fantasy that suggests that the 1587 Holinshed was open before him as he wrote. Holinshed writes:

> There were slain in all of the French part to the number of ten thousand men, whereof were princes and noble men bearing baners, one hundred twentie and six; to these, of knights, esquiers, and gentlemen so manie as made vp the number of eight thousand and four hundred (of the which fiue hundred were dubbed knights the night before the battle).  (III, sig. 3G6ʳ)

Shakespeare merely renders Holinshed's prose in hypermetric pentameter. "Field" and "yesterday" are the only consequential words Shakespeare adds to what he has read in the chronicle.

The same process is visible as Shakespeare's Henry reads the "number of our English dead":

> Edward the Duke of York; the Earl of Suffolk;
> Sir Richard Keighley; Davy Gam, esquire;
> None else of name, and of all other men
> But five-and-twenty.  (4.8.96–100)

Again, Shakespeare has followed Holinshed almost verbatim. The *Chronicles* read: "Edward duke [of] York, the earle of Suffolke, sir Richard Kikelie, and Davie Gamme esquire, and of all other people not aboue fiue and twentie persons" (III, sig. 3G6ʳ).

But something slightly different has happened here. First, Shakespeare adds the status distinction: "None else of name." This isn't Henry's (or even Shakespeare's) erasure of individuality but history's own, although I have seen a production in which Henry can't be bothered to read the names of the common soldiers who have died, crumpling up the paper in his rush to give God the victory. Holinshed, however, did not provide the "fiue and twentie" with names, and the bodies of common soldiers would inevitably be unidentifiable by the heralds who counted casualties in the battle's aftermath.

Mountjoy asks Henry permission to "wander o'er this bloody field" after the fighting at Agincourt,

> To sort our nobles from our common men.
> For many of our princes, woe the while,
> Lie drowned and soaked in mercenary blood;
> So do our vulgar drench their peasant limbs
> In blood of princes.   (4.7.64, 66–70)

Even in death, nobles must be separated from common men. But Mountjoy, after all, is a Frenchman, and Henry had promised his "band of brothers" better: "he today that sheds his blood with me / Shall be my brother. Be he ne'er so vile, / This day shall gentle his condition" (4.3.60–63). Henry, however, exactly like his father, knows "at what time to promise, when to pay" (*1 Henry IV*, 4.3.53).

There is, however, another oddity in Shakespeare's version of Holinshed's account of the English dead. Agincourt is of course an English victory of incredible proportion: ten thousand Frenchmen die and only twenty-nine English. But Holinshed's casualty report does not end where Shakespeare's does. Holinshed says immediately that this is only "as some doo report; but other writers of greater credit affirme, that there were slaine aboue fiue or six hundred persons" (III, sig. 3G6ʳ). Holinshed's version is taken almost verbatim from Edward Hall, who, even more incredulously, adds, "if you will give credite to such as write miracles."[19] Both chroniclers had read earlier historians who provide accounts of what Holinshed calls "The whole order of this conflict which cost manie a mans life and procured great bloodshed before it was ended."

Shakespeare, however, rejects the credible for the miraculous and ignores the historical logic of probable cause for the poetic logic of giant killing. All the historical accounts of Agincourt make much of the king's tactics and the skill of the English bowmen. But Shakespeare includes neither of these. The archers are never mentioned, though English skill with the longbow was renowned (and indeed could still be invoked as late as 1590 as an argument against the growing dependence on firearms, as it is in Sir John Smythe's *Certain Discourses Military*). Indeed, in the history plays Shakespeare's only reference to bowmen is at Bosworth Field in *Richard III*, when Richard desperately calls: "Draw, archers, draw your arrows to the head" (5.3.337). And tactically the most notable fact of the Battle of Agincourt, in addition to the well-chosen ground on which to fight it, was that the King

> caused stakes bound with iron sharpe at both ends, of the length of fiue or six foot to be pitched before the archers, and of ech side the footmen like an hedge, to the intent that if the barded horsses ran rashlie vpon them, they might shortlie be gored and destroied.

A printed marginal note in Holinshed marks this as "A politike inuention" (III, sig. 3G5$^r$).

In *The Famous Victories of Henry V*, the tactic is given prominence. We see Henry order

> That euery archer prouide him a stake of
> A tree, and sharpe it at both endes,
> And at the first encounter of the horsemen,
> To pitch their stakes downe into the ground before them,
> That they may gore themselues upon them,
> And then to recoyle backe, and shoote wholly altogither,
> And so discomfit them.

And after the fighting has ended, this is the only aspect of the battle that elicits comment from John Cobbler and Robin Pewterer:

> JOHN: But Robin, didst thou see what a pollicie the king had, to see how the French men were kild with the stakes of the trees,
> ROBIN: I, Iohn, there was a braue pollicie.[20]

Shakespeare, however, omits all reference to anything that might make the extraordinary victory plausible. The defeat of the French against the "fearful odds" (4.3.5) might be explicable if mention were made of the superior English strategy, but Shakespeare's Henry pointedly insists that victory came "without stratagem, / But in plain shock and even play of battle" (4.8.102–3).

Henry, unlike Hall or Holinshed, *will* credit miracles. He is quick to acknowledge God's agency. Five times in nineteen lines he rings changes on the theme, "O God, thy arm was here; / And not to us but to thy arm alone / Ascribe we all" (4.8.100–2); and he orders "Let there be sung *Non nobis* and *Te Deum*" (4.8.117). Shakespeare is again following what he finds in Holinshed. There Henry

> gaue thanks to almightie God for so happie a victorie, causing his prelats and chapleins to sing this psalme: *In exitu Israel de Aegypto*, and commanded euerie man to knéele downe on the ground at this verse: *Non nobis Domine, non nobis, sed nomini tuo da gloriam*. Which doone, he caused *Te Deum*, with certeine anthems to be soong, giuing land and praise to God, without boasting of his owne force or anie humane power.

The marginal note calls this "A worthie example of a godlie prince (III, sig. 3G6r).

But that doesn't seem to be exactly the king that Shakespeare portrays. The almost obsessive expression of Henry's gratitude in the play marks it as something other than simple piety. Henry *performs* "godlie prince," just as he has performed ranting tyrant before Harfleur in act 3, out-Heroding Herod, and will perform "plain soldier" in act 5; and also just, as Hal in the *Henry IV* plays, he had performed prodigal son. Henry has an enormous repertory of momentarily compelling roles and rhetorical registers, but each finally seems too well calculated to be convincing, too much a part of his knowing performance of power and never persuasively a spontaneous expression of feeling or belief.

In this case, the sheer reiteration of Henry's claim that "God fought for us" (4.8.114) might itself suggest that his piety is held up for critical examination, but if not, Fluellen's scarcely convincing or convinced agreement must: "Yes, in my conscience, he did us great good" (4.8.115). The short conversation between Fluellen and the king seems likely to be a later interpolation, interrupting two half-lines spoken by the king and the continuous thought of his now-two speeches.[21] Shakespeare won't quite let us take Henry's piety at face value.

Shakespeare finds and exposes the sharp edges of the history buried in Holinshed's seemingly straightforward account, and even when they are not there he seems happy to produce them himself. A minor episode in Holinshed, used to illustrate Henry's control of his troops and insistence on their discipline, sparks a moment in Shakespeare's play:

> Yet in this great necessitie, the poore people of the countrie were not spoiled, nor anie thing taken of them without paiment, nor anie outrage or offense doone by the Englishmen, except one, which was, that a souldiour took a pix out of a church, for which he was apprehended, & the king not once remooued till the box was restored and the offendor strangled.

The marginal note here instructs the reader to "Note $y^e$ force of iustice" (III, sig. 3G4$^v$).

In *Henry V*, we hear that "Fortune is Bardolph's foe, and frowns on him, / For he hath stol'n a pax, and hanged must 'a be" (3.7.35–36). In Holinshed, a nameless soldier steals a "pix," a jeweled box in which the consecrated wafers for the mass were kept. Shakespeare gives the thief a name and changes the stolen item. What Bardolph steals is a "pax of little price" (3.7.41), the engraved tablet, often with a picture of the crucifixion, kissed by the priest and passed through the congregation, an "osculatory" for the "kiss of peace."

It is no surprise to discover that Bardolph is a thief. He and Nym, as the Boy says, "are sworn brothers in filching" (3.2.39–40), and Nym we later learn has also been hanged, presumably for a similar offense (4.4.63). So much for the two soldiers who first appear onstage immediately after the Chorus's claim that "honor's thought / Reigns solely in the breast of every man" (2.0.3–4).

But why does Shakespeare change Holinshed's "pix" to a "pax," especially as it makes the theft somewhat more trivial? Perhaps that is the very point, showing Henry's insistence upon the absolute discipline of his troops, unwilling to forgive one of his former tavern acquaintances even for a relatively minor crime. But the implications of the change seem to be more consequential than merely showing Henry's mastery of the instructions of the military manuals, one of which specifically does say that "the prince or Generall" must ensure that no soldier "upon payne of hanging neither take nor spoyle any Churches."[22] Here, however, something else seems to be at stake, not in terms of what Holinshed wrote but in how Shakespeare read. Holinshed's "pix" prompted the possibility of something better: a better word not a better object.

Just as in *1 Henry IV*, where Falstaff's robbery of crowns headed for the king's treasury at Gadshill reflects on the stolen crown that has brought Henry to the throne, in *Henry V*, the pun in the stolen "pax" (of course the Latin "peace") seems designed to reflect on Henry's presence in France. Before the battle, the king laments the "hard condition" (4.1.210) of kingship and idealizes the ease of the peasant's life: "What infinite heartsease / Must kings neglect that private men enjoy?" (213–14). But soon the private man is the "wretched slave" (245) who has the "forehand and vantage of a king" (257), working hard by day and sleeping soundly at night, mainly because he is free of the terrible burden of "What watch the King keeps to maintain the peace" (260).

The king's complaint, of course, might be more persuasive if it weren't delivered while Henry is in France at the head of an invasion force. And the justice of his presence there would be more convincing were it not dependent upon a claim to the throne of France resting on a legal principle (the ability to inherit through the female) that would deny his claim to the throne of England.

That is the deep irony of the archbishop's convoluted speech disproving the ability of the Salic Law to disbar Henry's "claim to France" (1.2.36), and also of the strange moment in act 2, when, after the Chorus's passionate lament that "the gilt of France" (2.0.26) has corrupted three nobles, the following scene has only two of them admit the bribe. Cambridge, however, weirdly says: "For me, the gold of France did not seduce, / Although I did admit it as a motive / The sooner to effect what I intended" (2.2.153–55). It would seem essential that the king ask about what it was that Cambridge *did* in fact intend, but Henry lets the provocative statement pass without comment or question. Holinshed, however, provided the "motive" that Shakespeare ignores:

> Diuerse write that Richard earle of Cambridge did not conspire with the lord Scroope & Thomas Graie for the murthering of king Henrie to please the French king withall, but onelie to the extent to exalt to the crowne his brother in law Edmund, earle of March as heire to Lionell duke of Clarence.
>
> (III, sig. 3G2ᵛ–3G3ʳ)

Cambridge hoped to elevate his brother-in-law to the throne, whose claim through the line of Lionel, Duke of Clarence, the third eldest son of Edward III might well be thought stronger than Henry's (derived from John of Gaunt, the fourth son), except that it depends on the ability to succeed through the female, Phillipa, Lionel's daughter.

So, if Henry has a legitimate claim to the French crown, as the archbishop argues, his right to the English crown disappears, and if his claim to the English throne is legitimate, he has no claim to that of France. "No king of England, if not king of France" (2.2.192), Henry boldly says as he prepares for war, but the truth is, rather, "no king of England" if he *is* king of France. But subtle and precise thinking is not Henry's strongest suit. He likes the simplicity of a world where the truth "stands off as gross / As black on white" (2.2.101–2). The complexity of dynastic controversy is ignored and collapsed into "this dangerous treason lurking in our way," which "God so graciously hath brought to light" (2.2.184–85).

Henry doesn't listen to the archbishop's sixty-line genealogical justification of his right. It too is closely based on Holinshed's report of the archbishop's speech, though Shakespeare provides the archbishop's breathless claim at the end that this is all "as clear as is the summer's sun" (which inevitably gets a laugh in the theater [1.2.86]). When the archbishop finally finishes, Shakespeare's Henry simply asks, "May I with right and conscience make this claim," and his archbishop provides the exact answer the king is hoping for: "The sin upon my head, dread sovereign" (1.2.96–97). For Henry there is no complexity and, even better for him here, responsibility has been shifted onto the archbishop. But this too is Shakespeare's addition. And those same qualities of mind determine Henry's deafness to Cambridge's hint of dynastic controversy, refusing to hear the earl's firm denial of the charge that "for a few light crowns," he has "lightly conspired / And sworn unto the practice of France" (2.2.87–88).

Henry is convinced of "his cause being just and his quarrel honorable," but an attentive audience must be much less confident. As the soldier Michael Williams says, "That's more than we know" (4.1.119–20). Williams reminds the disguised king that

> if the cause be not good, the King himself hath a heavy reckoning to make when all those legs and arms and heads chopped off in battle shall join together at the latter day and cry all, "We died at such and such a place" – some swearing, some crying for a surgeon, some upon their wives left poor behind them, some upon the debts they owe, some upon their children rawly left. I am afeard that there are few die well that die in a battle.... Now if these men do not die well, it will be a black matter for the King that led them to it.                              (4.1.125–34)

Henry has no real reply to this, though he goes on at length. He responds neither to Williams's poignant register of the soldiers' risk of body and soul, nor to his affecting reminder of the embedded social lives they have left behind; and he completely evades the central question of the king's responsibility in undertaking the war in France. Henry's answer is simple: "Every subject's duty is the King's, but every subject's soul his own" (4.1.162–63).

The question about the king's "heavy reckoning" for those soldiers who are unlikely to die well has long been forgotten by the king. Any moral problem has been displaced onto his subjects, but that is one of Henry's characteristic moves. At the beginning of the play the archbishop is warned about "what your reverence shall incite us to" (1.1.20) and that "the sin" is on his head if the cause be unjust (97); the dauphin's mockery is responsible for the invasion that will follow and "his soul / Shall stand sore charged for the wasteful vengeance" (1.2.282–89); the three noble traitors bear responsibility for their own execution ("The mercy that was quick in us but late / By your own counsel is suppressed and killed" [2.2.77–78]); and Harfleur is "guilty in defense" (3.4.43), itself responsible for what threatens the city ("What is't to me, when you yourself are cause" [19]). Even when he prays before Agincourt that God not think about any royal misdeeds, it is his father's actions that he hopes God will forgive or, rather, forget: "think not upon the fault / My father made in compassing the crown" (4.1.270–71), the enjambment elegantly making the point about Henry's own refusal of accountability. And now the soldiers are themselves made responsible for the danger to their bodies and souls. Henry doesn't like responsibility and is very good at shrugging it off onto others.

If Henry is Shakespeare's most successful king, he is so, then, precisely because his uncritical moral intelligence always allows him to forge the unambiguous moral environment his political energies and ambitions demand. Recall his response to his father's admission of "what bypaths and indirect crooked ways" led him to the throne: "You won it, wore it, kept it, gave it me; / Then plain and right must my possession be" (2 *Henry IV*, 4.3.313, 349–50). The seventeen monosyllables perfectly speak the over-simplifications of the single polysyllabic word: "possession."

His father knew better, aware that the nobles who helped him to the throne know far too much about how to depose a king:

> Which to avoid,
> I cut them off, and had a purpose now
> To lead out many to the Holy Land,
> Lest rest and lying still might make them look
> Too near unto my state. Therefore, my Harry,
> Be it thy course to busy giddy minds
> With foreign quarrels, that action hence borne out
> May waste the memory of the former days.
>
> (2 *Henry IV*, 4.3.337–44)

Warfare is a strategy of rule, both so-called holy wars and those more obviously diversionary foreign quarrels; and if Henry V never admits, or maybe even never recognizes, the problematics of his possession, he instinctively commits to defending it: "Which I with more than with a common pain / 'Gainst all the world will rightfully maintain" (4.3.351–52). That "rightfully" turns out to be more complicated than Henry will ever admit, but his international adventurism seems evidence of his determination to "maintain" and even extend his possession, especially if the "common pain" might be something that would mainly be felt by the soldiers who will namelessly fight and sometimes die for it.

*Henry V* is Shakespeare's play most fully engaged with war, though it is an engagement thoroughly mediated by Holinshed, who is never the simple Tudor apologist that Hall sometimes seems to be (if only from his title: *The Union of the Two Noble and Illustre Families of Lancastre and Yorke*). Certainly, Holinshed refuses to mystify an imagined heroic past, but, then again, so does Hall. Both chronicles are, of course, intended as national histories, though Holinshed has a more capacious political imagination of what that might mean.

But when it comes to warfare, although there is clear English partisanship in both accounts, there is an undeniable honesty about what war usually looks like, if not much particularity. People fight and people die; the motives for action are pragmatic, and the ethics are often questionable. Holinshed writes about Henry giving the order to kill the French prisoners, an order that Gary Wills has recently argued is merely evidence of Henry's "regard for his troops' safety."[23] But that is not exactly how Holinshed saw it. He begins much as Wills suggests, but continues further, making it clear that this explanation isn't really good enough:

> he doubting least his enimies should gather togither againe and begin a new field; and mistrusting further that the prisoners would be an aid to his enimies, or the verie enimies to their takers in deed if they were suffered to liue, contrarie to his accustomed gentlenes, commanded by sound of trumpet, that euerie man (vpon paine of death) should incontinentlie slaie his prisoner. When this dolorous decre was pronounced, pitie it was to see how some Frenchmen were suddenlie sticked with daggers, some were brained with pollaxes, some slaine with malls, other had their throats cut, and some their bellies panched, so that in effect, hauing respect to the great number, few prisoners were saued.　　　　　　　　　　　　　　　(III, sig. 3G5ᵛ)

Holinshed will insist that this is "contrarie to [Henry's] accustomed gen-tlenes," and perhaps it is. But there isn't much gentleness in the chronicles' Henry or in Shakespeare's. The interjected phrase is the patriotic Holinshed speaking not the historian. Reading the historian's account of his reign makes it clear the truth is otherwise. Modern skeptical readings of Shakespeare's play are not imposing anachronistic values upon it. They are registering the results of Shakespeare's patient and alert reading of the chronicles. What he found there was the inescapable, dismaying evidence of the price, both phys-ical and moral, that human beings pay for the conduct of war, even as these accounts admit that wars always will and sometimes even must be fought.

As Shakespeare turns their history into his history plays, it is hard to think that the chronicles' encouragement to "valiancy," or even their sometime confidence that God was on their side, was quite enough for him or for his audience. Does *Henry V* thrill and inspire? Only at times, and then usually only as Shakespeare's text is cut and rearranged. Played as he wrote it, it does something different with its often-unsettling juxtapositions. It may be no mere gap in the records of theatrical history that, in spite of the 1600 Quarto's claim on its title page that the play "hath bene sundry times playd by the Right honorable the Lord Chamberlaine his servants," there is only a single record of an early performance of the play (at court on January 7, 1605). A nation wearied by and anxious about war might well have found that Shakespeare's skeptical history cuts, one might say, a little too close to the bone.

*Further Reading*

Cahill, Patricia A. *Unto the Breach: Martial Formations, Historical Trauma, and the Early Modern Stage*, Oxford, Oxford University Press, 2008.

Cavanagh, Dermot, Stuart Hampton Reeves, and Stephen Longstaffe (eds). *Shakespeare's Histories and Counter-Histories*, Manchester, Manchester University Press, 2006.

Djordjevic, Igor. *Holinshed's Nation: Ideals, Memory, and Practical Policy in the "Chronicles,"* Farnham, Ashgate, 2010.

Jorgensen, Paul A. *Shakespeare's Military World*, Berkeley, University of California Press, 1956.

Kewes, Paulina, Ian W. Archer, and Felicity Heal (eds). *The Oxford Handbook of Holinshed's "Chronicles,"* Oxford, Oxford University Press, 2013.

Knapp, James. *Illustrating the Past in Early Modern England: The Representation of History in Printed Books*, Farnham, Ashgate, 2003.

Patterson, Annabel. *Reading Holinshed's "Chronicles,"* Chicago, University of Chicago Press, 1994.

Rackin, Phyllis. *Stages of History: Shakespeare's English Chronicles*, Ithaca, Cornell University Press, 1990.

Somogyi, Nick de. *Shakespeare's Theatre of War*, Aldershot, Ashgate, 1998.

Woolf, Daniel. *Reading History in Early Modern England*, Cambridge, Cambridge University Press, 2000.

## NOTES

1 Ben Jonson, *The Devil Is an Ass* (London, 1616), 2.4.8–14. Some material in this chapter has been adapted from my essay, "Shakespeare and English History," in Margreta de Grazia and Stanley Wells (eds.), *The Cambridge Companion to Shakespeare* (Cambridge: Cambridge University Press, 2001), pp. 167–82.

2 Thomas Heywood, *Apology for Actors* (London, 1612), sig. f3$^r$; and Samuel Taylor Coleridge, "A Selection of the Essays, Notes and Lectures of Samuel Taylor Coleridge on the Poems of Shakespeare," in Terence Hawkes (ed.), *Coleridge's Writings on Shakespeare* (New York: Capricorn, 1959), p. 223.

3 Felicity Heal and Henry Summerson, "The Genesis of the Two Editions" and Matthew Woodcock, "Narrative Voice and Influencing the Reader," in Paulina Kewes, Ian W. Archer, and Felicity Heal (eds.), *The Oxford Handbook of Holinshed's "Chronicles"* (Oxford: Oxford University Press, 2013), pp. 3–20, 337–53.

4 Alexandra Gillespie and Oliver Harris, "Holinshed and the Native Chronicle Tradition," in Kewes et al. (eds.), *Oxford Handbook*, pp. 135–51; F. J. Levy, *Tudor Historical Thought* (San Marino: Huntington Library Press, 1967), esp.

pp. 167–201; May McKisack, *Medieval Historians and the Tudor Age* (Oxford: Clarendon Press, 1971), pp. 95–126; and Daniel Woolf, *Reading History in Early Modern England* (Cambridge: Cambridge University Press, 2000), pp. 11–78.

5 *Chronicles* (London, 1577), I, sig. ¶4ʳ. On the potential distraction, see, for example, Peter Heylin, who writes of "Voluminous *Stow* and *Holingshead*," whose pages are inevitably "full of confusion, and commixture of unworthy relations," in *Mikrokosmus: A Little Description of the Great World* (Oxford, 1625), sig. B4ʳ.

6 Aaron T. Pratt and David Scott Kastan, "Printers, Publishers, and the Chronicles as Artefact," in Kewes et al. (eds.), *Oxford Handbook*, pp. 21–42.

7 Fynes Moryson, in Charles Hughes (ed.), *Shakespeare's Europe: Unpublished Chapters of Fynes Moryson's "Itinerary"* (London: Sherratt and Hughes, 1903), p. 476.

8 Andrew Gurr, *Playgoing in Shakespeare's London* (Cambridge: Cambridge University Press, 1996), p. 11.

9 Paul E. J. Hammer, *Elizabeth's Wars: War, Government and Society in Tudor England, 1544–1604* (Basingstoke: Palgrave Macmillan, 2003); Mark Charles Fissel, *English Warfare, 1511–1642* (London: Routledge, 2001); and Hammer's chapter in this book (Chapter 1).

10 Wallace McCaffrey, *Elizabeth I: War and Politics* (Princeton: Princeton University Press, 1992), p. 46; and John S. Nolan, "The Militarization of the Elizabethan State," *The Journal of Military History*, 58 (1994), pp. 391–420.

11 T. Proctor, *Of the Knowledge and Conduct of Warres* (London, 1578), sig. ¶4ᵛ.

12 For example, Roger Williams, *A Brief Discourse of War* (London, 1590); John Smythe, *Certain Discourses Military* (London, 1590); William Garrard, *The Arte of Warre* (London, 1591); Matthew Sutcliffe, *The Practice, Proceedings, and Laws of Armes* (London, 1593); Robert Barret, *The Theorike and Practike of Modern Warres* (London, 1598); and Jacob de Gheyn, *The Exercise of Armes for Caliures, Muskettes, and Pikes* (London, 1608). See Paul A. Jorgensen, *Shakespeare's Military World* (Berkeley: University of California Press, 1956); Nina Taunton, *1590s Drama Militarism: Portrayals of War in Marlowe, Chapman, and Shakespeare's "Henry V"* (Aldershot: Ashgate, 2000); and Patricia A. Cahill, *Unto the Breach: Martial Formations, Historical Trauma, and the Early Modern Stage* (Oxford: Oxford University Press, 2008).

13 Victor Scholderer, "The Illustrations to the First Edition of Holinshed," *Edinburgh Bibliographic Society Transactions*, 2 (1946), pp. 398–403, 400; and Ruth S. Luborsky and Elizabeth M. Ingram, *A Guide to English Illustrated Books 1536–1603* (Tempe: Medieval and Renaissance Texts and Studies, 1998), pp. 1, 452–68.

14 James Knapp, *Illustrating the Past in Early Modern England: The Representation of History in Printed Books* (Aldershot: Ashgate, 2003), pp. 204–5; and Annabel Patterson, *Reading Holinshed's "Chronicles"* (Chicago: University of Chicago Press, 1994), p. 57.

15 See Holinshed, *Chronicles* (1577), I, sig. N2ᵛ; and Agustin de Zárete, *The Discoverie and Conquest of the Provinces of Peru*, trans. T. Nicholas (London, 1581), sig. O2ᵛ.

16 Luborsky and Ingram, *A Guide to English Illustrated Books*, pp. 455–60.

17 Arthur F. Kinney, "Scottish History, the Union of the Crowns and the Issue of Right Rule: The Case of *Macbeth*," in Jean R. Brink and William F. Gentrup (eds.), *Renaissance Culture in Context: Theory and Practice* (Aldershot: Scolar, 1993), pp. 18–53.

18 Sir Philip Sidney, *An Apology for Poetry*, ed. R. W. Maslen and Geoffrey Shepherd (Manchester: Manchester University Press, 2002), p. 111.

19 Edward Hall, *The Union of the Two Noble and Illustre Families of Lancastre and Yorke* (London, 1548), sig. I2$^r$.

20 *The Famous Victories of Henry the Fifth* (London, 1598), sig. E4$^v$, F2$^r$.

21 T. W. Craik (ed.), *King Henry V*, by William Shakespeare, The Arden Shakespeare (London: Routledge, 1995), p. 331nn118–22.

22 Garrard, *The Arte of Warre*, sig. 2Q4$^v$.

23 Garry Wills, *Making Make-Believe Real: Politics As Theater in Shakespeare's Time* (New Haven: Yale University Press, 2014), p. 117.

# 7

GAIL KERN PASTER

# Instrumentalizing Anger

## *Warfare and Disposition in the Henriad*

### Assuming the Port of Mars

"Oh, for a muse of fire, that would ascend / The brightest heaven of invention," the Chorus famously exclaims in the Prologue of *Henry V*, suggesting hyperbolically that only the workings of the hot breath of the heavens' highest element could inspire a play adequate to the epic deeds of England's royal military hero, victor of the Battle of Agincourt – the creation onstage of a "swelling scene" with "princes to act, / And monarchs to behold" (1–4). But then, six lines later, heat's creative power metamorphoses into the destructive violence of warfare. With such a force at work, the Chorus says,

> Then should the warlike Harry, like himself,
> Assume the port of Mars, and at his heels,
> Leashed in like hounds, should famine, sword, and fire
> Crouch for employment.   (5–8)

With these first words of the play, Shakespeare introduces into its dominant vocabulary of epic aspiration the caloric economy of early modern humoralism and the explanations of human behavior that it made possible. This was an economy of the elemental forces of fire, air, water, and earth, and their qualities of hot, cold, wet, and dry at work in the human body. Bodily heat stimulated action both mental and physical; cold depressed it. The young warrior's hot, dry choler gave him impulsiveness and the capacity for rage; cold, wet phlegm helped to produce his cowardly opposite's lethargy and was responsible for the general inconstancy and weakness of women. Sound judgment and prudent action required the free flow of clear fluids in the brain, but choler or melancholy darkened those fluids and muddled decision-making. Youth was hot and moist, age cold and dry. "The Minds inclination follows the Bodies Temperature," said John Selden, repeating a Galenic commonplace of the age.[1]

As we shall see, the Chorus's depiction of the caloric economy of early modern cosmology and its capacity to create and destroy runs throughout Shakespeare's history play about the lopsided victory of Henry V at Agincourt. Here, despite the Chorus's mock-humble emphasis on theater's inability to properly bring epic action to fictional life onstage, Shakespeare seems to have understood that the sociality of theater – collaborative, communal, and interactive – was in fact ideal for underscoring the ethical challenges of representing the violence of warfare. In order for the "swelling scene" to come to dramatic life, the Chorus invokes the audience's "imaginary forces" (Prologue, 4, 18) as the necessary ingredient to be added to the playwright's creative arsenal. The Chorus tasks the spectators to collaborate with the "muse of fire" and to engage in the hot, cognitive work of the imagination – asking them to "suppose," to "piece out our imperfections," to "think," and finally to "carry" the narrative in their minds (19–29) over time and space these partly embodied, partly imagined fictions of kings, horses, and their retinues. At this moment, the playhouse becomes a cognitive ecology, a place where "we remember, feel, think, sense, communicate, imagine, and act."[2] What matters, the Chorus implies, is the human warmth of strenuous engagement on both sides of the diegesis – cognitive, emotional, and embodied work from the "flat unraisèd" but nonetheless daring "spirits" (8) of the actors who are attempting this collective enterprise and the participatory agency of the spectators. This is the creative work of heat, a dualistic framework for the depiction of violence to come.

For those of us interested in the Henriad and represented emotions on the Shakespearean stage, what is also striking in this Chorus is the tension implied in the allegorical representation of Harry as Mars, with the violent forces of warfare likened to hounds crouching submissively before him, waiting only for his command to be unleashed. Indeed, the tension between discipline and violence, between cold and hot emotions, seems inherent to the overarching conceptualization of war. Such tension is also prominent in Vincenzo Cartari's allegorical portrait of Mars and his double-natured animal emblem:

> Some also haue appropriated vnto him the wolfe, being a most rauenous & deuouring beast, and therefore attributed vnto him; in that all souldiers and men of warre, vpon their first furie and heate are giuen much to spoiling and consuming of goods, ruinating and ouerthrowing all things whatsoeuer, that happen vnto them in the pride of their choler, & first inflamation of their blud: or else because this beast ... seeth most perfectly in the darkest night, as wise and prouident captaines and commaunders ought to doe, that is, that they with all all-foreseeing aduisednesse and circumspection, preuent and frustrate the secret, darke, and hidden plots, and close-contriued stratagemes of the

enemie whatsoeuer, for by the sharpe-sighted eyes of this beast is vnderstood the farre-reaching capacitie and wittie braine of a politicke commaunder, in discouering and seeing through the secret and concealed intendements of his aduersarie.[3]

Cartari does not decide between the relevant qualities of the wolf as Mars's emblematic animal – the destructive ravening of blood's "first inflammation" as contrasted to the animal's sharp-eyed calculation. He juxtaposes hot and cold, ravening fury and prudent calculation, aggressiveness and defensiveness in a careful refusal to judge between them as attributes of Mars.

Henry Peacham, too, in his emblematic representation of choler shows a lion crouching beside a naked, sword-wielding man in a desert landscape. Like Cartari, he proposes that the allegorical beast of choler has the seemingly incompatible attributes of unrestrained cruelty or generosity of spirit:

> We paint him young, to shew that passions raigne,
> The most in heedles, and vnstaied youth:
> That Lion showes, he seldome can refraine,
> From cruell deede, devoide of gentle ruth:
>     Or hath perhaps, this beast to him assign'd,
>     As bearing most, the braue and bounteous mind.[4]

Is the man of choler impulsive, unstable, and merciless or the bearer of a valiant spirit? Is the activity's heat creative or destructive? Like Cartari, Peacham will not choose between these attributes of war (see Figure 7.1).

## An Aristotelian Taxonomy of Anger

Shakespeare's imagination, too, seems to be engaged in this tension in the nature of the martial spirit embodied in a successful military commander – his cool and hot emotions, his mixing of creation and destruction, forcefulness and calculation. He dramatizes a career for Henry V from truant Prince of Wales upholding "the unyoked humor" of his tavern companions' "idleness" (*1 Henry IV*, 1.2.170–71), to energetic prankster at Gad's Hill, to newly resolute son promising "hereafter, my thrice-gracious lord, / Be more myself" (3.2.92–93), to leader of embattled troops over the rebellious Percies, and finally to victorious king and enraged agent of wartime atrocity as he orders the slaughter of French prisoners of war: "we'll cut the throats of those we have, / And not a man of them that we shall take / Shall taste our mercy" (*Henry V*, 4.7.55–57). I suggest that, in Henry's words and actions, Shakespeare stages the instrumentalization of anger – epic's emotion. But, despite the Chorus's invocation of Henry as Mars, the king's anger is not an individualistic rage – the "explosive touchiness" or "sublime irascibility" of

Figure 7.1 Emblem of choler, from Henry Peacham, *Minerva Britanna* (London, 1612), leaf T2 recto (page 128). Folger Shakespeare Library Shelfmark: STC 19511. Used by permission of the Folger Shakespeare Library

the Senecan tragic protagonist, or the Herculean hero. In this play, Shakespeare – like the early moderns generally – understands anger in Aristotelian terms as a social, gendered, and hierarchical emotion, a privilege reserved for elite men tasked with the maintenance or restoration of social order. It is the king's deft use of his emotions from the decision to invade France until his overwhelming success there that distinguishes him from the men who serve under him and that makes him a modern man of wrath. Furthermore, Shakespeare's depiction of anger instrumentalized operates quasi-independently from the ethical evaluation of the king so troubling to critics. Henry's capacity for disciplined anger is an attribute of demonstrable efficacy that is especially striking against the background of the earlier plays in the tetralogy, when instrumentalization of anger is juxtaposed with the vivid emotional contrasts in *1 Henry IV* between the ineffectual coldness of his father and the reckless tempestuousness of Hotspur.

It is not difficult to find martial anger in the canon. Shakespeare's association of epic heroes with the first heat of fury is evidenced in *Hamlet* when the First Player recites Aeneas's account of Pyrrhus rampaging through Troy:

> "Now is he total gules, horridly tricked
> With blood of fathers, mothers, daughters, sons,
> Baked and impasted with the parching streets
> That lend a tyrannous and a damnèd light
> To their lord's murder. Roasted in wrath and fire
> And thus o'ersizèd with coagulate gore,
> With eyes like carbuncles, the hellish Pyrrhus
> Old grandsire Priam seeks." (2.2.379–86)

As with Peacham's man of choler, Aeneas emphasizes reciprocal causality between the warrior and his environment, with Pyrrhus's hot core and the raging fires of Troy suggested in the humoralism of "roasted in wrath and fire."[5] The strategic calculation of the cool side of Mars's wolf is absent in this man of wrath, the heat of his rage baking his black armor from within as the fires bake that armor from without, making him one with the heat of his hellish environment.

Shakespeare's portrait of wrath is more attractive in Hotspur (whom we never see rampaging through a city) but there is a similar emphasis on explosiveness, as when Hotspur rages after the king who has demanded release of his prisoners of war:

> An if the devil come and roar for them
> I will not send them. I will after straight
> And tell him so, for I will ease my heart,
> Albeit I make a hazard of my head. (1.3.124–27)

"Drunk with choler?" his father exclaims (128), while the son inveighs against the king's disciplinary strictures and longs for release of his raging blood through battlefield purgation: "I'll empty all these veins / And shed my dear blood drop by drop in the dust" (132–33). Hotspur's rage here is a verbal incontinence that his father, seeking to control him with shame, brands as female: "Why, what a wasp-stung and impatient fool / Art thou to break into this woman's mood" (234–35). Though they rely on his daring, Hotspur's male relatives criticize his impulsiveness, understanding that the king may forgive his rebelliousness only because of his youth:

> My nephew's trespass may be well forgot;
> It hath the excuse of youth and heat of blood,
> And an adopted name of privilege,
> A hare-brained Hotspur governed by a spleen. (5.2.16–19)

In the end, Shakespeare presents Hotspur's impulsive longing for warfare: "Die all; die merrily," Hotspur exclaims (4.1.133), as the rebel faction considers doing battle against the royal forces.

These passages reveal Shakespeare's interest in the ambiguities – social, moral, ethical – attached to the warrior and his emotions. It was important for men in battle to access their capacity for the vehement passions.[6] But a lack of appropriate anger was also dangerous. Henry IV blames the onset of rebelliousness on his lack of appropriate royal heat and the discipline it imposes:

> My blood hath been too cold and temperate,
> Unapt to stir at these indignities,
> And you have found me, for accordingly
> You tread upon my patience. (1.3.1–4)

In future, he tells them,

> I will from henceforth rather be myself,
> Mighty and to be feared, than my condition,
> Which hath been smooth as oil, soft as young down,
> And therefore lost that title of respect
> Which the proud soul ne'er pays but to the proud. (5–9)

Restoration of civil peace, he suggests, will require an increased display of royal anger as the key to commanding respect. But the opposite problem – excess of anger and the impulsive, mania-like hyperactivity it breeds in restless noblemen accustomed to military activity – is clearly denoted in the nickname of Harry Percy, his explosiveness, and his tragic trajectory. Even though Hotspur's spiritedness is opposed to Prince Hal's initial idleness and forms the core of what the beleaguered Henry IV finds to praise as "a son who is the theme of honor's tongue" (1.1.80), by play's end he has been marked as socially archaic, part of an outmoded feudal past.[7]

Where, then, is evidence for the other side of the martial spirit, the cool wiliness of Cartari's emblematic wolf? It is found in Shakespeare's Henry V. No matter how we judge his actions before and after Agincourt, no matter how full of tonal contradictions we judge the Chorus and its protagonist to be, this king embodies military success – which in the hindsight of a history play frames all his actions. "I was not angry since I came to France / Until this instant," declares Henry (4.7.47–48) as he learns of the luggage boys' slaughter and orders the execution of French prisoners. This atrocity is committed with uncharacteristic choler. But – despite what Henry says about his anger – Shakespeare gives us a performatively angry king not only before this revenge but also throughout the play, for his actions offer a textbook taxonomy of the militarily correct uses of anger and the successes that its appropriate instrumentalization can accomplish. And it is this difference in the quality of their anger and the character of their dispositions – between destructive recklessness and instrumental deployment, between ineffective or belated anger and its deft opposite – that marks the contrasts among Henry IV, Hotspur, and Henry V. It is the difference between a king who cannot access his anger to control rebellion, the suicidal warrior who cannot control his anger, and the commander who knows how to access, modulate, perform, and wholly instrumentalize it in order to rally troops, threaten destruction, and achieve military success.

## Accessing Anger

As an introduction to the taxonomy of anger in *Henry V*, it is worth looking at its immediate social context, specifically certain events of 1598–99 that epitomize why the issue of anger was important to Shakespeare's audience. Writing *Henry V*, Shakespeare must have been thinking about the martial temperament, because we know from the Chorus to act 5 that he was also thinking about Robert Devereux, the Earl of Essex – England's supreme military man, the commander of the recent Irish expedition. Shakespeare's reference to Essex constitutes his only explicit reference to a living nobleman when the Chorus hopefully imagines Essex's return:

> Were now the General of our gracious Empress,
> As in good time he may, from Ireland coming,
> Bringing rebellion broachèd on his sword,
> How many would the peaceful city quit
> To welcome him! (5.0.30–34)

In thinking about Essex here, was Shakespeare also asking his audience to recognize the temperamental disparities between the king whose nearly miraculous military conquest he had just realized on stage and a military commander whose temperamental volatility and emotional excesses were well known?

In Elizabethan England, waging war remained a preserve of the nobleman, despite the advent of militias and the rise of the professional soldier. Managing aristocratic emotions and temperaments was clearly important in the choice of commanders over the two decades of Elizabethan militarism, especially recognizing temperamental differences in soldiers and commanders. Montaigne, who felt that "there is no passion that so shakes the clarity of our judgment as anger," was nevertheless willing to grant the role of soldierly anger, "for in that profession there are certainly occasions that cannot do without it."[8] But the Spanish philosopher Juan Huarte, in his influential treatise on innate differences among men, warns:

> martiall affaires are so dangerous, and of so deep counsell: and it falleth out a matter so important for a king to know well vnto whom he credits his power and state, that we shall perform no lesse thanks worthie a part of seruice to the common wealth, to teach this difference of wit and his signs.[9]

For Huarte it is the importance of temperament that elevates wisdom and prudence over bravery and hotheadedness:

> Yea wisdom is more highly to be regarded and rewarded in a generall, than courage and manlinesse: for as *Vegetius* well said, Few ouer-couragious captains bring their enterprises to luckie passe. Which groweth for that wisdom is more necessarie in warre, than courage in bickering. (201)

For the early moderns, thinking about anger in contexts other than war was influenced by Aristotle and the church fathers like Aquinas who followed him. Anger was both natural (a desire) and hierarchical (moving from low to high). It was a social emotion rather than the individual psychological experience that it became in the eighteenth century. According to Aristotle, anger was the natural response (here that of a male) to a slight received from a lower-ranking person not entitled under prevailing protocols to render such an insult. He defines anger as

> desire, accompanied by [mental and physical] distress, for apparent retaliation because of an apparent slight that was directed, without justification, against oneself or those near to one ... a kind of pleasure follows all experience of anger from the hope of getting retaliation.[10]

Here, even the first flush of anger seems to involve evaluation (the perception of injustice, the calculation of affiliation), the agency of desire, and an instant orientation to action. What is also important to note is that such a conception of anger not only intermixes pleasure and pain, but also invokes a larger ethical purpose – anger justified as restoration of the social order.[11] Anger thus becomes a duty, a natural form of social necessity, with resemblances to revenge and implications for accountability.

The anger of highborn men and their social permission to express it was a privilege attached to the hierarchy of emotions in the early modern social order, its possession being gendered male and reserved for the elite. Montaigne writes about the privilege attached to anger, instructing "those in my family who have the *right* to get angry" about how to husband their anger, "not expend it at random" (543, emphasis added). But in the highly competitive Elizabethan court world, even more than in a French nobleman's household, managing the anger of a high-strung group of honor-conscious noblemen was of considerable importance. In his *Passions of the Minde in Generall*, Thomas Wright displays anxiety over the passions of noblemen when he reports to "haue seen some, Gentlemen by blood, and Noblemen by birth" who were "so appassionate in affections, that their company was to most men intolerable."[12] Choleric men, he explains later, "are all fiery, and in a moment, at euery trifle they are inflamed, and, till their hearts be consumed (almost) with choller, they neuer cease, except they be reuenged" (37). The apparent tidiness of Aristotle's taxonomy collapses, it seems, when the slight is performed between equals, or near-equals, or when anger is not subject to perception and evaluation. In Wright, the personal and social sweetness of revenge in Aristotelian terms collides with the maintenance of social harmony, especially in times of war – and the many anecdotes surrounding the tempestuous careers of military men like Ralegh and Essex may help to explain why.

It is against this background of social anxiety over aristocratic anger, over the nature of sweetly vengeful emotions in wartime, that we can assess Shakespeare's portrait of the instrumentalization of anger as felt and performed by King Henry – including what seems to be a break in self-control when he orders the execution of French prisoners in retaliation. There is no requirement here to make a moral or ethical evaluation of the king's conduct. I will mostly refrain from doing so, if for no other reason than the notorious difficulty of judging the play's tone, whether as nostalgic celebration of Agincourt or as savage satire on the false claims and bad faith of Elizabethan militarists. What I will emphasize is Shakespeare's interest in Henry's self-control and its efficacy, as contrasted with his father's self-wounding coolness, Hotspur's intemperateness, and the comical choler of soldiers like Fluellen and MacMorris. What we see in Henry is clear access to his vehement passions, an understanding of passion as motive for action, the ability to instrumentalize anger for a larger, strategic goal, and the performative ability to threaten fury and rampage without actually feeling it. The representation of the king's anger does not account for all his behavior – his appalling willingness to shift moral responsibility for his decisions onto others, for example, or his questionable tactics as wooer. But anger is the affective center of *Henry V* as Shakespeare considers the means and costs of military victory.

## Performing Anger

In his treatment of the passions, Philip Fisher regards anger as the work of a moment (71–92). But in *Henry V*, Shakespeare stages the action to reveal a time-line taxonomy of the king's anger, dramatizing its phases from first flush to sweet revenge, anger stimulated by different triggers, anger unfolding in dramatic time. This close link between time and anger may explain why Shakespeare reverses a sequence of events in Holinshed regarding the clerics' interpretation of the Salic Law and the dauphin's insulting gift.[13] In the opening scene, Henry invites the clerics to deliver their verdict about the Salic Law in his favor so that he can regard the French king's refusal as a national injury giving him the right to wage war. But their self-interested interpretation offers him only general permission – the option to redress an old injustice that cannot be construed as personal to Henry himself. It is difficult to find the note of personal anger in his decision to invade France:

> Now are we well resolved, and by God's help
> And yours, the noble sinews of our power,
> France being ours, we'll bend it to our awe,
> Or break it all to pieces.   (1.2.223–26)

He therefore has reason to welcome a personal motive when it comes in the form of the dauphin's gift of the tennis balls – a personally framed insult of the king in full view of his court and the foreign nation represented by the ambassadors, who report the dauphin

> bids you be advised: there's naught in France
> That can be with a nimble galliard won:
> You cannot revel into dukedoms there.
> And therefore sends you, meeter for your spirit,
> This tun of treasure.   (252–56)

Henry's response sounds the note of angry self-justification requisite for the claim to be righting the wrong to England's honor as vested in him by waging war in France against the dauphin himself: "I will dazzle all the eyes of France, / Yea, strike the Dauphin blind to look on us" (280–81). Here is Henry's affective search for motivating anger – moving from a search for dynastic justification for aggression to a personal desire for pleasurable revenge. The insult registers Aristotle's requirements precisely: it comes with intent from a social inferior; it intends to shame his opponent. Henry is virtually required to revenge this insult to himself and his nation and to claim it as restoration of a social order he embodies. Thus Exeter, his representative in France, retaliates verbally with "scorn and defiance, slight regard, contempt, / And anything that may not misbecome / The mighty sender" (2.4.117–19) and attributes it to the king's transformation:

> you'll find a diff'rence,
> As we his subjects have in wonder found,
> Between the promise of his greener days
> And these he masters now.  (2.4.134–37)

The scenes that follow the decision to invade France – from the capture of the treacherous lords to the siege of Harfleur to Bardolph's hanging and the slaughter of the French prisoners – seem designed as a display of Henry's capacity to instrumentalize and perform anger in particular contexts, for particular goals. Shakespeare chooses not to restage the first flush of anger when his friends' betrayal provides another reason for personal revenge. Instead, we witness that anger's aftereffects in his cool entrapment of the treacherous peers. For Aristotle, the premeditation and planning of this entrapment would be the pleasure to be found in righteous anger, here highly theatricalized: "because people dwell in their minds on retaliating; then the image that occurs creates pleasure" (*Rhetoric*, 2.2). For Henry it is perhaps the even greater voyeuristic triumph of watching his treacherous friends receive their death sentences:

> – Look ye, how they change!
> Their cheeks are paper. – Why, what read you there
> That have so cowarded and chased your blood
> Out of appearance?  (2.2.71–74)

While Henry denies that he is moved by revenge "touching our person," he justifies his sentence and the social anger it represents as redressing injury: "But we our kingdom's safety must so tender, / Whose ruin you have sought, that to her laws / We do deliver you" (173–76). Henry's calm at achieving retaliation is "a settling down and quieting of anger," says Aristotle (*Rhetoric*, 2.3), here phrased to dishonor his treacherous peers with the embarrassing bodily evidence of cowardice.

When the action moves to France, Shakespeare presents the king's anger as no less committed to rhetorical performance and more instrumentalized, as we see in his speeches at the siege of Harfleur, first to his soldiers and second to the mayor. Before these two audiences the king does assume the port of Mars – exhorting his soldiers to become his companion beasts of cruelty, telling the mayor of the savagery that would ensue from their unleashing. Harry offers his men a model of bravery achievable through willed mimesis, bravery enabled by actions of flesh and spirit presented as voluntary. Military service to the king becomes a sophisticated performance, the men being asked to become like beasts of cruelty and model warriors, imitating "the action of the tiger" (3.1.6) through hardened flesh, heated blood, controlled breath, a terrifying visage. This performative model accepts that the soldiers are not themselves angry or vengeful, but that their capacity for cruelty would have instrumental efficacy to a motivated king. Two ideas of bodily transformation are at work here – one, that imitation of an affect can move the actor closer to experiencing emotion itself and the actions it would generate; two, that a look of cruelty can move the onlooker into submission. For anger's taxonomy, it matters little whether or not the king is merely rhetorical, much more that he tropes the animal tonus of wartime fury as natural, beautiful, even ennobling. And given that warfare heats and thins the blood, his exhortation to "Be copy now to men of grosser blood / And teach them how to war" (24–25) can be understood literally – if wishfully.

In sacking Harfleur as Henry describes it, there is no emblematic animal beauty, but only the horror of Pyrrhus-like cruelty that Henry claims for himself and the soldiers "yet . . . in my command," but soon to be "blind and bloody" (3.4.29, 34). The king's speech recalls the tension between violence held and released in the Prologue. Here the allegorized majesty of "the port of Mars" morphs into Peacham's man of choler – "impious war, / Arrayed in flames like to the prince of fiends" (15–16). What is striking is the particularity of the violence that Henry's bravura rhetorical performance brings before the audience's imagination, as the Prologue's generalized threats of "famine, sword, and fire" morph into specific bodily violations to "shrill-shrieking daughters," silver-bearded fathers "their most revered heads dashed to the walls," "mad mothers with their howls confused" (35–39), and other wartime horrors.

In a play that has asked its audience to do the work of imagining battlefield actions it cannot represent, the speech before Harfleur is horrific, especially when Henry ruthlessly places blame on the mayor himself, rather than on himself or his soldiers. For Cartari, the hot emotions of rampage were common to all soldiers and havoc was indiscriminate: "*all souldiers and men of warre*, vpon their first furie and heate are giuen much to spoiling and consuming of goods, ruinating and ouerthrowing *all things whatsoeuer*, that happen vnto them in the pride of their choler, & first inflammation of their bloud" (sig. Xi v, emphases added). But it is important to recognize how much of this portrait of wartime fury is performative; the emotions are not those of the king himself and, like Cartari, he represents the actions of his soldiers, once unleashed, as an unstoppable animal force rather than purposive, motivated human anger: "What rein can hold licentious wickedness / When down the hill he holds his fierce career?" (3.4.22–23).

The indistinction between threat and performance, the purposelessness of this threat as anger, become clearer once the mayor surrenders, announcing "we no longer are defensible" (50), for Henry not only instructs Exeter to "use mercy to them all" but also acknowledges his soldiers' inability to have performed such ruthless savagery – "the winter coming on and sickness growing / Upon our soldiers" (54–56).

The performativity of this rhetorical anger signifies the king's instrumental ability to separate himself from the passions of his environment in order to use passion's power more effectively. What we recognize in his soldiers is precisely the opposite – an inability to separate at all from the passions of their environment, an inability that Shakespeare registers alternately as shameful cowardice or comic bluster. Thus, at Harfleur Nym refuses to obey Bardolph's command to move "to the breach" on the grounds of the humors of his environment: "The knocks are too hot, and for mine own part I have not a case of lives. The humor of it is too hot" (3.2.2–4). The Boy professes himself effectively allergic to their cowardice and thievery: "I must leave them and seek some better service. Their villany goes against my weak stomach, and therefore I must cast it up" (45–47). But even some of the professional soldiers – Fluellen, MacMorris, and Jamy – carry themselves with a hair-trigger quarrelsomeness so unmotivated, so bizarrely directed at each other that it seems to be more an involuntary venting of choler – an expression of collective battlefield vehemence – than the result of individual self-expression. Fluellen describes MacMorris as "an ass, as in the world" (3.3.15); MacMorris scolds them all for talking rather than fighting (" 'tis shame to stand still, it is shame, by my hand. And there is throats to be cut, and works to be done" [3.3.50–52]) and explodes at Fluellen for referring to his nation, until they end up ready to cut off each other's heads and are pacified by Gower with difficulty. Fluellen is so taken with the ferocity of Pistol's rhetoric – his "prave words at the pridge" (3.7.58) – that Gower has trouble persuading him of Pistol's roguery, so well has Pistol learned how to mimic soldierly discourse. The most outrageous performance of this socially useless anger belongs to Nym, who ridiculously terrifies the poor French soldier who does not understand a word of his threats and relies on the Boy to translate his hyperbolic bluster about throat-cutting, "Owy, cuppele gorge, permafoy, / Peasant, unless thou give me crowns, brave crowns; / Or mangled shalt thou be by this my sword" (4.4.34–36).

In terms of Shakespeare's interest in the taxonomy of anger in *Henry V*, I would argue, it is the function of these quarrelsome lower characters to demonstrate the ineffectuality, even the irrelevance of such anger when compared to the instrumental anger of the king. Their anger does not seem motivated by personal injury or slight; they do not – as Aristotle would wish them to do – harbor pleasurable thoughts of revenge at righting their wrongs or restoring the social order. Their anger is not the socially productive anger that anger's advocates like Aristotle would have it be. Rather, their choleric moodiness seems almost the affective consequence of their battlefield environment – the almost automatic oppositional stance toward other human beings that military combat requires of the lower orders. Thus, when Fluellen accepts Gower's characterization of Pistol as "a gull, a fool, a rogue" (3.7.61), his natural reaction is to look for a means of challenging him: "If I find a hole in his coat," the querulous Welshman tells Gower, "I will tell him my mind" (76). Montaigne warns against just such socially purposeless anger: "They go after their own shadow, and carry this tempest into a place where no one is punished or affected by it, except someone who has to put with the racket of their voice. I likewise condemn in quarrels those who bluster and fume without an opponent; these rhodomontades must be kept for where they will strike home" (544).

Such combativeness among Fluellen and his mates is in direct contrast to the self-control the king displays in his conversations with his soldiers on the eve of Agincourt when he encounters their skepticism about the king's refusal to be ransomed ("he said so to make us fight cheerfully" [4.1.175]), when Williams says that he does not know if the king's quarrel is just and honorable: "That's more than we know" (120). Such insubordination might well have provoked another king's wrath, rather than the call to a post-battle quarrel that the disguised king pretends to engage with Williams, as his presumptive social equal, in an exchange of gloves. It is because of his demonstrable self-control in the face of such insubordination that his break after the slaughter of the luggage boys is so striking. In reporting this to Fluellen, Gower complicates the picture of the king's motivation:

'Tis certain there's not a boy left alive. And the cowardly rascals that ran from the battle ha' done this slaughter. Besides, they have burned and carried away all that was in the King's tent, wherefore the King most worthily hath caused every soldier to cut his prisoner's throat. Oh,'tis a gallant king!    (4.7.4–8)

Fluellen makes the king's motivation even less clear in his notoriously and oddly redundant comparison of Henry and Alexander the Pig, "in his rages, and his furies, and his wraths, and his cholers" (29). His byplay with Gower, making comedy of Alexander's epic wrath in killing his friend Clytus and underlining Fluellen's ridiculous querulousness, is juxtaposed with the horrifying power of the king's sudden fury as he arrives onstage, declaring the onset of his wrath and his decision to order the execution:

> I was not angry since I came to France
> Until this instant. Take a trumpet, herald;
> Ride thou unto the horsemen on yond hill.
> If they will fight with us, bid them come down,
> Or void the field: they do offend our sight.
> . . .
> Besides, we'll cut the throats of those we have,
> And not a man of them that we shall take
> Shall taste our mercy.   (4.7.47–57)

Holinshed offers several motivations for the atrocity, suggesting that Henry worried "that the prisoners would be an aid to his enimies, or the verie enemies to their takers in deed if they were suffered to live," and he clearly finds the episode uncharacteristic of the king, "contrarie to his accustomed gentleness."[14] In his chronicle account, the king not only threatens his own soldiers with pain of death should they fail to obey his command but also unleashes an uncontrolled bloodbath – "some Frenchmen were suddenlie sticked with daggers, some were brained with pollaxes, some slaine with malls, other had their throats cut, and some their bellies panched." But Holinshed is unsparing in his judgment of the episode, calling it a "lamentable slaughter." The moment is one not of socially purposive Aristotelian anger – the anger that the king has demonstrated and performed strategically heretofore – but a flare of epic wrathfulness, brought on by the slaughter of the defenseless boys and serving no social purpose except for the emotional release of bloodshed.

Henry has been merciless at earlier moments in the play – at his cool entrapment of his treacherous friends, or his refusal to acknowledge or grant clemency to Bardolph, for example, on the grounds of instilling discipline in his soldiers. But it is only here that mercilessness blends seamlessly with outrage, his savagery in ordering a clear violation of military codes of conduct pointing up by contrast the instrumentality of his control throughout the play – beginning with his angry response to the dauphin's insulting gift in 1.2, and his apparent recognition of the usefulness of this insult as he prepares to launch a morally questionable military campaign. As the final

Chorus makes clear, Shakespeare has no intention of allowing his audience to forget the ultimate failures of English militarism on the Continent or the brevity of Henry's life. But unless we read the tone of this Chorus as savagely ironic, he also insists upon the career of this king as one of personal success: "Small time, but in that small most greatly lived / This star of England" (Epilogue, 5–6). It is a success in which the strategic use of socially and militarily instrumental anger has played a huge part, as Shakespeare's taxonomy of anger in *Henry V* has brilliantly made clear. And the importance of this anger is even clearer in the context provided by the contrast of this instrumental anger with that of his father and Hotspur in the earlier play – no matter how we judge the ethical trajectory of Henry's reformation from undutiful Prince of Wales in *1 Henry IV* to strategically angry military conqueror in *Henry V*.

*Further Reading*

Altman, Joel. "'Vile Participation': The Amplification of Political Violence in the Theater of *Henry V*," *Shakespeare Quarterly*, 42 (1991), pp. 1–32.

Barker, Simon. *War and Nation in the Theatre of Shakespeare and His Contemporaries*, Edinburgh, Edinburgh University Press, 2007.

Breight, Curtis C. *Surveillance, Militarism and Drama in the Elizabethan Era*, New York, St. Martin's Press, 1996.

Cahill, Patricia A. *Unto the Breach: Martial Formations, Historical Trauma, and the Early Modern Stage*, Oxford, Oxford University Press, 2008.

Enenkel, Karl A. E., and Anita Traninger. "Introduction: Discourses of Anger in the Early Modern Period," in Enenkel and Traninger (eds.), *Discourses of Anger in the Early Modern Period*, Leiden, Brill, 2015, pp. 1–15.

Fisher, Philip. *The Vehement Passions*, Princeton, Princeton University Press, 2002.

Fraser, R. Scott. "*Henry V* and the Performance of War," in Ros King and Paul J. C. M. Franssen (eds.), *Shakespeare and War*, Basingstoke, Palgrave Macmillan, 2008, pp. 71–83.

Meron, Theodor. *Henry's Wars and Shakespeare's Laws: Perspectives on the Law of War and the Later Middle Ages*, Oxford, Clarendon Press, 1993.

Paster, Gail Kern. "Belching Quarrels: Male Passions and the Problem of Individuation," in *Humoring the Body: Emotions and the Shakespearean Stage*, Chicago, University of Chicago Press, 2004, pp. 189–241.

Somogyi, Nick de. *Shakespeare's Theatre of War*, Aldershot, Ashgate, 1998.

## NOTES

1 John Selden, *Titles of Honor* (London, 1614), sig. b4. For fuller explanations of the humoral economy, see Gail Kern Paster, *The Body Embarrassed: Drama and the Disciplines of Shame in Early Modern England* (Ithaca: Cornell University Press, 1993), pp. 1–17; *Humoring the Body: Emotions and the Shakespearean Stage* (Chicago: University of Chicago Press, 2004), esp. pp. 1–21; and "Nervous

Tension: Networks of Blood and Spirit in the Early Modern Body," in David Hillman and Carla Mazzio (eds.), *The Body in Parts: Fantasies of Corporeality in Early Modern Europe* (New York: Routledge, 1997), pp. 107–25.

2 Evelyn Tribble and John Sutton, "Cognitive Ecology as a Framework for Shakespearean Studies," *Shakespeare Studies*, 39 (2011), pp. 94–103, 94.

3 [Vincenzo Cartari], *The Fountaine of Ancient Fiction*, trans. Richard Linche (London, 1599), sigs. Xi v, Xii r. I am indebted for this reference to Virginia Mason Vaughan.

4 Henry Peacham, *Minerva Britanna* (London, 1612), p. 128.

5 Paster, *Humoring the Body*, pp. 28–48.

6 I borrow this phrase from Philip Fisher, *The Vehement Passions* (Princeton: Princeton University Press, 2002).

7 Paster, "Nervous Tension," p. 121.

8 Michel de Montaigne, "Of Anger," in *The Complete Essays*, trans. Donald M. Frame (Redwood City: Stanford University Press, 1957), pp. 540, 543.

9 J. Huarte Navarro, *The Examination of Mens Wits* (London, 1594; repr. Amsterdam: Da Capo Press, 1969), pp. 201–2.

10 Aristotle, *On Rhetoric*, trans. George Kennedy (Oxford: Oxford University Press, 2007), 2.2.

11 Karl A. E. Enenkel and Anita Traninger, "Introduction: Discourses of Anger in the Early Modern Period," in Enenkel and Traninger (eds.), *Discourses of Anger in the Early Modern Period* (Leiden: Brill, 2015), pp. 1–15, 2–3.

12 Thomas Wright, *The Passions of the Minde in Generall*, ed. Thomas O. Sloan (London, 1604; repr. Urbana: University of Illinois Press, 1971), p. 6; and Paster, *Humoring the Body*, pp. 191–93.

13 Geoffrey Bullough (ed.), *Narrative and Dramatic Sources of Shakespeare*, 8 vols. (New York: Columbia University Press, 1962), vol. IV, pp. 376–77.

14 Quoted in Bullough, *Narrative and Dramatic Sources of Shakespeare*, p. 397.

# 8

DAVID SCHALKWYK

# War and *Eros*

"Love and warre are all one."
                                    Miguel de Cervantes[1]

"Language ... has long since posited the equivalence of love and war: in both cases, it is a matter of *conquering, ravishing, capturing,* etc."
                                    Roland Barthes[2]

Both of my epigraphs capture the conjunction of love and war, but they do so differently. The proximity and the separation of *eros* and violence, at least as old as Homer, is exemplified in the poet's founding narratives of Western storytelling: the *Iliad* and the *Odyssey*. To which we may add Virgil's later *Aeneid*. In these foundational epics, love and war are both inseparable and violently disjoined. The Trojan War begins with a sexual liaison that is itself, at the very least, ambiguous in relation to sex and violence: Paris "rapes," "ravishes," or "abducts" Helen, the most beautiful woman ever, carrying her from her husband Menelaus to his hometown of Troy. He thereby launches Marlowe's "thousand ships," the ships that ultimately "burnt the topless towers of Ilium," as Cassandra predicts.[3] The destruction of Troy is therefore the result, not only of a founding act of violent sexual desire, but also the martial underwriting of that act in the name of honor. Troy's downfall in the form of the entrance of the Trojan Horse, within its formerly impenetrable walls, is itself an analogue for the inherent violence of sexual penetration. Male desire is figured as siege.

This is tellingly encapsulated by the king of France's remark to Shakespeare's Henry V, when he likens his daughter to a maiden city besieged by troops desirous of penetration and violation:

> Yes, my lord, you see them perspectively,
> the cities turned into a maid – for they are all girdled with
> maiden walls that war hath never entered.  (*Henry V*, 5.2.292–94)

In accordance with Barthes's maxim above, in Shakespeare the language of desire often runs parallel with that of violent conquest: sometimes metaphorically, as in Don Pedro's assurance to Claudio about winning Hero on his behalf in *Much Ado About Nothing* – "in her bosom I'll unclasp my heart / And take her hearing prisoner with the force / And strong encounter of my amorous tale" (1.2.279–81) – at other times erupting into real violence, like the attempted rape of Silvia at the end of *The Two Gentlemen of Verona*, where Proteus threatens to "love" Silvia " 'gainst the nature of love" (5.4.58), or in Tarquin's achieved brutality in *The Rape of Lucrece*.

*The Rape of Lucrece* returns us to the *Aeneid*, where *eros* is finally eschewed, even punished, in favor of the grander, masculine project of founding a nation. The allure of a Carthaginian queen must be abjured if Rome is to be reborn out of Troy's ashes. The destruction of Troy thus leads to new life in Aeneas's escape and founding of Rome and, ultimately, via the legendary Brutus of Geoffrey of Monmouth's *Historia Regum Britanniae*, the founding of Britain and the establishment, on the river Thames, of a New Troy: Shakespeare's London. The tragic epic turns out to be a comedy and all turns out well in the end.

## War and *Eros*: Essential Conjunction or Accidental Affinity?

It is striking how many of Shakespeare's erotic plays have war either as their setting or are born out of a recent state of violent conflict. *Troilus and Cressida* and *Antony and Cleopatra* fall most clearly into the former camp, where war is both the condition of desire and its nemesis. But think of *Much Ado About Nothing* and *A Midsummer Night's Dream*, where *eros* emerges from a newly forged peace only to constitute a new battleground of its own. In *All's Well That Ends Well*, war allows Bertram to avoid sex with his loathed wife, but it also provides the opportunity for a predatory sexuality that in the end allows Helen to trap him in the toils of his own desire: "But, oh, strange men, / That can such sweet use make of what they hate!" (4.4.21–22). *All's Well*'s equally enigmatic companion, *Measure for Measure*, sets Shakespeare's most explicit treatment of free sexuality and the attempts to control it within the context of a threatening war with the king of Hungary. *Cymbeline* sets up a national war against an imperial force with the deepest, and most murderously violent, anxieties about sexual infidelity, as does *Othello* in relation to the Ottoman Empire. *Titus Andronicus* offers a Stoic, Senecan perspective on the inherent violence contained not merely in sex, but also in love as a passion beyond control, that is, of the burning hatred that lies at the heart of any kind of commitment to that which is different from the self. *Romeo and Juliet* harnesses the irrational violence of the family feud to demonstrate the complementary intensities of love and hatred. *Macbeth* and *Hamlet* offer the violent sexuality of Claudius and Gertrude, Hamlet and Ophelia, and the Macbeths against a backdrop of internecine conflict, territorial aggression, and murder. Even *Twelfth Night*, like *The Comedy of Errors*, is set in a state of permanent war in which its most devoted protagonists of devotion are trapped. And *The Two Noble Kinsmen* integrates these disparate instances of sexual contests within a bellicose setting, with war as the driving condition of violent sexual desire.

Given this conjunction of war and *eros* in almost half of Shakespeare's plays (and I'm ignoring instances such as Kate and Hotspur's marital spat in *Henry IV*, expressions of love between Richard II and his wife, or the erotic conflicts involving Henry VI, Margaret and Suffolk) we need to ask whether these are merely contingent, theatrical conjunctions, or whether they indicate and reinforce a deep *conceptual* connection between *eros* and violence. Is it *language* itself, as Barthes suggests, that "posit[s] the equivalence of love and war"? When Henry V talks of the maid of his desire, the French king's daughter, as a fair city to be besieged and entered, is the tenor of sexual penetration yoked violently to the vehicle of military conquest in a mere metaphor? Or does language itself – and therefore a whole culture – already contain this identity?

One doesn't have to look far for theories of *eros* in which its association with war is not simply contingent (that is, sexual desire can sometimes be violent) but at its very heart (sex is war). That violence stems from the now almost universal theory, offered most powerfully by Plato, that desire is essentially predicated upon a lack. From Lucretius to Lacan the aggression of sexuality arises from the desiring subject's anger at needing another to fill an essentially unfillable emptiness. Plato avoids that aggression by sublimating it into an idealized desire for union, not with another person, but with the transcendent forms of Truth and Beauty. But for Lucretius such idealization is precisely the problem. Lovers literally inflict pain upon one another: "eagerly they nail their body to the other's and mingle the moisture of mouths and breathe deeply, clenching the other's lips in their teeth – all for nothing, since they cannot scrape anything off, or penetrate or get their body lost in that body."[4] Lovers suffer endless frustration because the desired union with a physical, yet idealized, other is impossible. The lover therefore, as Martha Nussbaum puts it, punishes the "partner ... for her very otherness, for resisting an incorporation that would remove love's bondage."[5] In sex, Lucretius asserts, lovers "cause pain to the body ... batter [it] with kisses ... there are hidden stings that goad them to hurt that very thing, whatever it is, that is the source of those seeds of madness."[6] But such violence is not inevitable. For Lucretius it arises from the inappropriate idealization of the desired object that cannot assuage the lack felt by the lover. Abandon the idealization, treat the other as simply human, and a mutual enjoyment of sexual pleasure is entirely possible.

Seneca's Stoic philosophy allows no such reprieve. The passionate life is necessarily both open to violation and contains a reciprocal desire to violate. In Nussbaum's words, "Love itself is a dangerous hole in the self, through which it is impossible that the world will not strike a painful and debilitating blow ... none of us, if we love, can stop ourselves from the wish to kill."[7] In the twentieth century, Georges Bataille offers his own version: "love spells suffering for us insofar as it is a quest for the impossible, and at a lower level, a quest for union at the mercy of circumstance. ... If the union of two lovers comes about through love, it involves the idea of murder, death, suicide ... the urge to love, pushed to its limit, is the urge towards death."[8] The deepest modern conjunction of sex and death comes in Freud's declaration that hatred is older, more fundamental, than love. Julia Kristeva offers an uncompromising application of the violence at the heart of *eros* in her reading of *Romeo and Juliet*. "Under the guise of sex," she writes, "it is hatred that prevails"; the play reveals "the intrinsic presence of hatred in amatory feeling itself. As soon as the *other* appears different from myself, it becomes alien, repellent, repugnant, abject – hated."[9] Desire, in this scenario, is indeed death, as Shakespeare writes in sonnet 147.

There is thus a powerful philosophical and literary tradition that regards both sexual desire and the need for love as inherently violent conditions, ranging from Lucretius to popular contemporary notions of the "war of the sexes." But what of the erotics of war itself? Pierre Guiraud writes in *Sémiologie de la sexualité*: "The military metaphor is so coherent, so relevant, that all the modes, means, and phases of combat and all the phrases describing them contain a powerful sexual image."[10] This is not a statement about the violence of sexuality but rather the underlying sexuality of war. In her study of Homer's *Iliad*, Hélène Monsacré finds the affinities between the beauty of the hero's body that provokes fear and that which provokes desire in its foundational images:

> Narrowing the field of observation still further to the heroic site *par excellence*, the body of the warrior, we find a more deeply complex relationship between his masculine nature and what would seem to be its absolute opposite: the world of women and love. There is a permanent slippage between the level of beauty that provokes fear and the level of beauty that awakens desire; the warrior's body does not only emit warlike signals. At the most intense moments of war, the heroic and the erotic are joined in the hero's body. It is at these moments that, by appropriating portions of positive femininity while

maintaining a distance, the wholly masculine ideology of the *Iliad* constructs its heroic specificity.[11]

Shakespeare follows this Homeric eroticization of the warrior's body in *Troilus and Cressida* as an object of beauty and admiration and also of intense desire; something to be embraced, but also to be penetrated in the intense coming together of two bodies in hand-to-hand combat. If Cressida will "war with" Troilus in a "virtuous fight" of mutual pledges of fidelity ("When right with right wars who shall be most right!" [3.2.158–59]), Aeneas invokes Venus, not Mars, in his pledge:

> By Venus' hand, I swear
> No man alive can love in such a sort
> The thing he means to kill more excellently.
> DIOMEDES: We sympathize. Jove, let Aeneas live –
> If to my sword his fate be not the glory –
> A thousand complete courses of the sun,
> But in mine emulous honor let him die
> With every joint a wound, and that tomorrow.
> AENEAS: We know each other well.
> DIOMEDES: We do, and long to know each other worse.
> PARIS: This is the most despiteful'st gentle greeting,
> The noblest hateful love, that e'er I heard of.  (4.1.23–34)

"The noblest hateful love." The paradox condenses all the erotic intensities of violent desire: loving the thing one "means to kill" conveys a bond that stems not from mere aggression but is tied to protocols and courtesies that mark war as much as they might have informed honorable sexual conduct. War binds enemies in an admiring embrace in which the desire for conquest, the heating of the blood, has all the intensity of *eros*.

In my epigraph from Cervantes, "Love and warre are all one," sex and violence are conjoined in the claim that they escape the norms or rules or protocols of communal existence: in Bataille's terms, they abrogate the very taboos regarding violence and reproduction that enable a social existence of communal and productive work. But taboos are meant to be broken, albeit in circumscribed, paradoxically regulated ways, as Bakhtin's work on carnival makes clear.[12] War is the clearest abrogation of the taboo against killing. But it is not an institution (and I use that word advisedly) without or beyond rules. Especially in Shakespeare's time, the conduct of war was circumscribed by what Fluellen in *Henry V* repeatedly calls the "laws" or "prerogatifs" or "disciplines" of war (e.g., 4.1.67, 3.3.5), codified among other places in Pope Gregory IX's *De truega et pace*, which established categories of people "who should have full security against the ravages of war" and the broader codes of chivalry that governed the conduct of knights and the nobility in warfare.[13] That is to say, like sexuality, warfare is always engaged with a series of taboos that circumscribe certain kinds of violence.

To declare, therefore, as Lyly does, that there are no rules in war abrogates a series of taboos within the abrogation of the general social taboo against violence. It's taboos all the way down. Just as Foucault reminds us that sexuality is a construct to enable a peculiarly modern discipline of bodies and desires, so war must be regarded not as a natural state of aggression but rather a social institution as complex and circumscribed as sexuality itself, involving similar constructions of subjectivity.[14] And just as war in the early modern period is subject to prohibition or regulation, so sexuality, too, is bounded by strict rules. The most elaborate of these is what has become known as "courtly love," which bound and channeled sexual desire in very rigid ways, but which also cloaks the intense violence of desire behind the protocols of restrained fantasy.

In order to develop this argument, I want to make two moves: first, I want to illustrate the interplay of subjective desire with social regulation with reference to *The Two Noble Kinsmen*; and second, I want to use two plays, *Troilus and Cressida* and *Romeo and Juliet*, to explore the conceptual affinities, following Hegel, between the human quest for acknowledgment or recognition from another person, either subjugated as a slave or killed (and thereby dehumanized), or achieved by transcending the struggle for mutual recognition in a reciprocal "toil of grace" (*Antony and Cleopatra*, 5.2.344).

### Desire and Regulation: *The Two Noble Kinsmen*

The violence of desire permeates *The Two Noble Kinsmen*: from the opening marriage ceremony between Theseus, duke of Athens, and Hippolyta, the defeated Amazonian queen, to the final proxy battle between Mars and Venus in the rival lovers' contest to the death over Emilia. The play represents a continual struggle between that violence and the urge to contain such aggressive intensity within constraining ritual – within taboo – even if such a ritual merely channels and manages destruction without eliminating it.

The opening plea by the three queens, to be permitted to bury their husbands in defiance of Creon's prohibition (in an echo of *Antigone*), stages the obligation to observe the taboos on the maltreatment of the dead in war. But it also interrupts Theseus's sexual enjoyment of his vanquished queen and allows the Second Queen to offer a conventional reflection on the degree to which Theseus's war with Hippolyta has restored a supposedly natural hierarchy between men and women:

> Honored Hippolyta,
> Most dreaded Amazonian, that hast slain
> The scythe-tusked boar; that with thy arm, as strong
> As it is white, wast near to make the male
> To thy sex captive, but that this thy lord –
> Born to uphold creation in that honor
> First nature styled it in – shrunk thee into
> The bound thou wast o'er-flowing, at once subduing
> Thy force and thy affection. (1.1.78–85)

"I wooed thee with my sword," Theseus declares in Shakespeare's *A Midsummer Night's Dream*, fusing sexual desire, war, and rape (1.1.16). The early comedy takes that conjunction of war and *eros* little further, but *The Two Noble Kinsmen* develops it in disturbing ways. It is clear from the beginning that Emilia and her sister are prisoners of a sort, even if their prison is a garden. They revel nostalgically in their memories of the specifically Amazonian hunt and affirm their irreversible identities as soldiers in the most brutal terms:

> We have been soldiers, and we cannot weep
> When our friends don their helms, or put to sea,
> Or tell of babes broached on the lance, or women
> That have sod their infants in – and after ate them –
> The brine they wept at killing 'em. (1.3.18–22)

Same-sex relationships are a special source of conflict. Immediately after urging Pirithous to join Theseus in the war against Creon, Hippolyta and Emilia speculate on the degree to which he is a rival for her husband's love:

> Their knot of love
> Tied, weaved, entangled, with so true, so long,
> And with a finger of so deep a cunning,
> May be outworn, never undone. I think
> Theseus cannot be umpire to himself,
> Cleaving his conscience into twain and doing
> Each side like justice, which he loves best. (1.3.41–47)

This knot of love between the two men is forged through their shared experience of violence and suffering in war:

> They two have cabined
> In many as dangerous as poor a corner,
> Peril and want contending; they have skiffed
> Torrents whose roaring tyranny and power
> I'th' least of these was dreadful; and they have
> Sought out together where Death's self was lodged. (1.3.35–40)

This anticipates the more prominent friendship between Palamon and Arcite, whose closeness arises as much from their military experiences together as their kinship. But it also leads on to Emilia's reflection on a very different kind of same-sex love:

> The flower that I would pluck
> And put between my breasts – oh, then but beginning
> To swell about the blossom – she would long
> Till she had such another and commit it
> To the like innocent cradle where, phoenix-like,
> They died in perfume. (1.3.66–71)

Hippolyta declares that she loves her husband precisely for his devotion to Pirithous through mutual hardship and war, and it is against the backdrop of this admiration for male friendship that Emilia declares her different memory and commitment to her desire for women rather than men: that she, as Hippolyta concludes, "shall never, like the maid Flavina, / Love any that's called man" (1.3.83–84). The mimetic desire of the two kinsmen for Emilia is contextualized by this declaration.[15] Their imitative desire, in which the one desires Emilia *because* the other does, leads to an intense antagonism that bears all the ferocity of Lucretian or Senecan *eros*. This is a rewriting of *The Two Gentlemen of Verona*, in which, instead of forgiving each other and in effect abandoning the woman as an object of idealizing desire, the friends fight to the death. Like Theseus, they woo her with their swords, channeling the aggressiveness of the fantasy of the early comedy into a destructive energy focused on each other. They embody and displace the erotic language of combined admiration and aggression we shall see in the soldiers on the plains of Troy.

Why does Theseus not simply allow them to kill each other? Because he is determined to maintain a monopoly on the exercise of violence and its relation to desire. This accounts for the puzzlingly elaborate martial contest he arranges, in which the victor is not permitted to kill the vanquished, but the latter must be slain by Theseus's executioners. The ritual killing of the loser is the prerogative of the man who needs not only to control the taboos on violence and sexuality in his society, but also the ways and degrees to which they may be transgressed or interact. War is the permitted transgression of the general taboo against violence, marriage the permitted transgression of the general taboo against free sexual desire. And the ruler is the one who permits, prohibits, and controls both.

The play ends with the classical contest between Venus and Mars. We know from myth and countless Renaissance paintings that it is Venus who finally subjugates Mars. But it is telling that in *Venus and Adonis* the goddess of love describes her seduction of the god of war in *martial* terms:

> "I have been wooed as I entreat thee now,
> Even by the stern and direful god of war,
> Whose sinewy neck in battle ne'er did bow,
> Who conquers where he comes in every jar;
> > Yet hath he been my captive and my slave,
> > And begged for that which thou unasked shalt have.
>
> . . .
>
> "Thus he that overruled I over-swayed,
> Leading him prisoner in a red-rose chain.
> Strong-tempered steel his stronger strength obeyed;
> Yet was he servile to my coy disdain.
> > Oh, be not proud, nor brag not of thy might,
> > For mast'ring her that foiled the god of fight."   (97–114)

There is a paradox here: Venus wins the battle, but Mars triumphs in the discourse. Emilia may echo Venus in her tender recollection of her beloved Lavinia in the perfumed flower pressed between her breasts, but she is finally abandoned by her own goddess, Diana, as she must be, in the conquest of Mars by Venus. And in the contest between Venus and Mars, for which Arcite and Palamon stand proxy, both god and goddess win, even if Venus, following tradition, has the last word.

This is a very un-Shakespearean ending: not only in its carelessness regarding the autonomy of female desire, but also in its eschewing of Shakespeare's habitual insistence on love's singular vision, of its refusal of any substitute, its projection of value independently of any socially agreed qualities of the beloved.[16] Shakespeare is finally confronting and extrapolating what it means to woo a woman with the sword and what it means to be wooed with such violence. If *Two Gentlemen of Verona* finally avoids the physical violence of desire attached to pure, narcissist fantasy by averting Silvia's rape, *The Two Noble Kinsmen* ends with a double rape. In the sorry fate of the jailer's daughter, who leaves the stage to have sex with a man she has been deluded into accepting with the words "But you shall not hurt me. / . . . / If you do . . . I'll cry" (5.2.110–12). And in Emilia's helplessness before the brutal violence of her impending marriage – tortured emotionally, trapped, and violated by an order in which sex is merely war fought by another means. *The Two Noble Kinsmen* reveals the Lucretian destructiveness of sexual desire, merely diverted and contained by the violent sway of a warrior ruler (and lover) like Theseus; *Troilus and Cressida* embodies the chiasmic presence of erotic intensity in the very protocols of warfare.

## The Quest for Acknowledgment: *Troilus and Cressida*

For a much more skeptical, not to say cynical, appraisal of the attribution of value, I turn to a very different play about love in the time of war – *Troilus and Cressida*:

> TROILUS: What's aught but as 'tis valued?
> HECTOR: But value dwells not in particular will;
>    It holds his estimate and dignity
>    As well wherein 'tis precious of itself
>    As in the prizer. 'Tis mad idolatry
>    To make the service greater than the god,
>    And the will dotes that is inclineable
>    To what infectiously itself affects
>    Without some image of th'affected merit.   (2.2.53–60)

This is a chicken and egg question about value: *are we spilling so much blood over Helen because she is worthy of that sacrifice; or is she made worthy by our willingness to spill blood – death and injury being the cosmetics that create beauty?* "Helen must needs be fair / When with your blood you daily paint her thus" (1.1.85–86). It is not Helen's loveliness that justifies the war; it is rather the fighting, and its bloody sacrifices, that bestow value upon her. This may be a throwaway line by a Troilus in torment for his desire for Cressida, which has in turn robbed him of any will to fight – "I cannot fight upon this argument; / It is too starved a subject for my sword" (87–88) – but it evokes a standard imbrication of war and sex in the chivalric values that informed each form of desire:

>                    "Kings, princes, lords,
>    If there be one amongst the fair'st of Greece
>    That holds his honor higher than his ease,
>    That seeks his praise more than he fears his peril,
>    That knows his valor and knows not his fear,
>    *That loves his mistress more than in confession*
>    *With truant vows to her own lips he loves,*
>    *And dare avow her beauty and her worth*
>    *In other arms than hers*, to him this challenge.
>    Hector in view of Trojans and of Greeks,
>    Shall make it good, or do his best to do it:
>    *He hath a lady wiser, fairer, truer*
>    *Than ever Greek did compass in his arms,*
>    *And will tomorrow with his trumpet call*
>    *Midway between your tents and walls of Troy*
>    *To rouse a Grecian that is true in love.*

> If any come, Hector shall honor him;
> If none, he'll say in Troy when he retires
> The Grecian dames are sunburnt and not worth
> The splinter of a lance." (1.3.261–80, my emphasis)

Here love is not only the occasion of war – in a merging of sexual and military honor – but it is also given value by the outcome of combat. No honorable, non-truant love confined to the arms of the beloved is possible – it has to be tested and proven "in other arms than hers."

And those "arms," with their double meaning, themselves have a homo-erotic intensity in the oft-noted erotic discourse of male contest, especially in the embrace and emblazoned noting of Hector's body by Achilles's gaze in preparation for its ultimate, deadly penetration. Desire and admiration come together, the wonder of affinity accompanied by an equal delight in the prospect of conquest and death:

> HECTOR: Let me embrace thee, Ajax.
> By him that thunders, thou hast lusty arms!
> Hector would have them fall upon him thus.
> Cousin, all honor to thee.
> AJAX: I thank thee, Hector.
> Thou art too gentle and too free a man.
> I came to kill thee, cousin, and bear hence
> A great addition earnèd in thy death. (4.5b.19–25)

The erotic quality of this exchange is intensified by Achilles's aggressive determination to "oppress" Hector "with [his] eye," to "view [him] limb by limb" (125, 122) – asking, as he puts it, in which part of his body

> Shall I destroy him – whether there, or there, or there –
> That I may give the local wound a name
> And make distinct the very breach whereout
> Hector's great spirit flew. (4.5b.127–30)

Before we see this exchange too quickly as a sign of homoerotic desire, however, it may help to clarify the intensity of that desire in Hegelian terms. Hegel's master-slave dialectic offers a model that encompasses the intensity of erotic desire, the need for acknowledgment by the other that is the essence not only of love but of humanity itself, and the drive toward obliteration or subjugation that is the essence of war. Hegel, in other words, offers a model of the human desire for acknowledgment that encompasses Mars and Venus alike: the human need to be recognized as a *being-for-itself* rather than the merely animal existence *in-itself* leads to a struggle to the death as each antagonist demands recognition from the other, unless one gives in and accepts the inferior status of slave to the other, in which case he gives up his freedom as a human being.[17] The intensity of the need and desire for the other is erotic; the violence of the demand martial.

Crucially, in the pursuit of this desire one has to be willing to risk one's life for such recognition. This means that the desire for human recognition is agonistic. It necessitates a relationship with at least one other, each determined to wrest from the other the acknowledgment he needs. This means a fight to the death, unless one capitulates as a slave in service to the other as master. If that doesn't happen, the quest for recognition develops into an endless fight with serial others, since once the other is killed he can no longer provide the human acknowledgment demanded, and a contest with another ensues.[18]

This dialectic enables us to see that the encounter between Hector, Ajax, and Achilles is not necessarily homoerotic, but it does have an intensity of desire that has close conceptual affinities with *eros*.

If we compare the Hector/Ajax/Achilles agon with Troilus's fantasy of his engagement with Cressida, important differences appear. He is a lover bewailing his amatory lack, not an opponent reveling in the erotics of bloodletting:

> I tell thee I am mad
> In Cressid's love; thou answer'st she is fair,
> Pour'st in the open ulcer of my heart
> Her eyes, her hair, her cheek, her gait, her voice;
> Handlest in thy discourse – oh, that her hand,
> In whose comparison all whites are ink
> Writing their own reproach, to whose soft seizure
> The cygnet's down is harsh, and spirit of sense
> Hard as the palm of plowman. This thou tell'st me,
> As true thou tell'st me, when I say I love her.
> But saying thus, instead of oil and balm,
> Thou lay'st in every gash that love hath given me
> The knife that made it.   (1.1.48–60)

Whereas Ajax and Achilles entertain the prospect of penetrating Hector, here Troilus is the one who sustains the wound, pierced to his infected heart by "Her eyes, her hair, her cheek, her gait, her voice." Whereas Hector's body, both in embrace and as an object of scrutiny, has a solid physicality, Cressida dissolves into pure fantasy: her hand is all softness; it offers no resistance at all. Indeed, there is none of the friction that is the condition of any sexual encounter, of any sexual pleasure:

> I am giddy; expectation whirls me round.
> Th'imaginary relish is so sweet
> That it enchants my sense. What will it be

> When that the wat'ry palates taste indeed
> Love's thrice-repurèd nectar? Death, I fear me,
> Swooning destruction, or some joy too fine,
> Too subtle-potent, and too sharp in sweetness
> For the capacity of my ruder powers.
> I fear it much, and I do fear besides
> That I shall lose distinction in my joys,
> As doth a battle when they charge on heaps
> The enemy flying.   (3.2.16–27)

Like an archetypal Lucretian lover, Troilus fears what he desires most: the complete loss of the self in the delirium of sexual pleasure: "death," "swooning destruction," or, to the same effect, an unbearable intensity of feeling that induces fear rather than delight. This is an expression of the Senecan view that *eros* is always a breach of the integrity of body and soul: an opening of the self to a world that is ultimately as hostile as it is fearfully desirable. And in contrast to Ajax and Achilles's sense that the conquest of a noble and honorable enemy will bring honor and distinction upon the victor – like Prince Hal's claim that Hotspur is but his "factor" (*1 Henry IV*, 3.2.147) – and especially *recognition*, Cressida's complementary fear is her own loss of value by giving in too easily: "Things won are done" (1.2.265). And she proves to be right. The consummation is no "thrice-repurèd nectar." Not only does Troilus refuse to "tarry" the next morning; he offers no resistance to her being transferred to the enemy, the Greeks.

Troilus, unwilling to fight because of love, is also unwilling to fight for love. *Troilus and Cressida* finally suggests that erotic desire is sustained by warfare, and consummation and surrender leads to impotence. Furthermore, that intensity, which combines a passionate aggression to the death with an absolute desire for acknowledgment or recognition from the other, prefigures Hegel's master-slave dialectic. The paradox of the dialectic cannot be resolved. The agonistic nature of the desire for recognition from another, *free* human being ends either in the death of that person (as in Achilles's slaying of Hector), or the reduction of that subject to slavery, whose loss of freedom means that they are incapable of rendering the required recognition. Is there a way out of this impasse? To see, we need to take a final detour through *Romeo and Juliet*.

## The Quest Fulfilled: *Romeo and Juliet*

*Romeo and Juliet* is technically not set in a time of war. But it weaves together the intensities of love and hatred as much as any of the plays discussed so far. We should take care not to equate war and hatred. They are not synonymous. Indeed, as we have seen, war in every sense may involve love; it certainly encompasses desires that may be as intense as any erotic devotion. When Romeo belatedly comes upon the aftermath of the brawl between the Montagues and Capulets in act 1, he declares, "Here's much to do with hate, but more with love," before continuing in a Petrarchan invocation of the warfare of antithetical elements that love encompasses (1.1.170–78).

Romeo's Petrarchan oxymorons extend the fundamental relation of hatred and love as intertwined through a similar intensity of passion. The intensities of desire are matched and encompassed by the irrationality of animosity, in the form of the family feud. This forms both the condition of impossibility and the condition of possibility of the young lovers' attraction, in which the aggression of retainer rivalry is expressed in sexual terms throughout the play. This encapsulates Hegel's dialectic insofar as the *agon* between individuals needing recognition from the other *to the death* has no ground or reason other than a fundamental, mortal desire.

Romeo and Juliet's willingness to sacrifice themselves for the other (like Antony and Cleopatra) recalls the Hegelian position that in order to fulfill the fundamental human desire for recognition by another human being one has to be willing to risk one's life. But we have seen that the master-slave struggle ends in an impasse: either in the death of the opponent from whom recognition or acknowledgment is required, or else in an asymmetrical relationship between master and unfree, subhuman slave.

Hegel offers a political path out of this impasse through love that escapes the violence of desire. Love retains the structure of the self discovering its own self-consciousness, and therefore its humanity, in relation to another who is different, as in the master-slave dialectic. But instead of the agonistic, hierarchical nature of the latter, love forges the possibility of a unifying reciprocity of mutual recognition:

> Love means in general the consciousness of my unity with another, so that I am not isolated on my own, but gain my self-consciousness only through the renunciation of my independent existence and through knowing myself as the unity of myself with another and of the other with me.[19]

Hegel in fact quotes from *Romeo and Juliet* to illustrate this theory of love:

> Love is stronger than fear. It has no fear of its fear, but, led by its fear, it cancels separation.... The lover who takes is not thereby made richer than the other; he is enriched indeed, but only so much as the other is. So too the giver does not make himself poorer; by giving to the other he has at the same time and to the same extent enhanced his own treasure (*compare Juliet in* Romeo and Juliet [ii. ll. 175–77: "My bounty is as boundless as the sea, My love as deep;] the more

*I give to thee, The more I have"*). This wealth of life love acquires in the exchange of every thought, every variety of inner experience, for it seeks out differences and devises unifications ad infinitum.... What in the first instance is most the individual's own is united into the whole in the lovers' touch and contact; consciousness of a separate self disappears, and all distinction between the lovers is annulled.[20]

Shakespeare's most celebrated romantic tragedy thus helps to clarify, at a conceptual or philosophical level, the affinities and the differences between *eros* and war, if we read the play through a Hegelian lens. The deaths of the lovers from this perspective are not accidental, but absolutely necessary. Jacques Derrida remarks on the peculiarity of the fact that Romeo and Juliet "*in turn* live the death of the other, for a time ... not in 'objective reality' ... but in the experience."[21] This turns Hegel's master-slave confrontation on its head. For the warlike initiation of that encounter must end either in the death of one of them or in his subjugation as slave. The mutual deaths of Romeo and Juliet (and Antony and Cleopatra) invert this dialectic. For it is by each lover's living the death of the other in mourning that the other is in fact recognized fully, accepted as a human being like myself, and for whom I am prepared to risk myself to the death. This event is symmetrical, shared equally and reciprocally.

Bataille, reading Hegel, illuminates the ways in which the mutual suicides of Romeo and Juliet and Antony and Cleopatra enable us as theater audiences to see and experience this impossible death for ourselves, without having to undergo it:

> In order for Man ultimately to reveal himself to himself, he would have to die, but he would have to do it while living – watching himself ceasing to be. In other words, death itself would have to become (self-) consciousness at the very moment that it annihilates the conscious being. In a sense, this is what takes place (what is at the point of taking place, or takes place in a fugitive, ungraspable manner) by means of a subterfuge. In the sacrifice, the sacrifice identifies himself with the animal that is struck down dead. And so he dies in seeing himself die, one in spirit with the sacrificial weapon. But it is a comedy![22]

Bataille is commenting on the paradox of Hegel's assertion that what has to die in the *human* forging of self-consciousness is the *animal* self. But since the human self subsists upon the animal self, that death involves the annihilation of both. The theater, however, especially the Shakespearean theater, enables us, "in the experience," though "not in 'objective'" fact, to pass through that necessary death – just as Romeo and Juliet can impossibly experience the deaths of each other – unharmed and the richer in our consciousness and self-consciousness. The whole event is finally a comedy, as Bataille unexpect-edly declares.

Barthes seems to be right that the affinities of *eros* and war are written into our language, embedded in cultural forms of life that conjoin desire with violence, in which war and sexuality are chiasmically intertwined. I have argued that Hegel's master-slave dialectic offers a model or a picture of the degree to which the human quest for acknowledgment from another to rise above a merely animal existence necessarily involves a battle either to the death or submission by the other, who is then ironically deprived of the capacity to afford the recognition sought. Love, rather than merely desire, offers a possible path out of this impasse insofar as it offers the possibility of a reciprocal acknowledgment without the necessity of violence or conflict. But Shakespeare's great tragedies of love, *Romeo and Juliet* and *Antony and Cleopatra*, force the reciprocity of love through the passage of death. Freud insisted that there is finally no separating *eros* and *thanatos*. But the impulse to death that lies at the heart of love, and which Shakespeare reiterates relentlessly at the microlevel of the word "die" as much as on the larger field of his tragedies, may be experienced vicariously in the form of his theater. We do not *have* to die to know what it is to love.

## Further Reading

Barker, Simon. *War and Nation in the Theatre of Shakespeare and His Contemporaries*, Edinburgh, Edinburgh University Press, 2007.

Bataille, Georges. *Erotism: Death and Sensuality*, trans. Mary Dalwood, new ed., San Francisco, City Lights Publishers, 2001.

Bowen, Barbara E. *Gender in the Theater of War: Shakespeare's "Troilus and Cressida,"* New York, Garland, 1993.

Girard, René. *A Theatre of Envy: William Shakespeare*, Leominster, Gracewing Publishing, 2000.

Johnson, James Turner. *Just War Tradition and the Restraint of War: A Moral and Historical Inquiry*, Princeton, Princeton University Press, 1981.

Jorgensen, Paul A. *Shakespeare's Military World*, Berkeley, University of California Press, 1956.

Kristeva, Julia. *Tales of Love*, trans. Leon S. Roudiez, New York, Columbia University Press, 1987.

Meron, Theodor. *Bloody Constraint: War and Chivalry in Shakespeare*, New York, Oxford University Press, 1998.

Monsacré, Hélène. *The Tears of Achilles*, trans. Nicholas J. Snead, Hellenic Studies Series 75, Washington, DC, Center for Hellenic Studies, 2018.

Nussbaum, Martha Craven. *The Therapy of Desire: Theory and Practice in Hellenistic Ethics*, Princeton, Princeton University Press, 1994.

Schalkwyk, David. *Shakespeare, Love and Language*, Cambridge, Cambridge University Press, 2018.

## NOTES

1 Miguel de Cervantes, *Don Quixote*, trans. T. Shelton (London, 1620), II, p. xxi.
2 Roland Barthes, *A Lover's Discourse*, trans. Richard Howard (New York: Hill and Wang, 1974), p. 188.
3 Christopher Marlowe, *Dr. Faustus* (London, 1604), 1.3.88–89.
4 Titus Lucretius Carus, *On the Nature of Things*, trans. Martin Ferguson Smith (Indianapolis: Hackett, 2001), ll. 1105–11.
5 Martha Craven Nussbaum, *The Therapy of Desire: Theory and Practice in Hellenistic Ethics* (Princeton: Princeton University Press, 1994), p. 171.
6 Lucretius, *On the Nature of Things*, ll. 1079–83.
7 Nussbaum, *The Therapy of Desire*, pp. 442–43.
8 Georges Bataille, *Erotism: Death and Sensuality*, trans. Mary Dalwood, new ed. (San Francisco: City Lights Publishers, 2001), pp. 20, 44; and "Hegel, Death and Sacrifice," trans. Jonathan Strauss, *Yale French Studies*, 78 (1990), pp. 9–28.
9 Julia Kristeva, *Tales of Love*, trans. Leon S. Roudiez (New York: Columbia University Press, 1987), pp. 220, 222.
10 Pierre Guiraud, *Sémiologie de la sexualité* (Paris: Payot, 1978), quoted in Hélène Monsacré, *The Tears of Achilles*, trans. Nicholas J. Snead, Hellenic Studies Series 75 (Washington, DC: Center for Hellenic Studies, 2018), 1.3: https://chs.harvard .edu/CHS/article/display/6805.i-4-the-feminine-and-the-warrior. Last accessed December 14, 2019.
11 Monsacré, *The Tears of Achilles*, 1.4.
12 Mikhail Bakhtin, *Rabelais and His World*, trans. Hélène Iswolsky, new ed. (Bloomington: Indiana University Press, 2009).
13 James Turner Johnson, *Just War Tradition and the Restraint of War: A Moral and Historical Inquiry* (Princeton: Princeton University Press, 1981), p. 127; and also Franziska Quabeck's chapter in this collection (Chapter 2).
14 Simon Barker, *War and Nation in the Theatre of Shakespeare and His Contemporaries* (Edinburgh: Edinburgh University Press, 2007); and Michel Foucault, *The Will to Knowledge*, trans. Robert Hurley, vol. 1 of *The History of Sexuality* (London: Penguin, 1998).
15 René Girard, *A Theatre of Envy: William Shakespeare* (Leominster: Gracewing Publishing, 2000).
16 My thanks to Elena Pellone for drawing this to my attention.
17 Georg Wilhelm Friedrich Hegel, *Phenomenology of Spirit*, trans. A. V. Miller, new ed. (Oxford: Oxford University Press, 1976); *Early Theological Writings*, trans. T. M. Knox, with Richard Kroner (Philadelphia: University of Pennsylvania Press, 1971); and *Elements of the Philosophy of Right*, ed. Allen W. Wood, trans. H. B. Nisbet, Cambridge Texts in the History of Political Thought (Cambridge: Cambridge University Press, 1991).
18 I have retained Hegel's use of masculine pronouns in my summary.
19 Hegel, *Philosophy of Right*, p. 199.
20 Hegel, *Early Theological Writings*, pp. 306–7, my emphasis.
21 Jacques Derrida, *Acts of Literature*, ed. Derek Attridge (London: Routledge, 1991), p. 422.
22 Bataille, "Hegel," p. 19.

# 9

LYNNE MAGNUSSON

# Shakespeare's Language and the Rhetoric of War

This chapter explores the verbal and rhetorical challenges and opportunities that the representation of war created for Shakespeare. In *Henry V*, for instance, as Shakespeare's Chorus in act 3 calls upon the audience's imagination to offset the problems he encounters in staging war, he also signals two kinds of challenges war poses for theatrical language. The first kind is obvious and concerns how the scenes of war with their vast scale and technical complexity challenge not only onstage representation but also its alternative, poetic narration. Yet even as he signals the problem, the heightened diction and metaphors with which the Chorus evokes the warships en route as "[a] city on th'inconstant billows dancing" or the siege weapons "With fatal mouths gaping on girded Harfleur" (3.0.15, 27) are themselves reminders of the highly developed verbal resources available to a poetic dramatist who was schooled in classical rhetoric and epic poetry. The challenge to linguistic invention posed by war was an invitation to exploit the high or "grand style," the highest of the three levels of style theorized by Cicero and Quintilian. In the grand style and its rhetorical techniques for bringing complex scenes vividly to life in poetic narration, war came pre-packaged for Elizabethan poets. In its heightened language, redolent of Virgilian and epic contexts mediated in Shakespeare's day by grammar-school rhetoric exercises in amplification and larger-than-life diction, the exploits of Talbot, Hotspur, Henry V, or Macbeth could readily be colored in heroic glory. Yet style is not only a matter of brave or splendid ornamentation, a solution to problems for bringing war onto the stage. Style is always ideology, and, as we shall see, the stylistic choices for narration of war scenes inevitably position and condition the questions raised about war and the attitudes expressed.

The second kind of challenge – or opportunity – posed by war for dramatic language concerns dialogue and how Shakespeare parses the characteristic speech interactions associated with war. Where the Chorus invites playgoers to "Suppose th'ambassador from the French comes back, / Tells

Harry that the King doth offer him / Katherine his daughter, and ... Some petty and unprofitable dukedoms," concluding dismissively "The offer likes not" (3.0.28–32), what we are asked to imagine turns on conversation and diplomatic negotiation. As an action of war this imagined situation of face-to-face speech exchange is quite different from a sea crossing or a siege. While narrated by the Chorus in this instance, such war negotiations are typically developed as onstage dialogue. From one perspective, war is what happens where dialogue ends, where words cease and civil conversation bears witness to its failure to sustain peaceful cooperation. In the ur-myth of Ciceronian rhetoric, the excellence of human language and its highest attainment in the skilled eloquence of the orator are the foundational instruments of civilization, the conciliatory power that brought "rude and savage people" together into "communities," enabling them to enjoy the fruits of "peace and tranquillity." "[W]hat other power," Cicero asks, "could have been strong enough either to gather scattered humanity into one place, or to lead it out of its brutish existence in the wilderness up to our present condition of civilization as men and as citizens, or, after the establishment of social communities, to give shape to laws, tribunals, and civic rights?"[1] The Renaissance ideal of language upon which Elizabethan playwrights were bred in the grammar school's education in classics and language arts was this celebratory story of linguistic intercourse as the antithesis and counterweight to violence and warfare.

Of course, the Elizabethan stage, with its drum rolls, trumpet blasts, and clashing swords, was equipped for the "noise" of war as a counterpart to speech. Nonetheless, Renaissance drama was, at its core, a theater of words and dialogue; they are the Shakespearean theater's primary mode of action. Whatever the seeming contradiction involved, wars in Shakespeare remain primarily linguistic constructs. War in the Renaissance theater offered Shakespeare both the challenge and opportunity to imagine the actions of war as encompassing a rich range of verbal interaction genres or conversational situations. Shakespeare takes up the invitation, bestowing rhetorical invention on war councils and embassies elaborating justifications and declarations of war, divisive quarrels that spark armed aggression, threatening and offensive speech acts that fuel hostilities, the negotiation and betrayal of alliances, parleys amidst combat, and condition-making amidst surrender. Some of these speech events and dialogic scripts are opportunities to highlight ceremonial rhetoric, war parsed as high occasion, performative oration. Some take us deeper into the politics of human relationships and the politics of war.

This chapter looks first at Shakespeare's "words of war," at the grand style and poetic diction typically exploited for the narration of war scenes.

Then it turns to the exploration of war as dialogue in Shakespearean drama, examining how the playwright parses war as dysfunctional communication and what possibilities (if any) he models for its remediation. It explores the contradictions inherent in a rhetorical culture that, on the one hand, makes eloquence the default language for violent militarism and, on the other hand, idealizes eloquence as peacemaking.

## Words of War: The Grand Style and Narrated Scenes of War

For a theater poet experimenting in the 1590s with war as a principal theme of history plays and tragedies, the classical doctrine of the three levels of style (*genera dicendi*), taught as a part of the Ciceronian rhetorical tradition emphasized in Elizabethan grammar schools, strongly suggested a match to the grand style, the style associated with elevated subject matter. If there was any leap of imagination at all needed to transfer the Virgilian matter of "arms and the [heroic] man" from the genre of epic to plays featuring heroism in war, the model was already firmly in place when Shakespeare came onto the English theatrical scene. Christopher Marlowe's venture into the "stately tent of war" in *Tamburlaine* (c. 1587) had supremely and self-consciously modeled the translation of the grand style's "high-astounding terms" to the Elizabethan stage.[2] Shakespeare clearly came to be seen by contemporaries as heir and challenger to "Marlowe's mighty line," exploiting his precursor's innovations not only in tragedy but also as he explored European warfare and English civil war in developing the genre of the English history play. The grand style is not readily confused with the other two recognized styles, low and middle, inherited as doctrine from the classical tradition, but Sylvia Adamson has provided a helpful "identikit" for it, derived from Thomas Wilson's "englishing" of its qualities in his *Art of Rhetoric*.[3] In Wilson's words, the grand style uses "great words," "vehement figures" (including especially "metaphors" and "translated words"), "stirring sentences," and "amplifications." When Shakespeare introduces the great subject matter of the Trojan War into English drama in the Prologue of *Troilus and Cressida*, he illustrates (and, perhaps, parodies) these features:

> In Troy there lies the scene. From isles of Greece
> The princes orgulous, their high blood chafed,
> Have to the port of Athens sent their ships,
> Fraught with the ministers and instruments
> Of cruel war. Sixty and nine that wore
> Their crownets regal from th'Athenian bay
> Put forth toward Phrygia, and their vow is made
> To ransack Troy, within whose strong immures

> The ravished Helen ... / sleeps – ...
> To Tenedos they come,
> And the deep-drawing barks do there disgorge
> Their warlike freightage. Now on Dardan plains
> The fresh and yet unbruisèd Greeks do pitch
> Their brave pavilions. Priam's six-gated city –
> Dardan, and Timbria, Helias, Chetas, Troien,
> And Antenorides – with massy staples
> And corresponsive and fulfilling bolts
> Spar up the sons of Troy.  (1–19)

"Great words" are illustrated here by unusual Latinate loanwords or derivatives ("immures," "corresponsive"), word choices incorporating extra syllables ("freightage" for "freight"), compound epithets ("deep-drawing," "six-gated"), and exotic names. Great words and a habit of amplification come together in the expansively compounded noun phrases ("the ministers and instruments / Of cruel war," "The fresh and yet unbruisèd Greeks," "with massy staples / And corresponsive and fulfilling bolts"), a habit reworked and varied with great virtuosity throughout Shakespeare's career in phrasal constructions coupling Latinate and Saxon synonyms or deploying the heightening tactic of hendiadys. Hendiadys was recognizable as a common rhetorical figure in Virgil's *Aeneid*, distributing a single complex idea into two compounded substantives. George T. Wright offers "'*membris et mole valens*' 'powerful in limbs and weight' (*Aeneid* v.431)" as a Virgilian example.[4] "Before the eye and prospect of your town" is one of several examples fitting the strict definition of hendiadys from Shakespeare's *King John* (2.1.208), but many of Shakespeare's compounded adjectives are also suggestive of the figure.

In the Prologue, the high style's "stirring sentences" take the form of exaggeratedly inverted and suspended syntax. Suspended syntax is by no means the norm of Shakespeare's dramatic style, for it pulls against the need for ready intelligibility and ease in dialogue. Nonetheless, Shakespeare's battle narrations and war orations frequently do incorporate or suggest the "stirring" syntax of suspended constructions, delaying the revelation of outcomes as in the bleeding sergeant's narration before King Duncan of the rebel Macdonald's conflict with "the brave Macbeth":

> For brave Macbeth – well he deserves that name –
> Disdaining Fortune with his brandished steel,
> Which smoked with bloody execution,
> Like valor's minion carved out his passage
> Till he faced the slave,

Which ne'er shook hands nor bade farewell to him,
Till he unseamed him from the nave to th' chops,
And fixed his head upon our battlements.

(*Macbeth*, 1.2.16–23)

In the Prologue to *Troilus and Cressida*, the "vehement" (or strongly forceful) figuration is mainly confined to a metaphoric diction that animates the machinery of war ("disgorges") or endows it with purpose ("corresponsive and fulfilling"). In Shakespeare's English history plays, this mode of figurative animation is typically employed to heighten the terrifying prospect of siege weaponry, as in King John's "great words" in 2.1 describing the French weaponry that is threatening the "winking gates" and "sleeping stones" of Angers' fortifications:

These flags of France that are advancèd here
Before the eye and prospect of your town,
Have hither marched to your endamagement.
The cannons have their bowels full of wrath,
And ready mounted are they to spit forth
Their iron indignation 'gainst your walls.

(*King John*, 2.1.207–12)

Both the Prologue and John's speech before Angers bring prospective violence vividly into view through a proleptic tactic of negating attributive adjectives: we are asked to imagine "the fresh and yet *unbruisèd* Greeks" (*Troilus and Cressida*, Prologue, 14), and the citizens are implored "To save *unscratched* your city's threatened cheeks" (*King John*, 2.1.225, emphasis added). This "vehement" device contributes to the much-valued rhetorical heightening associated with "*enargeia*," Aristotle's term for description so vivid that it makes an event seem as if before your very eyes. In fact, a great innovation of Shakespeare's war rhetoric is its invention of prospective rather than retrospective scenes of action and violence. However familiar the long speeches of messengers narrating past and offstage actions may be from classical drama, these are remarkably infrequent in Shakespearean drama. Where they do occur, Shakespeare usually endeavors to rewrite static narration and replicate the "fog of war" through a stream of contradictory news and half-knowing messengers, as when Northumberland receives contradictory "certain news from Shrewsbury" (2 *Henry IV*, 1.1.12), first of Hotspur's triumph, then his death. More often the terror of war scenes is cast as future prospect. King Henry V's threatening oration before the gates of Harfleur (*Henry V*, 3.4) does not specifically deploy the verbal trope previously illustrated, which *does* precisely what it seems to *undo* – "your yet unviolated maidens," "your unwasted town" – but the entire speech can be understood as amplifying that rhetorical strategy. It makes vivid, present, and alarmingly *actual* the future *possibility* of Harfleur's brutalized citizenry and devastated city. "Stirring" sentences are created, not so much by suspended syntax, as by the forward rush of repeated questions ("What is it then to me if impious war, / ... / Do with his smirched complexion all fell feats / Enlinked to waste and desolation? / What is't to me ... / If your pure maidens fall into the hand / Of hot and forcing violation?" [3.4.15–21]), momentarily interrupted by the "out" clause ("Therefore, you men of Harfleur, / Take pity of your town and of your people" [27–28]), but then immediately reverting to and driving home through specific imagery the imminent violence. Just as military machines are animated and rendered purposeful, so human action in the war is dissociated from its regular controls and patterns of causation. Henry washes his hands of responsibility, disavowing control over "impious war" or the "blind and bloody soldier," and it is not the soldier who dashes fathers against walls and spits infants upon pikes but either "heady murder, spoil, and villany" or (in the frequent use of synecdoche) "foul hand" or some other disassociated body part (3.4.32–34). Transforming what might have been cast as a static war narration into a threatening oration, turning description into terrorizing speech action, Shakespeare harnesses rhetoric's power to arouse powerful emotion and to move hearers to action. Versions of the "if ... if not" scenario, casting description as fearsome prospect, recur frequently in Shakespeare's deployment of the grand style for scenes of warfare (e.g., Bolingbroke before Flint Castle in *Richard II*, 3.3.31–61). The "endamagement" war produces, then as now, lies in the psychology of fear as well as in ruined lives and walls. In this strategy of prospective narration, Shakespeare illustrates the power of speech itself to constitute an act of war.

## Words of War: Updating the Lexicon

Specialized military vocabulary is one of the most obvious ways to impart a sense of specificity about military engagements in plays, where the weaponry that can actually be brought onto the stage is necessarily limited. If Shakespeare's military diction draws on age-old classical rhetorical figuration, it also shows evidence of being up-to-date in vocabulary, new-made in the English language. When the "gallant Hotspur" (*1 Henry IV*, 1.1.52) is so consumed with anticipation of glorious exploits in "iron wars" that he shouts out in his sleep, his wife, Lady Percy, hears him rehearse elaborate terms of warfare:

> Speak terms of manage to thy bounding steed,
> Cry, "Courage! To the field!" And thou has talked
> Of sallies and retires, of trenches, tents,

> Of palisadoes, frontiers, parapets,
> Of basilisks, of cannon, culverin,
> Of prisoners' ransom, and of soldiers slain,
> And all the currents of a heady fight.  (2.3.44–50)

The speech shows off what another Shakespearean character calls "fire-new words" (*Love's Labor's Lost*, 1.1.176) – here, specifically, loanwords freshly imported into early modern English from European languages and combat zones. Siege warfare is an ancient practice, but it is updated here with modern terminology to acknowledge the latest in defensive and offensive armaments. For *palisado*, borrowed from Spanish, the *Oxford English Dictionary* (OED) cites Paul Ive's 1589 *Practise of Fortification* for its first recorded English use.[5] Ive writes of how vulnerable old towns and frontier forts "enclosed with weake walles of stone" are to the weaponry of modern siege warfare, "insufficient to abide the mallice and offence that an enemy at this day may put in practise, the Cannon being an engine of much more force then any before it inuented."[6] "Palisadoes" and "parapets" (borrowed from Italian around 1575) are constructions Ive commends among the military engineer's added defenses against modern ordinance weapons. Hotspur's terms, "basilisks" and "culverin" name newer cannons regarded as devastating threats in siege warfare (also used, in recent memory, in naval engagement with the Spanish Armada). With reference to a weapon said to weigh "9000 pounds, eight inches, and thrée quarters within the mouth," and clearly as terrifying as the mythical reptile from which it takes its name by metaphorical transference, the "basilisk" is first recorded in English use (according to the *OED*) in William Harrison's *Description of England*, where all three of Hotspur's terms for artillery appear in a list of the "names of our greatest ordinance."[7]

The period from 1570 to 1630 witnessed the "fastest vocabulary growth" in English in proportion to overall vocabulary, with lexical borrowing a key contributor to the enhanced copiousness of the word stock.[8] Overall, Latin was the primary source language, but for specialized military vocabulary English imported wholesale from French, Italian, Spanish, and other European languages. In the later sixteenth century, "words such as *ambush*, *alarm*, *squadron*, *infantry*, *cavalry*, and *artillery* comprised a linguistic invasion altogether more successful than any of Philip of Spain's armadas."[9] In the theater, Marlowe had led the way in bringing high-tech novel military vocabulary together with the poetic grandeur of his overreaching conqueror's style. Marlowe not only borrowed new terms from specialized military works like Ive's *Practice of Fortification* but took care to gloss the unfamiliar vocabulary: lecturing on the "rudiments of war," Tamburlaine, for example, explains how forts "must have high argins and covered ways / To keep the bulwark fronts from battery, / And parapets to hide the musketeers, / Casemates to place the great artillery" (2 *Tamburlaine*, 3.2.54, 75–78).[10] Shakespeare's assimilation of this new military vocabulary related especially to siege warfare of his time is not simply a matter of borrowing specialized terms in imitation of Marlowe to update and amplify descriptions of war scenes. To see how some of the specific terminology takes hold in Shakespeare's imagination, one has only to consider the evocative metaphors in *Hamlet* that apply or "translate" various modern European words for siege or land warfare to other spheres of activity, as where Old Hamlet's ghost "work[s] i'th' earth" like a "*pioneer*" (1.5.164–65), or where Hamlet imagines outwitting an opponent who, like the "engineer" setting explosives to breach a fortification, is "Hoist with his own *petard*" (3.4.207–8), or where "sorrows" assail Claudius not as "single spies, / But in *battalions*" (4.2.77–78, emphasis added).

The meeting up of modernized war technology with the grand style fired the imagination of the young Winston Churchill as he shaped his account of his early experience with frontier warfare in *The Story of the Malakand Field Force*, first published in 1898. As the epigraph for what he described as the most technical of his chapters, "Military Observations," Churchill specifically chose Kate's report of Hotspur's obsession with the machinery of modern war – "And thou hast talk'd / Of sallies and retires, of trenches, tents, / Of palisadoes, frontiers, parapets, / Of basilisks, of cannon, culverin."[11] It is clear that an immersion in Shakespeare's war rhetoric had an enormous shaping influence on Churchill's own military imagination, which (as Paul Stevens has discussed) never wholly shook off an apprehension of warfare as a "grand imperial adventure."[12] The identification in the epigraph of his interests with Hotspur's is only one sign among others of the Shakespearean influence in *The Story of the Malakand Field Force* upon his military self-fashioning. The epigraph for the volume as a whole is drawn from Shakespeare's *King John*, specifically the Bastard Falconbridge's words as he takes upon himself an embassy of war in the final act: "According to the fair play of the world, / Let me have audience" (5.2.118–19). The *OED* defines the "theatre of war," an expression often used by Churchill in *The Story of the Malakand Field Force* and elsewhere, rather colorlessly as "a particular region ... in which a war is being fought," but for Churchill it clearly provided a guiding metaphor, constructing the war scene as a testing place for manly endeavor, a stage (like the one Hotspur seeks) upon which to perform greatness.

## The Ideology of the Grand Style

Adopting the grand style as the default for war has consequences. First, obviously enough, it takes for granted, and invites its audience to take for granted, that war is a dignified and elevated subject matter, a fit match for the heightened style. This is not to say that Shakespeare invariably represents war in a uniform way as positive, or glamorous, or among the highest of heroic activities. Shakespeare can, and does, explore ways to answer back to the ideological resonances of his predominant stylistic choice. For example, in *Troilus and Cressida*, the high style rises in the mouth of Agamemnon and others to grandiosity and tips into parodic bombast reinforced by a surround of satiric voices. Nonetheless, the default choice helps set the questions that are implicitly being raised about war and the basic terms of any talk-back or countering debate that might suggest instead that war can be a trivial matter or a pernicious and degrading pursuit, that its quarrel-picking can (as Hamlet suggests of Fortinbras) be over "a straw" (4.1.54). A pacifist or a skeptical or a realist attitude is not the base chord when you begin with the grand style.

Second, the classical principle of decorum that dictates the choice of styles is not merely an aesthetic or literary tradition. It is also a social doctrine. To choose the high style is coextensive with the choice of kings, nobility, and generals as the main cast of characters. Richard Helgerson argued that Shakespeare's histories "are based on *exclusions*": among "historical players," they favor "the monarchical-aristocratic bloc," and "render others invisible or marginal."[13] A principle of identification and generalization is often brought forward to justify the king- or nobility-centric point of view of Shakespeare's Elizabethan theater, as if these "great ones" model behaviors viewers can emulate. As Thomas Heywood described this potential identification in Shakespeare's own day, "what English blood seeing the person of any bold English man presented and doth not hugge his fame, and hunnye at his valor, pursuing him in his enterprise with his best wishes ... as if the Personator were the man Personated, so bewitching a thing is liuely and well spirited action, that it hath power to new mold the harts of the spectators and fashion them to the shape of any noble and notable attempt."[14] But neither a king's motivation nor a prince or general's experience of war can be shared and emulated by the wide range of the population. Erasmus's *Complaint of Peace* (1517) emphasizes this lack of common ground between princes or military leaders and common people, commenting on how recent European wars, mostly competitions for territory, "were all started in the interests of princes and carried on with great suffering for the people, although they were in no sense the people's concern": "As things are now, princes wage war unscathed and their generals thrive on it, while the main flood of misfortune sweeps over the peasants and humble citizens, who have no interest in war and gave no occasion for it."[15]

Shakespeare's plays do, of course, repeatedly remark upon this problem, debating the significance to the greater majority of combatants or to affected noncombatants of Helen's seizure and secured possession in *Troilus and Cressida* or of the "little patch of ground" in Poland that young Fortinbras, "with divine ambition puffed," seeks to gain (*Hamlet*, 4.1.17, 48). The point that the political motivation of the war is not the citizens' concern is strikingly made in *King John*, where the warring kings entirely fail in their effort to engage the besieged citizens of Angers to make their voices known on the matter of legitimate possession of the city. To a limited extent then, Shakespeare's plays take note of this divergence of interests and include some citizens' or women's or conscripts' voices, but never in any proportion that can truly offset the built-in bias of the default grand style and its implicit social ideology. That is not to denigrate losing ourselves in enjoyment of Shakespeare's plays, which, for the most part are not actively warmongering, but, as with all ideological rhetoric we should also be ready to call seriously into question the effects of a stirring elevated style capable of making spectators lose themselves, feeling like the co-participants they cannot be. It is easy enough to regard rhetorical style as innocent, style as ornamental, but with the alliance of the grand style to the violence of war, with its power to rouse and stir emotions, it is not inert. Cicero distinguished the grand style from the simple and middle style not solely in relation to subject and speaker, but especially in relation to its forceful kind of action upon the listener: whereas the simple style is "for proving," the middle style "for pleasing," the "vehement style [is] for moving."[16] Rushing "along with the roar of a mighty stream," the grand style has "power to sway men's minds and move them in every possible way. Now it storms the feelings, now it creeps in; it implants new ideas and uproots the old."[17]

Sylvia Adamson contends that Renaissance ideals of eloquence and corresponding interpretations of rhetoric pulled in two opposite directions: toward the "ornamental" or the "armamental."[18] On the one side she points to John Colet's ideal in founding St. Paul's school of Christianizing classical rhetoric, of educating children by reading authors "that hathe with wisdome joyned the pure chaste eloquence."[19] On the other side she points to evocations of the "power" accorded in an orator's forceful persuasions, so that (in Henry Peacham's words in *The Garden of Eloquence*) – he "is in a maner the emperour of mens minds."[20] Peacham, as Adamson points out, characterizes rhetoric "as an arsenal of 'martiall instruments both of defence & inuasion ... weapons alwaies readie in our hands.'"[21] Wayne Rebhorn also reflects on the contradictory ideals ascribed to Renaissance eloquence. In its peacemaking aspect it invites "a fundamentally dialogic view of life," encouraging skepticism by teaching students to argue cases from different perspectives; but, where "animated by a fantasy of power," it often construes "the orator, wielding words more deadly than swords, tak[ing] on the world and emerg[ing] victorious" (like Tamburlaine) as "a conqueror, a ruler – even in some treatises, something close to a god."[22] Rebhorn expresses strong concern about the "fantasy of imperial, absolutist power at the heart" of eloquent discourse.[23] When powerful leaders in times of war (like Winston Churchill or Margaret Thatcher) turn for inspiration to the stirring words of Shakespeare's grand style from Falconbridge in *King John*, from Hotspur in *1 Henry IV*, or from Henry V, it is often this "armamental" power they harness (whether consciously or unconsciously) as, sweeping people into the embrace of what may serve their masters more than them and without full control over potential "endamagement," they "let slip the dogs of war" (*Julius Caesar*, 3.1.275).

## Dialogue and the Limits of Verbal Negotiation: The Case of *King John*

"We start wars by words also, and carry them on in that way too."
Alberico Gentili[24]

Clearly, it would be naive to expect Shakespeare's plays to separate out war as the province of violent blows and armed conflict from a peaceful sphere of words and linguistic engagement. But, if the verbal representation of past battles and of threatened future violence tends in Shakespearean accounts of war to rise dangerously in pitch toward an "armamental" grand style, what about the dialogic interactions we might expect to foster mutual understanding, and especially the diplomatic conversations that constitute specific efforts at peacemaking? Surely both Shakespeare's humanist schooling and a wider rhetorical culture promoting civil conversation fostered faith in dialogic intercourse as a peacemaking alternative to force and violence. Even if an orator's or a leader's "armamental" rhetoric could intensify and glorify violent conflict as heroic adventure, surely diplomacy and dialogue could supply a countervailing dynamic, conducive to mutual cooperation and peaceful coexistence?

*King John* is an unusually illuminating play in which to explore the dialogic intercourse of war. Unlike many Shakespearean plays in which war is the occasional backdrop to the overall action or the condition of extreme breakdown (or necessary remedy) in situations focused on other themes, the state of war is very nearly a constant in *King John*, either as imminent or actual. Nonetheless, while the play does incorporate a few battle scenes, Shakespeare expended little energy on choreographing physical combat, relying on the stereotypical stage direction, "Alarums, excursions" to cover the occurrence of fighting offstage. What is foregrounded to represent the omnipresence of war is instead a series of highly charged dialogic encounters. Most begin with an appearance of civility and formal decorum and quickly deteriorate into impassionate outbursts and spectacular quarrelling, ingenious in their rhetorical coloring even as everything spins out of control. As we have seen, some of this dialogue consists in the prospective narration of violent conflict I have previously characterized, with threatening speeches of the "if ... if not" structure exchanged, as exemplified by King Philip of France's ultimatum to the citizens of besieged Angers to accept Arthur Plantagenet (over John) as their ruler or suffer ruinous defeat:

> For this downtrodden equity we tread
> In warlike march these greens before your town,
>
> . . .
>
>               Be pleasèd then
> To pay that duty which you truly owe
> To him that owes it, namely this young prince,
> And then our arms, like to a muzzled bear,
> Save in aspect, hath all offense sealed up.
> Our cannons' malice vainly shall be spent
> Against th'invulnerable clouds of heaven,
> And with a blessèd and unvexed retire,
> With unhacked swords and helmets all unbruised,
> We will bear home that lusty blood again
> Which here we came to spout against your town,
> And leave your children, wives, and you in peace.
> But if you fondly pass our proffered offer,
> 'Tis not the roundure of your old-faced walls
> Can hide you from our messengers of war.

$$(2.1.241-42, 246-60)$$

Nonetheless, a high proportion of the dialogue occurs during "parles" or short truces, with the exchange presented quite explicitly either as a "conference" in which opponents aim at persuasion through reasoned arguments or as a diplomatic negotiation in which a formally appointed ambassador or informal envoy works to secure "peace and fair-faced league" (2.1.417).

Confidence in the possibility of reasoned dispute resolution (or of the virtue of compromise) is expressed at the outset of the play by King John's mother, Queen Eleanor, who comments, after the French ambassador has delivered an ultimatum of "fierce and bloody war" (1.1.17) that the situation "might have been prevented and made whole / With very easy arguments of love, / Which now the manage of two kingdoms must / With fearful bloody issue arbitrate" (1.1.35–38). What is openly disputed between the two kings and their allies once a face-to-face parley preceding the combat before Angers is called are their respective justifications of war, hinging on whether John or his nephew Arthur is the rightful claimant to the crown of England and to rule of the Angevin territories. This dispute, of course, touches upon the premises of "just war theory," which imagines hellish war not as indifferently amoral (or immoral) but as (at least in some circumstances) a principled and moral practice for the side defending right.[25] Historical scholars may have very decided opinions about the right or wrong of King John's claims (whether those of the historical man or the dramatic character), but Shakespeare engineers the rhetoric of the play and the quarreling factions in such a way as to set up equivalences between the disputing opponents. Two strong women – Queen Eleanor (John's mother) and Constance (Arthur's mother) – go head to head in the quarrel and repeatedly are made to sound identical in their charges against one another:

> QUEEN ELEANOR: Thou monstrous slanderer of heaven and earth!
> CONSTANCE: Thou monstrous injurer of heaven and earth!
>
> (2.1.173–74)

The complete symmetry between one side and the other is reinforced in a number of ways, with the kings each in his way characterizing the women's quarrels as "ill-tunèd repetitions" (2.1.197) and with symmetrical word repetition, as in King John's initial response to the French ambassador Chatillon's threat of war as "Here have we war for war and blood for blood, / Controlment for controlment" (1.1.19–20), accenting the likeness rather than moral difference of the two sides. As the episode degenerates into name-calling and quarrels, it becomes clear that the prospect for reasoned "conference" deteriorates into what one character calls an "abundance of superfluous breath" (2.1.150, 148). Clearly, the rhetorical argumentation on display cannot be construed as a show of that humanist "wisdom with eloquence" conducive to the dialogic weighing of right and wrong and a peaceful resolution of a conflict. In this play at least, Shakespeare appears to express extreme skepticism about speech acts justifying war, making them indistinguishable from one another, inefficacious, and apparently more motivated by self-interest than justice. This is in line with the views of a key jurist of Shakespeare's time, Alberico Gentili, who "broke away from the classical just war doctrine with its view of war as a unilateral instrument of justice," imagining war more often to be "a contest for victory between equal parties."[26] He broached the idea of a "subjectively just cause" and reliance of leaders on "individual conscience": a prince had the right to decide for himself, but "whatever the result of his decision may be, it never affects the legality of his action, since war is nothing more than a procedural device that may be resorted to even for the redress of a probable wrong."[27] Far from the argumentation in *King John* conducing to rational weighing of the justice of either side, so that argumentative dialogue discovers right and conduces to peaceful resolution, speech acts of justification in this play are "words of war." If these speech acts and the political objective they articulate have a role in persuading anyone, it appears to be as self-persuasion or as rhetorical motivation to secure the adherence of one's own fighting forces and allies to a shared aim. The play's skepticism about the role of argumentation in war is also in line with the skepticism about rational guiding motives for war expressed by the pragmatic nineteenth-century military theorist, Carl von Clausewitz, who defines war as "an act of force to compel our enemy to do our will."[28] Indeed, as the respective arguments of John's and Arthur's sides of the controversy unravel in *King John* 2.1, the polysemous word "will" and accusations of willfulness on either side are bandied about:

> QUEEN ELEANOR: Thou unadvisèd scold, I can produce
>  A *will* that bars the title of thy son.
> CONSTANCE: Ay, who doubts that? A *will*, a wicked *will*,
>  A woman's *will*, a cankered grandam's *will*.
> (2.1.191–94, emphasis added)

Any opposition between peacemaking words and death-dealing war that a believer in rational dialogue might try to hold on to is powerfully deconstructed in King John's speech warning the citizens of Angers that King Philip's persuasive words are just substitute weapons:

> Behold, the French, amazed, vouchsafe a parle;
> And now, instead of bullets wrapped in fire
> To make a shaking fever in your walls,
> They shoot but calm words folded up in smoke,
> To make a faithless error in your ears.   (2.1. 226–30)

### Ambassadors and the Dialogue of War: The Case of *King John*

If the quarrels of *King John* bear out Gentili's observation that "We start wars by words also, and carry them on in that way too," can we nonetheless salvage a positive role for civil conversation in the war-ending labors of ambassadors and diplomatic mediators? Usually in Shakespeare, the outcomes of wars are determined by force not words. *King John* stands apart in its investigation of negotiated outcomes and its interest in diplomatic communication. Among the cast we encounter a host of professional diplomats – including Chatillon, the French ambassador to England; the Heralds of France and England; and, most prominent in stopping (and starting!) wars, Cardinal Pandulph, the papal legate. In addition to the performances of these professionals, key acts of diplomacy are highlighted in 2.1 when a Citizen of Angers emerges as an impromptu international negotiator, offering the two "great Kings" a route to "peace and fair-faced league" (2.1.416–17), and in 5.2 when Philip Falconbridge briefly and self-consciously plays at undertaking an ambassadorial role.

The perspective *King John* offers on the civil conversation of peacemaking diplomacy is also surprisingly negative. Gentili's observations both in his treatise on embassies (1585) and his work on war provide useful context. First, Gentili writes against the long-standing truism that the "business" of an ambassador "is peace": as the fifteenth-century writer Bernard du Rossier put this idealistic position, "An ambassador labours for the public good."[29] Citing his direct disagreement with Tasso's observation that "every ambassador is a man of peace," Gentili insists on the category of the "ambassador of war."[30] Chatillon's mission to England (like the French ambassadors with their tennis balls in *Henry V* 1.2) fits the bill of Gentili's "ambassador of war," the spokesperson commissioned to stay within a prearranged script and, supported by the "fair play" conditions that guarantee his personal safety even when inflaming hostility, "wages war by means of words, the only weapons he can use."[31] Chatillon's business in the English court is to deliver King Philip's insult, demand (without expectation of result) that John relinquish his "borrowed" sovereignty to Arthur, speak the "if not" threat of "fierce and bloody war," and pronounce "my King's defiance from my mouth, / The farthest limit of my embassy" (1.1.4, 17, 21–22). Even more programmatically, the role of French and English heralds in the play is represented as furthering the business of war, even where (without expectation of peacemaking) its customs require parleys before direct use of force and outright acts of slaughter.

That said, the play highlights mediators' roles and their linguistic interventions in halting combat. We shall see how Gentili's reflections on preferred ways to end wars and Erasmus's complaints about the dubious advantages of league-making can provide illuminating context to help us understand why peacemaking diplomatic language is ultimately cast in a very negative light in *King John*. Counterintuitively, Gentili regarded a negotiated peace as inferior to a resolution of conflict by victory: "In Gentili's system, peace by agreement was only arrived at through a chain of human failings. If war was a substitute for adjudication in the face of man's failure to discern right from wrong, peace without victory was a failure thereof.... Under Gentili's system, peace through agreement was one step further removed from the ideal workings of justice than peace through victory."[32] In *King John*, two types of diplomatic peacemaking are foregrounded: one that seeks resolution by means of league-making and marital alliance and the other that accepts guidance from the supposedly higher wisdom of the church. The first negotiated "peace" comes about when a bold Citizen of Angers steps forth to propose a marital alliance between Lady Blanche of Spain, who is "near [i.e., close kin] to England" (2.1.424), and Louis the dauphin of France. Blanche quickly bends her "will" (2.1.513) to "My uncle's [King John's] will" (2.1.510) in this matter and Louis the dauphin's protestation of love quickly resolves King Philip to agree. "We will heal up all" (550), John concludes, and all looks rosy for the moment until Constance's spectacular performances of her grief make it clear how this "healing" papers over broken vows by France and his allies supporting Arthur and ignores the implications for everyone's claims about why they came initially to conflict. From here on, the play's pendulum swings wildly back and forth between "peace" and "war," in what increasingly looks like ongoing and potentially endless cycles of violent conflict.

However commonsensical it may seem to prefer alliance to armed combat, the play undermines and critiques such shortsighted league-making, beginning with the Bastard's comments on the kings' "purpose-chang[ing]" (567). "Mad world, mad kings, mad composition!" (561), he exclaims, and pronounces "tickling commodity" (573) to have been the true "broker" of the agreement. This character – Coeur-de-lion's natural son, Philip Falconbridge (later Sir Richard Plantagenet) – plays an interesting role in the play's critique of diplomatic negotiation, serving the audience throughout the play as a sort of surrogate ear and linguistic interpreter. In 1.1, he entered the English court as a newcomer and outsider, and part of his initial characterization turned on his bemused anatomy of the routinized question-and-answer structure of courtly "dialogue[s] of compliment," which sounded like empty catechizing to him: "'My dear sir' – / Thus ... I begin – / 'I shall beseech you.' That is Question now, / And then comes Answer like an Absey book: / 'O sir,' says Answer, 'at your best command, / At your employment, at your service, sir'" (1.1.193–98). He brings this metalinguistic turn toward analysis to bear on the well-crafted persuasive oration of the actual broker of the peacemaking deal, the Citizen of Angers. In his assessment of the Citizen's speech, we are once again confronted with a viewpoint that deconstructs any idealistic opposition between words and weapons:

> Here's a large mouth indeed,
> That spits forth death and mountains, rocks and seas,
> . . .
> What cannoneer begot this lusty blood?
> He speaks plain cannon-fire and smoke and bounce;
> He gives the bastinado with his tongue.
> Our ears are cudgeled; not a word of his
> But buffets better than a fist of France.
> Zounds! I was never so bethumped with words.   (2.1.457–66)

The play's critique of this kind of league-making is in line with Erasmus's critique in *The Complaint of Peace*: "Peace is not to be found in various leagues or confederations of men, which are ofttimes the very sources and cause of wars."[33] How can this be? It is well to remember that *King John* interrogates warfare and league-making diplomacy within a specific historical landscape: not a landscape of clearly delimited nation-states but of medieval European Christendom, where, according to Mattingly, "large parts of the political map of Europe presented an intricate puzzle of partial and overlapping sovereignties."[34] Philip's initial challenge made through his ambassador Chatillon on behalf of Arthur Plantagenet is to a widely dispersed range of lands – "To this fair island and the territories – / To Ireland, Poitou, Anjou, Touraine, Maine" (1.1.10–11), a collectivity of lands variously assembled as Angevin possessions under Henry II through such mechanisms as armed aggression and dynastic marriage and inheritance. They were held, as Chatillon mentioned, under "several titles" (as king of England, duke of Normandy, count of Anjou, etc.); with "several titles" (13) went "several" mechanisms of administration and succession, complicated by the Angevins owing feudal homage in the case of some French possessions to the king of France as overlord. No wonder the citizens of Angers deny any clear-cut opinion on who is their rightful ruler. This is the kind of situation Erasmus describes as obtaining in Europe when he writes his *Complaint of Peace*, a Europe where, he laments, Christians, "members of one body," war against themselves: "how often do 20,000 armed Christians fight 20,000 armed Christians?"[35] At the root of the problem of warfare within the family of Christendom, in Erasmus's view, is not only a lust for power but also, critically, the dispersed lands and impermanent borders of kingdoms, which promote a "constant change of empire." He proposes a vision of peaceful kingdoms keeping within defined bounds, secured not by marriages creating far-flung dynastic alliances that potentially multiply future contenders for thrones but by royal marriages made within the country and by increased clarity over rules of succession.[36]

In *King John*, the same dynamic appears to be at work, with the "friendly treaty" (2.1.481) promoted by the citizen mediator ultimately triggering renewed conflict in England between Dauphin Louis and King John, no longer justified by Arthur's claims but by Louis's own enhanced claims through marriage to title and sovereignty. As Constance puts it, what the league-making peace helps to trigger is "War, war, no peace! Peace is to me a war" (3.1.39). And it is, of course, her own dynastic ambitions and her opponent Eleanor of Aquitaine's Angevin empire-advancing marital contributions that have helped to inflame earlier conflicts.

Nonetheless, before the full consequences of this first "inglorious league" (5.1.65) are felt, another style of diplomatic communication comes into play with the entrance of the pope's legate, Cardinal Pandulph. The church, while claiming it seeks "universal peace," regularly fomented the wars (Erasmus claims) between "20,000 armed Christians fight[ing] 20,000 armed Christians,"[37] and that is precisely what Pandulph proceeds to do. He excommunicates and curses John (not for any wrongs hitherto in the play attributed to him, but for not bowing to the pope's edicts regarding ecclesiastical appointments and tithes) and he orders Philip, "on peril of a curse, / Let go the hand of that arch-heretic, / And raise the power of France upon his head" (3.1.117–19). The commandment precipitates a crisis of "faith" in Philip. As Pandulph sums up Philip's situation, "So mak'st thou faith [pledged in league-making] an enemy to [Christian] faith, / And like a civil war sett'st oath to oath, / Thy tongue against thy tongue" (3.1.189–91). Pandulph's brand of diplomacy is pure abuse of power. He seems to relish the chaos he stirs up and to delight in his warmongering in the name of "mother" church (3.1.67). Later in the play, having egged Louis on "by the honor of [his] marriage bed, / After young Arthur [to] claim this land [of England] for mine" (5.2.93–94), a land Louis has by this time "half-conquered" (95), Pandulph abruptly does an about-turn and commands peace. He claims that since "King John hath reconciled / Himself to Rome," therefore Louis should "thy threatening colors now wind up, / And tame the savage spirit of wild war, / That, like a lion fostered up at hand, / It may lie gently at the foot of peace" (5.2.69–70, 73–76). *King John*'s depiction of the commodity-serving papal legate is consistent with Erasmus's complete cynicism in *The Complaint of Peace* about the pope's authority in relation to war-making and peacemaking: "When the pope issues a summons to war," he comments, "men obey. Why is it that they cannot exhibit a similar obedience when he calls for peace? If they prefer peace, why did they obey Pope Julius, the author of war? Hardly anyone has obeyed Pope Leo in his exhortation to peace."[38] Indeed, Louis does not obey Pandulph's injunctions to peace in 5.2 and fierce battle ensues.

Thus, contrary to the optimism voiced in classical and Renaissance rhetoric and in humanist pedagogy about eloquent language creating cooperative communities, in Shakespeare's *King John*, dialogic art – whether as reasoned argument or diplomatic negotiation – is far from peacemaking. Even where dialogue contributes through league-making to temporary cessations of violence, the play repeatedly suggests that these alliances contain the seeds of future conflict. Of course, if we seek to generalize about Shakespeare's views on civil conversation – to ask whether he considers verbal dialogue an affordance more conducive to war or to peace – we must consider how he writes each play as a fresh experiment. Still, while no other play is so explicitly critical of diplomatic endeavor in wartime as *King John*, it is hard to think of counterexamples demonstrating the efficacy of rhetorical pleading or dialogic negotiation to counter the violence of war. Volumnia's intervention in *Coriolanus* might be said to offer an isolated example. A longer analysis might consider the planning of large-scale warfare in Shakespeare as itself an accomplishment dependent on highly choreographed collaborative action and successfully coordinated communication. His wars certainly demonstrate how any massive mobilization of forces demands alliance building as a key prerequisite for the effective conduct of warfare. The depiction of dialogue among military allies (and not just between enemies) deserves further analysis. Yet even a quick survey of alliances (Talbot and Somerset, Henry IV and Hotspur, Hotspur and Glyndŵr, Octavius and Antony, Brutus and Cassius) is enough to remind us how often quarrels, fallings off, and betrayal beset cooperative pacts in Shakespeare's plays. Even if Antony and Octavius emerge as victorious allies at Philippi in *Julius Caesar*, what the art of Shakespeare's dialogue captures is their tension-filled contrariety and collision of wills:

> ANTONY: Octavius, lead your battle softly on
>     Upon the left hand of the even field.
> OCTAVIUS: Upon the right hand, I. Keep thou the left.
> ANTONY: Why do you cross me in this exigent?
> OCTAVIUS: I do not cross you, but I will do so.
>     *March.*
>
> *(Julius Caesar,* 5.1.16–20)

On the whole, Shakespeare reserves for comedy and romance the exploration of dialogue as a vehicle for reconciliation. Military engagement in the histories and tragedies affords more often a space to explore how the linguistic gift said to be humankind's "greatest advantage over the brute creation" – "that we can hold converse one with another"[39] – contributes to those forceful conflicts of will Clausewitz identifies as warfare.

## Further Reading

Adamson, Sylvia. "The Grand Style," in Adamson, Lynette Hunter, Lynne Magnusson, Ann Thompson, and Katie Wales (eds.), *Reading Shakespeare's Dramatic Language: A Guide*, London, Arden Shakespeare, 2001, pp. 31–50.

"Literary Language," in Roger Lass (ed.), *The Cambridge History of the English Language, Vol. 3, 1476–1776*, Cambridge, Cambridge University Press, 1999, pp. 539–653.

Erasmus, Desiderius. *A Complaint of Peace Spurned and Rejected by the Whole World*, ed. A. H. T. Levi, trans. Betty Radice, vol. XXVII of *The Collected Works of Erasmus*, Toronto, University of Toronto Press, 1986, pp. 292–322.

Gentili, Alberico. *De Iure Belli Libri Tres (Three Books on the Law of War)* (1612 ed.), trans. John C. Rolfe, 2 vols., Oxford, Clarendon Press, 1933.

*De Legationibus Libri Tres (Three Books on Embassies)* (1585), ed. Ernest Nys, 2 vols., New York, Oxford University Press, 1924.

Hampton, Timothy. "The Slumber of War: Diplomacy, Tragedy, and the Aesthetics of the Truce in Early Modern Europe," in Nathalie Rivere de Carles (ed.), *Early Modern Diplomacy, Theatre and Soft Power: The Making of Peace*, London, Palgrave Macmillan, 2016, pp. 27–45.

Jorgenson, Paul A. *Shakespeare's Military World*, Berkeley, University of California Press, 1956.

Mattingly, Garrett. *Renaissance Diplomacy*, London, Jonathan Cape, 1963.

Quabeck, Franziska. *Just and Unjust Wars in Shakespeare*, Berlin, Walter de Gruyter, 2013.

Rebhorn, Wayne A. *The Emperor of Men's Minds: Literature and the Renaissance Discourse of Rhetoric*, Ithaca, Cornell University Press, 1995.

Somogyi, Nick de. *Shakespeare's Theatre of War*, Aldershot, Ashgate, 1998.

## NOTES

1 Cicero, *De oratore*, trans. E. W. Sutton and H. Rackham (Cambridge, MA: Harvard University Press, 1948), bk. 1, 8.30, 8.33–34. For the three levels of style, *Orator*, trans. H. M. Hubbell and G. L. Hendrickson (Cambridge, MA: Harvard University Press, 1962), 5.20–23, 21.69–29, 101; and Quintilian, *Institutio Oratoria: The Orator's Education*, trans. Donald A. Russell (Cambridge, MA: Harvard University Press, 2001), bk. 12, 10.58.

2 Christopher Marlowe, *Tamburlaine, Parts One and Two*, ed. Anthony B. Dawson, New Mermaids, 2nd ed. (London: A & C Black, 1997), pt. 1, Prologue, 3–5.

3 Sylvia Adamson, "The Grand Style," in Adamson, Lynette Hunter, Lynne Magnusson, Ann Thompson, and Katie Wales (eds.), *Reading Shakespeare's Dramatic Language: A Guide* (London: Arden Shakespeare, 2001), pp. 31–50, 35–41; and "Literary Language," in Roger Lass (ed.), *The Cambridge History of the English Language, Vol. 3, 1476–1776* (Cambridge: Cambridge University Press, 1999), pp. 539–653, 570–74.

4 George T. Wright, "Hendiadys in *Hamlet*," *PMLA*, 96 (1981), pp. 168–93, 168.

5 For uses of "palizado," see Paul Ive, *The Practise of Fortification* (London: Thomas Orwin, 1589), pp. 36, 37, 38.

6 Ive, *The Practise of Fortification*, p. 36.

7 Raphael Holinshed, *Chronicles of England, Scotland, and Ireland* (1587), vol. 1, bk. 2, ch. 16. The *OED*, citing a Victorian edition, gives the date as 1577, but the parallel texts in *The Holinshed Project* make it clear that the relevant list of ordinance does not appear until 1587: www.cems.ox.ac.uk/holinshed/. Last accessed May 1, 2019.

8 Terttu Nevalainen, "Early Modern English Lexis and Semantics," in Lass (ed.), *Cambridge History of the English Language*, pp. 332–458, 336, 358.

9 Nick de Somogyi, *Shakespeare's Theatre of War* (Aldershot: Ashgate, 1998), p. 76.

10 Somogyi, *Shakespeare's Theatre of War*, p. 73.

11 Winston L. Spencer Churchill, *The Story of the Malakand Field Force: An Episode of Frontier War* (London, Edinburgh, and New York: Thomas Nelson and Sons, 1916), p. 321. The epigraph came to my attention thanks to the Folger Shakespeare Library's exhibition on "Shakespeare's Churchill," October 6, 2018–January 6, 2019, where Churchill's manuscript notes to his publisher concerning chapter epigraphs were displayed.

12 Paul Stevens, "Churchill's War Horse: Children's Literature and the Pleasures of War," in Lissa Paul, Rosemary Ross Johnston, and Emma Short (eds.), *Children's Literature and Culture of the First World War* (New York: Routledge, 2016), pp. 11–29, 11.

13 Jean Howard, "Other Englands: The View from the Non-Shakespearean History Play," in Helen Ostovich, Mary E. Silcox, and Graham Roebuck (eds.), *Other Voices, Other Views: Expanding the Canon in English Renaissance Studies* (Newark: University of Delaware Press, 1999), pp. 135–53, 137–38, summarizing Richard Helgerson, "Staging Exclusion," in *Forms of Nationhood: The Elizabethan Writing of England* (Chicago: University of Chicago Press, 1992), pp. 195–245.

14 Thomas Heywood, *Apology for Actors* (London: Nicholas Okes, 1612), sig. B4r, also quoted in Howard, "Other Englands," p. 136.

15 Desiderius Erasmus, *A Complaint of Peace Spurned and Rejected by the Whole World*, ed. A. H. T. Levi, trans. Betty Radice, vol. XXVII of *The Collected Works of Erasmus* (Toronto: University of Toronto Press, 1986), pp. 292–322, 307, 312; and *The Complaint of Peace*, in *The Essential Erasmus*, trans. John P. Dolan (New York: New American Library), pp. 177–204.

16 Adamson, "The Grand Style," p. 33.

17 Cicero, *Orator*, 28.97.

18 Adamson, "Literary Language," pp. 546–47.

19 Statutes of St. Paul's School, quoted in Adamson, "Literary Language," p. 542.

20 Henry Peacham, *The Garden of Eloquence* (London: Richard Field, 1593), sig. AB3v.

21 Adamson, "Literary Language," p. 546, quoting Peacham, sig. AB4r.

22 Wayne A. Rebhorn, *The Emperor of Men's Minds: Literature and the Renaissance Discourse of Rhetoric* (Ithaca: Cornell University Press, 1995), p. 15.

23 Rebhorn, *The Emperor of Men's Minds*, p. 17.

24 Alberico Gentili, *De Legationibus Libri Tres (Three Books on Embassies)* (1585), ed. Ernest Nys, 2 vols. (New York: Oxford University Press, 1924), vol. II, p. 16.

25 Franziska Quabeck, *Just and Unjust Wars in Shakespeare* (Berlin: Walter de Gruyter, 2013).
26 Randall Lesaffer, "Alberico Gentili's *ius post bellum* and Early Modern Peace Treaties," in Benedict Kingsbury and Benjamin Straumann (eds.), *The Roman Foundation of the Law of Nations: Alberico Gentili and the Justice of Empire* (Oxford: Oxford University Press, 2010), pp. 210–40, 238; and Alberico Gentili, *De Iure Belli Libri Tres (Three Books on the Law of War)* (1612 ed.), trans. John C. Rolfe, 2 vols. (Oxford: Clarendon Press, 1933), vol. II, p. 12.
27 Mary Ellen O'Connell, "Peace and War," in Bardo Fassbinder and Anne Peters (eds.), *The Oxford Handbook of the History of International Law* (Oxford: Oxford University Press, 2012), pp. 272–93, 276, quoting the summary of Gentili's position from Joachim von Elbe, "The Evolution of the Concept of the Just War in International Law," *American Journal of International Law*, 33 (1939), pp. 665–88, 678.
28 Carl von Clausewitz, *On War*, trans. Michael Howard and Peter Paret (New York: Oxford University Press, 2006), p. 13.
29 Garrett Mattingly, *Renaissance Diplomacy* (London: Jonathan Cape, 1963), p. 48.
30 Gentili, *De Legationibus*, p. 17.
31 Gentili, *De Legationibus*, p. 16.
32 Lesaffer, "Alberico Gentili's," pp. 226, 239.
33 Erasmus, *Complaint of Peace*, trans. Dolan, p.193.
34 Mattingly, *Renaissance Diplomacy*, p. 26.
35 Erasmus, *Complaint of Peace*, trans. Dolan, pp. 188–89.
36 Erasmus, *Complaint of Peace*, trans. Dolan, p. 194.
37 Erasmus, *Complaint of Peace*, trans. Dolan, p. 189.
38 Erasmus, *Complaint of Peace*, trans. Dolan, p. 193.
39 Cicero, *De oratore*, 1.8.32.

# 10

MICHAEL HATTAWAY

# Staging Shakespeare's Wars in the Twentieth and Twenty-First Centuries

This chapter will focus on climates of war and the staging of battles in stage and screen versions of Shakespeare's history plays in Britain since the beginning of the twentieth century. It is keyed to the procession of wars over that period, but it is not confined to productions that took place during or soon after them. Two world wars and a handful of lesser conflicts, to say nothing of the Cold War, which lasted from 1947 some forty-five years and beyond, as well as struggles for liberation from colonialism, some of which led to genocides and wars of religion, left deep imprints on the politics and culture of the period that affected the production and design of performances. So did the militarization of criminality: today we commonly speak of "gang warfare." The trope has a long lineage: St. Augustine observed, "Remove justice, and what are kingdoms but gangs of criminals on a large scale? What are criminal gangs but petty kingdoms?"[1] Pastiche commonplaces of gangster movies informed sequences of stage productions, as in the Hall and Barton *Wars of the Roses* (1963), where the sons of York appeared as "solipsistic amoralists, [occupying] a space outside order,"[2] and in Richard Loncraine's film of *Richard III* (1995). Sequences depicting disorderly behavior in civil war – the Cade scenes in 2 *Henry VI*, for example – once seemed simple riots against established order. Some more recent productions have interpreted them as insurrections against unjust establishments. When reflecting on his 1988 production, Adrian Noble decided that "while satirizing Cade's populism ... it is also clear that what the rebels most want is strong government and a revival of national pride – a Peronist rebellion ultimately suppressed by another conservative orator (Clifford)."[3]

"Postwar" means not simply "after war" but "formed by war." The early wars of the twentieth century were, because of technological advances, self-evidently "modern." They were waged when the potencies of globalization were strengthening, and their particular savagery engendered deep moral skepticism, drawing scrutiny to notions of "just wars" as well as the links between morality and actions. Outward residues of the iconology of chivalry disappeared: knights or officers on horseback, glamorous war garb conspicuously badged with heraldic devices, elaborate "colors" or banners, challenges and ritual duels in the middle of battles, and even, to a degree, hand-to-hand fighting. In Noble's Royal Shakespeare Company *Henry V* (1984), soldiers shivered under tarpaulins as rain pelted down on the battlefield. In 1997, Roy Daniels, also for the RSC, conjured ghostly presences from a set, again for *Henry V*, that was "part American Vietnam memorial, part Menin Gate."[4]

We have to acknowledge that the whole period from 1900 to the present is more infused by war than we like to admit. Evocations of the so-called *Pax Americana* conceal ongoing struggles against neocolonialism. Not surprisingly, therefore, Shakespeare's history plays have been decoupled from particular *historical* events and instead become *political* documents – invitations to offer, particularly after Brecht, reflections *on* rather than reflections *of* periods and ideologies. War becomes as much a condition as a subject for theatrical narrative, particularly in the case of plays written largely in verse, which generalizes upon what is shown. The aim of theater directors was once to purvey varieties of realism, often centering on episodes of violence. In contrast, certain more recent productions have, when rendering battles, foregrounded stylized evocations of past values and fighting styles. Sometimes balletic movements have been deployed, sometimes spectacular fantasy, as when, in his 2007 RSC production of *Henry V*, Michael Boyd had the French trapezing across the theater like glorious golden eagles until they were brought down by tracers of white paper to the sound of shooting arrows. Sometimes conflict and struggle are rendered largely through music and sound effects – as was also the custom at early modern performances.[5] In Jane Howell's television version of *3 Henry VI* for the BBC (1981–83) the filming of the battles turned them into nightmarish commentaries on the political narratives. They thereby comprised a diegetic rather than mimetic sequence. Another way of putting this is to say that Shakespeare anatomizes wars rather than, in the manner of blockbuster movies, merely depicting battles.

The gendering of war has proved to be another issue. Uncritical advocacy for macho heroism has been challenged: for instance, in 2014 by Phyllida Lloyd in an all-female *Henry IV* at the Donmar Warehouse, with the two parts combined, and in 2016 when Michelle Terry played Henry V in an Open Air Theatre production in London's Regent's Park directed by Robert Hastie. The effect? Audiences learned, yet again, that both war and authority are essentially performances.

## The Histories and the British Empire

Queen Victoria died in the second year of the twentieth century, her reign having seen British nationalism hugely boosted by the wealth that the industrial revolution and colonialism had generated. In 1877, the Conservative Prime Minister, Benjamin Disraeli, had the queen proclaimed empress of India. This partial conversion of the monarchy was marked, on January 1, 1877, by a huge theatrical spectacle steeped in archaizing iconology, the political pageant known as the Delhi Durbar. As in playhouses, spectacle could be coupled to power.

However, confidence in the Empire was shortly threatened in another part of the world – South Africa. Wars broke out from 1880 between the Dutch settlers of the Transvaal and the British in the Cape Colony. In 1896, the abortive "Jameson Raid" on the Boers was intended to generate what the critic William Archer termed a "spasm of patriotism."[6] In that year too Beerbohm Tree played Falstaff in the rarely seen 2 *Henry IV*: it rekindled awareness of the enduring myths of British monarchy.[7] This was followed three years later by Tree's immensely popular production of *King John*, a play that can be appropriated as another strong evocation of English nationalism.[8] Eventually, Lord Kitchener's "scorched earth policy," the torching of Boer homesteads, and the establishment of concentration camps wherein women and children were imprisoned, brought about a victory, albeit rendered inglorious by its appalling moral costs.

This was the background to two important productions of *Henry V*. The first, by the actor-manager Frank Benson, was a triumphalist rallying cry. Benson was an uncomplicated man of action, playing on sets like those used by Charles Kean (1811–68) – designed to present "realities" rather than to kindle audience imagination. Benson had first directed the play, playing Henry himself, at the Shakespeare Memorial Theatre in Stratford in 1897.[9] He regularly revived it for the next thirty years, often to commemorate St. George's Day – this, conveniently, is also Shakespeare's birthday. The first night of the 1900 London season coincided with the lifting of the Siege of Kimberley when outnumbered British troops were rescued in the Transvaal.[10]

Not surprisingly, Benson played Harry the warrior rather than Henry the man. He reduced 250 lines from the beginning of the play to 20. The moral and political dilemmas raised by the invasion of France disappeared. The fustian account of the roistering Prince Hal's reformation into an "ideal king" (1.1.25–69), and Henry's key demand of the Archbishop of Canterbury, "May I with right and conscience make this claim?" (1.2.96), were cut, as were four of the five choruses.[11] Benson always expunged any traces of sexual explicitness,[12] although the text strongly suggests connections between the male libido and bellicosity.

On stages where spectacle ruled over speech, where scaling-ladders and battering-rams filled the stage,[13] where costumes were matched with sets in order to fix an historical period, and heraldry and antiquarian accuracy trumped the exploration of the possibilities of verse – war became a kingly sport. Benson, in full armor, pole-vaulted onto the walls of Harfleur and installed in the French camp a particularly Edwardian delight: dancing girls (among whom Isadora Duncan made her first appearance on the English stage).[14] We may care to remember that on Ash Wednesday 1599 the popular preacher Lancelot Andrewes (1555–1626) preached a sermon at court, "At what time the Earl of Essex was going forth upon the Expedition for Ireland," in which he pronounced, "War is no matter of sport."[15]

The production generated a scathing review by the young Max Beerbohm: "As a branch of university cricket, the whole performance was, indeed, beyond praise."[16] Decades later, in her BBC television versions of *1–3 Henry VI* and *Richard III*, Jane Howell took an engagingly quizzical look at the "war as sport" topic: in the studio she created a circular playground, ringed with old doors salvaged from curbside skips, within which the players, costumed to look like American footballers, played out their manly games.[17]

However, games can turn nasty, and there were also explicit shots of dying and violence. Stuart Hampton-Reeves and Carol Rutter suggest that the funeral of Henry V was "ghosted" by the televised funeral of Earl Mountbatten, last Viceroy of India, killed by the IRA in 1979, a ceremony which, 102 years after the Delhi Durbar, marked "a symbolic end of Britain's imperial story."[18]

The kinds of decor that were used in Benson's productions may be glimpsed in a film of *Richard III* he made in 1911. Benson maintained his manly bearing – there was no prosthetic hump for his back – and his wife, Constance Benson, played the Lady Anne. It opens with a pageant depicting the triumph of Edward IV over Henry VI at what a title card calls "the Battle of Tewkesbury": a feast of heraldic devices with many armored extras crowding in front of a painted backdrop showing the town from across the River Severn. Despite Shakespeare's injunction against actual horses in the Prologue to *Henry V* (26–27), there is at least one in shot – a paradigmatic example of a reality effect. Elaborately painted backdrops of London streets materialize – a group of children dances before Richard when he offers his brother Edward IV evidence of Clarence's treachery, and many shots include a score of extras to amplify the displays of emotion (Kean had done likewise). Toward the end, Henry Richmond arrives into a painted forest scene, and yet another painted backdrop with a meandering river stands behind Richard's tent at Bosworth. The period's emphasis on historical accuracy and geographical prompting makes it much more difficult to understand that the "histories" are political texts rather than historical pageants, whether these be "true chronicles" or "authentic" representations.

The terminal fight that brings the Wars of the Roses to their conclusion is a virtuoso piece of swordsmanship between Richmond the hero and Richard the antihero. The wars therefore end with a triumph of very English valor and virtue in a duel, a trial by combat, the outcome of which was taken to be God-ordained. Those who saw the production when it was repeated during the Great War perhaps realized this was a sort of propagandist dream: twentieth-century wars were, in great part, won not by well-honed masculinity but by material and technological advantage – as Shakespeare suggests in the first sequence of *1 Henry VI*.

With the outbreak of the First World War, Shakespeare was quickly requisitioned as a weapon: twenty-five of his plays were performed at the Old Vic, and thousands of schoolchildren were brought to matinee performances. Although the quarter-centenary celebrations of his death in 1916 were muffled, many festivities, artistic and political, took place, even if the Easter Uprising in Dublin, which began the day after Shakespeare's birthday, was an insurrection against Britishness.[19] However, that same year, at a matinee in Nottingham, "the whole of the Theatre Royal [was] filled with men in hospital blue. Benson [as Henry V], in full armour, with his helmet surmounted by the fox's brush, gave Henry's speech; for this he had chiming bells to ring in the feast of Crispin."[20] That was a one-day battle: meanwhile, in the "real" France, the Battle of Verdun raged from February till December of that year.

It is scarcely surprising that *Henry V* should again be of prime significance during the Second World War, the focus being Laurence Olivier's 1944 film. Olivier had taken the lead on stage at London's Old Vic in 1937. In fact, the director, Tyrone Guthrie, opened a dialogue with directors who sought theatrical illusion:

> The stage of the Old Vic glows with colour from emblazoned shields and surcoats … and from banners which fall forward and fold themselves into tents for the camp scenes, but this polychromatic splendour is not set off by realistically painted vistas but by a simple arrangement of curtains. The appeal is to a more adult aestheticism.[21]

Guthrie also took a quizzical look at the traditions of heroic performances: this Henry V had a smack of Hamlet in him, and the conniving divines who authorized the conflict with France were not comic caricatures but hard-bitten and self-serving politicians (see Figure 10.1).

Figure 10.1 Tyrone Guthrie's 1937 production of *Henry V* at London's Old Vic, scenery and costumes by Motley, starring Laurence Olivier

However, shortly after, in time of war, the thrust of the film that followed the production, starring and directed by Olivier, needed to inculcate heroic, patriotic, and Christian values. It endorses the virtues of the "common man": the comic "humor'" characters – Pistol and his crew – are not vile parasites upon the body politic but exhibit the grim optimism of British Tommies (privates) in both world wars. In the taverns, decency is sustained and sexual puns are underplayed (although they remain in 3.5, the Princess's English lesson).

Part of the film, especially the epic Battle of Agincourt, exhibiting numerous troops of horses, was shot on location at the Powerscourt Estate in Ireland, in Technicolor and using the conventions of cinematic realism – although there is no blood at Olivier's Agincourt. The film in fact deploys varieties of the "adult aestheticism" that the reviewer in *The Times* found in Guthrie's earlier stage version. Moreover, Olivier drew upon a range of genres and styles. The visual tropes of medieval illuminations inform its portrayal of the countryside, and the music by William Walton moves from early modern dance (played by a full symphony orchestra) to Elgaresque religiosity.

One of the distinctive features of the text is how little space it devotes to Agincourt. Most of the action, in fact, focuses on a messy encounter between

Pistol and a French soldier (4.4). There is no montage of hand-to-hand encounters like those in *1–3 Henry VI*. Not surprisingly, Olivier cut 4.4, along with Henry's order to his soldiers to kill all their prisoners (4.6.37). But he eschewed any economies: he crammed within his screen dozens of horses and extras, particularly when the French cavalry made their charge. However, it is not simple realism but unembarrassed pastiche: "It is … Hollywood, with a great charge of French horseman taken from Griffiths, an Eisenstein-like flight of arrows through the sky, and English soldiers dropping from branches as in Errol Flynn's Robin Hood films."[22] In this film, moral outrage, aroused when the French kill all of the English boys and fire the English camp, spurs Henry into an inserted single combat with the Constable of France who, as in medieval romance, wears black armor and rides a black horse.

The film abandons battle for a pageant of musical merriment and painterly cheer. Jump to a picture-postcard scene of a snow-covered village where Fluellen humiliates Pistol: perhaps the wintriness is a fit setting for Pistol's narrative of his Nell's death from the pox (5.1.72–73). From this icy interlude we switch to a shot of a castle painted in the style of a medieval illustration and bathed in glorious spring sunshine; inside, the court is singing merry roundelays. The scene begins to cloud with Burgundy's lament for the state of France, abandoned by Peace (5.2.23–67), accompanied by a flashback to panning autumnal shots of the ruined countryside. Yet this is but a contrasting prelude to a completely unironic treatment of the handfasting of Henry and Katherine (Renée Asherson). They flirt in comic prose, although the improprieties (5.2.241–47) of the French word *baiser* (to kiss or to copulate) are suppressed. Their kiss is romanticized by a choir aloft in a kind of apotheosis. As in Spenser's *The Faerie Queene*, mutability is displaced by a pageant of the seasons:[23] Hal and Kate progress in matching robes, perhaps inspired by the gown worn by Spring/Flora in Botticelli's *Primavera*, to chairs of state in the "castle" that morph into their equivalents back in the Globe. Kate is now played by a "boy actress" (George Cole).

## After World War II

In 1944, during the Second World War, E. M. W. Tillyard published his immensely influential *Shakespeare's History Plays*. He offered a moralizing interpretation:

> Shakespeare's history plays endorsed the Tudor myth [that] presented a scheme fundamentally religious, by which events evolve under a law of justice and

under the ruling of God's providence, and of which Elizabeth's England was the acknowledged outcome.[24]

This kind of certitude did not last long. In the British theater of the 1960s, the influence of Bertolt Brecht and the Berliner Ensemble was widely felt. Power seemed secular in origin, not ordained by God, and royal authority was not authenticated by divinity. The motives of great men mattered less than analyses of political systems. Illusionism was vanquished, theater companies served not their stars but ideals of collective endeavor, and moral commonplaces were scrutinized. The RSC was established as a permanent and democratic repertory company.

Twenty years after Tillyard, when Europe arguably continued to struggle with the aftermath of the war and continued to reflect on the rise of the totalizing and absolutist regimes of the twentieth century, Jan Kott published an equally historicist and equally influential generalization:

> Emanating from the features of individual kings and usurpers in Shakespeare's History plays, there gradually emerges the image of history itself. The image of the Grand Mechanism. Every successive chapter, every great Shakespearean act is merely a repetition. . . . Feudal history is like a great staircase on which there treads a constant procession of kings. Every step upwards is marked by murder, perfidy, treachery. Every step brings the throne nearer. Another step and the crown will fall. One will soon be able to snatch it. . . . From the highest step there is only a leap into the abyss. The monarchs change. But all of them – good and bad, brave and cowardly, vile and noble, naive and cynical – tread on the steps that are always the same.[25]

Just twenty years after 1945, after a great victory in a "just war," Kott deemed history to be a dark and inscrutable force. The images of staircase and abyss appeared in John Barton's 1973 production of *Richard II* for the RSC. The action took place between two escalators or staircases that led to a gallery running high above the stage.

Richard Pasco and Ian Richardson alternated the two principal roles: in the scene pictured in Figure 10.2, Bolingbroke visits the King in his base prison, disguised as one of his keepers and shielding his face with a tray, its center punched out, which resembles the mirror called for by the King in 4.1. Loncraine's 1995 film of *Richard III* ends memorably with Ian McKellen as Richard leaping into a blazing abyss.

The year 1964 marked the quarter-centenary of Shakespeare's birth, and among the Stratford productions was an offering, prepared the year before, entitled *The Wars of the Roses*, devised by John Barton and Peter Hall (see Figure 10.3). The three parts of the Henry VI sequence were condensed into two plays, *Henry VI* and *Edward IV*, and followed by *Richard III*.[26] In his

Figure 10.2 Richard Pasco as the King and Ian Richardson as Bolingbroke in *Richard II*, 5.3, directed by John Barton for the RSC in 1973 at Stratford

introduction to the published text, Hall acknowledged the presence in his mind of both Tillyard and Kott, and this obviously affected the company's thinking about *mise-en-scène*: "We ... had a clear purpose in our task. With our designer, John Bury, we found a strong visual image for our production – a cruel, harsh world of decorated steel, cold and dangerous."[27]

The Barton and Hall "*Henry VI*," written before the *Richard II* to *Henry V* sequence, is an "after-war" play, here well-suited to an after-war period. Bury's set proclaimed its approach. Although full of battles, the stage was often dominated by a council table that could be thrust up from the stage. It suggested evolution from later medieval *court* to early modern *state*. It "enabled the directors to show swiftly and succinctly the fluctuations of power": it was a metonym for the summit conferences that often punctuated Cold War politics. Barton and Hall had in part supplanted the warlord archetype with the politician archetype: the text, Hall wrote, uncovered in the *Henry VI* plays "a perceptive analysis of power and the inevitable corruption of politicians."[28] Bury wrote of the set:

> On the flagged floors of sheet steel tables are daggers, staircases are axeheads, and doors the traps on scaffolds. Nothing yields: stone walls have lost their seduction and now loom dangerously – steel-clad – to enclose and to imprison. The countryside offers no escape – the danger is still there in the iron foliage of the cruel and, surrounding all, the great steel cage of war.[29]

Figure 10.3 *Henry V*, 1.2, in John Barton and Peter Hall's 1964 RSC Stratford production

These were productions for an age when totalitarianism loomed, an age of iron curtains. The Tory party, "the natural party of government," had recently been defeated twice by Labour politicians. Many young people were alienated by American participation in the Vietnam War (1955–75). Freshly prominent were roles for strong and determined women: in this trilogy, Joan La Pucelle and Margaret of Anjou. Peggy Ashcroft, who played the Queen in 1963, and later Helen Mirren in Terry Hands's version of 1977–79 and Penny Downie in Noble's rendering of 1988, proved that women too could imitate the action of the tiger. These performances, of their time and for their time, were enlivened and carried along by surges of cultural change. When Trevor Nunn staged a tribute revival of the Hall and Barton some fifty years later in 2015, at the Rose Theatre, Kingston on Thames, his production was damned as "more pageant than revolution."[30]

In the television version of the Hall and Barton "*Henry VI*," broadcast by the BBC in 1966, the throne was first seen through an iron grille. England and its institutions were contained within a cage or prison house – this visual trope recurred. This was the Cold War, with ideological struggles between east and west Europe – analogous to the Hundred Years' War that is the background to the Wars of the Roses as portrayed in the play. To establish the Temple Garden where, in 2.4, the undefined "case of truth" sparks the civil conflict, the grille was threaded with long-stemmed roses. Politicians were constrained by varieties of false consciousness and took no responsibility for the lives of those who lived under their yokes. Behind, incongruous in the midst of the metallic plates, was a shadowy archaic image of Christ: this was postwar, an age, in Nietzsche's formulation, unfolding after a perceived death of God, perhaps a Kafka-like world in which the truths of religion could be but dimly remembered. Joan of Arc (Janet Suzman), with a gamine haircut, was a good swordswoman, but her surprising victory over Talbot was cut, and Warwick without difficulty outfought her – supernatural aid was no longer available.

Some audiences found the callousness depicted in *The Wars of the Roses* disturbing, particularly in a scene like 1.4 of *3 Henry VI* where Queen Margaret smears the face of the Duke of York with a napkin, soaked in the blood of his son, the Earl of Rutland. An alternative to Shakespeare's simple realism (often linked to Artaud's advocacy for a theater of cruelty)[31] was extreme stylization: for a 1988 production of *King John* in a black box setting at Stratford's Other Place, Deborah Warner deployed a set with "three dozen plain ladders, used as siege instruments at Angiers, and six plain chairs – minimalist trappings that placed the play's conflicts within a cage or forest to figure power, in this metallic age, as the ability to scale heights and remain 'on top.'"[32] Thirteen years later in 2001, Edward Hall directed the Propeller Company in a shortened all-male version of the *Henry VI* plays where the bodies of the actors – sometimes dressed as Edwardian gentlemen, sometimes as butchers – were not impacted. Instead, animal entrails were chopped and giant cabbages slashed in a macabre feast of absurdity and horror (see Figure 10.4).[33]

In 1975, Terry Hands directed, for the centenary season of the RSC, the "Falstaff plays," *1–2 Henry IV*, *Henry V*, and *The Merry Wives of Windsor*. The sequence was designed by Farrah, and the nature of the *mise-en-scène* was foregrounded by having the players on a very bare stage in rehearsal costumes as the audience entered. In *Henry V*, period dress was donned as the production unfolded: until 2.4, the costuming remained "largely modern, the costumes drawing inspiration from both world wars."[34] However, from 2.4, a scene that depicts the French court, a fifteenth-century

Figure 10.4 Civil war as butchery: the Duke of Somerset killed by Richard Duke of Gloucester, in 2 *Henry VI*, 5.2, in Edward Hall's 2001 production for the Propeller Company, Watermill Theatre, Newbury

element was added, suggesting "an etiquette-bound remnant of the age of chivalry, the age of Richard II."[35] The aim was to enhance collaborative work between actors and audience.

These productions fostered agnosticism – by classic Brechtian means. The director often built scenes around a well-defined *gestus*, a moment when the gist of the scene was caught by the gesture of the player.[36] Memorable among these was Henry's exit at the end of 2.2. In the words of the director:

> Fully costumed he [Alan Howard, who played the King] leaps "heroically" upon the cart carrying the cannon, and "heroically" leads his army away.
>
> > Cheerly to sea. The signs of war advance.
> > No king of England, if not king of France. [2.2.191–92]
>
> At this point Guy Woolfenden introduced a marching song – *Deo Gracias* – which was to become the theme tune of the play. Here it was used triumphantly, the exterior pageant of war, covering the interior anguish and unease we have just witnessed [as the traitors were arrested].[37]

Some forty lines later, Pistol quotes the King's words: "Yokefellows in arms, / Let us to France, like horse-leeches, my boys, / To suck, to suck, the very blood to suck!" (2.3.45–47), and he and his companions 'quote' the exit, although it is "a thin straggly line, with tattered clothes, beaten up equipment."[38]

As for the Battle of Agincourt, the English were, unexpectedly, shocked by their victory. In fact, they fell on their knees after the King proclaimed:

> O God, thy arm was here;
> And not to us, but to thy arm alone
> Ascribe we all.   (4.8.100–2)

Alan Howard wrote: "The determination he had, and his army had before the battle, is not enough to explain what has happened. It is a mystery, or a miracle. He accepts it as such."[39] After much debate within the cast a very ambiguous double song was decided upon, a "*Te Deum*" sung by Fluellen over the army's version of their normal marching song.[40] The soldiers from the four nations of Britain perpetually squabble and scrap: did the play demonstrate that patriotism and warmongering were no longer tools for busying giddy minds? This was the time of the Troubles in Northern Ireland,[41] and the doubt that imprinted the production echoed the doubt that gripped the United States and its allies in the early 1970s as the Vietnam War demonstrably failed.

In 1977, Hands went on to direct the *Henry VI* plays uncut, with Alan Howard returning to play the title role, the son of Henry V. The productions were notable for foregrounding struggles between female and male power as well as the sometimes riotous dissensions between commoners and nobles that had been all but cut from *The Wars of the Roses* of the previous decade.[42]

The English Shakespeare Company emerged in the early 1980s under the leadership of Michael Bogdanov and Michael Pennington. With substantial help from the Arts Council, the mission of this repertory company was to be different from those of the RSC and the National Theatre – to tour large-scale productions to the larger regional theaters and also to London's Old Vic and abroad. The project began in 1985, and by spring 1988 the company was staging eight history plays in seven parts under the title *The Wars of the Roses*. A tight budget fostered a "practical" sense of ensemble: there were only twenty-five members, everyone had to appear in every play, "everyone had to understudy everyone else," dialogue and action were to be accessible – "accurate and fastidious"[43] – and music was generated by cast members. This was a nonmetropolitan venture: actors with regional accents retained them, and sometimes accents fitted the cities and counties from which nobles took their titles.

The productions were fired by a sense of political injustice. Thanks to the iniquity of the British electoral system, Margaret Thatcher had been propelled into office, despite losing in Scotland, Wales, and the North:

> Boadicea had rallied her troops around her with a senseless war of expediency, sailing heroically (in some people's eyes) twelve thousand miles to the

Figure 10.5  Falstaff (Barry Stanton) plays the King in *1 Henry IV*, 2.4, from the English
Shakespeare Company's version of 1988

Falklands to do battle for "a little patch of ground / That hath in it no profit
but the name. / To pay five ducats – five – I would not farm it."[44]

On his deathbed, Henry IV had advised his son to "busy giddy minds / With
foreign quarrels" (*2 Henry IV*, 4.3.342–43): Bogdanov and Pennington
exposed the weaponization of jingoism (see Figure 10.5).

*Mise-en-scène* was all-important: this was no feast of heraldry, for
costumes were eclectic, leaping over centuries and glancing at varieties of
the English establishment. Bishops wore wristwatches, courts were peopled
by men in Victorian frock coats. In *1 Henry IV*, Bolingbroke, Hal, and
Hotspur at the Battle of Shrewsbury wore medieval chain mail with heraldic
tabards and fought with broadswords, while Falstaff sported camouflage
gear and a tin hat. A kit of props remained on the stage, and the set was a
brutal steel structure that provided a

> theatre within a theatre, the audience able to see the mechanics of flying, the
> lighting bridge, the iron-clad framework of the walls of a stage. The bridge
> should be able to go up and down and operate at several levels. Two sections
> should be moveable towers to provide upper levels. [We originally] dreamed of
> fights and chases up and down the towers.... We added a white border to the

floor and a back-projection screen with a door to the back.... Our ingrained modernity was asserting itself. *Henry V*, with its war of expediency, ruthless manipulation, bribery and corruption, palpable pacificism, the French superior in numbers but beaten by superior technology, felt modern ... the English army [wore] modern battle fatigues, the French powder-blue uniforms, echoing the futile French cavalry charges of the First World War, their battalions mown down by automatic weapons.[45]

A variety of music from a variety of periods matched the eclecticism of the costumes.[46] Surrounding the black square painted on the stage cloth with a white border created a stage upon a stage, an index of metatheatricality.

This was "Shakespeare with attitude": here national pride had degraded into jingoism, and war and sport became again identical. But the mode could not have been more different from that created in the Benson era. Two moments acquired a degree of notoriety: first, into the scene in *King Henry VI House of Lancaster* (the title of the fifth part of the adapted series) where Suffolk captures and woos Margaret (*1 Henry VI*, 5.6), Bogdanov inserted a brief wordless sequence, the capture and offstage rape of a French peasant girl. She was a figure standing for France and for Joan La Pucelle, and also for the future Queen Margaret – and a reminder of the way rape, in certain wars of the late-twentieth century, was not just opportunistic but often a weapon, systematically used.

The second moment was the "going-to-war" scene for Pistol and his drunken crew (*Henry V*, 2.3). After the Hostess's narrative of Falstaff's death (2.3.9–23), "I Did It My Way" played on a guitar was heard, the ragbag soldiers burst out into the football chant "Ere we go," and the lights came up on the balcony from which hung a Union Jack, the cross of St. George, and a banner reading "Fuck the Frogs." The music morphed into "Jerusalem," and the Chorus crossed the stage bearing a football rattle and placard that read "Gotcha," the headline the *Sun* had displayed after the sinking of the Argentine cruiser *Belgrano* in the Falklands War in 1982. In his account of the production, Bogdanov quoted a letter of complaint: "The use of the word was offensive and the term 'Frogs' hardly helps promote racial harmony and dispel old prejudices. I was ashamed to be English."[47] Precisely. The case rests.

Kenneth Branagh directed his film of the play in 1989, a moment when the Cold War was coming to an end, the year when Francis Fukuyama published his essay "The End of History." The idea of a new age is rendered by incorporating flashbacked Falstaff sequences to enhance Mistress Quickly's account of his death. Branagh retains the scene (2.2) in which Henry disposes of the aristocratic traitors Cambridge, Grey, and Scrope, who had tried to kindle revolt of the kind that had plagued his father, Henry IV.

Like Olivier, Branagh took the principal role himself. It is an homage to the master, opening not in a mock-up Globe but in a film studio. The lights are down, and the Chorus, Derek Jacobi, illuminates himself by striking a match. This is a film that celebrates heroism even more than Olivier's did: Branagh makes his first appearance, shot, as Welles might have done, from below, as a huge silhouette framed by the massive loading doors of the film studio that morph into the entrance of a council chamber. Where appropriate he rides a white steed. There are a lot of intimate sequences, heads in close-up, but the mode switches to epic and the fights are spectacular, and here, once let slip, the dogs of war (Pistol and his crew) are more prominent. Olivier had one volley of arrows mid-air, Branagh offers seven. But the glorifying shots of battle are intercut with glimpses of vicious cruelty and bodies being despoiled.

The film stresses morality rather than history. Branagh had taken the lead in a 1984 stage production by Noble, significantly the first at the RSC for ten years. Branagh wrote that he was trying to eschew a *"Boy's Own* adventure," and "tried to realise the qualities of introspection, doubt and anger which I believed the text indicated."[48] These, he felt, could best be served by cinematic close-ups and low-level dialogue. There is a stunning shot when the two cowled bishops appear on either side of the frame, like two tempting devils in a morality play, when the King, center-frame, asks, "May I with right and conscience make this claim" (1.2.96). The focus is on the conscience of the King, on tugs between mercy and punishment. War seems to have receded into the past: a fleeting reference to Harry having crossed the Somme spurs a sequence of pelting rain and clinging mud – a motif from the First World War. Harry's order that his soldiers should kill the prisoners was again cut (4.6.37). Having commanded the singing of *"Non Nobis, Domine,"* Branagh the king picks up the body of a slaughtered English boy to carry him off the field and remains at the center of a very long tracking shot.[49] Patrick Doyle's setting of the psalm is a brainworm tune (it was first heard in the thick of the battle), repeated three times after Agincourt and once over the final titles, which evokes attempts in twentieth-century film music to turn common men into heroes, the sort of music, as a friend remarked, that used to accompany cinematic exhortations to greater industrial productivity in Stalinist Russia. Its melodiousness and orchestral accompaniment minimize the gory details and glimpses of French women despoiling the bodies. This was patriotism de-ironized: "God fought for us" (4.8.114).

By 1994 that kind of easy patriotism was not an option, a cultural shift that was memorialized by Katie Mitchell's stand-alone production of

3 *Henry VI* at the Other Place in Stratford. The director stated that "I wanted to do something in response to what's been happening in Bosnia and Rwanda," and indicted Britain's refusal to intervene.[50]

In 2003, the year the Iraq War began, Nicholas Hytner directed *Henry V* in modern dress at the National Theatre, with a black actor, Adrian Lester, as the King. As Michael Billington wrote:

> Hytner's intentions are clear from the start: to undercut the rhetorical glamour surrounding war. William Gaunt's pragmatic Archbishop of Canterbury has prepared fat dossiers supporting Henry's dubious claim to the French throne. No sooner has Penny Downie's cardiganed Chorus told us "Now all the youth of England are on fire" [2.0.1] than we cut to the pub where Nym zaps TV channels preferring the snooker to the king's bellicose warmongering.[51]

However, Charles Spence further commented that "the battle scenes are both deafening and thrilling, and with inventive use of live video, the production also shows how war has become a media event, with Henry's big moments projected onto a screen at the back of the stage."[52]

In the 1580s, Raphael Holinshed, compiler of Shakespeare's principle source for the histories, had wondered, "What should be the meaning of all those foughten fields?"[53] Particular answers inform particular productions at particular times. But there is not, and should not be, any overarching or final elucidation.

## Further Reading

Alexander, Catherine M. S. "Shakespeare and War," *Use of English*, 65 (2014), pp. 6–21.

Barker, Simon. "Shakespeare, Stratford, and the Second World War," in Irena R. Makaryk and Marissa McHugh (eds.), *Shakespeare and the Second World War: Memory, Culture, Identity*, Toronto, University of Toronto Press, 2012, pp. 199–217.

Brown, Karin, and Jan Sewell. "*Henry V* in Performance: The RSC and Beyond," in Jonathan Bate and Eric Rasmussen (eds.), *Henry V*, The RSC Shakespeare, Basingstoke, Macmillan, 2010, pp. 146–201.

Dickson, Lisa. "The Blazon and the Theater of War: *The Wars of the Roses* and *The Plantagenets*," in Deborah Uman and Sara Morrison (eds.), *Staging the Blazon in Early Modern English Theater*, Farnham, Ashgate, 2013, pp. 137–47.

Fernie, Ewan. "Action! *Henry V*," in Hugh Grady and Terence Hawkes (eds.), *Presentist Shakespeares*, London, Routledge, 2007, pp. 96–120.

Fraser, R. Scott. "*Henry V* and the Performance of War," in Ros King and Paul J. C. M. Franssen (eds.), *Shakespeare and War*, Basingstoke, Palgrave Macmillan, 2008, pp. 71–83.

Heijes, Coen. "'Strike up the Drum': The Use of Music in the Boyd History Cycle," *Shakespeare Bulletin*, 27 (2009), pp. 223–48.

Hiscock, Andrew. "'More Warlike than Politique': Shakespeare and the Theatre of War – A Critical Survey," *Shakespeare* (British Shakespeare Association), 7 (2011), pp. 221–47.

Hoenselaars, Ton (ed.). *Shakespeare's History Plays: Performance, Translation, and Adaptation in Britain and Abroad*, Cambridge, Cambridge University Press, 2004.

Kennedy, Dennis. *Looking at Shakespeare: A Visual History of Twentieth-Century Performance*, Cambridge, Cambridge University Press, 1993.

## NOTES

1 St. Augustine of Hippo, *Concerning the City of God against the Pagans*, trans. Henry Bettenson (Harmondsworth: Penguin Books, 1972), bk. 4, ch. 4, p. 139.

2 Stuart Hampton-Reeves and Carol Chillington Rutter, *The Henry VI Plays*, Shakespeare in Performance (Manchester: Manchester University Press, 2006), p. 70.

3 Adrian Noble (ed. and intro.), *The Plantagenets*, by William Shakespeare (London: Faber and Faber, 1989), p. ix.

4 Rex Gibson, "Horrified Fascination," *Times Educational Supplement*, September 19, 1997.

5 Paul A. Jorgensen, "A Fearful Battle Rend'red You in Music," in *Shakespeare's Military World* (Berkeley: University of California Press, 1956), pp. 1–34; Michael Hattaway, "'Thou Laidst No Sieges to the Music-Room': Anatomizing Wars, Staging Battles," in Emma Smith (ed.), *Shakespeare and War*, Shakespeare Survey 72 (Cambridge: Cambridge University Press, 2019), pp. 48–63.

6 William Archer, "'Henry IV' in Manchester," in *The Theatrical 'World' of 1896* (London: Walter Scott, 1898), pp. 29–34.

7 Richard Foulkes, *Performing Shakespeare in the Age of Empire* (Cambridge: Cambridge University Press, 2002), p. 134.

8 Foulkes, *Performing Shakespeare in the Age of Empire*, p. 133.

9 J. C. Trewin, *Benson and the Bensonians* (London: Barrie and Rockliff, 1960), pp. 92–93; and Patrick Rucker, "Benson and Shakespeare: Passing on the Grand Tradition," *Theatre Southwest*, 18 (1990), pp. 18–24.

10 Sally Beauman, *The Royal Shakespeare Company: A History of Ten Decades* (Oxford: Oxford University Press, 1982), p. 43; and (ed.), *The Royal Shakespeare Company's Production of "Henry V"* (Oxford: Pergamon, 1976).

11 John Courtenay Trewin, *Going to Shakespeare* (London: Allen and Unwin, 1978), pp. 149–50.

12 Beauman, *The Royal Shakespeare Company*, p. 36.

13 Gordon Crosse, *Shakespearean Playgoing, 1890–1952* (London: A. R. Mowbray & Co., 1953), p. 33.

14 Emma Smith (ed.), *King Henry V*, by William Shakespeare, Shakespeare in Production (Cambridge: Cambridge University Press, 2002), p. 35.

15 Lancelot Andrewes, *Ninety-Six Sermons* (London, 1629), p. 188.

16 Max Beerbohm, review of *Henry V*, directed by Frank Benson, *Saturday Review*, February 24, 1900, repr. in J. C. Trewin, *Benson and the Bensonians*, p. 111.

17 Michael Hattaway (ed.), *The First Part of King Henry VI*, by William Shakespeare (Cambridge: Cambridge University Press, 1990), pp. 51–52.

18 Hampton-Reeves and Rutter, *The Henry VI Plays*, p. 120.

19 Richard Foulkes, "The Theatre of War: The 1916 Tercentenary," in *Performing*, pp. 180–204, 198; and Catherine M. S. Alexander, "Shakespeare and War: A Reflection on Instances of Dramatic Production, Appropriation, and Celebration," *Exchanges: The Warwick Research Journal*, 1 (2014), pp. 279–96.

20 Trewin, *Benson and the Bensonians*, p. 214.

21 Review of *Henry V*, Old Vic, London, *Times*, April 7, 1937, p. 14.

22 Andrew Gurr (ed.), *Henry V*, by William Shakespeare, The New Cambridge Shakespeare, 2nd ed. (Cambridge: Cambridge University Press, 2005), p. 49.

23 Edmund Spenser, *The Faerie Queene* (1596), bk. 7, canto 7, st. 28–31.

24 E. M. W. Tillyard, *Shakespeare's History Plays* (London: Chatto and Windus, 1944), pp. 320–21.

25 Jan Kott, *Shakespeare Our Contemporary*, trans. Boleslaw Taborski (Garden City: Anchor Books, 1966), pp. 10–11, 53–54.

26 Beauman, *The Royal Shakespeare Company*, pp. 266–72; and Hampton-Reeves and Rutter, *The Henry VI Plays*, pp. 54–79.

27 John Barton and Peter Hall, *The Wars of the Roses: Adapted for the Royal Shakespeare Company from William Shakespeare's "Henry VI," Parts I, II, III and "Richard III"* (London: BBC, 1970), pp. x–xi.

28 Barton and Hall, *The Wars of the Roses*, p. ix.

29 Barton and Hall, *The Wars of the Roses*, p. 237.

30 Susannah Clapp, "*The Wars of the Roses* Review," *Observer*, October 11, 2015.

31 Antonin Artaud, *The Theater and Its Double*, trans. Mary Caroline Richards (New York: Grove Press, 1958).

32 Barbara Hodgdon, *The End Crowns All: Closure and Contradiction in Shakespeare's History* (Princeton: Princeton University Press, 1991), p. 42.

33 Lyn Gardner, "Blood Flows at Newbury's Watermill," *Guardian*, February 9, 2001.

34 Beauman, "*Henry V*," pp. 101, 137.

35 Beauman, "*Henry V*," p. 137.

36 Bertolt Brecht, *Brecht on Theatre*, trans. John Willett (London: Methuen, 1964), p. 42.

37 Beauman, "*Henry V*," p. 134.

38 Beauman, "*Henry V*," p. 137.

39 Quoted in Beauman, "*Henry V*," 212n, cf. p. 60.

40 Beauman, "*Henry V*," pp. 46, 213–14.

41 Beauman, "*Henry V*," p. 84.

42 Hampton-Reeves and Rutter, *The Henry VI Plays*, pp. 82–107.

43 Michael Bogdanov and Michael Pennington, *The English Shakespeare Company: The Story of "The Wars of the Roses," 1986–1989* (London: Nick Hern Books, 1990), pp. 17, 19.

44 Bogdanov and Pennington, *The English Shakespeare Company*, p. 23, quoting *Hamlet*, 4.1.17–19.

45 Bogdanov and Pennington, *The English Shakespeare Company*, pp. 29–31.

46 Bogdanov and Pennington, *The English Shakespeare Company*, p. 109.

47 Bogdanov and Pennington, *The English Shakespeare Company*, p. 48.

48 Kenneth Branagh, *"Henry V" by William Shakespeare: A Screen Adaptation by Kenneth Branagh* (London: Chatto and Windus, 1989), pp. 9–10.

49 Branagh, "Henry V" by William Shakespeare, pp. 113–14.

50 Lawrence Christon, "She Delivers More than a Message," *Los Angeles Times*, October 30, 1994; and Barbara Hodgdon, "Making It New: Katie Mitchell Refashions Shakespeare-History," in Marianne Novy (ed.), *Transforming Shakespeare: Contemporary Women's Re-Visions in Literature and Performance* (London: Palgrave, 1999), pp. 13–33.

51 Michael Billington, "*Henry V,*" *Guardian*, May 14, 2003.

52 Charles Spence, "A Tale for Our Time Summons the Blood," *Telegraph*, May 15, 2003.

53 Raphael Holinshed, *Chronicles of England, Scotland, and Ireland* (1587), 6 vols. (London: J. Johnson et al., 1808), vol. III, p. 273.

# 11

GREG SEMENZA

# Reading Shakespeare's Wars on Film

## Ideology and Montage

Relative to the other arts, cinema amazes and troubles us for its peculiar ability "to hold ... the mirror up to nature" (*Hamlet*, 3.2.20) or, as Jean Louis Baudry states the matter: "the cinematographic technique is the only one that makes possible a succession of images rapid enough to roughly correspond to our faculty for producing mental images."[1] The Renaissance theater's anxiety about its own insufficiency to do the same is often most pronounced in relation to the staging of battle scenes, its inability to bring forth "famine, sword, and fire" on so "unworthy" a "scaffold" as the stage (*Henry V*, Prologue, 7, 10). Ben Jonson famously mocked the types of battles Shakespeare attempted in the history plays, wherein the players would, "with three rusty swords, / And help of some few foot-and-half-foot words, / Fight over *York* and *Lancaster*'s long jars, / And in the tiring-house bring wounds to scars."[2] Yet more famously did Sir Philip Sidney describe the interpretive burden that battle scenes imposed on audiences: "While in the meane time two Armies fly in, represented with four swords and bucklers, and then what hard heart will not receive it for a pitched field?"[3] In these and other contemporary commentaries on staged wars, early modern playgoers repeatedly lamented the significant mismatch between the technologies of the theater and the scale, shape, and intrinsic spectacle of warfare. Whereas the stage was easily, and unfairly, ridiculed as a mere shadow of the real, the cinema would often be celebrated, even by its early commentators, for blurring the lines between art and reality.

Consequently, because the depiction of battles poses so significant a challenge to playwrights, it also grants a major opportunity to cinematic adaptors of plays about war. Indeed, the cinema has reveled, since the earliest days of the silent era, in its ability to improve on the theater through on-location shooting ("vasty fields" and all), the employment of massive sets, and the use of special effects, all in the service of a powerful realism – and nowhere more obviously and profoundly than in its depiction of war (*Henry V*, Prologue, 12). Adaptations of Shakespeare have played a notably important role in the evolving history of war on film. The Prologue to *Henry V* invoked a "muse of fire" capable of making monarchs "assume the port of Mars" (1, 6); the cinema ascended the heights of invention 300 years later, offering a belated but magnificent response to that conjuration. By the late 1920s, with the invention of sound and especially the incorporation of non-continuity-based montage techniques, filmmakers were capable of depicting battles on a monumental scale to frighteningly realistic effect.

Of course, Shakespeare's battles were conceived by a playwright who understood the gap between the real and the representative, lamented it even, but knew he could never bridge it. Thus, the meanings and impact of the approximately fifteen Shakespeare plays featuring prominent battle scenes hinge specifically on the literal absence of, rather than the figurative presence of, realism. In other words, because the true muse of fire, the cinematographic apparatus, did not exist in the early modern period, the plays were written around its *absence*. What have been the effects, then, of the muse's eventual arrival, not just on the meanings of the plays but on our reception of them? In light of apparatus theory's insistence on the intrinsically ideological nature of the cinema, how especially does the formal shift from stage to screen – from realism's absence to its presence – affect the ways in which we respond to Shakespeare's warlike monarchs?

This chapter considers how, in six successful Shakespeare films, exclusively cinematic formal methods of depicting battle serve to interpret and transform the plays' perspectives on warfare. Because the number of Shakespeare films featuring battles has surpassed what any one chapter can possibly cover, emphasis will be further drawn around the concept (and deployment) of dialectical montage first developed by Sergei Eisenstein in his seminal 1929 essay "The Dramaturgy of Film Form." Though Eisenstein's relatively rigid theory of montage has been endlessly appropriated, expanded, and, at times, openly rejected by filmmakers and scholars alike, it remains ground zero for realist cinematic treatments of warfare and a key of sorts for deciphering individual filmmakers' ideological orientations to their subject matter.

Eisenstein dismissed hitherto-assumed straightforward links between montage and the continuity system associated with Hollywood cinema; those links are implicit even etymologically in the French term "*montage's*" meaning of "assembly," which connotes ideas of building, unity, and flow. In its place, Eisenstein offered a dialectical approach to montage that recognizes editing in terms of "collision" or conflict specifically: "But in my view montage is not an idea composed of successive shots stuck together but an idea that DERIVES from the collision between two shots that are independent of one another."[4] For Eisenstein, the power of montage rested not in an erasure of difference between two shots – an illusion of continuity, that is – but in the logical juxtaposition of those shots' differences. Eisenstein's language might be said to celebrate a certain violence in montage, both in terms of the literal "cutting" of film through the editing process and the more figurative notion of colliding shots; montage itself emerges as a microcosmic scene of battle, suggesting perhaps why the emblematic examples of Eisensteinian montage – the army massacre of the laborers in *Strike* (1925), the "Odessa Steps" sequence in *Potemkin* (1925), the Battle on the Ice in *Alexander Nevsky* (1938) – all happen to center on and around epic scenes of violence. In a sense, the filmed battle scene, and scenes of violent conflict more generally, emerge early in film history as the exemplars par excellence of Soviet montage practice.

To consider the matter yet further: if dialectical montage comes for many filmmakers and audiences to symbolize the essence of cinema, and the battle scene the essence of montage, then we might productively isolate the constituent components of the filmed battle scene as perhaps the most basic formal units able to "solve the problem of film as such," to use Eisenstein's own words for the conundrum posed by medium specificity.[5] For our purposes, the question of medium specificity will be most important in relation to specific films' adaptations of specific plays, so that we might also say the following: the formal qualities of the many memorable battle montages within filmed Shakespeare clarify how the realist potential of the cinema renders intrinsically political the adaptation of specifically nonrealistic theatrical elements central to the plays' meanings.

I say "intrinsically political" because the power that directors and editors have to control audience receptions of film images and narratives is most obviously epitomized by their choices surrounding montage. Perhaps no other element of cinema warrants such attention in relation to its ability to intensify or weaken audience agency than montage. How ironic were Eisenstein's intentions, we might ask, when he declared that "[w]hereas the conventional film directs and develops the *emotions*, here [through montage] we have a hint of the possibility of likewise developing and directing the entire *thought process*"?[6] In any case, what was Eisenstein acknowledging other than the idea that montage itself (the very soul of the technology that in many ways most troubled contemporary thinkers such as Walter Benjamin) could most effectively advance the specifically fascist, democratic, or other aims of filmmakers? And what form of montage could better distill – and, for audiences, reveal – those aims than scenes of violent conflict, especially of nations at war, in films whose very subject matter is political in nature?

Few Shakespeare films serve such obvious propagandizing intentions as Laurence Olivier's *Henry V* (1944) or Vishal Bhardwaj's *Haider* (2014). Yet,

Figure 11.1 Dialectical montage and the chaos of war in Orson Welles's *Chimes at Midnight* (1965)

as we shall see, even the least overtly political film adaptations of Shakespeare's most political plays tend to reveal a certain preoccupation with the ethical, ideological, and of course hermeneutic implications of representing battle scenes in a medium that all but demands their representation. Since at least the 1920s, two basic approaches have dominated cinematic representations of battles, and both of them have influenced Shakespeare on film. The first, somewhat obviously, is the use of dialectical montage techniques to capture the chaotic realism of large-scale military conflict. In fact, Orson Welles's *Chimes at Midnight* (1965) offers one of the most powerful and influential homages to Eisenstein's Battle on the Ice in all of film history (see Figure 11.1), and numerous non-Shakespearean examples could be cited as key modern instances of the method – most memorably the D-Day sequence in *Saving Private Ryan* (1998).[7]

Generally speaking, the rapid intercutting, volume, and variety of shots used in such scenes serve to undermine any arguments for the "glory" of battle precisely by rendering impossible audience identification with – or even tracking of – individual human subjects.

The other approach, influenced by the classical Hollywood style – in which "the character must act as the prime causal agent"[8] – minimizes the clash of noncontiguous images so that narrative continuity and spatial/temporal unity are prioritized, allowing audiences to track, and identify with, individual subjects and thereby evaluate their deeds positively or negatively. The camera's steady focus on battling heroes and villains in the western and superhero genres certainly supports, and is supported by this editing approach; so too are the battle scenes from unabashedly character-centered Shakespeare films such as Kenneth Branagh's *Henry V* (1989) or Richard Loncraine's *Richard III* (1995). This style accommodates relatively easily the forms or impressions of battle we find within the plays themselves; indeed, David Bordwell, Janet Staiger, and Kristin Thompson have noted that – unlike dialectical montage – the continuity system could "come from the other arts: the film frame is analogous to the proscenium of a stage."[9] Directors of battle scenes need not employ the classical Hollywood continuity style in politically regressive ways, of course, but the style can serve conservative ideological functions quite well, including the forms of Hollywood utopianism theorized so poignantly by Fredric Jameson.[10]

I wish to emphasize that this binary between dialectical montage, on the one hand, and Hollywood continuity editing, on the other, need not be overstated – regardless of its influence on film criticism and historiography. Especially after the European New Wave and art house first absorbed Hollywood techniques, and America, in turn, experienced its own New Wave and thriving independent film scene beginning especially in the late 1960s, cinematic styles have become mixed – often deliberately so. Furthermore, the more recent international influence of Asian and other global cinemas means that montage styles tend to be much more playful and capacious than what D. W. Griffith or Eisenstein envisioned while elucidating their own principles of editing. As we will see, certain directors' skills in combining basic elements of dialectical montage and continuity editing, more or less simultaneously, can produce distinctive and highly specific commentaries on war, which more exclusive formal approaches alone may fail to communicate.

In what follows, then, I turn to six important filmed Shakespeare battle scenes. Though the films differ in their treatments of the plays and their politics, sometimes quite dramatically, all are demonstrably thoughtful about the relationship between ideology and montage. I would argue that this concern, in fact, trumps smaller ones – sometimes presumed to be larger ones – about remaining faithful to the plays' own presentations of battle; rather than preoccupying themselves overly much with Shakespeare's presumed ethical and political positions on warfare, that is, these directors seem to wrestle primarily with the ethical and political questions raised by their attempts (and perhaps their obligations) to depict warfare more or less realistically. Whether a particular film's treatment of warfare happens to be "accurately" Shakespearean or not proves less important than whether it facilitates more progressive or regressive ways of thinking about the aestheticizing of warfare. Film does not merely enable artists to adapt

Shakespeare's wars; it changes the very questions they, and their audiences, must ask about those wars.

## Laurence Olivier's *Henry V* (1944): The Battle of Agincourt

Few Shakespeare films can be more directly linked to specific wartime imperatives than Olivier's *Henry V*, which was commissioned and partly financed by the British government as a late-war morale booster for troops and audience members alike. The scene in question is, of course, the unlikely triumph of the badly outnumbered English army at Agincourt. It has sometimes been misunderstood by post-Branagh *Henry V* scholars who anachronistically highlight its relative nonrealism while ignoring its complex intertextual engagement with previous war films. The scene is in fact directly, profoundly, influenced by Eisenstein's Battle on the Ice, not just in terms of cinematography but also sound design and editing. Especially in relation to the overall style of the film, the montage is notable for the variety of shots employed (low and high angles, Dutch angles, tracking shots, shifting points of view, overhead shots), the speed of the cuts once the battle begins (3 to 5 seconds is typical), and the deliberately jarring nature of contrasted images (e.g., the extreme 1-second close-up of a horse's braying mouth in between shots of hand-to-hand fighting and running archers). The scene is not as lyrical as Eisenstein's, and in this regard, it is more realistic, emphasizing coherency and clarity of action above the generation of metaphorical or allegorical meanings achieved through the collision of images (see Figure 11.2).

The French charge takes place on a clearly established horizontal plane, screen right to screen left. In a clear tribute to Eisenstein's German charge (also screen right to screen left and quite prolonged), Olivier films the French charge in a rousing tracking shot more than a minute long. Just as Eisenstein's terrified Novgorodian army prays and waits screen left (often in medium shots and close-ups), so do Henry's badly outnumbered British soldiers. In establishing a clear plane of action with relatively few cuts or perspective shots, Olivier insists on clarity about where the action takes place and who its participants are. However, once the first salvo of arrows is fired by the British archers, a brief montage-within-the-montage takes place that serves to highlight the confusion of battle. In this roughly 90-second sequence, Olivier exploits nearly every type of shot and perspective available to him and cuts them extremely rapidly. He then breaks off and begins tracking Henry again, reestablishing the film's interest in the king as an individual subject and reorienting the audience by defining the realistic battle's importance in

Figure 11.2  Director Laurence Olivier's temporary use of dialectical montage in *Henry V* (1944)

relation to the brave young king's life and deeds. Throughout the battle scene, the montage style produces a realistic impression of battle, which is required if it is to serve its allegorical function, but its brand of realism ultimately serves to bolster our sense of English heroism – both at Agincourt and on the continent circa 1945 – and especially of Henry's own prowess and leadership qualities. In short, the montage mode complements a wartime propaganda imperative that demands suppression of the brutal side of Henry that the play explores, including his threats at Harfleur to rape the French women and spit their babies on pikes. Montage, in other words, demands that we read Henry as heroic and honorable; it allows no other way.

## Orson Welles's *Chimes at Midnight* (1965): The Battle of Shrewsbury

*Falstaff*, more often referred to as *Chimes at Midnight*, amalgamated elements of the Henriad and *The Merry Wives of Windsor* to lament the "tragedy" of Sir John and the decline of Merry England. As one might expect from such a project, the film's perspective on war and its chief perpetrators is hardly flattering. In noting how Welles appropriated the Falstaff plays "to denounce modern political hypocrisy and militarism," Tony Howard pin-points the importance of the film's commentary on the horrors of warfare and, perhaps, modernity itself.[11]

Still the most radical of all filmed Shakespeare battle scenes and certainly the most influential one in film history, the Battle of Shrewsbury runs only about six minutes long but required nearly two months of editing. The scene employs a relentlessly fast-paced dialectical montage style, stringing together hundreds of glaringly noncontiguous shots – including low-angle, overhead, dolly, swish pans, freezes, and fast motion shots, to mention only some. Influenced, like *Henry V*, by Eisenstein's Battle on the Ice but now engaging Olivier's film as an intertext, the sequence begins on a clear horizontal plane of action, with the king's army charging right to left, and the rebels left to right. During the entire sequence, the only identifiable individual figure is Falstaff – his incongruous fatness resonating as a type of visual counterpoint to the "honorable" military deeds performed by the hundreds of other men.

Unlike Eisenstein's gradual, lyrical buildup to battle or Olivier's minute-long French charge, both of which work to establish the bravery of the "good" armies, Welles quickly brings the two sides together through cross-cut 2- to 5-second shots of each army's charge. Once the battle begins, the rapidness of the cuts increases, as does the variety of shots – and at no point does the action allow the viewer to identify with any participants in the melee, or even to differentiate loyalist and rebel soldiers. Whereas Olivier's editing eventually slows down, so to speak, to reestablish identification with Henry, leading us all the way up through his one-on-one fight with the dauphin, Welles's montage ends symbolically, with a quasi-surreal sequence of exhausted survivors either wrestling one another or lying dead in the mud and filth of the battlefield. "Honor" proves, indeed, to be "a mere scutch-eon" (*1 Henry IV*, 5.1.138–39).

*Chimes at Midnight* highlights war's erasure of human dignity and individuality. Neither side wins or loses. In battle, humanity crawls back into the filth out of which it supposedly evolved. Unlike Olivier twenty years earlier, Welles is free from Ministry of Information commissions and guidelines. His total commitment to dialectical montage theory serves to highlight the horrors of war without qualification, and the Shrewsbury scene epitomizes how the method can, somewhat counterintuitively, pro-duce a level of realism unachievable on the stage. Moreover, such a realistic depiction of warfare serves to control audience interpretation and identification, ensuring that Falstaff remains the film's most sympa-thetic and beloved character by obliterating the individuality and iden-tifiability of nearly every other character.

## Akira Kurosawa's *Ran* (1985): The Siege of the Third Castle

Kurosawa's late masterpiece, and his third and final Shakespeare adaptation, transports *King Lear* to the Sengoku period (1467–c. 1568) of Japanese history, which was marked by incessant military upheaval and civil conflict. As the film's title might suggest ("*ran*" translates roughly to "chaos"), it is no less cynical about war and violence as inevitable outgrowths of human depravity than is its radical source play. In this regard, *Ran* can be more neatly aligned with *Chimes at Midnight* than films such as Olivier's *Henry V*.

The monumental "Third Castle siege" scene – in which Hidetora's (Lear) retinue is attacked and he is taken captive by his sons Taro and Jiro – lasts approximately twelve minutes and is divided into two clearly marked sections: one featuring a haunting Toru Takemitsu score and a shorter one without music. The subject of the scene is not war per se but, rather, the revelation that life on earth is itself hell and, more generally speaking, that both gods and nature are indifferent to humanity's endless suffering. Indeed, the scene is introduced formally by the first note of Takemitsu's elegiac score, which follows immediately upon the declaration of Hidetora's guard that "we truly are in hell." Civil war and familial discord epitomize the state of chaos into which human ambition and treachery have thrust Japan, paralleling those "late eclipses in the sun and moon" characterized by the distraught Gloucester in the opening of *King Lear*: "in cities, mutinies; in countries, discord; in palaces, treason; and the bond cracked twixt son and father" (1.2.94, 98–100). Perhaps unsurprisingly, the scene is shot in a lyrical rather than realist mode, and the editing is non-dialectical.

The montage does feature several rapid cuts, though generally these appear toward the end of the scene, in the section where more naturalistic sounds – of screams, gunfire, frantic horses – punctuate the score's sudden cessation. Symbolic montage techniques, such as the frequent cutting away to the sun being eclipsed by clouds and smoke, serve mainly to reinforce the hellish themes. The majority of cuts, however, are paced systematically enough to spotlight the importance of *mise-en-scène* over shot collision, calling attention especially to the grotesque formal arrangements of corpses, the mannerist use of color (especially blood red) to accentuate the horrors of the massacre, and the decidedly artificial images that entrance us, such as waterfalls of blood flowing through the castle's floorboards and down its stairways, and especially one seated warrior holding his own detached arm and laughing maniacally at his existential predicament (see Figure 11.3).

Still, however gorgeous and moving these images may be, Kurosawa's juxtaposition of scored and non-scored sections of the scene constitutes its own crucial collision, a declarative rejection of warfare's pure

Figure 11.3 *Mise-en-scène* and meaning in Akira Kurosawa's *Ran* (1985)

aestheticization. The two extended sequences, rather than multiple individual shots, collide to clarify the meaning of the larger scene – producing a unique type of dialectical montage. About eight minutes into the siege, at the moment Taro – Hidetora's eldest son – is betrayed by his younger brother, Jiro, a piercing gunshot abruptly cuts off the score, and the realistic sounds of warfare and death take over the soundtrack for several minutes. The cuts come faster as chaos triumphs. At this point, war ceases to be metaphorical and becomes all too real. In *Ran*, the collision of the seemingly incongruous – of the poetic and the realistic, the metaphorical and the literal – produces one of the more cogent expressions of anguish in world cinema, let alone in the history of Shakespeare adaptation.

## Richard Loncraine's *Richard III* (1995): The Battle of Bosworth at Battersea

The subject of this modernization, cowritten by Ian McKellen and Loncraine, is the rise and fall of a World War II–era English fascist with whom we are forced to identify for nearly two hours. As opposed to the central characters of Olivier's, Welles's, and Kurosawa's films, Richard is unequivocally marked as a villain by film and source play alike, so it is no mistake that continuity (and other formal) techniques associated with the western, gangster, and sci-fi genres work to frame McKellen's "bad guy" even during scenes of major military conflict. These techniques not only contribute to our ability to track Richard through the chaos of war; they present an alternative to a more realist formal approach that would make audience identification with Richard nearly impossible – thereby surrendering the crucial dynamic that makes *Richard III* such a powerful, entertaining play.

In the adapted "Battle of Bosworth Field" scene, filmed at the long-decommissioned Battersea Power Station on the South Bank, the isolated visuals of Richard serve not to reinforce heroism but, instead, to expose acts of duplicity and selfishness, such as when Richard shoots one of his own guards who is attempting to help him escape. The camera focuses on Richard nearly the whole time, even allowing the audience to view this violent scene from the antagonist's perspective. In his notes on the screenplay, McKellen laments the lack of detail Shakespeare provides about the progression of the battle scene, and he admits, "I left it to RL [Loncraine] to invent the progression of the battle in its modern urban setting. His instructions were hand-drawn on a 'story-board,' like a kid's comic, so we could all understand each detail between Richard's last line in the play and his last line in the film."[12] The comment suggests the degree to which concerns about war realism were subordinate for Loncraine and McKellen to concerns about maintaining clear character and plot trajectories. More important, it reveals the degree to which the entire battle scene must revolve around Richard himself.

The scene unsurprisingly winds up being relatively theatrical, Shakespearean, less a clash of two armies than one between two men whose armies recede into background. Jarringly noncontiguous shots occasionally follow one another, and rapidly, but they are also often longer than ten seconds, the combination serving to prioritize narrative clarity in spite of the chaos of war. In the memorable showdown between Richard and Richmond, the large-scale impact of war becomes a blurry background; the camera holds tight in medium shots and close-ups of the two "dueling" men. Only after Richard is shot and/or leaps to his death does the camera's primary commitment to his perspective shift to Richmond's point of view. In a whimsical close-up, the victorious Richmond smiles directly at the camera, breaking the fourth wall and thereby suggesting his replacement of Richard at the seat of English power – and as the primary subject of audience attention and perhaps even identification. The film's critique of war is achieved not merely through the suggestion that Richmond will, like Richard III and the historical Henry VII, become a tyrant, but also through an editing process that limits the audience's awareness of war's atrocities and scale precisely by linking its functionality to the ambitions and self-serving manipulations of morally dubious noblemen.

Loncraine sets *Richard III* specifically in the context of the rise of European fascism, drawing direct parallels between Richard and Hitler

and, eventually, the Tudor monarchs and Hitler. To highlight these connections, he limits dialectical montage techniques in something like a parody of
traditional Hollywood battle sequences, thereby exposing the lies they often
tell. Like the Renaissance stage, the film seems to be arguing, the Hollywood
dream factory produces a version of "heightened reality," to use McKellen's
own term, rather than a truly realistic vision of the world[13] This particular
form of reality often pushes over that thin separating line into surrealism or,
at least, as James Loehlin notes, "The ending of Loncraine's film seems ... to
go beyond its 'realist' mode into this realm of layered and elusive meanings"
established through its constant intertextual engagement of Hollywood
conventions.[14] Such a formal approach suits well a film produced in the
alternate history format of fantasy, incorporating enough realistic details to
establish poignancy and relevancy, but remaining self-conscious and playful
enough to keep audiences willingly complicit in Richard's machinations.

## Ralph Fiennes's *Coriolanus* (2011): The Battle of Corioles

Fiennes's *Coriolanus*, written by John Logan, modernizes the play's setting
into a vaguely twenty-first-century, eastern European country similar to the
Serbia in which it was filmed. The remarkable "battle of Corioles" scene
extends over nearly fifteen minutes of the film's two-hour runtime. Fiennes
condenses and combines scenes 1.3 through 1.5 of Shakespeare's play to
dramatize the conditions according to which human beings will agree to
trade their personal liberties in exchange for the protections and even
tyranny of strong men. The montage style works differently from most of
the other examples in building more directly on the collision of shots, not
merely with one another (the key to the scene's frenetic realism), but with the
poetic lines that Fiennes freely reorganizes to expose the old lie, *dulce et
decorum est*. ... Unlike in the play, where often the only cues for understanding the soldiers' reactions to Martius's speeches and commands are signaled
by vague stage directions and unanswered commands such as "Follow's!"
(1.4.43), the film contextualizes the dilemma of the soldiers – and, consequently, the dilemma of the viewers – through reaction shots and cutting
techniques that offer direct commentary on Martius's words and actions.

Five isolated seconds of film time exemplify the approach:

| | |
|---|---|
| 11:49–50 | Shot from behind Roman soldier's head of distant Volscian building |
| 11:51–53 | Cut to shot of building exploding from bomb impact |
| 11:53–54 | Cut to extreme close-up of Martius's face screaming the beginning of lines 1.4.29–30: "He that retires ..." |

| | |
|---|---|
| 11:54–55 | Cut to close-up of Roman soldier redirecting his eyes from the exploding building to Martius: "I'll take him for a Volsce ..." |
| 11:56–57 | Cut back to extreme close-up of Martius's partial face continuing his speech: "... And he shall feel mine edge" (1.4.30) |
| 11:57– | Cut to second Roman soldier redirecting his eyes toward Martius |
| 11:58– | Cut back to close-up of original Roman soldier still staring at Martius. The command "Go!" is appended here onto Martius's speech |
| 11:59– | One-second zoom-in on dead Roman soldier whose head lies in a pool of gore on the street |
| 12:00– | Cut to long shot of this carnage from anonymous Volscian perspective from atop a distant building |

Eight rapid cuts and nine shots mark the 5-second, 2-line warning and command of Martius, lending the moment its chaotic, realistic quality, but also communicating its critical stance on the human costs of Martius's campaign.

Up to this point, Fiennes has rendered warfare in notably realistic terms, granting the viewer a godlike view of the action from both Roman and Volscian perspectives; so far, Martius has been a mere participant in the battle, however much more vocal his participation has been than that of his subordinates. A moment later, however, after he and his men are debilitated by a booby trap, Martius alone rises up from the ground to continue his siege on the "gates" of Corioles, and the camera settles for nearly the duration of the scene behind him in what appears to be an homage to first-person perspective shooter video games such as *Doom* and *Halo*. This perspective takes to an extreme even the classical Hollywood glorification of the martial hero by erasing the distance between us and him – by putting us into his shoes and tricking us into believing that his survival is our survival, his brutality our salvation (see Figure 11.4). As the masculine hero bravely enters into a blown-out building and kills numerous faceless enemies one by one, Fiennes's noticeable stylistic departure from the montage method Eisenstein used to capture the horrors of battle suggests the ways in which the Hollywood style can be effectively used to glorify individual, martial heroism. But in a move much more deliberate than Olivier's break in *Henry V*, Fiennes has also conditioned us through the earlier dialectical montage sequence – and by rendering so visible the shift away from that style of montage – to loathe the perspective we've been forced to take on

Figure 11.4 First-person shooter perspective in Ralph Fiennes's *Coriolanus* (2011)

here. Just moments prior to a one-on-one knife fight between Martius and Aufidius that would make John Ford proud, we have been made witness by the abruptness of that shift to the logic of our own ideological manipulation. Like the Romans Martius so despises, we loathe him and feel in awe of him; thus, largely as a result of the battle scene Fiennes constructs so meticulously, we are brought into an understanding of the central dilemma that Martius – and leaders of his ilk – represents for the people he is entrusted to protect.

## Vishal Bhardwaj's *Haider* (2014): The Graveyard Conflict

For his third Shakespeare adaptation since 2003, the award-winning Hindi cinema director Vishal Bhardwaj sets *Hamlet* in the context of the India-Pakistan Kashmir conflict in the year 1995. The film's final scene – the equivalent of the fencing scene in the play – occurs in a graveyard where Haider discovers Arshia's (the Ophelia character) body and, as a result of his dramatic reaction to her death, exposes his location to the enemy forces of his uncle Khurram (Claudius), his father's murderer. The play's final scene, with its relatively narrow focus on the destruction of a royal family, is expanded into an extended battle scene whose scale is more appropriate for the larger cultural conflict with which the adaptation concerns itself. The battle is fought between Khurram's forces and the pro-separatist militant group with which Haider has allied himself. Khurram's men charge the graveyard house in which Haider and the heavily armed militants have holed themselves up.

After dozens of men are taken out by the ensuing storm of grenade explosions and gunfire, Haider's mother Ghazala Meer (Gertrude) walks into the center of the graveyard and reveals herself to be wearing a suicide vest. In pulling the grenade pin, she kills herself and all the surviving men except for Haider and a severely wounded Khurram. Haider presses a gun toward Khurram's face but, heeding the final warnings of his mother that "Revenge only begets revenge" and that "Revenge does not set you free," he puts down the weapon and walks away, leaving the screaming Khurram behind, begging to be put out of his misery. Thus, Haider ostensibly rejects the revenge burden imposed upon him as a result of his father's foul murder, choosing personal redemption over the cycle of violence that has torn apart families and destroyed thousands of lives on both sides of the Kashmir conflict. In seeking a way forward through the rejection of violence, *Haider* embraces *Hamlet*'s (and nearly all Elizabethan and Jacobean revenge dramas') famous critique of revenge as base and futile but without killing off the philosopher king who is potentially capable, as both Hamlet and Haider appear to be, of teaching others a more productive way forward. The ending can be reasonably accused of being naive and heavy-handed, but it engages the source text's critical meditations on revenge in direct and complex ways.

Of the films featured in this chapter, *Haider*'s battle scene is edited in the least experimental manner – essentially highlighting classical continuity techniques in order to keep clear the two sides, perhaps in homage to the countless Hollywood westerns whose siege scenarios Bhardwaj's film recreates. The scene takes turns between the assailants' and the defenders' points of view, in part to set up the eventual meeting between Haider and Khurram in the central space where Ghazala blows herself up. Slow motion ratchets up the tension that culminates in the climactic explosion, producing a character-centered focus – all eyes are on the two male leads running toward Ghazala as her finger reaches for the grenade pin – which is nearly the opposite of Welles's dialectical montage approach to war in *Chimes at Midnight*. Bhardwaj's film, like Olivier's, uses a violent Shakespearean conflict to comment on a contemporary military conflict, but unlike *Henry V*, *Haider* is unequivocally pacifist. So why does the film eschew those montage techniques that have become so directly associated with gritty war realism in favor of more classical continuity editing techniques?

The answer may have to do with the way Bhardwaj pens himself in by choosing *Hamlet* as a major source text for his film about Kashmir. Though *Haider* can be said to treat battle, and violence more generally, in a realistic manner – showing the gory carnage and collective trauma it causes – the source dictates that the focus be on one family in particular, and especially one particularly charismatic protagonist. Here the costs of war are measured primarily through the toll they take on a single family and its extended circle; furthermore, the commentary on war is measured best through Haider's own gradual realization of war's futility, so that his rejection of war serves as the logical culmination of a basic coming-of-age narrative. Because wars are driven largely by powerful and charismatic men, those men too, the film suggests, have the ability to end the cycle of violence that feeds wars. Eisenstein's dialectical montage approach to war tends to erase the individual, but Haider, like Hamlet, cannot be erased precisely because this narrative's statement on war is communicated through his individual character arc.

## Conclusion

In four of the six cases discussed above (*Henry*, *Chimes*, *Ran*, and *Coriolanus*), directors use dialectical montage techniques for at least several moments of a given battle scene's total running time. Only Welles, though, can be said to invest wholeheartedly in the dialectical montage approach. Precisely because directors need not commit entirely or exclusively to the technique but, instead, may employ it sporadically, partially, or even symbolically, their adherence to and departures from Eisensteinian methods often constitute keys to understanding both their own politics and their engagement with Shakespeare's politics. In the films of Welles and Kurosawa, human beings are so dwarfed by the scale and atrocity of warfare that even their monumental Shakespearean protagonists disappear into the smoke and dust and blood-strewn earth. Whereas Welles's clear political project of condemning warfare explains his adherence to Eisenstein's dialectical montage method, Kurosawa's cynical vision of warfare as something like the natural condition of debased humanity prompts a more experimentally symbolic approach to both dialectic structure and montage. In the films of Olivier and Fiennes, dialectical montage techniques are employed but gradually give way to more classical forms of editing precisely to illustrate the relationship between the horrors and glories of warfare, on the one hand, and the roles of powerful military leaders, on the other. Though the films of Loncraine and Bhardwaj also highlight the crucial importance of this relationship between war and charismatic men, they more freely embrace their extraordinary individual characters – ironically or sincerely – by eschewing almost entirely all dialectical montage techniques.

To return, then, to a central binary articulated earlier in this chapter regarding the depiction of war in theater versus the cinema: can the Shakespearean battle be depicted in such a way that its monumental scale and its dehumanizing impact – its service to tyrants and tyrannical systems – might be realistically captured? Or must war's true ugliness always be minimized, impressionistically rendered, largely in the service of personal narratives about great men and their singular deeds? Whereas Renaissance drama struggled so hard to depict war in the former way, it excelled at depicting it in the latter way. Shakespeare and contemporaries such as Sidney and Jonson expressed frustration about this fact; crucially, they were not oblivious to it, as *Henry V*'s Prologue makes clear. Filmmakers, on the other hand, have benefited from technologies allowing tremendous creative freedom to depict war in infinitely varied and highly realistic ways. It's tempting to feel that, wherever Eisenstein seems most present in these films, Shakespeare will be most absent. But cinematic montage might also be regarded as the artistic development best capable of revealing that the Prologue's problem was really an opportunity the whole time. Shakespeare could not have imagined the discovery of cinema, and yet his plays are incalculably richer for having anticipated the questions raised by that unborn muse of fire.

*Further Reading*

Aumont, Jacques. *Montage Eisenstein*, trans. Lee Hildreth, Constance Penley, and Andrew Ross, Bloomington, Indiana University Press, 1987.

Bordwell, David, Janet Staiger, and Kristin Thompson. *The Classical Hollywood Cinema: Film Style and Mode of Production to 1960*, New York, Columbia University Press, 1985.

Eisenstein, Sergei. "The Dramaturgy of Film Form," in Leo Braudy and Marshall Cohen (eds.), *Film Theory and Criticism*, 8th ed., Oxford, Oxford University Press, 2016, pp. 23–40.

Jorgensen, Paul A. *Shakespeare's Military World*, Berkeley, University of California Press, 1956.

MacIntyre, Jean. "Shakespeare and the Battlefield: Tradition and Innovation in Battle Scenes," *Theatre Survey*, 23 (1982), pp. 31–44.

Murch, Walter. *In the Blink of an Eye: A Perspective on Film Editing*, 2nd ed., Hollywood, Silman-James Press, 2005.

Potter, Lois. "Scenes and Acts of Death: Shakespeare and the Theatrical Image of War," in Marie-Thérèse Jones-Davies (ed.), *Shakespeare et la Guerre*, Paris, Belles Lettres, 1990, pp. 89–100.

Rothwell, Kenneth S. *A History of Shakespeare on Screen: A Century of Film and Television*, 2nd ed., Cambridge, Cambridge University Press, 2004.

Salt, Barry. *Film Style and Technology: History and Analysis*, 3rd ed., London, Starword, 2009.

Semenza, Greg (ed.). "Shakespeare and the Auteurs: Rethinking Adaptation through the Director's Cinema," special issue, *Shakespeare Bulletin*, 34 (2016).

## NOTES

1 Jean-Louis Baudry, "The Apparatus," trans. Jean Andrews and Bertrand Augst, *Camera Obscura*, 1 (1976), pp. 104–26, 106.

2 Ben Jonson, *Every Man in His Humour*, 2nd version (1616), in Robert M. Adams (ed.), *Ben Jonson's Plays and Masques* (New York: W. W. Norton, 1979), Prologue, 9–12.

3 Sir Philip Sidney, *An Apology for Poetry*, ed. Forrest G. Robinson (New York: Macmillan, 1970), p. 76.

4 Sergei Eisenstein, "The Dramaturgy of Film Form," in Leo Braudy and Marshall Cohen (eds.), *Film Theory and Criticism*, 8th ed. (Oxford: Oxford University Press, 2016), pp. 23–40, 26.

5 Eisenstein, "The Dramaturgy of Film Form," p. 26.

6 Eisenstein, "The Dramaturgy of Film Form," p. 39.

7 Greg Semenza, "Radical Reflexivity in Cinematic Adaptation: Second Thoughts on Reality, Originality, and Authority," *Literature/Film Quarterly*, 41 (2013), pp. 143–53, 146–47.

8 David Bordwell, Janet Staiger, and Kristin Thompson, *The Classical Hollywood Cinema: Film Style and Mode of Production to 1960* (New York: Columbia University Press, 1985), p. 13.

9 Bordwell, Staiger, and Thompson, *The Classical Hollywood Cinema*, p. 194.

10 Fredric Jameson, "Reification and Utopia in Mass Culture (1979)," in *Signatures of the Visible* (London: Routledge, 1990), pp. 11–46.

11 Tony Howard, "Shakespeare's Cinematic Offshoots," in Russell Jackson (ed.), *The Cambridge Companion to Shakespeare on Film* (Cambridge: Cambridge University Press, 2000), pp. 295–313, 296.

12 Ian McKellen, *William Shakespeare's Richard III: A Screenplay* (Woodstock: Overlook, 1996), p. 282.

13 McKellen, *William Shakespeare's Richard III*, p. 44.

14 James N. Loehlin, "'Top of the World, Ma': *Richard III* and Cinematic Convention," in Richard Burt and Lynda E. Boose (eds.), *Shakespeare, the Movie, II: Popularizing the Plays on Film, TV, Video, and DVD* (London: Routledge, 2003), pp. 173–85, 179.

# 12

## GARRETT A. SULLIVAN JR.

# Shakespeare and World War II

This chapter will argue that, while Shakespeare was deployed in World War II Britain for propaganda purposes, references to the playwright or his works also exposed rifts or contradictions within the national culture he was called upon to embody. Additionally, the precise nature of his deployment varied depending upon the medium in which he or his works appeared. To make these points, I will focus on three major venues in which Shakespeare was staged, adapted, or appropriated: the theater, the radio, and the cinema. By doing so, I will suggest that gauging Shakespeare's place in World War II Britain necessitates that we not only catalog signs of his cultural presence but also examine the variable, contested, and sometimes even minor roles he played within different media.

While my chapter will focus on Britain, it should be noted that Shakespeare's role in World War II was an international one. Irena R. Makaryk observes that "[m]ost, if not all, of the belligerents of the Second World War have, at one time or another, laid claim to Shakespeare and have called upon his work to convey their society's self-image."[1] The Nazi appropriation of Shakespeare, which represents the most notorious example of such cultural stake-claiming, was built upon a long-standing German affinity for the playwright.[2] With the Nazis, assertions about Shakespeare's "Germanness" were strongly inflected by race theory.[3] Not only was Shakespeare determined to be "luminously Aryan," in part by using a portrait to take his cranial measurements, but the eugenicist Hans Günther also argued that his writings, especially the "procreation" sonnets, demonstrated the importance of the genetically fit male choosing an appropriate mate.[4] Moreover, the nature of Shakespeare's work was understood to derive from his racial origins: "Since Shakespeare was thus indisputably Nordic, it followed that he had written Nordic plays and verse. (Of course, with classic nazi circular reasoning, his work had earlier helped authenticate his own Nordic status.)"[5] Additionally, Shakespeare was recognized as having potential propaganda value:

Elizabethan England, which had produced Shakespeare, was itself annexed and explicitly equated with the Third Reich: two youthful nations, with strong leaders, opposing corrupt, crumbling empires.... Usefully, this also helped explain why Germany had so far failed to produce a Shakespeare of her own: the bard's England, unlike Germany, had been free of Jews for 300 years (now, of course, there was no holding back the "New Elizabethans" led by Adolf Hitler).[6]

That being said, Nazi admiration for Shakespeare was neither uniformly nor constantly held and, at the height of the war, regard for the playwright was undoubtedly mitigated by his national origins.

Those same origins helped make Shakespeare a propaganda weapon for the British. Consider, for example, the eminent literary critic G. Wilson Knight's *This Sceptred Isle: Shakespeare's Message for England at War*, which was published in 1940 and reprinted three times in less than a year. Knight arranges extracts from Shakespeare's works that are exemplary of "What England is," "How England should act," "What England must oppose," and "What England stands for." The book's concluding passage clearly articulates his conceptual interweaving of Shakespeare and "Englishness":

This war has awaked England, awaked the world, to its own futurity; and, if we are not to slip back miserably into old failures, we need something bigger than ourselves, to which we can go for wisdom and power; something which is nevertheless our own deepest and most royal selfhood, as men and women, as a nation; something which speaks to us not alone of our historic past but, prophetically, of that higher destiny which we serve; something which we shall find in Shakespeare, and in Shakespeare alone – the authentic voice of England.[7]

In asserting that Shakespeare emblematizes both an historic past and a higher destiny, Knight channels and modifies the famous speech by *Richard II*'s John of Gaunt quoted in his book's title. Knight does so, of course, in the name of national unity. "Something bigger than ourselves" that is at the same time "our own deepest and most royal selfhood ... as a nation." Shakespeare is "the authentic voice of England," and it is our Englishness, Knight suggests, that makes of all of us a band of brothers (and sisters).

Knight's unifying rhetoric is of a piece with one of the period's most powerful conceptions: that the British were fighting "a people's war." This idea encompassed both official propaganda initiatives and popular sentiment; it spoke to the felt sense of many that the war had leveled class differences and created a shared sense of purpose.[8] The "old failures" that

Knight mentions would, for many of his wartime readers, include the disparities of rank, wealth, and opportunity that were understood to have been ameliorated (at least temporarily) by the collective response to German aggression. With this in mind, it is worth noting that Knight's appeal to national unity threatens to undermine itself. The "higher destiny" is not Britain's, but England's. The problematically Anglocentric nature of such slippages did not go unnoticed during the war. For example, the BBC received complaints about radio programs that "typically celebrated 'England' rather than 'Britain,' to the increasing resentment of Scotland, Wales, and Northern Ireland. The [Ministry of Information] was sensitive to this problem, and warned the BBC as early as October 1939 to avoid using 'England' as a synonym for 'Britain' ('it causes irritation among the minorities')."[9] Even as Knight identifies Shakespeare as the voice of national destiny, he attests to potential fault lines within his conception of the nation (where exactly do "minorities" such as the Scots and Welsh fit into this picture?). Whether by intention or not, Knight's Shakespeare signals difference as much as he does commonality.

## Theater

Of the three media under examination in this chapter, theater is unsurprisingly the one in which Shakespeare looms largest and functions least equivocally. Moreover, during the war the reach of Shakespearean theater was arguably more truly national than ever before:

> Shakespeare's plays received an increasing number of productions, attracted the country's greatest actors and producers, and were seen by record audiences. In August 1942 alone three new Shakespeare revivals started their runs in London with Gielgud's *Macbeth*, the Old Vic's *Othello*, and Robert Atkins's open-air productions in Regent's Park. And in 1944 the Old Vic at the New [Theatre] as well as Gielgud at the Haymarket established their classical repertory. These ventures more than anything else appeared to contemporaries as the dramatic highlight of the war, the quintessence of what Britain was fighting for.... Although the use of Shakespeare for political purposes was not new, the scale and quality of the revival not only in London but also in the provinces seems unparalleled in British history.[10]

This nationwide flourishing of interest in Shakespeare did not occur spontaneously; it was enabled by state intervention. Although theaters were briefly closed at the beginning of the war, the importance of musical and dramatic entertainment for maintaining the morale of both civilians and the military soon came to be widely recognized. As a result, the state provided regular arts subsidies "for the first time in British history," primarily by means of two organizations.[11] The mandate of the Entertainments National Service Association (ENSA) was to arrange performances for the armed forces at home and abroad, although they also came to be responsible for regular lunchtime concerts at munitions factories. The Council for the Encouragement of Music and the Arts (CEMA), on the other hand, focused entirely on the home front. The differences between the two organizations were not merely jurisdictional. CEMA offered support to the performing arts throughout the nation and "sought to provide audiences even in the remotest parts of the British Isles with works of high art from the established canon."[12] ENSA provided a range of entertainments while skewing toward the popular. Shakespeare was certainly not absent from ENSA's offerings; for example, John Gielgud gave a series of ENSA-sponsored lectures on "Shakespeare in War and Peace."[13] On the other hand, Donald Wolfit, who was well known for lunchtime Shakespeare performances undertaken in London at the height of the Blitz, was rebuffed when he attempted to secure ENSA's backing; the organization's director Basil Dean informed him that "the visit of the Stratford Memorial Theatre [a precursor to the Royal Shakespeare Company] to the camps, whilst much appreciated for the quality of the performances, has not proved to the liking of a large majority of the troops."[14] It is possible that Dean is being diplomatic here, as Wolfit's old-fashioned histrionics were not to everyone's taste. Nevertheless, it is likely that, absent the involvement of a screen star like Gielgud or Olivier, performed Shakespeare and the military were not entirely comfortable bedfellows.

To return to CEMA, one of the primary beneficiaries of the organization's largesse was the aforementioned Old Vic Company, Britain's foremost purveyor of Shakespearean and classical drama in this period. While its home theater was located in London, the company also toured the nation. With the Blitz, it left London: "Save for a few weeks in the spring of 1940 the Old Vic Theatre remained closed for the duration, and from May 1941 onwards suffered increasing damage. The Old Vic Company was to play away for the next ten years."[15] It established a new headquarters in Burnley, from which it sent touring companies throughout Britain – for instance, Sibyl Thorndike and Lewis Casson led several tours to Welsh mining villages.

For all the praise heaped upon the Old Vic, its actions were not universally lauded. Writing immediately after the war, theater director and producer Norman Marshall is dismissive of the Old Vic's "much criticised" decision to abandon its metropolitan home (although it returned to the city for occasional productions). In Marshall's estimation, the Vic showed no sense of duty towards its London audience. The fact that [its home theater] had been destroyed by bombing in May of 1941 was not sufficient excuse for shrugging off its responsibilities so easily. There were other available theatres in London. Besides, the Old Vic had assumed the role of Lady Bountiful in the provinces at a time when its own theatre still stood undamaged and empty.[16]

With his reference to Lady Bountiful, a character from George Farquhar's *The Beaux Stratagem* (1707), Marshall intimates that the Old Vic's touring constituted a patronizing display of theatrical generosity to the less fortunate – meaning, those in the provinces. Meanwhile, the company neglected its true constituents in the metropole. Contrastingly, Marshall praises Wolfit's company for doing what the Old Vic did not: "Although the dressing-rooms were bombed and the costumes in them destroyed, the company continued to play one hour excerpts from Shakespeare for more than a hundred consecutive performances to an average audience of four hundred people a day."[17]

We have encountered two different narratives, then. In one, CEMA and the Old Vic are agents of a theatrical golden age marked by the expansion of interest in Shakespeare and classical drama – "the quintessence of what Britain was fighting for" – across the nation. In the other, the Old Vic Company, like some other Londoners with the resources to do so, abandons the city at the height of the Blitz and thus brings Shakespeare to the provinces to the detriment of inhabitants of and visitors to the metropole: "It is regrettable that for so much of the war London was without its own Shakespearian company, especially at a time when it was thronged with service men from the Dominions, the colonies, the United States and the continent."[18] Of course, these narratives are not mutually exclusive, and Marshall's complaint does not undermine our sense that Shakespeare flourished on the nation's stages. It does, however, articulate by means of the Old Vic's departure the tensions between a London-centered theatrical worldview – the Old Vic was the city's "own Shakespearian company" – and a national one. Perhaps lurking behind Marshall's grievance is the sense that, for all the rhetoric of a collective national endeavor, it was London that bore the brunt, especially but not only during the Blitz. Whether or not Marshall held this view, it is clear that for him the Old Vic's national agenda was to the detriment of its London audience.

## Radio

As Susanne Greenhalgh observes, "British radio Shakespeare means BBC radio Shakespeare."[19] This is because the BBC held a monopoly on radio broadcasting in the nation (although Radio Luxembourg and Radio Normandie reached British audiences until they were shut down at the beginning of the war, and Radio Hamburg's broadcasts from the Nazi propagandist William Joyce ["Lord Haw-Haw"] were widely listened to throughout the war).[20] While this monopoly survived World War II, the BBC underwent dramatic changes during the conflict that entailed a reimagining of both its charge and its relationship to the listening public. Shakespeare was less an agent than a barometer of these changes.

Greenhalgh convincingly demonstrates the abiding role of Shakespeare on BBC radio, even arguing for "the self-identification of BBC broadcasting with Shakespeare throughout its history."[21] However, the war foregrounded the disconnect between the BBC's historical mission, to which Shakespeare was central, and popular tastes. That sense of mission went back to the organization's stewardship by Sir John Reith, who became general manager of the BBC in 1922, the year of its first broadcasts.[22] (The British Broadcasting Company became the British Broadcasting Corporation in 1927; it was "a publicly funded yet quasi-autonomous organization.")[23] Reith's ambition was to educate the BBC's listeners, and his values were undoubtedly elitist. As Thomas Hajkowski puts it, "Reith envisioned British broadcasting as a public service, answerable neither to the government nor to the listeners, but only to a higher cultural ideal. 'Our responsibility,' he wrote in 1924, 'is to carry into the greatest possible number of homes everything that is best in every department of human knowledge.'"[24] Needless to say, this included Shakespeare. Val Gielgud, who was in charge of radio drama at the BBC, notes that

> Shakespeare had been represented in BBC drama schedules from [the beginning]. *Romeo and Juliet* ... was broadcast in July, 1923; and the general directive given me by [Director of Programmes] Roger Eckersley in 1929 included the stipulation that at least eight of Shakespeare's plays should appear in our programmes each year. This stemmed from the unexceptionable point of view that representation of Shakespeare should axiomatically find a place in the Corporation's general cultural and educational policy.[25]

In addition to full adaptations of plays, the BBC presented scenes and extracts from Shakespeare from very early on in its history.[26] We see, then, that Shakespeare is central to the BBC's stated mission. This is not, however, because of overwhelming popular demand, but because the BBC's sense of public service entailed giving listeners what it believed to be good for them.

Tensions between the BBC's mission and the realities of popular taste were present from the beginning:

> Reith and those of his colleagues who shared his sense of mission were unimpressed by what became a seasonal round of newspaper polls which showed

what the public "wanted." ... One of the first of such polls, that in the *Daily News* in May 1924, gave in order as the top twenty programme preferences: popular music, dance music, classical music, *Children's Hour*, humorous items, light opera, grand opera, news, general talk, modern plays, sport, education, classical plays, sacred music, fashion talks, literature, hobbies, domestic economy, religious addresses, decorative schemes and clothing. Most later polls placed classical music (particularly chamber music) far lower in the order and sport far higher.[27]

So, if "classical plays" like those of Shakespeare were integral to the BBC's self-definition and its efforts to educate the masses, for listeners they ranked behind numerous other categories.

Before the war, the BBC was a national service that included six regional networks; while the regions derived content from the London-based national service, they also generated their own programming. (For example, on May 25, 1939, BBC Wales broadcast *Y Marsiandiwr o Venice*, an hour-long Welsh-language version of *The Merchant of Venice*.)[28] With the war, "the BBC synchronized all of its transmitters to the same wavelength and suspended the regional networks for the duration.... [T]he great benefit of synchronization was that it allowed the BBC to be heard, without interruption, throughout the whole of Britain."[29] The Home Service adhered to the model of mixed programming established by Reith, which encompassed, as the abovementioned *Daily News* poll shows, "a heterogeneous variety of programmes that catered in turn to a variety of different tastes."[30] However, during the so-called Bore War – the period of approximately eight months between Britain's declaration of war against Germany (September 1939) and Germany's invasion of France and the Low Countries (May 1940) – the BBC recognized its failure to keep up the morale of restless troops, many of whom chose "Lord Haw-Haw" over the BBC. This recognition led not only to the formation of the Forces Programme, but also to a concomitant transformation of BBC domestic programming.

Siân Nicholas dubs the establishment of the Forces Programme "probably the single most significant wartime decision that the BBC made."[31]

> This was the first British radio station conceived to attract a particular and narrow audience. Programmes were planned to be appropriate to the conditions in which servicemen listened, i.e., in groups, and for the most part as background noise. The new service would be 90 per cent "light." A.P. Ryan ... noted that "if we give them serious music, long plays, or peacetime programme talks, they will not listen."[32]

"Light" programming included, among other things, popular and dance music, variety shows, sports, and advice programs. While designed for the armed forces, the Forces Programme (later redubbed the General Forces Programme) soon became more popular with the general public than the Home Service[33] – and it deviated sharply from the original Reithian model of general mixed programming designed to elevate and educate radio listeners. In 1943, the BBC began planning for its postwar reorganization: the General Forces Programme would effectively become the Light Programme; the Home Service would "continue as in essence a London-based network, which a federation of regional services – Scottish, Northern, Midland, West, Welsh and Northern Irish – could draw upon." Additionally, there would be a Third Programme that hewed closest to the BBC's original vision: "a highbrow network dedicated to the arts, philosophy, serious discussion and experimental programmes."[34] It is with the Third Programme, or Radio 3, that Shakespeare has come to be most closely aligned.[35]

Shakespeare was not entirely absent from the General Forces Programme; for example, half-hour episodes of a series on "Shakespeare's Characters" either originated or were rebroadcast there in 1944 and 1945. Nevertheless, the Home Service was more amenable to Shakespeare during the war years. Bard-centric offerings included either scenes from or full adaptations of plays produced in a radio studio; condensed versions of theatrical productions, including two by the Old Vic Company; programs centered on Shakespeare's songs; broadcasts designed for schools; and even new radio dramas centered on the playwright's life and works (such as *Will Shakespeare* [January 13, 1940] and *Her Majesty Desires, Mr. Shakespeare...* [November 21, 1943]). The wartime broadcast history of *Romeo and Juliet* shows the different ways in which Shakespeare's works were treated on the Home Service. On October 25, 1939, the BBC broadcast a 30-minute program, featuring Alec Guinness and Nova Pilbeam, centered on the balcony scene; on April 6, 1941, an hour-long program presented portions of the play accompanied by extracts from Lamb's *Tales from Shakespeare*; and on June 30, 1944, listeners tuned in for a nearly 3-hour (including the interval) radio adaptation of *Romeo and Juliet*. *Henry V* was represented in similarly diverse ways. A 55-minute broadcast of scenes from the play was heard on November 5, 1939. A small extract appeared in a 75-minute program dedicated to "The Immortal Falstaff" on August 10, 1941, while a version of the entire work, also 75 minutes and featuring Laurence Olivier, was broadcast on April 19, 1942. On February 28, 1943, Leslie Banks starred in *Henry Agincourt: Scenes from "Henry V"* (50 minutes), while a recurring schools program entitled *Senior English II* devoted 40 minutes to the play on May 29, 1945, just weeks after VE day.

While radio productions of Shakespeare had long been a staple of BBC domestic programming, G. Wilson Knight's patriotic exegesis of Shakespeare suggests how such productions could take on new significance during the war, serving to rally the populace or remind it of the values and heritage for which it was fighting.[36] Shakespeare also played a role in the BBC's Overseas (formerly Empire) Service, which expanded dramatically during the war, covering parts of Europe, the Americas, Africa, and Asia.[37] A case in point is a series of thirteen 30-minute broadcasts entitled *The Man Shakespeare*, which were transmitted via the North American Service. Episodes were centered on a single play or a cluster of related ones. For example, the second episode, entitled "World in Arms," took up scenes from *Henry V*, *1 Henry IV*, and *King John* in order to demonstrate, as Knight did, the ties between the Bard and British national identity. The final episode, "The Isle is Full of Noises," made *The Tempest* its focal point, presumably for a pointed propaganda reason: to recall to American listeners, by way of a play often interpreted in terms of the history of the New World, the strong cultural bonds between Britain and the United States. Indeed, that was undoubtedly a purpose of the series as a whole, which concluded on August 28, 1941, just over three months before the United States entered the war. We have seen, then, that radio Shakespeare could serve both to consolidate British national identity and to gesture toward transnational cultural bonds. However, the transformation of the BBC's domestic programming indicates how Britain's national poet was also associated with an elitist model of broadcasting the hegemony of which was overturned during the war years.

## Cinema

The April 19, 1942, radio broadcast mentioned above inspired the production of one of the landmarks of film Shakespeare, Laurence Olivier's 1944 *Henry V*.[38] (For more on Shakespeare and film, see Greg Semenza's contribution to this volume [Chapter 11].) Famous for its formal innovations, the film is also unabashedly propagandistic. Its depiction of the invasion of France strongly evoked the Normandy landings in June of that year, and the movie was intended, in part, to rally the British people for the tough final slog of the war. As James Chapman puts it, the film offers "an historical narrative which used ... a famous English victory over a larger European enemy to draw a parallel with the present; but ... it is also a celebration of English culture and heritage, bringing Shakespearean drama to the screen in a vivid and dramatic form."[39] Olivier's *Henry V* attests to Shakespeare's status as, in Chapman's words, "the supreme embodiment of what is best about national culture."[40]

What do we make of the fact, then, that *Henry V* is the *only* British feature-length Shakespeare film made during the war? Or that it was likely the first Shakespeare feature-length film to be profitable during its initial release?[41] The success and importance of Olivier's movie distracts us from the fact that, during the war, Shakespeare was largely a stranger to British cinemas. A stranger, that is, if we focus exclusively on feature-length adaptations of the plays. If we consider more elliptical cinematic references to the playwright and his works, we see that Shakespeare appears occasionally as a cultural reference point in a wide range of movies, from documentaries to romantic comedies to spy thrillers to costume melodramas. Additionally, we encounter a Shakespeare who sometimes functions in complicated relation to both propaganda objectives and some of the central tenets of the war effort.

From relatively early on in the war, the Ministry of Information (MOI) recognized the need to fight Hitler not only with troops, bombers, and tanks, but also with ideas and images. Anthony Aldgate and Jeffrey Richards are correct when they note that "the story of the British cinema in the Second World War is inextricably linked with that of the [MOI]."[42] Many feature film directors, documentarians, actors, producers, and exhibitors, among others, cooperated extensively with the MOI in order to produce cinematic works compatible with the war effort. Generally speaking, this entailed following the "Programme for Film Propaganda" laid out by Kenneth Clark (the second director of the MOI Films Division) in 1940. The "Programme" stressed three broad themes to be addressed in movies: "What Britain is fighting for"; "How Britain fights"; and "The need for sacrifices if the fight is to be won." Most relevant to our purposes is the first of these themes. Clark describes "What Britain is fighting for" in terms of (1) *British life and character*, "showing our independence, toughness of fibre, sympathy with the under-dog, etc." and (2) *British ideas and institutions*, encompassing "[i]deals such as freedom, and institutions such as parliamentary government."[43] While no literary figures are mentioned in the three brief paragraphs on this topic, Shakespeare fits comfortably within the rubric as an emblem of the virtues and values in the name of which the British are supposedly fighting.

It is one thing for a government ministry to come up with a plan for wartime propaganda; it's another for that plan to be widely adopted throughout the film industry. Cinema owners and audiences were often leery about movies that smacked of propaganda, as Sue Harper discusses:

A *Kinematograph Weekly* article on 11 January 1940, "Do Propaganda Films Pay at the Box-Office?," quoted the owner of two Plymouth cinemas: "People do not want films dealing with war and its horrors or propaganda films which preach at patrons who pay to be entertained." ... [Another] article on

11 January 1945 attack[ed] "the higher cinema being prattled about by the Higher Brows." The British RKO [Studios] sales manager felt that "uplift" was incompatible with audience pleasure and studio profit.[44]

Certain studios – most notoriously, Gainsborough, which produced a series of extremely popular historical melodramas starting in 1943 – broke decisively with propaganda objectives in the name of pleasure and profit. It is remarkable, however, the extent to which film producers, distributors, and exhibitors – not to mention directors, film technicians, and movie stars – subscribed to and advanced the view of film propaganda articulated by the MOI Films Division. As Chapman puts it, "the extensive use of film propaganda had been made possible by the good relations between cinema and state."[45] These good relations informed film production during what is widely regarded to be a golden age of British cinema.

Shakespeare and his works make cameo appearances in a wide range of period movies. Olivier and John Gielgud, the latter of whom is seen preparing to play Othello, appear as themselves in Michael Powell and Emeric Pressburger's tribute to the Fleet Air Arm, *The Volunteer* (1944); Gielgud reappears in Humphrey Jennings's lyrical documentary *A Diary for Timothy* (1945), this time in the role of Hamlet. Herbert Wilcox's spy thriller *The Yellow Canary* (1943) begins with a debate between two fire-watchers over the authorship of Shakespeare's plays. The authorship controversy and *Hamlet* are also central to Leslie Howard's *Pimpernel Smith* (1941), which, among other things, considers Shakespeare's possible Germanness; the film conflates *Hamlet*'s graveyard scene with the protagonist's search for skeletal remains that would prove the existence of an ancient Aryan civilization. Anglo-American relations are explored in Powell and Pressburger's *A Matter of Life and Death* (1945) by staging the rehearsal scene from *A Midsummer Night's Dream*.[46] In Harold French's *The Day Will Dawn* (1942), a German spy does not recognize a quotation from *Romeo and Juliet*, while a Norwegian masquerading as a quisling proves herself an ally by being a lover of both Shakespeare and Dickens. Knowledge of Shakespeare also differentiates the female protagonist from a group of aspiring "chorus girls" in the spy thriller *They Met in the Dark* (1943), directed by Carl Lamac (Karel Lamač). Anthony Havelock Allen's imperial propaganda film *From the Four Corners* (1941), also featuring Leslie Howard, invokes Shakespeare as part of the shared heritage of the Commonwealth countries. And Shakespeare's importance to English nationalism is underscored by the fact that three films take their titles from John of Gaunt's famous "royal throne of kings" speech in *Richard II*: David MacDonald's *This England* (1941), Anthony Asquith's *The Demi-Paradise* (1943), and David Lean's *This*

*Happy Breed* (1944). In most instances, Shakespeare functions in ways that are commensurate with propaganda imperatives – most, but not all.

In the space remaining, I will discuss three films that suggest how Shakespeare can trouble propaganda imperatives as well as support them. Humphrey Jennings's documentary *Fires Were Started* (1943), which was produced for the MOI's Crown Film Unit, focuses on the crew of an Auxiliary Fire Service (AFS) substation at the height of the Blitz. The film's climax is the death of a firefighter during a dockside blaze that threatens supply ships. After finally extinguishing the fire, the remaining members of the crew return to their substation. While the bone-weary men try to recover from their ordeal, Rumbold reads these lines from *Macbeth*:

> Ay, in the catalogue ye go for men,
> As hounds and greyhounds, mongrels, spaniels, curs,
> Shoughs, water-rugs, and demi-wolves are clept
> All by the name of dogs. The valued file
> Distinguishes the swift, the slow, the subtle,
> The housekeeper, the hunter – every one
> According to the gift which bounteous nature
> Hath in him closed.   (3.1.92–99)

The general function of the scene is telegraphed by B. A.'s assertion, in the wake of Rumbold's reading, that the men need to "snap out of it"; they must rally and prepare for another night of fighting fires. This scene is squarely focused on the propaganda themes of sacrifice and of all pulling together.

Given this, one might have expected Rumbold to have turned to, say, *Henry V's* "St. Crispin's Day" speech. Instead, we hear Macbeth's lines to the First and Second Murderers. In comparing men to dogs, Macbeth insinuates that the murderers are not among those breeds to be valued by the king; they will need to prove themselves otherwise by slaughtering Banquo and Fleance. If the film's conclusion stresses group cohesion, this allusion to *Macbeth* foregrounds both inequality and exploitation; Shakespeare becomes the occasion for articulating the AFS's grievances, widely disseminated early in the war, at being overworked, underappreciated, and in harm's way. When B. A. demands that his fellow firemen "snap out of it," he's referring to the temptation to fall into cynicism about the idea of a "people's war" in which class differences are ameliorated and all suffer equally. Shakespeare appears here as a marker of internal difference rather than an expression of who "we" are and what "we" are fighting for.

Leslie Arliss's *The Man in Grey* (1943) and *Love Story* (1944) each offer jaundiced views of Shakespearean drama. The former film, one of the Gainsborough melodramas mentioned above, features a Regency theatrical staging of Desdemona's murder in *Othello*. The performance is comically bad, with "Othello" (Rokeby) and "Desdemona" (Hester) carrying on an onstage conversation between recitations of their lines. Importantly, the scene resonates with two others in the film, both of which evoke not only Othello's famous line, "Put out the light, and then the light" (5.2.7), but also a bed-borne death. An early scene finds Clarissa (who will become first the wife of the vicious Lord Rohan and later Rokeby's lover) pretending to pray at her bedside in order to postpone the symbolically resonant extinction of her candle. Toward the end of the film, the feverish Clarissa, who is murdered in her bed by Hester, evokes the earlier moment, as well as the staged scene from *Othello*, by raving about not "put[ting] out the light." Through the linkage of these three scenes, Arliss smudges the difference between Shakespearean tragedy and Regency melodrama. In doing so, he thumbs his nose not only at propaganda imperatives – so much for Shakespeare as "what we are fighting for" – but also at the canons of taste on display at the BBC or the Old Vic. To put it differently, Arliss gives the people what he believes they want at Shakespeare's expense, even while citing Shakespeare to do so.

The three main characters of *Love Story* – Felicity, a concert pianist with only months to live; Kit, a former engineer and RAF pilot who has learned he will soon go blind; and Judy, a childhood friend of Kit's who secretly loves him – have all escaped the war by moving to Cornwall. There, Judy restores a cliffside amphitheater in order to produce *The Tempest*. Arliss does not stage any of the play, though we witness some rehearsals. Instead, he references *The Tempest* in order to suggest an analogy between remote Cornwall and the play's unnamed island; Felicity, Kit, and Judy's willed self-removal from the war forms an ironic counterpoint to the banishment of Prospero and Miranda. Felicity's eventual return to society takes the form of ENSA-sponsored concerts performed for troops overseas. Contrastingly, Judy's staging of *The Tempest* is part of a broader plan to prevent Kit from reentering the world. In a film that is explicitly critical of those who do not contribute to the war effort, Shakespeare serves as a vehicle for Judy and Kit's evasions. In this way, *Love Story* casts a skeptical glance at the notion animating both CEMA and the BBC Home Service: that Shakespearean drama has an important and salutary part to play in the war.

While Shakespeare was a cornerstone of British wartime nationalism, we can see that, by attending to his place in theater, on radio, and in film, he additionally served as a register of cultural, regional, and social difference. G. Wilson Knight would have it that Shakespeare was at the heart of a "people's war," but the poet also emblematized an elitist worldview at odds with that conception. The point is not to adjudicate between these positions. Instead, it is to suggest that, as the British people – theater professionals and playgoers, radio broadcasters and listeners, filmmakers and cinema audiences – contemplated in their own ways the reality of their nation at war, Shakespeare gave them invaluable material with which to do so.

## Further Reading

Aldgate, Anthony, and Jeffrey Richards. *Britain Can Take It: British Cinema in the Second World War*, 2nd ed., London, I. B. Tauris, 2007.

Chapman, James. *The British at War: Cinema, State and Propaganda, 1939–1945*, London, I. B. Tauris, 1998.

Davies, Anthony. "The Shakespeare Films of Laurence Olivier," in Russell Jackson (ed.), *The Cambridge Companion to Shakespeare on Film*, Cambridge, Cambridge University Press, 2000, pp. 163–82.

Greenhalgh, Susanne. "Shakespeare Overheard: Performance, Adaptations, and Citations on Radio," in Robert Shaughnessy (ed.), *The Cambridge Companion to Shakespeare and Popular Culture*, Cambridge, Cambridge University Press, 2007, pp. 175–98.

Heinrich, Anselm. "Theatre in Britain during the Second World War," *New Theatre Quarterly*, 26 (2010), pp. 61–70.

Makaryk, Irena R., and Marissa McHugh (eds.). *Shakespeare and the Second World War: Memory, Culture, Identity*, Toronto, University of Toronto Press, 2012.

Oesterlen, Eve-Marie. "'Full of Noises, Sounds and Sweet Airs': Shakespeare and the Birth of Radio Drama in Britain," in Olwen Terris, Oesterlen, and Luke McKernan (eds.), *Shakespeare on Film, Television and Radio: The Researcher's Guide*, London, British Universities Film and Video Council, 2009, pp. 51–73.

Semenza, Greg, and Bob Hasenfratz. *The History of British Literature on Film, 1895–2015*, London, Bloomsbury, 2015.

Strobl, Gerwin. *The Swastika and the Stage: German Theatre and Society, 1933–1945*, Cambridge, Cambridge University Press, 2007.

Sullivan, Garrett A., Jr. "'More Than Cool Reason Ever Comprehends': Shakespeare, Imagination and Distributed Auteurism in *A Matter of Life and Death*," *Shakespeare Bulletin*, 34 (2016), pp. 373–89.

## NOTES

1 Irena R. Makaryk, "Introduction," in Makaryk and Marissa McHugh (eds.), *Shakespeare and the Second World War: Memory, Culture, Identity* (Toronto: University of Toronto Press, 2012), pp. 3–21, 4.

2 Anselm Heinrich, "'It Is Germany Where He Truly Lives': Nazi Claims on Shakespearean Drama," *New Theatre Quarterly*, 28 (2012), pp. 230–42, 231; "Theatre in Britain during the Second World War," *New Theatre Quarterly*, 26 (2010), pp. 61–70; and *Entertainment, Propaganda, Education: Regional Theatre in Germany and Britain Between 1918 and 1945* (Hatfield: University of Hertfordshire Press, 2007).

3 Gerwin Strobl, "The Bard of Eugenics: Shakespeare and Racial Activism in the Third Reich," *Journal of Contemporary History*, 34 (1999), pp. 323–36; *The Germanic Isle: Nazi Perceptions of Britain* (Cambridge: Cambridge University Press, 2000), pp. 36–60; and "Shakespeare and the Nazis," *History Today*, 47 (1997), pp. 16–21.

4 Strobl, "The Bard of Eugenics," pp. 332–33.

5 Strobl, "The Bard of Eugenics," p. 333.

6 Strobl, "Shakespeare and the Nazis, " pp. 19–20.

7 G. Wilson Knight, *This Sceptred Isle: Shakespeare's Message for England at War* (Oxford: Blackwell, 1940), p. 36.

8 Angus Calder, *The People's War: Britain 1939–1945* (New York: Pantheon Books, 1969); and *The Myth of the Blitz* (London: Pimlico, 1994).

9 Siân Nicholas, *The Echo of War: Home Front Propaganda and the Wartime BBC, 1939–45* (Manchester: Manchester University Press, 1996), p. 231.

10 Heinrich, "Theatre in Britain during the Second World War," pp. 65–66.

11 Heinrich, "Theatre in Britain during the Second World War," p. 62.

12 Heinrich, "Theatre in Britain during the Second World War," p. 63.

13 Heinrich, *Entertainment, Propaganda, Education*, p. 47.

14 Ronald Harwood, *Sir Donald Wolfit, C.B.E.: His Life and Work in the Unfashionable Theatre* (New York: St. Martin's Press, 1971), pp. 146–47.

15 George Rowell, *The Old Vic Theatre: A History* (Cambridge: Cambridge University Press, 1993), p. 129.

16 Norman Marshall, *The Other Theatre* (London: John Lehmann, 1947), pp. 133, 134.

17 Marshall, *The Other Theatre*, p. 133.

18 Marshall, *The Other Theatre*, p. 133.

19 Susanne Greenhalgh, "Shakespeare Overheard: Performance, Adaptations, and Citations on Radio," in Robert Shaughnessy (ed.), *The Cambridge Companion to Shakespeare and Popular Culture* (Cambridge: Cambridge University Press, 2007), pp. 175–98, 177; and "Shakespeare and Radio," in Mark Thornton Burnett, Adrian Streete, and Ramona Wray (eds.), *The Edinburgh Companion to Shakespeare and the Arts* (Edinburgh: Edinburgh University Press, 2011), pp. 541–57.

20 Andrew Crisell, *An Introductory History of British Broadcasting*, 2nd ed. (London and New York: Routledge, 2002), p. 52.

21 Greenhalgh, "Shakespeare Overheard," p. 195.

22 David Cardiff and Paddy Scannell, "Broadcasting and National Unity," in James Curran, Anthony Smith, and Pauline Wingate (eds.), *Impacts and Influences: Essays on Media Power in the Twentieth Century* (London and New York: Methuen, 1987), pp. 157–73, 158–59.

23 Crisell, *An Introductory History of British Broadcasting*, p. 28.

24 Thomas Hajkowski, *The BBC and National Identity in Britain, 1922–53* (Manchester: Manchester University Press, 2010), pp. 10–11.

25 Val Gielgud, *Years in a Mirror* (London: The Bodley Head, 1965), p. 180.

26 John Drakakis, "Introduction," in Drakakis (ed.), *British Radio Drama* (Cambridge: Cambridge University Press, 1981), pp. 1–36, 3.

27 Asa Briggs, *The BBC: The First Fifty Years* (Oxford: Oxford University Press, 1985), p. 62; and *The War of Words* (1970) (Oxford: Oxford University Press, 1995), p. 517.

28 Unless otherwise specified, information about BBC broadcasts is derived from the invaluable "International Database of Shakespeare on Film, Television and Radio," hosted by the British Universities Film and Video Council: http://bufvc .ac.uk/shakespeare/. Last accessed January 12, 2017.

29 Hajkowski, *The BBC and National Identity in Britain*, p.121.

30 Nicholas, *The Echo of War*, p. 12.

31 Nicholas, *The Echo of War*, p. 41.

32 Nicholas, *The Echo of War*, p. 51.

33 Briggs, *The BBC*, p. 187.

34 Crisell, *An Introductory History of British Broadcasting*, p. 67.

35 Greenhalgh, "Shakespeare Overheard," p. 186.

36 Eve-Marie Oesterlen, "'Full of Noises, Sounds and Sweet Airs': Shakespeare and the Birth of Radio Drama in Britain," in Olwen Terris, Oesterlen, and Luke McKernan (eds.), *Shakespeare on Film, Television and Radio: The Researcher's Guide* (London: British Universities Film and Video Council, 2009), pp. 51–73, 68–69.

37 Briggs, *The War of Words*, pp. 442–77.

38 Anthony Davies, "The Shakespeare Films of Laurence Olivier," in Russell Jackson (ed.), *The Cambridge Companion to Shakespeare on Film* (Cambridge: Cambridge University Press, 2000), pp. 163–82, 167.

39 James Chapman, *The British at War: Cinema, State and Propaganda, 1939–1945* (London: I. B. Tauris, 1998), p. 247.

40 Chapman, *The British at War*, p. 244.

41 Greg Semenza and Bob Hasenfratz, *The History of British Literature on Film, 1895–2015* (London: Bloomsbury, 2015), p. 220.

42 Anthony Aldgate and Jeffrey Richards, *Britain Can Take It: British Cinema in the Second World War*, 2nd ed. (London: I. B. Tauris, 2007), p. 4.

43 This document is reproduced in Ian Christie (ed.), *Powell, Pressburger and Others* (London: BFI, 1978), pp. 121–24. See also Chapman, *The British at War*, p. 26.

44 Sue Harper, *Picturing the Past: The Rise and Fall of the British Costume Film* (London: BFI Film Publishing, 1994), p. 97.

45 Chapman, *The British at War*, pp. 249–50.

46 Garrett A. Sullivan Jr., "'More than Cool Reason Ever Comprehends': Shakespeare, Imagination and Distributed Auteurism in *A Matter of Life and Death*," *Shakespeare Bulletin*, 34 (2016), pp. 373–89.

# 13

PAUL STEVENS

# *Henry V* and the Pleasures of War

As this volume makes abundantly clear, it is difficult to talk about Shakespeare and war without referring to its extraordinarily influential representation in *Henry V*. Indeed, from the seventeenth century to the most recent wars, from *Paradise Lost* to *Blood Meridian*, Shakespeare's drama has played a central role in Anglophone representations of war. It is woven into the fabric of our culture: when its lines are quoted by Colonel Collins of the Royal Irish on the eve of the Iraq War or more recently by the eulogist at Senator McCain's funeral, no one has to explain where phrases like "band of brothers" come from. But at the same time, no one fully understands the play from which they come, for the play is, of course, complex and highly ambivalent, especially about war. The text of *Henry V* that has dominated the play's reception over the last four centuries, the 1623 First Folio edition of Shakespeare's *Comedies, Histories, & Tragedies*, is remarkable for the way it contains passages that simultaneously intensify both the play's skepticism about the value of war and its exhilaration in the practice of war.[1] At the center of any comprehensive understanding of the play lies the relation between these two contradictory or countervailing tendencies, especially the degree to which the latter, the play's delight in war, complicates the former and so denies any clear-cut moral critique. It is true that in performance either one of these tendencies might be heightened and the play redirected to a more pointed end, obvious examples being Laurence Olivier's film emphasizing the exhilaration of war and Kenneth Branagh's the skepticism.[2] But in the text, in F itself, they remain unresolved. The text is, as Claire McEachern observes, anamorphic.[3] Change your angle of vision and the play changes with it.

No modern response foregrounds the confusion this ambivalence produces more succinctly than that of the great antiwar poet, Wilfred Owen. Owen loved *Henry V*, a play that, he says to his mother in September 1911, "I have read, and learnt, and spouted these last two years." In the same letter, he appears animated by the Chorus's appeal to "a muse of fire that would ascend / The brightest heaven of invention" (Prologue, 1–2). Caught "between two fires" or manifestations of Shakespeare's muse, caught between going to see a performance of *Macbeth* and one of *Henry V*, Owen assures his mother that he will draw something of value from either one: depend upon it, "whichever Fire indraws me, I shall extract the brilliance and the fervour of the flames, and shall come out unscathed."[4] Seven years later, in October 1918, far from being unscathed by the fires of war, if not by Shakespeare's muse, he can still disconcertingly write of war's Shakespearean joys. Long after he had written his most famous antiwar poems, in the aftermath of a bloody assault on the village of Joncourt, he writes of war's ecstasy: "I can find no word to qualify my experiences except the word SHEER," he explains to his mother. Those experiences transcend abhorrence: "I lost all my earthly faculties and fought like an Angel." With a young corporal "who stuck to me and shadowed me like your prayers I captured a German Machine Gun and scores of prisoners ... I only shot one man with my revolver (at about 30 yards!); the rest I took with a smile."[5] Almost incomprehensibly, after all he's been through, it's not the fire of *Macbeth*'s horror that animates or "indraws" him but the fire of *Henry V*'s exhilaration.

Written in 1599 during one of the most intense periods of the Anglo-Spanish War of 1585–1604, Shakespeare's play insists on the pleasures of war, on precisely the kind of exhilaration Owen feels, on emotional elevation or transcendence, on the deeds of England's "mighty men" in "the full course of their glory" (Epilogue, 3–4). But the significance of those joys, I want to suggest, is more complex than either a reflex gesture toward "nationalism" or a superficial reading of Owen's letters might allow. Indeed, so much of the play's staying power lies in the very distinctive way it represents war's pleasure or the peculiar experience of fighting like an angel – that is, in the specific way it aestheticizes war. Before trying to explain how it does this – how it makes war seem sublime, attractive, or a thing of great joy – let me say something about its antithesis, the play's recurrent skepticism.

### Few Die Well that Die in a Battle

That skepticism and the class divide it marks are hard to miss. If war at its most exhilarating is articulated by the Chorus, the king, and the play's aristocrats, so war at its most troubling is given voice in the behavior and concerns of the play's common soldiers. This is not surprising since England's ancient aristocracy is historically committed to war in a way that common people are not.[6] This double-register is evident from the beginning.

It is strikingly epitomized in act 2, for instance, when the Chorus's epic imagination of England's youth as winged "Mercuries," heroes in whose breasts only honor reigns (2.0.1–7), is immediately confounded by their first appearance on stage. The "youth of England" may be "on fire" but all we actually see is the "flashing fire" (2.1.49) of ancient Pistol and his antic rabble, the ensign's strutting braggadocio and Bardolph's poxed-up face. The Homeric reach of the Chorus is parodied in a kind of mock-heroic, lower-class antimasque where Nym plays Troilus to Pistol's Diomedes as they struggle over Mistress Quickly's Cressida. Hence Pistol's allusion to Robert Henryson's late medieval *Testament of Cressid* in rebuking Nym: "think'st thou my spouse to get? . . . / Fetch forth the lazar kite of Cressid's kind, / Doll Tearsheet she by name, and her espouse" (2.1.68–72). The two groups who most bear the burden of the play's skepticism are then, first, this one, the broken remnant of Falstaff's old company (Bardolph, Pistol, and Nym) and, second, the much more soldierly community of Captain Gower's men-at-arms (Court, Bates, and Williams). Both these companies of the king's infantry are deployed to question the value of war, the first in its caricature-like rapaciousness and the second in its conscientiousness.

The trajectory of Falstaff's old company is one of increasing, self-defeating disintegration. Overwhelmed by the death of Falstaff himself – the king "has killed his heart" (2.1.82) – the company, despite its attempts to reconstitute itself, goes from bad to worse. In this great national war, the comic exuberance of the *Henry IV* plays turns sour. It's true that they still talk of "brotherhood" (2.1.101), that Bardolph urges them to storm the breach at Harfleur, and that Pistol movingly pleads for Bardolph's life, but they are leaderless. They have no captain, only a confusion of lieutenants, ensigns, and corporals: it's never clear who's in charge or indeed what their purpose is other than "filching" (3.2.40). More than anything else they appear as the parasites war encourages: "Let us to France, like horse-leeches, my boys," says Pistol, "To suck, to suck, the very blood to suck" (2.3.46–47). The Boy, Falstaff's former page, serves as a kind of anti-Chorus charting the course of their accelerating corruption: "As young as I am, I have observed these three swashers . . . three such antics do not amount to a man. . . . Their villainy goes against my weak stomach, and therefore I must cast it up" (3.2.25–47). Their ultimate fate is hanging and humiliation. While their villainy may be there to illustrate the deleterious effects of war, it is also there to highlight its virtues, that is, to justify the king's stern discipline and validate the new professionalism of England's archipelagic captains: "Go, go, you are a counterfeit cowardly knave," Captain Gower reproves the incompetent Pistol in defense of his professional comrade, the Welsh Captain Fluellen. "You thought because he could not speak English in the native garb, he could not therefore handle an English cudgel. You find it otherwise. And henceforth let a Welsh correction teach you a good English condition" (5.1.62–70). All four of the archipelagic captains, despite Fluellen's doubts about MacMorris, are at one in their professionalism: they all have "good knowledge and literature in the wars" (4.7.135–36). In details like these, the criticism of war so evident in the actions of the Eastcheap Company is contained, put in perspective. But things prove more difficult with Captain Gower's soldiers.

It is a measure of the pervasive influence of Shakespeare's play that the infantry companies of both Falstaff and Gower are reproduced in David Jones's First World War company of Welsh fusiliers. In Jones's great prose poem, *In Parenthesis*, he explains how "trench life brought the play [*Henry V*] pretty constantly to mind."[7] Jones's London Welsh companions are the "children of Doll Tearsheet,"[8] he says, and before the climactic assault on Mametz Wood, "some bastard woods as Jerry was sitting tight in,"[9] Privates Ball, Olivier, and Lewis rehearse the anxieties of their ancestors, "privates" Court, Bates, and Williams (4.1.215). In Jones's poem, these "three loved each other" and tried to talk of "ordinary things," but they have no doubt about the impending battle and how it is likely to be a "first clarst bollocks and murdering of Christen men."[10] In Shakespeare's play, war and the murdering of Christian men is very much on the mind of Private Williams. He knows that if the king's cause is unjust, "if the cause be not good" (4.1.125), Henry's guilt will be irredeemable: he will have "a heavy reckoning to make," when, in a nightmare parody of Ezekiel's valley of dry bones "all those legs and arms and heads chopped off in a battle shall join together at the latter day and cry all, 'We died at such a place' – some swearing, some crying for a surgeon, some upon their wives left poor behind them, some upon the debts they owe, some upon their children rawly left" (4.1.125–31). The emphasis here is on the king's possible failure in making the case *jus ad bellum*, that is, the justice of his cause in going to war, but Williams's following reflection that "few die well that die in a battle" (4.1.131–32) allows the king to quietly switch the charge to *jus in bello*, that is, the justice of his soldiers' behavior in war.[11] While the force of this justification has been prepared for by the king's obsessive concern with his soldiers' discipline, in the immediate context of his response to Williams it constitutes an extraordinary act of equivocation. Williams's question is not "is the king responsible for his soldiers' personal behavior?" but "is the war the king initiated just?" Williams remains pointedly silent and the effect of Henry's equivocation on the play is dramatically anamorphic. It opens up an oblique angle or skeptical perspective on everything. Innocently seeking common ground on the hardness of their common bivouac, Sir Thomas

Erpingham's response to the king, for instance, suddenly sounds ominous: "Now lie I like a king" (4.1.17).

As the king absolves himself of guilt, so he proceeds in anger and self-pity to strip his own kingship bare – if not his very grounded sense of self. In this, he inadvertently reveals the taint of his Cheapside education. That is, in his deconstruction of ceremony, Henry sounds a lot like Falstaff in his famous deconstruction of honor (*1 Henry IV*, 5.1.127–39). Not that the king dislikes honor, but the process of dismantling an inconvenient ideal is similar. He has learned well. Even so, as he does this and one complex pattern pushes the play increasingly toward a skeptical critique of war, a powerful countervailing pattern begins to emerge – one that speaks directly to the peculiar pleasure the play's representation of war produces.

## Political Theology and the King's *Virtù*

In this new, critically important pattern, Shakespeare reveals a distinctive understanding of "political theology," or the way theology informs politics. Not knowing who his interlocuter is, Williams speaks to the king without ceremony, like an equal, and Henry doesn't like it. Despite Henry's earlier, somewhat complacent concession that the king is "but a man" (4.1.101), he finds the reality not to his taste. It is this chastening encounter with his "privates" that leads him to reflect on the thankless burdens of kingship. What might most sustain a medieval king is unexpectedly and revealingly trivialized and dismissed out of hand. The only thing that distinguishes a king from his people, Henry argues, is "ceremony" and what is that? What "art thou, thou idol ceremony?" he asks, not waiting for an answer (4.1.217). Although Henry acknowledges a version of the king's two bodies, that he is "Twin-born with greatness" (4.1.211) and that there is a difference between his "royal person" and his private person (2.2.165, 173), he has no real belief in the sacral power of monarchy.[12] For him, monarchy's divinity is a false god and its ceremony simply a matter of empty or idle forms: "Art thou aught else but place, degree, and form" only there to create "awe and fear in other men?" (4.1.223–24). In this Machiavellian moment, Shakespeare's character distinguishes himself from both his historical models, Richard II and Henry V, and more immediately important, from his fictional antecedent, Shakespeare's Richard II. Unlike them, the political theology of Shakespeare's Henry is entirely instrumental.

For Shakespeare's Richard, ceremony is central to kingship and his sense of being in the world – fragile as that sense turns out to be. For him, ceremony, drawing on its original Latin meaning of *caerimonia*, is a religious ritual that binds human and divine realms. Here, most importantly in the

coronation rite, it binds the king to his people and through him the people to
God. It is this that constitutes the very "soul" of ceremony's "adoration"
(4.1.222), the essence that Henry cannot quite see. For Richard, it has all the
power Henry denies: "Not all the water in the rough rude sea," says
Richard, "Can wash the balm from an anointed king. / The breath of
worldly men cannot depose / The deputy elected by the Lord" (*Richard II*,
3.2.49–52). For a moment, Richard convinces himself that for every man the
rebels raise, God will enlist a "glorious angel," and "if angels fight, / Weak
men must fall, for heaven still guards the right" (56–57). For Richard,
political theology means the degree to which the divine is a real presence:
that is, to which its immanence sustains the king and interpenetrates politics
even at its most quotidian. For Henry, this is a fantasy; the political theology
implicit in Richard's understanding of ceremony is nothing but a "proud
dream" (4.1.234). Ceremony has no intrinsic power, he says as though he
were speaking directly to Richard:

> I know
> 'Tis not the balm, the scepter, and the ball,
> The sword, the mace, the crown imperial,
> The intertissued robe of gold and pearl,
> The farcèd title running fore the king,
> The throne he sits on, nor the tide of pomp
> That beats upon the high shore of this world –   (4.1.236–42)

What attribute or power does then? The play seems pretty clear in its
answer, and it is this that emerges to confound or occlude the play's
skepticism about war.

For a Machiavellian prince like Shakespeare's Henry V, what beats upon
the high shore of the world is *virtù* – not virtue but manly prowess or the
king's will, what he calls his hawk-like "affections" or desires, ambitions
that are "higher mounted" than those of ordinary men (4.1.102). What
emerges to confound the play's skepticism about war is the way contingency
facilitates *virtù*; that is, the way the prince in his entirely human, apparently
amoral *virtù*, is more than willing to take advantage of occasion, and most
importantly, our pleasure in it. At Agincourt, feeling endangered, Henry's
sudden, instinctive, and utterly ruthless decision to cut his prisoners' throats
is greeted by the moderate, good-natured Gower with awe and joy: "Oh, 'tis
a gallant king!" (4.7.8). The king's decisiveness or "decisionism," his fer-
ocious prowess and supreme self-confidence in his own power to decide, is
absolute and thrilling. Like that of Machiavelli's Cesare Borgia, it is always
ready to swoop, in brute speed, valor and act, as it does here and on the
Southampton conspirators; or to galvanize and mold England's archipelagic

soldiers into one as he does before the breech at Harfleur; or to articulate itself in the form of carefully calculated policy as it does with just war theory throughout the play. Despite his opening insistence on *jus ad bellum* and his later resort to *jus in bello*, for instance, it's not clear that either of these arguments are anything but matters of expedience, both driven by the king's relentless will. His concern for discipline and the just behavior of his soldiers is similarly quite simply a matter of policy. The grace he offers the people of Picardy and Artois comes at the expense of the mercy he denies his old Cheapside comrade, Bardolph. Bardolph must die not to do justice but to win the hearts and minds of the local people, for, as Henry explains, "when lenity and cruelty play for a kingdom, the gentler gamester is the soonest winner" (3.7.100–1). Winning may be all and agency its own end, but that's not, of course, how it feels.

Although ceremony and the particular kind of political theology it signifies may have little meaning for the king, its forms or accidents live on and the contents of those forms provide an enabling sense of legitimation. They become masks of power. That is, the forms may still be used – even if they are used in ways that might have appalled the intensely religious, historical Henry V. Angels may not really fight but it is of enormous advantage, comfort, and indeed intense pleasure to behave as if they did. Not as Shakespeare's ineffectual Richard II does, but as his masterful Henry V does. What begins to emerge in Shakespeare's clash of "two mighty monarchies," massive polities whose "fronts" are imagined as "high, upreàred, and abutting" (Prologue, 20–21), is a new secular sense of political theology, one in which fighting like an angel and the agency or delight in life it articulates offers a peculiarly sublime pleasure. This is so because in *Henry V*, if not Owen, *virtù*'s violence is sacralized and functions as one of the German jurist Carl Schmitt's now famous "secularized theological concepts."[13] That is, as the play's biblical language suggests, the king's violence is quite consciously made to represent itself as a manifestation of God's freedom – even though it is quite clearly merely an arrogation of that freedom. In this new kind of political theology, the concept of God's freedom and the sheer terror it threatens is appropriated and transferred to the prince, not as God's deputy but as the nation's increasingly secular sovereign, its own "dread King" (3.4.47). To understand the genesis of this appropriation more fully, we need to turn, however briefly, to what we know of the historical Richard II and Henry V.

## God's Freedom and Its Violence

Both these medieval kings, the historical Richard II and Henry V, seem to have believed in the sacral power of monarchy. For almost a year during his father's exile in 1398–99, Henry of Monmouth, the historical model for Shakespeare's Henry V, was a member of King Richard's household. The king, his father's mortal enemy, treated the eleven-year-old hostage with great kindness, granting him an allowance of £500 a year and referring to him as our "good sonne Henry."[14] The boy's first experience of war was at the king's side in Ireland: Richard knighted him and it seems clear that an unlikely bond of affection grew up between the two. Henry showed no great desire to join his father when the rebellious Bolingbroke landed at Ravenspur in July 1399, and one of the first actions Henry took when he himself became king in 1413 was to reinter the murdered Richard with great ceremony in Westminster Abbey. This act of reverence is as important as it is because the Abbey, the place where Richard had always wished to be buried, was the center of his cult of sacral monarchy. That cult, so powerfully visualized in the Wilton Dyptich, insists on the divinity of the king's sovereignty: he was chosen not by the people or any of the nation's estates, but by God. His authority, as it's so powerfully remembered in Shakespeare's *Richard II*, was divine. In the Dyptich, a moveable altar piece intended to aid Richard in his personal devotions, the king appears in an "intertissued robe of gold and pearl"; he is presented to the Virgin Mary and her Son by John the Baptist and Anglo-Saxon England's royal saints, Edmund the Martyr and Edward the Confessor. Westminster Abbey had been founded by Edward and both these ancient English kings had chapels in the royal mausoleum. Yet, however much Richard revered and wanted to join his tragic forbears, he imagined himself not so much as Christ the suffering servant or even Christ the redeemer, but as Christ the King. At his coronation Richard became the "anointed" one of Psalm 2, the king whom God places on his holy hill of Zion and to whom he declares: "Thou *art* my Son; this day have I begotten thee" (Psalm 2:7). That is, in anointing the king with holy oil, the coronation ritual reenacted the election of David as Messiah, the king whose typological relation to Christ the King is made explicit in the New Testament's forceful reinterpretation of the royal psalm (Acts 4:24–26). Most importantly for the present argument, through the authority of the psalm the king's sovereignty is imagined not only as unqualified but as irresistible in its unrelenting violence: "Why do the heathen rage, and the people imagine a vain thing? ... He that sitteth in the heavens shall laugh: the Lord shall have them in derision.... Thou *art* my Son; this day have I begotten thee.... Thou shalt break them with a rod of iron; thou shalt dash them in pieces like a potter's vessel" (Psalm 2:1–9). High on a hill Yahweh smiles as his son breaks his enemies in pieces.

In Shakespeare's *Henry V*, the echoes of this psalm constitute a barely heard, but insistent base note of sacred violence reverberating throughout the play. God's violent resolution for his son is appropriated and reproduced in Henry's terrifying resolve: "Now are we well resolved" – by God's help and with France being ours, "we'll bend it to our awe, / Or break it all to pieces" (1.2.223–26). Violence is imagined as the most immediate and dramatic measure of agency: "How terrible in constant resolution" (2.4.35), says the French king as he identifies the coming of Henry with the violent exaltation of Edward III's son at Crécy. There, as he remembers it, the Black Prince breaks the French in pieces while his father, "his mountain sire, on mountain standing / Up in the air, crowned with the golden sun, / Saw his heroical seed, and smiled to see him / Mangle the work of nature" (2.4.57–60). The English Archbishop of Canterbury remembers the same battle but with unconcealed joy: while the king's son breaks the French, "his most mighty father on a hill / Stood smiling to behold his lion's whelp / Forage in blood of French nobility" (1.2.108–10). Nowhere in Scripture is the violence of God's agency more powerfully articulated than in Yahweh's final response to Job. Out of the whirlwind human reason is made to bend to God's *virtù*. In Shakespeare's play, one of the central images from Yahweh's response is assigned to the dauphin. The dauphin's apostrophe to his horse is any number of things but, most importantly, it is a redaction of Yahweh's apostrophe to his great war horse in Job.

The climax of the Book of Job is primarily an extraordinary expression of God's freedom – the will or *virtù* that overawes reason. The book does this through a series of images of immense, irresistible power, most importantly here images of the war horse and Leviathan. In his anguish, Job would curtail God's freedom and reduce him to the measure of human reason. He would subject God to a "natural" or human conception of justice as equity: "Let me be weighed in an even balance," he cries out in his suffering, "that God may know mine integrity" (Job 31:6). But Yahweh will not be held to account by one of his own creatures. He speaks out of the whirlwind: "Who is this that darkeneth counsel by words without knowledge?" Answer me this, he demands of Job: "Where wast thou when I laid the foundations of the earth?" Where were you when "the morning stars sang together, and all the sons of God shouted for joy?" (38:1–7). And then as if to emphasize the transcendence of his power, he turns to one of the most sublime of his creations, the war horse. Consider the horse, Yahweh says:

> Hast thou given the horse strength? hast thou clothed his neck with thunder? Canst thou make him afraid as a grasshopper? The glory of his nostrils *is* terrible. He paweth in the valley, and rejoiceth in *his* strength: he goeth on to meet the armed men. He mocketh at fear, and is not affrighted; neither turneth he back from the sword. The quiver rattleth against him, the glittering spear and the shield. He swalloweth the ground with fierceness and rage: neither

believeth he that *it is* the sound of the trumpet. He saith among the trumpets, Ha, ha; and he smelleth the battle afar off, the thunder of the captains, and the shouting.                                                                   (39:19–25)

In the Book of Job, the image of the war horse in all his power and glory serves as a metonym for the sublimity of God's freedom. In his majesty he soars like a hawk towering in the sky. "Doth the hawk fly by thy wisdom, *and* stretch her wings toward the south?" demands Yahweh (39:26). In so many subsequent, secular texts, however, the image becomes a metonym not for God's power but for the sublimity of human agency and, most importantly, its violent expression in warfare. Violence becomes the register of human freedom. In Job's war horse, says Edmund Burke, bearing witness to the aesthetic pleasure of war, "the terrible and sublime blaze out together."[15]

In *Henry V*, the image is separated from God and arrogated by the French dauphin, the character whose endless but foolish self-glorification is meant to parody Henry's very real *virtù*. Consider my horse, the play's counterfeit Henry says on the night before Agincourt, speaking as though he were Yahweh. I would not trade him for any that treads on four pasterns: "Ah ha!" he says, "He bounds from the earth as if his entrails were hairs – *le cheval volant*, the Pegasus, *qui a les narines de feu!* When I bestride him, I soar, I am a hawk. He trots the air. The earth sings when he touches it. . . . He is pure air and fire" (3.8.12–20). The dauphin and his horse become one; that is, his mount becomes a prosthetic extension of his agency and it allows him an unrivaled sense of violent mastery: "I will trot tomorrow a mile, and my way shall be paved with English faces" (3.8.73–74). Unlike the dauphin, Shakespeare is, of course, no fool. For while he has both English and French voices ridicule the dauphin's blasphemous vainglory, he quietly registers the English king's power in exactly the same terms, in terms of the war horse's cognate from the Book of Job, the terrifying figure of Yahweh's sea beast, Leviathan. "Canst thou draw out leviathan with an hook? . . . Canst thou fill his skin with barbed irons? or his head with fish spears?" Yahweh demands. "None *is so* fierce that dare stir him up." Who then, he continues, "is able to stand before me?" (41:1–10). When Henry claims his inability to control his triumphant army before Harfleur, he protests more than a little disingenuously of his powerlessness, explicitly his inability to do what Yahweh does and draw out Leviathan with a hook: "We may as bootless spend our vain command / Upon th'enragèd soldiers in their spoil," he says to the governor of Harfleur, "As send precepts to the leviathan / To come ashore" (3.4.24–27). But Henry doesn't need precepts; he is perfectly capable of using both halter and hook to control his formidable army, and so, as he disclaims his God-like power, he both invokes it and revels in its terror. As his wrath becomes an instrument of policy, the king presses the governor to work on his fancies and picture the "blind and bloody soldier with foul hand" defiling "the locks of your shrill-shrieking daughters."[16] The king dwells on the scene with pleasure and urges the governor to imagine "Your fathers taken by the silver beards / And their most reverend heads dashed to the walls; / Your naked infants spitted upon pikes, / Whiles the mad mothers with their howls confused / Do break the clouds" (3.4.34–40). Without any hope of succor and faced with this kind of terror, the governor submits: "Therefore, dread King, / We yield our town and lives" (3.4.47–48). As Exeter promises, when the king comes, he will come out of a whirlwind like Yahweh: "Therefore in fierce tempest is he coming, / In thunder and in earthquake, like a Jove, / That if requiring fail, he will compel" (2.4.99–101).

What the king expects is obedience, and what he wants especially from his followers is not dialogue or rational consent but the predicate of obedience, faith. But faith in what? Since the king is obviously not Yahweh, what cause or principle makes Henry's decisionism, his secular arrogation of God's *virtù* credible or even desirable? What allows Henry's soldiers and Shakespeare's audience to take such righteous or moral pleasure in war and glory in the king's violent agency?

## War as the Secular Nation's Eucharist

One obvious answer is the good of the country. Indeed, if we follow Carl Schmitt and his English mentor, Shakespeare's young contemporary, Thomas Hobbes, it might be specifically the security provided by the newly emerging secular state. In Hobbes, the state, like Henry's army, is imagined as Leviathan and it is clear that Hobbes takes enormous pleasure in the strength of this beast: "that great Leviathan, or rather (to speake more reverently) … that *Mortall God* to which wee owe under the *Immortall God*, our peace and defence."[17] Referring specifically to the Book of Job, he delights in the fact that the state is a "mortal god" whose strength cannot be contested: "*There is nothing*, saith [God], *on earth, to be compared with him. He is made so as not to be afraid. Hee seeth every high thing below him; and is King of all the children of pride.*"[18] The state is imagined as one mighty artificial or fictional person whose members are the state's "subjects" and soul the "sovereign." The sovereign animates or carries the state and by the authority given him by its subjects, by "every particular man in the Common-Wealth, he hath the use of so much Power and Strength conferred on him, that *by the terror thereof*, he is enabled to forme the wills of them all, to Peace at home, and mutuall ayd against their enemies abroad."[19]

Although they may be thinking in similar terms, Shakespeare's play precedes Hobbes's Civil War treatise by half a century and it is difficult to see Henry's soldiers and citizens as subjects created in the image and likeness of Hobbes's fears. What moves Henry's soldiers and what gives their war its sublimity is something more than Hobbesian fear or longing for security. Nowhere is this more evident than in the speech Henry makes to the army before Agincourt. There, while retaining all the force of Leviathan, Henry's army and the country it represents transcends Hobbes's vision of the state and metamorphoses itself into a new nation. As Benedict Anderson has shown, the nation is something more than the state.[20]

In the *Gesta Henrici Quinti* (1416–17), the book the historical Henry V commissioned immediately after Agincourt, the agency of our immortality is religious; it is the individual's belief in God's grace, an agency only made available through Christ crucified.[21] In Shakespeare's *Henry V*, the agency of our immortality seems to be much more secular; it appears to be the individual's belief in the life of the nation, an agency only made fully legible in war. Political theology in this case means the emotional force of the one is effectively transferred to the other. This does not mean that Henry's soldiers cease to be Christians, but that the story of Henry V shifts its emphasis or affective force from religion to the secular life of the newly imagined nation. In the medieval *Gesta*, Henry's speech is not so much a public act of encouragement to the army as a private act of faith made before his immediate household. When one of his stewards, Sir Walter Hungerford, expresses the desire for "ten thousand of the best archers in England who would have been only too glad to be there,"[22] the king rebukes him for his foolishness. He makes it clear that the impending battle is not about our agency but God's glory. The very paucity of the army is part of God's design: it is a necessary condition of his plan to demonstrate his freedom and test our faith. The climactic battle will reproduce the central miracle of Christianity – the impossible event of Christ crucified. It is a climactic occasion of grace. For these soldiers that "I have here with me," the king explains to Hungerford, are not mine but "God's people, whom he deigns to let me have at this time."[23] Their very paucity is the hinge of faith: "Do you not believe," he continues, "that the Almighty, with these His humble few, is able to overcome the opposing arrogance of the French who boast of their great number and their own strength"?[24] As he questions Hungerford's faith, he proceeds to justify his own. Of course, the Almighty is capable of overcoming the worldly arrogance of the French, the king insists, for, "as I myself believe," it is "not possible for misfortune to befall a son of His with so sublime a faith." This is so because grace is implicit in God's justice or "true righteousness [*vera iusticia*]."[25]

This confession of faith stands in stark contrast to Shakespeare's version of the same scene.

Shakespeare completely reverses the emphasis in the *Gesta*. The paucity of the army is not so much about God's glory as the "honor" of the king and his soldiers – "The fewer men, the greater share of honor" (4.3.22). God is certainly mentioned (as is Jove, in the same breath) but the emphasis falls on the king's appetite for renown, esteem, and the recognition of his *virtù*: "if it be a sin to covet honor / I am the most offending soul alive" (4.3.28–29). Honor becomes a commodity and what makes the king's spiritual avarice so palatable is the degree to which he is willing to share this wealth. In this, his *virtù* or potency becomes the property of all and he transforms the army into a "band of brothers" (4.3.60), the microcosm of a new nation. In this *ersatz* religion of the nation, what is exceptional and eternal is not God's grace but the acts and monuments of England's *virtù*.

The king's speech dwells on the particular day of the battle, that is, on "the feast of Crispian" (4.3.40). What is important is not so much that this feast remembers the martyrdom of an earlier band of brothers, Crispin and Crispianus, but that it is so obscure. The king seems completely unaware, for instance, that there were actually two saints. Henceforth, this day will be remembered not for the martyrdom of the old band of brothers but for the heroism of the new band, the new archipelagic English who can assimilate Welsh, Scots, and Irish into themselves. Henry can call himself Welsh (4.1.51), precisely because to be Welsh is no longer a mark of exclusion but one of inclusion in the new Anglocentric polity. As we've seen, the Welsh are now perfectly capable of teaching those who were born English the meaning of "a good English condition" (5.1.70). They can be more English than the English. In emphasizing the importance of St. Crispin's Day, the king is effectively re-writing and secularizing the annual calendar of religious observance;[26] he is re-enchanting the everyday world with a new story, not of Christ resurrected through God's grace but of the nation reborn through its own quickening power. As the Archbishop of Canterbury makes clear at the beginning of the play, the English (and not least Shakespeare's Elizabethan audience in a time of war) need to re-member themselves: "Look back into your mighty ancestors. / Go, my dread lord, to your great-grand-sire's tomb," touch the stone, and "Invoke his warlike spirit" (1.2.102–4). The English most truly become themselves only in war – when they "stand like greyhounds in the slips," most worthy of their breeding (3.1.31). What will be remembered on this day is, then, not the names of Christian saints, Crispin and Crispianus, but those of English soldiers in their "predeceased" valor, "our names, / Familiar … as household words" (4.3.51–52). In an endless, patrilineal sequence of memorials, handed down from father to son, no year shall go by from "this day to the ending of the world / But we in it shall be rememberèd" (4.3.58–59). War and remembrance. The speech's potency lies in the way it acts out its own meaning. The speech is an act of communion, a secular eucharist in which, as members are encouraged to share their blood, all binaries and the hierarchies they imply fall away: "For he today that sheds his blood with me / Shall be my brother. Be he ne'er so vile, / This day shall gentle his condition" (4.3.61–63). What the speech offers is not only war's delight in agency but, most importantly, that joy made sacred in a new secular story that will transform "fatality into continuity, contingency into meaning."[27] In this story, we shall be transubstantiated; our condition shall be both *Englished* and *gentled*: neither Welsh nor Scots, Cornish nor Irish, neither aristocrat nor commoner, but all one in the new national community. "What ish my nation" (3.3.61)? – the new Anglocentric polity or sovereign empire whose narrative embraces the whole archipelago.

Although there is no direct reference, the inclusivity of Henry's appeal imitates the great cry of Pauline universalism in the Epistle to the Galatians: "There is neither Jew nor Greek, there is neither bond nor free, there is neither male nor female: for ye are all one in Christ Jesus" (3:28). Shakespeare's imitation and its national narrative is, of course, deeply flawed. Welshmen, for instance, are included only as stage Welshmen – the greatest of Wales's princes, Llewelyn, becomes the comic Fluellen with his risible inability to pronounce the plosive "B" (somewhat ironically since the English are equally unable to pronounce the Welsh fricative "Ll"). Commoners are included only when occasion warrants; indeed, so vile do they remain that when the English dead are detailed only the noble are remembered – there are "None else of name" (4.8.99), the king brazenly reports. And women, as Henry's brutal wooing of Princess Katherine makes clear, are included only to be conquered, mastered, and domesticated as the bearers of male warriors: "If ever thou beest mine, Kate ... thou must therefore needs prove a good soldier-breeder" (5.2.190–93). What remains, however, is formidable.

The aesthetic power of a nationalist ideology in what is for us now the almost subliminal form of a secularized political theology continues to prove seductive. That is, as the nation's exceptional narrative is made to imitate the story of God's freedom, it still has the power to sacralize violence and legitimize the sublime pleasure of agency that war's physical sensations only fittingly realize. *Dulce et decorum est pro patria mori.* The sweetness, or in this case the sublimity, lies in the narrative's now barely heard political theology; take that away and all that is left are glad animal movements and dismembered "legs and arms and heads" (4.1.126–27). There is no intrinsic beauty in war. Whatever beauty there is lies in the memory and its representation – which is why the study of literature is so important. And so without its claims of just cause or echoes of political theology, without the aesthetic of its sacralized national narrative, *Henry V* becomes *Blood Meridian*. In order to emphasize the aestheticizing power of its political theology, let me conclude by looking at the play through the lens of Cormac McCarthy's great novel, a work deeply engaged with Shakespeare's work.

## Cormac McCarthy's *Henry V*

*Blood Meridian*, first published in 1985, is a western – but one remarkable for the way it revises the genre in the light of the disillusionment and horror of the Vietnam War.[28] One of its three central characters, Judge Holden, is a Leviathan-like figure of enormous size and strength: in the midst of a great storm, the judge stands "naked atop the walls, immense and pale in the revelations of lightening, striding the perimeter up there and declaiming in the old epic mode."[29] The judge is routinely identified with the devil, as is Leviathan in Christian revelation: "And the great dragon was cast out, that old serpent, called the Devil, and Satan" (Revelation 12:9). In *Paradise Lost*, Leviathan is the true form of Satan, the consolidated image of evil (1.193–210).[30] The judge may be irredeemably evil, but his *virtù* excites the admiration of all, not least the demonized descendants of *Henry V*'s captains and camp boys, Captain Glanton and the Kid. Like Bacon, the judge speaks for the empire of human knowledge and unfettered human agency. He would become the sovereign Hobbes imagines in *Leviathan*: "Only nature can enslave man," says the judge, "and only when the exist- ence of each last entity is routed out and made to stand naked before him will he be properly suzerain of the earth. . . . In order for the earth to be mine nothing must be permitted to occur upon it save by my dispensation."[31] His is the spirit that moves Captain Glanton's band of brothers – not an army inspired by just cause or the nation's aesthetic, its exceptional, life-giving narrative, but a "patrol condemned to ride out some ancient curse"[32] – a company of mercenaries driven to harvest Indian scalps, the novel's equiva- lent of body counts. Like Milton's damned angels they ride on: "Thus roving on / In confused march forlorn, the adventurous bands / With shuddering horror pale, and eyes aghast" discover a "universe of death," a landscape "where all life dies" and only "death lives" (2.614–28). The Mexican border country is such a demonic landscape, where nature breeds, perverse, all monstrous things, like trees of dead babies.[33] It is burnt by the sun and tortured by dustspouts, but "out of that whirlwind no voice spoke."[34]

In the gang's climactic slaughter of Gileno Apaches, the novel remembers Yahweh's war horse. In the early morning, before the assault on the sleeping village, a bird called and Captain Glanton "turned to his horse and unhooded it like a falconer at morning. A wind had risen and the horse lifted its head and sniffed the air."[35] In their exhilaration, they swoop, charging at full gallop; they offer no quarter, "hacking at the dying and decapitating those who knelt for mercy"; one of the Delaware scouts emerges from the carnage in a memory of Psalm 137 "with a naked infant dangling in each hand ... and swung them by the heels each in turn and bashed their heads against the stones"; and at the same time, "a young woman ran up and embraced the bloodied forefeet of Glanton's warhorse."[36] The slaughter has no purpose other than sensation, a few dollars, and the joy of killing. At the end of the novel, the judge identifies himself with Shakespeare's Henry V: "And some are not yet born who shall have cause to curse the Dauphin's soul."[37] The judge substitutes "soul" for "scorn" (1.2.289), because there is no cause, no meaning, only the human soul's unbounded desire for agency: "We are not speaking in mysteries," he says to the Kid. "You of all men are no stranger to that feeling, the emptiness and despair. It is that which we take arms against, is it not? ... What is death if not an agency?"[38]

One of the key stories in Ken Burns and Lynn Novick's film, *The Vietnam War*, is that of Mogie Crocker, a young paratrooper who begins with the exhilaration of *Henry V* and ends in a mental wasteland like that of McCarthy's novel.[39] As the story charts Mogie's progress from listening to his mother recite Henry V's "band of brothers" speech to his death in Vietnam, so it charts the gradual collapse of the US Army's belief in its own exceptionalism, in the aesthetic appeal of its nation's own sacred narrative. For some, like the soldiers of the army's notorious Tiger Force, the only value or pleasure left becomes quite literally that of Captain Glanton and the judge, which they pursue with a vengeance: "This is war. This is what we do." As this story and McCarthy's novel suggest, Shakespeare's *Henry V* is as important as it is because it illuminates so powerfully the complexity of our culture's profoundly conflicted attitude to war. In its ambivalence, the play takes us not only to the heart of war's darkness but to the power of a sacralizing aesthetic meant to occlude that darkness.

*Further Reading*

Allmand, Christopher. *Henry V*, New Haven, Yale University Press, 1992.
Dutton, Richard. "'Methinks the Truth Should Live from Age to Age': The Dating and Contexts of *Henry V*," *Huntington Library Quarterly*, 68 (2005), pp. 173–204.
Greenblatt, Stephen. "Invisible Bullets: Renaissance Authority and its Subversion," *Glyph*, 8 (1981), pp. 40–61.

Harriss, Gerald. *Shaping the Nation: England 1360–1461*, Oxford, Clarendon Press, 2005.

Keegan, John. *The Face of Battle*, New York, Viking Press, 1976.

Kerrigan, John. "Oaths, Threats, and *Henry V*," *Review of English Studies*, 63 (2012), pp. 551–71.

Maus, Katharine Eisaman. "Introduction to *Henry V*," in Stephen Greenblatt et al. (eds.), *The Norton Shakespeare*, 3rd ed., New York, W. W. Norton, 2016, pp. 1533–40.

Rabkin, Norman. "Rabbits, Ducks, and *Henry V*," *Shakespeare Quarterly*, 28 (1977), pp. 279–96.

Shapiro, James. "'What Ish My Nation?' Shakespeare's Irish Connections," *The Irish Times*, April 23, 2016.

Vale, Malcolm. *Henry V: The Conscience of a King*, New Haven, Yale University Press, 2016.

## NOTES

1 See Gary Taylor (ed.), *Henry V*, Oxford World Classics (Oxford: Oxford University Press, 1998), pp. 4, 12.
2 See Michael Hattaway's contribution to this volume (Chapter 10).
3 See her contribution to this volume (Chapter 4).
4 Wilfred Owen, *Collected Letters*, ed. Harold Owen and John Bell (London: Oxford University Press, 1967), p. 82.
5 Owen, *Collected Letters*, p. 580.
6 See David Schalkwyk's contribution to this volume (Chapter 8).
7 David Jones, *In Parenthesis* (London: Faber, 2014), p. 196.
8 Jones, *In Parenthesis*, p. x.
9 Jones, *In Parenthesis*, p. 138.
10 Jones, *In Parenthesis*, pp. 139, 138.
11 See Franziska Quabeck's contribution to this volume (Chapter 2).
12 See Ernst H. Kantorowicz, *The King's Two Bodies: A Study in Medieval Political Theology* (Princeton: Princeton University Press, 1957), pp. 24–41.
13 Carl Schmitt, *Political Theology: Four Chapters on the Concept of Sovereignty* (London: University of Chicago Press, 2005), p. 36.
14 John Matusiak, *Henry V* (London: Routledge, 2013), p. 43.
15 Edmund Burke, *A Philosophical Inquiry into the Origin of Our Ideas of the Sublime and the Beautiful* (London: Basil, 1792), p. 96.
16 On the king's use of anger, see Gail Kern Paster's contribution to this volume (Chapter 7).
17 Thomas Hobbes, *Leviathan*, ed. C. B. Macpherson (New York: Penguin, 1977), p. 227.
18 Hobbes, *Leviathan*, p. 362.
19 Hobbes, *Leviathan*, pp. 227–28, my emphasis.
20 Benedict Anderson, *Imagined Communities: Reflections on the Origin and Spread of Nationalism* (London: Verso, 1991), pp. 9–36.
21 Frank Taylor and John S. Roskell (eds.), *Gesta Henrici Quinti: The Deeds of Henry the Fifth* (Oxford: Clarendon, 1975).

22 Taylor and Roskell (eds.), *Gesta*, p. 79.
23 Taylor and Roskell (eds.), *Gesta*, p. 79.
24 Taylor and Roskell (eds.), *Gesta*, p. 79.
25 Taylor and Roskell (eds.), *Gesta*, p. 79.
26 See David Cressy, *Bonfires and Bells: National Memory and the Protestant Calendar in Elizabethan and Stuart England* (Berkeley: University of California Press, 1989).
27 Anderson, *Imagined Communities*, p. 11.
28 Cormac McCarthy, *Blood Meridian, or the Evening Redness in the West* (New York: Vintage, 1992).
29 McCarthy, *Blood Meridian*, p. 124.
30 Milton is quoted from Stephen Orgel and Jonathan Goldberg (eds.), *John Milton: The Major Works*, Oxford World Classics (Oxford: Oxford University Press, 2008).
31 Hobbes, *Leviathan*, p. 207.
32 Hobbes, *Leviathan*, p. 157.
33 McCarthy, *Blood Meridian*, p. 60.
34 McCarthy, *Blood Meridian*, p. 117.
35 McCarthy, *Blood Meridian*, p. 161.
36 McCarthy, *Blood Meridian*, p. 162.
37 McCarthy, *Blood Meridian*, p. 340.
38 McCarthy, *Blood Meridian*, p. 343.
39 Ken Burns and Lynn Novick (dirs.), *The Vietnam War* (Florentine Films, 2017).

# 14

# *Macbeth* and Trauma

The times has been
That, when the brains were out, the man would die,
And there an end.

(3.4.80–82)

This chapter aims to illuminate Shakespeare's disturbing Scottish tragedy in terms of several key military contexts: England's contemporary wars with Ireland, an important backdrop to *Macbeth*; William Wallace and late-medieval Anglo-Scottish wars; and the violence of early modern warfare and the psychological trauma it could produce. Such contexts can help historicize the play, as well as explain its memorable language of war and wounding.

## Headwounds

Macbeth's words quoted in the epigraph ring true, but in Shakespeare's day battlefield surgery was an advancing field and deep wounds could heal.[1] Philip Sidney's cousin Henry Harington is the subject of a memorable passage in Henry Sidney's Irish *Memoir*. Irish "rebel" Rory Oge O'More took Harington hostage in November 1577, to Sir Henry's great distress, "for I loved him and do love him as a son of my own." O'More "in sundry parts of his head so wounded him as I myself in his dressing did see his brains moving; yet my good soldiers brought him away, and a great way, upon their halberds and pikes, to a good place in that country, where he was relieved, and afterwards (I thank God) recovered."[2]

Rory was a slippery customer, his frequent escapes "attributed to 'Sorcerie or Enchauntement.'"[3] John Derricke called him "Rorie Roge."[4] John Harington recollected that Rory, besieged by Sidney and a hundred soldiers, "gat through them all without hurt, where a mouse almost could not haue got betweene them: and I haue heard it affirmed in Ireland, that it was with meere witchcraft."[5] This is a tale twice told, the second time with some skepticism, for in a letter written in 1599, Harington, referring to his men being spooked by the Irish, recalls his cousin's plight twenty years earlier when his English pursuers believed O'More eluded them "by dint of witchery, and had by magic compell'ed them not to touch him."[6] In fact, turning it around, Harington believed the soldiers' belief in witchcraft allowed Rory to evade them: "I verily think the idle faith which possesses the Irishry, concerning magic and witchcraft, seized our men and lost the victory."[7]

Rory's luck ran out on June 30, 1578. Trapped and hacked to death, his head – bought for a hundred pounds by Henry Sidney – was mounted on Dublin Castle.[8] Rory's promised end is twice told by Derricke, first as authorial announcement, then poetic conceit:

> *suppose that you see a monstrous Deuill, a trunckelesse head, and a hedlesse bodie liuyng, the one hid in some miskin & donghill, but the other exalted, yea mounted vppon a poule ... on the highest toppe of the Castell of Dublin, vtteryng in plaine Irishe the thynges that ensewe.* (sig. Kiiii^v)

Derricke then gives Rory his own posthumous pole speech:

> My hed from the bodie, parted in twaine:
> Is set on the Castell, a signe to remaine. (sig. Liii^r)

Thus "Rory Roge" went on talking as "a trunckelesse head." Such a great rebel's fate – first Macdonald, then Macbeth – as a twice-told tale is key to Shakespeare's "Scottish play" and its Irish subtext.

Banquo, unlike Henry Harington, does not survive his headwound and puts in an appearance at the castle. Banquo dies a double death, his throat cut (3.4.17), and, just to be sure, left "safe in a ditch ... / With twenty trenchèd gashes on his head" (3.4.27–28). Once dead, you are beyond surgery, but not beyond affecting the living, either through your offspring or the impact of your demise, as witness Banquo's reappearance with "twenty mortal murders" on his crown (3.4.83).

In *His Farewell to Military Profession* (1581), veteran soldier Barnabe Rich draws on a metaphor of deep wounding to advocate for colonial violence, asserting that "an old sore, being once overrun, will not be cured with any moderate medicine, but must be eaten with corrosives till it comes to the quick."[9] As Sidney Sondergard notes, this is "a metaphor of special significance to veterans of military conflict who had witnessed the devastating effects of deep wounding – a threat to life even after apparent healing."[10] Three years earlier, Rich had issued a wake-up call for a state with a neglected soldiery:

> But the warres being once finished ... howe be they rewarded ... what other thing gaine they then slaunder, misreporte, false impositions, hatred and despight?[11]

Though chiefly concerned with Ireland, where he saw long service, Rich singles out for special mention "that small garrison at *Barwicke*," scene of treaties, troubles, and witch hunts.

"Now for our Irish wars, / We must supplant those rough, rug-headed kerns" (*Richard II*, 2.1.155–56). So says Richard II, but the kerns are alive and skipping in *Macbeth*, and the Irish wars rumble on, with its "kerns and galloglasses" (1.2.13) fighting for Macdonald and "wretched kerns" (5.7.18) battling for Macbeth, its tanistry and subsequent conversion of native nobility to earls and its hiding place for Donaldbain – "To Ireland, I" (2.3.135). The Irish foot soldiers that frame the play, dismissed as mercenaries, are key to its context. John Kerrigan suggests "*Macbeth* helped pave the way for British colonialism in Ireland."[12] Stephen Orgel recognizes one dramatic dimension as "the enforced anglicization of Scotland, which Macbeth is resisting."[13] Although he never wrote an Irish play, the two countries were inseparable in the time of the historical Macbeth, sharing troubled landscapes, unsafe borders, and defensive walls. According to Brian Outhwaite, the Irish conflict, "as far as the professional soldiers were concerned, was the most hated war of their era: England's Vietnam."[14] Ireland underpins the play's source, with Malcolm's reign as bloody as Macbeth's: "Holinshed reports that Malcolm eventually died a gruesome death, his head skewered through the eye upon the spear of an English knight; after which Donalbain returned from Ireland, slew Malcolm's eldest son, and usurped the throne."[15] Yet despite Anne Barton's insistence that *Macbeth* "is surely as much a history play as *Richard II*," the "Scottish play" has not been historicized alongside Shakespeare's medieval "English" histories. The Irish wars are the backdrop to *Macbeth*, not just the newly ended Nine Years' War (1594–1603), but the ongoing process of expropriation, occupation, and settlement. When Banquo asks, "How far is't called to Forres?" we foresee the shade of Birnam Wood (1.3.40), mindful that "trees fill an important part in the history of the Irish Gael."[16] Gerard Boate noted the twofold benefits of deforestation, "to deprive the Theeves and Rogues, who used to lurk in the Woods in great numbers," and to secure "very good Pastures" and "excellent Arable and Meddow."[17]

The rebranding of thanes as earls in *Macbeth* entails more than the conversion of Scottish nobles. The struggle over titles has an Irish dimension in the colonial policy of "surrender and regrant" whereby Irish lords relinquished their native titles and assumed English ones.[18] It was Hugh O'Neill's decision to drop his adopted English title of Earl of Tyrone and revert to his Irish one – "The O'Neill" – that signaled the outbreak of the Nine Years' War. And, of course, Mac-Beth is a name that puns on son of Elizabeth, a fitting title for a play directed at the successor of a childless monarch. And as we have seen with Harington, Ireland's borderlands and backwoods were bound up with witches, faeries, and the supernatural.

Shakespeare's is a well-doctored corpus, *Macbeth* his most medicalized play – "More than four hundred medical allusions have been tallied."[19] Lacerated by words of war and wounding, it seems to speak to us today. The first act mentions Golgotha (1.2.40) and Aleppo (1.3.8). Macbeth declares: "Scarf up the tender eye of pitiful day" (3.2.46). Lady Macbeth would have "dashed the brains out" of the child she suckled to prove her resolve (1.7.58), a recurrent trope in atrocity literature, and an echo of her husband's earlier invocation of "Pity, like a naked newborn babe / Striding the blast" (1.7.21–22).[20] This is a play loaded with terms of the time. One succession tract spoke of "hurly burly and rumor."[21] The air was thick with phrases ripe for plucking. When Macbeth cries "Sleep no more! / Macbeth does murder sleep" (2.2.38–39) he echoes an Elizabethan sermon that asked: "What meanest thou ô sleeper? arise, sleep no more, and I will waken you no more."[22] Lady Macbeth's sleepwalking in 5.1, her "slumbery agitation" (5.1.10), is part of a sequence of late-night strolls, another aftereffect of trauma. Duncan's death makes Macduff want to wake the dead: "As from your graves rise up and walk like sprites" (2.3.74). Playing on walking and waking, Lennox notes that "Banquo walked too late" (3.6.5), concluding that "men must not walk too late" (3.6.7). News of his wife's death triggers Macbeth's "walking shadow" (5.5.24). There are echoes of earlier plays in forms of address and title. Duncan's address, "Sons, kinsmen, thanes" (1.4.35) conjures up Antony's "Friends, Romans, countrymen" (*Julius Caesar*, 3.2.71), which in turn recalls his earlier "Romans, countrymen, and lovers" (3.2.13). *Macbeth* is a disturbing play full of alarms, bells and trumpets, "drum and colors," warnings and wake-up calls. We need to lend our ears to these echoes.

*Macbeth* is a drama steeped in blood and the mental stain it leaves. Lady Macbeth tells her husband to "smear / The sleepy grooms with blood" (2.2.52–53), and when he refuses she resolves to do it herself. Indeed, she dismisses painted devils even as she uses face paint to shift the blame for Duncan's murder:

> The sleeping and the dead
> Are but as pictures; 'tis the eye of childhood
> That fears a painted devil. If he do bleed,
> I'll gild the faces of the grooms withal,
> For it must seem their guilt. (2.2.56–59)

Later, Macbeth tells his servant: "Go prick thy face and over-red thy fear" (5.3.14). According to Edmund Spenser, "the Gaules used to drinke their enemyes blood, and to painte themselves therewith," a practice also imputed to the Irish.[23] Face painting and giving suck had different meanings in Spenser's Ireland:

> at the execution of a notable traitor at Limericke, called Murrogh O-Brien, I saw an old woman which was his foster mother, take up his head, whilst he was quartered, and sucked up all the blood that runne thereout, saying, that the earth was not worthy to drinke it, and therewith also steeped her face and breast, and tore her haire, crying and shrieking most terribly.[24]

How many children had Lady Macbeth fostered? And is *Macbeth* a play about quartering as well as beheading and disemboweling?

## Unspeakable Grief

The previous section dealt with headwounds literal and metaphorical – establishing the key point that war damages all who partake of its violence – and with the corrosive subtext of the Irish wars. This section expands on the grief or suffering that Macbeth carries with him, integrating it into such subthemes as gender and masculinity, and, through the Scottish hero William Wallace – heroic even in English accounts – the burden of empire, for and against. In line with recent scholarship, including medical and military responses to *Macbeth*, the 2015 film version played down the demonizing and foregrounded the personal consequences of conflict.[25] Macbeth's early aside flags up how anxiety supplants battlefield courage:

> Present fears
> Are less than horrible imaginings.   (1.3.139–40)

Fresh from the fray and his fraught encounter with the camp followers/weird sisters, Macbeth's "dull brain [is] wrought / With things forgotten" (1.3.152–53). The emerging orthodoxy is that this drama depicts state hypocrisy in deploying soldiers to carry out acts condemned in civil contexts, and that war neuroses and traumatic memory are part of the play's texture. Post-traumatic stress disorder (PTSD) by any other name is an old condition – "shellshock" in the First World War, "battle fatigue" during World War II, PTSD after Vietnam. The word "trauma" has its own history. Early works tied it to injury.[26] Edward Phillips, Milton's nephew, glossed "Traumatick" as "(Greek) belonging to wounds."[27] For Steven Blankaart, "Troma, is a Wound from an external Cause," while "traumatica, are those things, which being taken in Decoctions and Potions, fetch the serous and sharp Humours out of the Body, and so attenuate the Blood, that it may be conveniently driven to the wounded, broken, or bruised parts."[28] According to Daniel Sennert, "if a soft part be dissolved by a thing that cutteth, it is called by the Greeks *Trauma*, by the Latines *Vulnus, i.e.* a wound."[29]

Beyond wounds lies the trauma of witnessing and remembering, "The grief that does not speak" (4.3.209). The dream activity recounted in a play heavy with sleep disturbed by wakefulness suggests remembrance or remorse:

> Better be with the dead,
> Whom we, to gain our peace, have sent to peace,
> Than on the torture of the mind to lie
> In restless ecstasy. (3.2.19–22)

*Macbeth* is a play about war's aftermath – guilt, hallucinations, insomnia at that stage where the theater of war becomes a drama of trauma, and the blades with keenest edges are the "dagger of the mind" (2.1.38), the "daggers in men's smiles" (2.3.137), and "the air-drawn dagger" (3.4.63). In *Macbeth*, the mental health of character and country are intertwined, so that Scotland is "Almost afraid to know itself" (4.3.165) while its hero-turned-villain is "a soldier and afeard" (5.1.32–33). This fear is integral to Macbeth's makeup as a soldier. Echoing an earlier speech – "The times has been / That, when the brains were out, the man would die" (3.4.80–81) – Macbeth in a revealing moment says:

> The time has been my senses would have cooled
> To hear a night-shriek, and my fell of hair
> Would at a dismal treatise rouse and stir. (5.5.10–12)

To fear "a night-shriek" or "a dismal treatise" appears at odds with the violence of war. These, like the "air-drawn dagger," seem "Impostors to true fear" (3.4.65).

Killing and its consequences are connected in the first act, when Ross praises Macbeth as:

> Nothing afeard of what thyself didst make,
> Strange images of death. (1.3.97–98)

When Macduff speaks of Scotland's tainted rule – "The title is affeered" (4.3.34) – he plays on affirmed and afraid.[30] Like Scotland, like soldiers, the title (the crown) and the play's very name are fearful.

*Macbeth* is also a play about militant masculinity. Stephen Orgel asks: "What constitutes acting like a man in this play: what other than killing?"[31] For David Willbern: "To be a man, in this tragedy's central terms, means to be bloody or bloodied. Wounds are the mark of manliness."[32] Macduff's not being born of woman is integral to the misogynistic structure: "surgery was a

male prerogative – the surgeon was always a man; midwives were not
allowed to use surgical instruments – and the surgical birth thus means ...
Macduff was brought to life by men, not women.... Such a birth, all but
invariably, involved the mother's death."[33] On this basis, Orgel concludes
that Macbeth "really is an astonishingly male-oriented and misogynistic
play." Childbirth is a scene of carnage. A Caesarean that kills the mother
is an act of murder on the battlefield of birth. Whether or not we ever make it
to a battlefield, no matter how we are delivered, we are all bloodied to begin
with.[34] But was the surgeon always a man, especially on a battlefield? It has
been argued that surgeons proved expensive, and that "female camp followers
quite often stepped into the gap and provided medical assistance to soldiers."[35] Barnabe Rich recalled those Spartan women who "would goe into
the fielde to see in what place their husbandes and friendes were wounded, if it
were before, they would with ioy and gladnes shewe them to euery man, and
so burie them with great solemnitie: if behinde, they al ashamed would depart
leauing them vnburied" (*Allarme*, sig. Biii^r). This anticipates Siward's question
of his dead son: "Had he his hurts before?" (5.7.76).

What is at stake in Lady Macbeth's call for gender reassignment? On the
battlefield, soldiers unseamed, unsexed, with their brains out were common
sights. Shakespeare knew of battlefield unsexing when he invoked – after
Holinshed – the English dead subjected to "beastly shameless transformation" by Welshwomen (*1 Henry IV*, 1.1.44). His source was more explicit:
"the women of Wales cut off their priuities, and put one part thereof into the
mouthes of euerie dead man, in such sort that the cullions hoong downe to
their chins."[36] Unsexing was a strategy suggested by Barnabe Rich, who
recommended castration for England's Irish enemies.[37] Irishwomen were
unsexed in another sense. According to Fynes Moryson, they "are not
straight laced ... and the greatest part are not laced at all."[38] Neither
swaddled in infancy nor corseted in adulthood, Irishwomen were, as Chris
Highley observes, "perceived as unencumbered by the ideological constraints that corsetting symbolized."[39] Perhaps Lady Macbeth, in calling to
be unsexed, was asking to be unraveled, as in Lear's "Off, off, you lendings"
(*King Lear*, 3.4.98–99).

Drugs are being developed of the sort Macbeth wished for his wife,
selective memory erasers:

> Canst thou not minister to a mind diseased,
> Pluck from the memory a rooted sorrow,
> Raze out the written troubles of the brain,
> And with some sweet oblivious antidote
> Cleanse the stuffed bosom of that perilous stuff
> Which weighs upon the heart? (5.3.40–45)

The doctor's ineffectiveness draws from Macbeth the cry "Throw physic to the dogs!" (5.3.47).

The stench of war – "the smell of the blood" (5.1.44), of hell, of sulphur – hangs over *Macbeth* from first stage direction to final image of severed head, doubling the rehearsed beheading of Macdonald in the second scene.[40] Tripling, because between times Duncan's death prompts Macduff to invite his fellow subjects to:

> Approach the chamber and destroy your sight
> With a new Gorgon. (2.3.66–67)

Here Macduff foreshadows his own decapitation of Macbeth, his head "Painted upon a pole" (5.7.56), as well as suggesting the three witches as Gorgons. The "blasted heath" on which the weary soldiers are greeted is a battlefield (1.3.78).[41] Malcolm compares Macbeth to Satan – "Angels are bright still though the brightest fell" (4.3.22) – so fittingly, in the wake of war, Milton's Satan "Stands on the blasted Heath" (1.615).[42] The play's action, unfolding on battlefields and under battlements, begins and ends with a beheading, the first greeted as a demonstration of courage. We hear of "brave Macbeth" (1.2.16), "valor's minion" (1.2.19), fighting the rebel Macdonald, whom he disembowels and decapitates:

> Till he unseamed him from the nave to th' chops,
> And fixed his head upon our battlements. (1.2.22–23)

Disemboweling precedes beheading – in this traitor's death Macbeth's "brandished steel, / ... / smoked with bloody execution" (1.2.17–18), but unlike an official executioner, he "ne'er shook hands nor bade farewell to" his victim (1.2.21). One seventeenth-century commentator claimed that "double Deaths of Strangling and Burning, or Strangling and Disemboweling" were the practices of "Papist Priests."[43]

This double death was one associated with a particular historical figure, William Wallace, whose "execution was the first in which a half-strangled man was disemboweled and beheaded; he was no ordinary enemy."[44] Wallace's death and dismemberment in London is recounted in Holinshed in a sympathetic light, filtered through the lens of Scottish chronicler Hector Boece.[45] As Roger Mason observes, Holinshed's *Description of Scotland* is complicated by the fact that William Harrison, commissioned to write it, "had chosen to English John Bellenden's Scots vernacular translation of Hector Boece's original *Scotorum Historia*, published in Paris in 1527."[46] Wallace is relevant to *Macbeth* not only because a character called "Mackbeth" appears in a 1637 play about Wallace, but because in 1617 on a visit to Scotland Wallace was invoked in order to remind James

I of his origins.[47] That Robert the Bruce's chief physician and surgeon was "Gaelic doctor Patrick MacBeth" of the *Clann Meic-bethad* reinforces the sense of a play haunted by history.[48]

If Harris on behalf of Holinshed could only anglicize Bellenden's Boece in the four days he had at his disposal, then what of John Speed, who in 1612 still managed, albeit in a more nuanced fashion, to preserve Wallace's heroism and indeed use it as an example to his own nation? In Speed's account, Wallace lives on as legend and lesson: "whom though (with *Hectors* translatour) we doe not call a *Martyr*, yet must we thinke his Countrey honoured in him, wishing many the like in our owne."[49] My suggestion here is that Wallace and the Anglo-Scottish wars of the thirteenth and fourteenth centuries, wars bound up with larger questions of empire, are as vital to our understanding of *Macbeth* as the Bothwell (1591), Gowrie (1600), or Gunpowder (1605) plots. If Macbeth is about empire as well as war – war for empire – it is so in an odd and oblique way.[50]

> Two truths are told,
> As happy prologues to the swelling act
> Of th'imperial theme.   (1.3.129–31)

Macbeth's aside on "th'imperial theme" sits oddly next to Malcolm telling Macduff, "A good and virtuous nature may recoil / In an imperial charge" (4.3.19–20). As critics have noted, "The phrase 'imperial theme' did not come into the play from Holinshed."[51] Despite Malcolm's loaded language, the commission he alludes to is religious rather than military, as when contemporaries speak of "the imperiall charge and command of Christ."[52] By contrast the imperial theme persists, and Banquo's line, James's line, "has endured as an imperial succession to this day."[53] In *The Prophetess*, Geta asks Maximinian:

> Do you think (Master) to be Emperor
> with killing Swine?[54]

Perhaps there's a more subtle dig at empire in Shakespeare's piggish image, echoing Fluellen's plosive pun on "Alexander the Great" as "Alexander the [Big] Pig"? (*Henry V*, 4.7.10), for "is not 'pig' great?" (13).[55]

In *Macbeth*, the report of Macdonald's disembowelment and decapitation draws from Duncan the exclamation: "O valiant cousin, worthy gentleman!" (1.2.24). Valiant and violent are synonymous, and since Duncan and Macbeth's mothers were sisters the salutation "cousin" is fitting, as is Duncan's subsequent allusion to Macbeth as "a peerless kinsman" (1.4.58).[56] In putting son before cousin, "Duncan was thus creating in Scotland an hereditary monarchy."[57]

The messenger bearing news of Macbeth's deeds is well-treated in a double sense:

> So well thy words become thee as thy wounds;
> They smack of honor both. – Go, get him surgeons.   (1.2.43–44)

Surgeons here, unlike the doctor later, have a purpose. Macbeth's actions, in which "justice had, with valor armed" (1.2.29) vanquished the king's enemies, are good. This image is mirrored at the play's end, where Macduff enters with Macbeth's severed head, declaring:

> Behold where stands
> Th'usurper's cursèd head.   (5.7.84–85)

Macbeth beheads Macdonald for Duncan (and reward); Macduff beheads Macbeth for Malcolm (and revenge). Justice is in the hands of the beheader.

Macbeth, a hero when butchering on behalf of the state, a demon when fighting against it, resembles modern combatants, praised in war zones, a problem back on Civvy Street. Displaying heads as trophies of war has a long history that runs into the present:

> One recurring motif is the parading of decapitated "insurgent" heads, demonstratively held up in front of the camera.... This continuous posting of ... a motif that the soldiers themselves callously call the "headshot," indicates a mode of pathological fixation in which the acts of taking and circulating these atrocious photographs function to reproduce traumatic war experiences in the form of a compulsive acting out.[58]

Veterans find homecoming hard because after what they witnessed or enacted a land fit for heroes does not await them, a familiar fact of military history.

Macbeth is the "Soldiers' play" as well as the "Scottish play." In 2004, as part of the National Endowment for the Humanities "Bard at the Bases" project, a production of Alabama Shakespeare Festival's *Macbeth* toured US military bases, prompting the headline: "Pentagon money is sending a stage play about a military hero who murders his commander in chief on a tour of 13 military bases."[59] At Maxwell Air Force Base, the cast posed in front of a stealth fighter. One officer, asked "Do you have a special interest in Shakespeare?" answered, "No, I have long-term interest in dropping bombs!"[60] For director Kent Thompson, speeches like Siward's about his son's death resonated with a military audience – closer to "Shakespeare's audience" than any he'd played to before – living with such loss.[61] Kathleen McCall as Lady Macbeth felt the drama was forged afresh in front of soldiers: "*Macbeth* seems to speak directly to them and their world."[62]

Asked by an army general after a performance, "How do you stay so emotionally connected night after night doing Lady Macbeth?" McCall said she'd acquired an added sense of what it meant when Lady Macbeth goaded her husband, saying "a soldier, and afeard?"[63]

Macbeth speaking directly to soldiers is nothing new. The kit bag of poet Edward Thomas, killed in France at the Battle of Arras on April 9, 1917, contained a volume of Shakespeare's plays and a diary. The entry for April 3, 1917, a week before his death, states: "Snow just frozen – strong S.E. wind. Feet wet by 8.15 a.m. Letters.... A fine day later, filling sandbags. MACBETH."[64] Neither is it new to talk of *Macbeth* in relation to the aftereffects of trauma or under the banner of war neuroses. As early as May 1947, an article appeared entitled "Was Macbeth a Victim of Battle Fatigue?" For its author, Robert Bossler, the only novel aspect of the condition was its name. Shakespeare lacked knowledge of modern psychology and medical terms, but understood "the reaction to an overdose of combat."[65] Bossler, a student at Allegheny College in Meadville, Pennsylvania, was a former GI with combat experience in Europe.[66] As a returning soldier, Bossler saw in Macbeth a fellow combatant. In 2007, sixty years after Bossler's essay, another former American soldier, Christy Clothier, a student at the University of New Hampshire, likewise identified Macbeth as "a fellow vet."[67]

Witnessing violence and treating the aftereffects of war has a long history. In the seventeenth century, care of soldiers was becoming crucial.[68] Picking up on John Kerrigan's claim for the "prophetic power" of drama, let us leave Shakespeare's Macbeth for a moment, standing in the field, valorous and loyal, bathed in blood, and look briefly at another Macbeth.[69] This Macbeth is our contemporary. Jesse MacBeth, a young man from Tacoma in Washington, fell victim to Operation Stolen Valor.[70] Found guilty of "falsifying a Department of Veterans Affairs claim and an Army discharge record," on September 21, 2007, he was sentenced to five months in jail and three years' probation, convicted as part of a year-long investigation based on the United States Stolen Valor Act, aimed at rooting out fake veterans claiming benefits intended for those engaged in combat operations. The judge in Jesse's case ordered the accused to get help for mental health problems "especially as they related to committing domestic violence."[71]

## Scotland

How is the problem of *Macbeth* relevant to contemporary Scotland? As a parody of Scottish resistance to anglicization, *Macbeth* is a play of containment, but as Alan Sinfield and David Norbrook have shown, there is subversion, too, in a republican subtext. Two postwar films that invoke the Scottish play through that country's traumatized soldiers reveal different aspects of its afterlife. *The Hasty Heart* (1949) and *Tunes of Glory* (1960) are each preoccupied with Scotland's "culture of violence" and its "soldiering tradition," largely cultivated in the service of empire. More recent dramas like *Black Watch* (2007) and *Dunsinane* (2010) explore the same strands of Scottish culture, including the aftermath of war and the reputation for belligerence.[72]

"Stands Scotland where it did?" (4.3.164). Or will it study war no more? *Macbeth* was written at a time of union, the makeup of Britain. Four centuries on we may be looking at the breakup. In Scotland, a culture of violence has accompanied a soldiering tradition harnessed to foreign wars bound up with the imperial theme. Is Scotland still afraid to know itself? Or ready to question the militarism that diverts vital resources to killing, resources better committed to constructing communities and building bridges? Shakespeare gave Macbeth a bad name in a play that, in dramatic tradition, dare not speak its name.

History is on a loop in *Macbeth*. Alan Sinfield pointed to the play's circular nature, bookended by beheadings.[73] My conclusion is in keeping with such circularity. I began with Henry Sidney and Rory Oge O'More. I end with their sons. Philip Sidney died in October 1586, slowly, of a gunshot wound to the left thigh that went gangrenous. He was thirty-one. In a remarkable passage in his *Life of Sidney*, Fulke Greville offers a drawn-out account of Philip's death from the moment he "cast off his Cuisses" (thigh armor) to the last act of "the too short Scene his life."[74] The passage begins the moment "an unfortunate hand ... brake the bone of Sir *Philip*'s thigh with a Musket-shot," prelude to a protracted period of surgery that features ineffectual doctors and unwelcome messengers, figures familiar from *Macbeth*.[75] Sidney's slow decline and the failure of battlefield surgery to save him are captured poignantly by Greville as is the stoicism, which prompts the biographer to declare that "greatness of heart is not dead every where; and ... war is both a fitter mould to fashion it, and stage to act it on, than peace can be."[76] Neither surgeon's skill nor soldier's resilience can save Sidney, who senses – smells – his own mortality, and this self-knowledge proves stronger than the delicate ministrations of the medics who attend him.[77] Unlike his cousin, Henry Harington, who cheated death nine years earlier even when his brains were out, Sidney's wounding was the end of him. Greville's narrative is the most dramatic, poetic, and sustained treatment of a soldier's death in the period, and in the effect it had on its author, evidence of the impact of warfare on those who are witnesses to death. Rebecca Lemon has noted Sidney's use of medical metaphors in his treatment of tragedy, "that openeth the greatest wounds, and showeth forth the ulcers that are covered with tissue."[78] For Sidney, Lemon argues, "tragedy is a genre that turns things inside out: what should be inside the body spills out for external, public view in the form of an ulcer or wound," and "*Macbeth* provocatively illuminates Sidney's view of tragedy as a genre that 'showeth forth the ulcers.'"[79] Sidney wrote his *Defense of Poetry* in the wake of his father's Irish service, with the wounds of war fresh printed in his mind. One need not be as pun-obsessed as Shakespeare to see a play on ulcer/ Ulster, more explicit in the original that capitalizes and italicizes that word (but not "wounds").[80] As Edward Bowles remarked: "It is the language of the times, and not mine. A filthy ulcer must have a sharpe lance; the massacre of Ireland is a bitter cup."[81]

So much for Sidney. What about that other father's son? Owny MacRory O'More was around twenty-three years old when fatally wounded in August 1600. He had been a baby when his mother and brothers were murdered and his father beheaded by Henry Sidney. Rather than have his head fixed on the battlements of Dublin Castle like his father's, Owny "wyled it to be cutt of after his death and buried."[82]

> This is more strange
> Than such a murder is.   (3.4.84–85)

The strangeness of *Macbeth* is its strength. It furnishes the finest example of a character whose brutality is condemned so soon after being celebrated. There is an exploration of doublethink in a play that upholds savagery as heroism in its opening act in the shape of the severed head of a rebel and holds up the head of the executioner, a hero-turned-villain, in its closing scene. With all the smoke and mirrors of witches and ghosts, audiences need to be alert to the play's exploration of hypocrisy and *realpolitik*, and its deep meditation on the experience and memory of conflict and survival.

### Further Reading

Bell, Millicent. "Macbeth and Dismemberment," *Raritan*, 25 (2006), pp. 13–29.
Boling, Ronald J. "Tanistry, Primogeniture, and the Anglicizing of Scotland in *Macbeth*," *Publications of the Arkansas Philological Association*, 25 (1999), pp. 1–14.
Cahill, Patricia A. *Unto the Breach: Martial Formations, Historical Trauma, and the Early Modern Stage*, Oxford, Oxford University Press, 2008.
Cantor, Paul A. "'A Soldier and Afeard': *Macbeth* and the Gospelling of Scotland," *Interpretation: A Journal of Political Philosophy*, 24 (1997), pp. 287–318.
Favila, Marina. "'Mortal Thoughts' and Magical Thinking in *Macbeth*," *Modern Philology*, 99 (2001), pp. 1–25.

Highley, Christopher. "The Place of Scots in the Scottish Play: *Macbeth* and the Politics of Language," in Willy Maley and Andrew Murphy (eds.), *Shakespeare and Scotland*, Manchester, Manchester University Press, 2004, pp. 53–66.

Kendall, Gillian Murray. "Overkill in Shakespeare," *Shakespeare Quarterly*, 43 (1992), pp. 33–50.

Nosworthy, J. M. "The Bleeding Captain Scene in *Macbeth*," *Review of English Studies*, 22 (1946), pp. 126–30.

Palmer, Patricia. *The Severed Head and the Grafted Tongue: Literature, Translation and Violence in Early Modern Ireland*, Cambridge, Cambridge University Press, 2013.

Pasupathi, Vimala C. "Locating *The Valiant Scot*," in Susan Bennett and Mary Polito (eds.), *Performing Environments: Site-Specificity in Medieval and Early Modern English Drama*, London, Palgrave Macmillan, 2014, pp. 241–59.

Wofford, Susanne L. "Origin Stories of Fear and Tyranny: Blood and Dismemberment in *Macbeth* (with a Glance at the *Oresteia*)," *Comparative Drama*, 51 (2017), pp. 506–27.

## NOTES

1 Franciscus Arcaeus, *A Most Excellent and Compendious Method of Curing Woundes in the Head*, trans. John Read (London: Thomas East, 1588); and B. Nathan and G. Evans, "The Treatment of Head Injury during the Renaissance," *Journal of Accident and Emergency Medicine*, 15 (1998), pp. 119–20.

2 Ciarán Brady (ed.), *A Viceroy's Vindication? Sir Henry Sidney's Memoir of Service in Ireland, 1556–1578* (Cork: Cork University Press, 2002), p. 98; David Finnegan, "O'More, Rory Oge [Ruaidhri Óg Ua Mordha] (c. 1540–1578), Chieftain and Rebel," and "O'More, Owny MacRory [Uaithne MacRuaidhri ua Mordha] (b. in or before 1577, d. 1600), Chieftain and Rebel" in *Oxford Dictionary of National Biography* (Oxford: Oxford University Press, 2004).

3 Finnegan, "O'More, Rory."

4 John Derricke, *The Image of Irelande* (London: John Day, 1581), title page; John Harington, *Orlando Furioso in English Heroical Verse* (London: Richard Field, 1591); and *Nugae Antiquae*, ed. Thomas Park and Henry Harington, 2 vols. (London: J. Wright, 1804).

5 Harington, *Orlando Furioso in English Heroical Verse*, p. 94.

6 Harington, *Nugae Antiquae*, 1, p. 268.

7 Harington, *Nugae Antiquae*, 1, p. 267.

8 Finnegan, "O'More, Rory."

9 Cited in Sidney L. Sondergard, "A Soldier's Allusion to Deep Wounding in Riche's *Farewell to Military Profession*," *ANQ: A Quarterly Journal of Short Articles, Notes and Reviews*, 27 (2014), pp. 49–51, 49.

10 Sondergard, "A Soldier's Allusion to Deep Wounding," p. 49.

11 Barnabe Rich, *Allarme to England* (London: Henry Middleton, 1578), sig. Eiiii$^v$.

12 John Kerrigan, "Archipelagic *Macbeth*," in *Archipelagic English: Literature, History, and Politics 1603–1707* (Oxford: Oxford University Press, 2008), pp. 91–114, 99.

13 Stephen Orgel, "*Macbeth* and the Antic Round," *Shakespeare Survey*, 52 (1999), pp. 143–53, 147.

14 R. B. Outhwaite, "Dearth, the English Crown and the 'Crisis of the 1590s,'" in Peter Clark (ed.), *The European Crisis of the 1590s: Essays in Comparative History* (London: Allen and Unwin, 1985), pp. 23–43, 32.

15 Donald W. Foster, "*Macbeth*'s War on Time," *English Literary Renaissance*, 16 (1986), pp. 319–42, 321.

16 Herbert F. Hore, "Woods and Fastnesses in Ancient Ireland," *Ulster Journal of Archaeology*, 1st ser., 6 (1858), pp. 145–61, 146.

17 Gerard Boate, "Of the Woods in Ireland," in *Irelands Naturall History* (London: John Wright, 1652), pp. 118–22, 119.

18 Kerrigan, "Archipelagic *Macbeth*," pp. 111, 458n68.

19 Ralph F. Sett, "Dunsinane Revisited: Medicine in Shakespeare's *Macbeth*," *The Linacre Quarterly*, 29 (1962), pp. 185–89, 185.

20 Joan Redmond, "Memories of Violence and New English Identities in Early Modern Ireland," *Historical Research*, 89 (2016), pp. 708–29, 712.

21 Irenicus Philodikaios, *A Treatise Declaring, and Confirming against All Obiections the Just Title and Right of the Moste Excellent and Worthie Prince, Iames the Sixt, King of Scotland, to the Succession of the Croun of England* (Edinburgh: Robert Waldegrave, 1599), p. 3.

22 Henry Smith, *Sixe Sermons* (London: Richard Field, 1592), p. 153.

23 Edmund Spenser, *A View of the State of Ireland (1633): From the First Printed Edition*, ed. Andrew Hadfield and Willy Maley (Oxford: Blackwell, 1997), p. 66.

24 Spenser, *A View of the State of Ireland*, p. 66.

25 Henry Barnes, "Michael Fassbender: '*Macbeth* suffered from PTSD,'" *Guardian*, May 23, 2015.

26 Andrew Boorde, *The Breuiary of Helthe* (London: W. Myddelton, 1547), p. 120; and John Brown, *A Compleat Discourse of Wounds* (London: E. Flesher, 1678), p. 11.

27 Edward Phillips, *The New World of English Words* (London: Evan Tyler for Nathaniel Brooke, 1658), sig. Pp3$^v$.

28 Steven Blankaart, *A Physical Dictionary* (London: J. D., 1684), pp. 285, 284.

29 Daniel Sennert, *Nine Books of Physick and Chirurgery*, trans. N. D. B. P. (London: Lodowick Lloyd, 1658), p. 40.

30 Kerrigan, "Archipelagic *Macbeth*," pp. 109, 457n64.

31 Orgel, "*Macbeth* and the Antic Round," p. 145.

32 David Willbern, "Phantasmagoric *Macbeth*," *English Literary Renaissance*, 16 (1986), pp. 520–49, 531–32.

33 Orgel, "*Macbeth* and the Antic Round," p. 150.

34 I owe this point to John Kerrigan.

35 Mary Elizabeth Ailes, "Camp Followers, Sutlers, and Soldiers' Wives: Women in Early Modern Armies (c. 1450–c. 1650)," in Barton C. Hacker and Margaret Vining (eds.), *A Companion to Women's Military History* (Leiden: Brill, 2012), pp. 61–92, 79.

36 Raphael Holinshed, *The Third Volume of Chronicles* (London: Henry Denham, 1587), p. 528.

37 Barnabe Rich, *A New Description of Ireland* (London: William Jaggard, 1610), p. 23; and Christopher Highley, *Shakespeare, Spenser, and the Crisis in Ireland* (Cambridge: Cambridge University Press, 1997), p. 101.

38  Graham Kew, *The Irish Sections of Fynes Moryson's Unpublished "Itinerary"* (Dublin: Irish Manuscripts Commission, 1998), p. 105.

39  Highley, *Shakespeare, Spenser, and the Crisis in Ireland*, p. 102.

40  Jonathan Gil Harris, "The Smell of *Macbeth*," *Shakespeare Quarterly*, 58 (2007), pp. 465–86, 466.

41  John Babington, *Pyrotechnia or, A Discourse of Artificiall Fire-Works* (London: Thomas Harper, for Ralph Mab, 1635), p. 63.

42  Alwin Thaler, "The Shaksperian Element in Milton," *PMLA*, 40 (1925), pp. 645–91, 662.

43  William Lawrence, *The Right of Primogeniture, in Succession to the Kingdoms of England, Scotland, and Ireland* (London: [s.n.], 1681), p. 173.

44  A. A. M. Duncan, "Our Kingdom Had No Head," in *The Nation of Scots and the Declaration of Arbroath (1320)* (London: Historical Association, 1970), pp. 10–18.

45  Raphael Holinshed, *The Firste Volume of the Chronicles of England, Scotlande, and Irelande* (London: John Hunne, 1577), pp. 310–11.

46  Roger Mason, "Scotland," in Paulina Kewes, Ian W. Archer, and Felicity Heal (eds.), *The Oxford Handbook of Holinshed's "Chronicles"* (Oxford: Oxford University Press, 2012), pp. 647–62, 648.

47  Kerrigan, "Archipelagic *Macbeth*," pp. 115, 141.

48  Iain A. MacInnes, "Heads, Shoulders, Knees and Toes: Injury and Death in Anglo-Scottish Combat, c. 1296–c. 1403," in Larissa Tracy and Kelly DeVries (eds.), *Wounds and Wound Repair in Medieval Culture* (Leiden: Brill, 2015), pp. 102–27, 121.

49  John Speed, *The Theatre of the Empire of Great Britaine* (London: William Hall, 1612), p. 550.

50  Henry N. Paul, "The Imperial Theme in *Macbeth*," in James G. McManaway, Giles E. Dawson, and Edwin E. Willoughby (eds.), *Joseph Quincy Adams Memorial Studies* (Washington: Folger Shakespeare Library, 1948), pp. 253–68.

51  Paul, "The Imperial Theme in *Macbeth*," p. 253.

52  William Gouge, *An Exposition on the Whole Fifth Chapter of S. Iohns Gospell* (London: John Bartlett, 1630), p. 158.

53  Paul, "The Imperial Theme in *Macbeth*," p. 256.

54  Francis Beaumont and John Fletcher, *Comedies and Tragedies* (London: Humphrey Robinson and Humphrey Moseley, 1647), p. 26.

55  Thomas Herron, "'Killing Swine' and Planting Heads in Shakespeare's *Macbeth*," in Larissa Tracy and Jeff Massey (eds.), *Heads Will Roll: Decapitation in the Medieval and Early Modern Imagination* (Leiden: Brill, 2012), pp. 261–88.

56  Paul, "The Imperial Theme in *Macbeth*," p. 257.

57  Paul, "The Imperial Theme in *Macbeth*," p. 265.

58  Kari Andén-Papadopoulos, "Body Horror on the Internet: US Soldiers Recording the War in Iraq and Afghanistan," *Media, Culture and Society*, 31 (2009), pp. 921–38, 927.

59  Kent Thompson, "Operation *Macbeth*: How the Alabama Shakespeare Festival Took the Front Line in a New Cultural Campaign," *American Theatre*, 22 (2005), pp. 22–24, 76–79, 78; Kathleen McCall, "Tour of Duty," *American Theatre*, 22 (2005), pp. 25–27, 80–82; and "The Bard at the Bases": www.arts

.gov/sites/default/files/nea_arts/neaARTS_2004_v3_0.pdf. Last accessed July 15, 2018.

60 Thompson, "Operation *Macbeth*," p. 79.

61 Thompson, "Operation *Macbeth*," p. 78.

62 Thompson, "Operation *Macbeth*," p. 25.

63 Thompson, "Operation *Macbeth*," p. 82.

64 Cited in Edmund G. C. King, "'A Priceless Book to Have out Here': Soldiers Reading Shakespeare in the First World War," *Shakespeare*, 10 (2014), pp. 230–44, 233.

65 Robert Bossler, "Was Macbeth a Victim of Battle Fatigue?," *College English*, 8 (1947), pp. 436–38, 436.

66 Bossler, "Was Macbeth a Victim of Battle Fatigue?," p. 436.

67 Christy Clothier, "Understanding Macbeth: A Returning Soldier," *Inquiry Journal* (2007), paper 1: http://scholars.unh.edu/inquiry_2007/1. Last accessed July 10, 2018.

68 Chris R. Langley, "Caring for Soldiers, Veterans and Families in Scotland, 1638–1651," *History*, 102 (2017), pp. 5–23; and Mark Stoyle, "'Memories of the Maimed': The Testimony of Charles I's Former Soldiers, 1660–1730," *History*, 88 (2003), pp. 204–26.

69 Kerrigan, "Archipelagic *Macbeth*," p. 96.

70 Mike Barber, "Fake Veteran Gets 5-Month Sentence," *SeattlePI.com*, September 21, 2007: www.seattlepi.com/local/article/Fake-veteran-gets-5-month-sentence-1250322.php. Last accessed July 22, 2018.

71 Barber, "Fake Veteran Gets 5-Month Sentence."

72 Gregory Burke, *Black Watch* (London: Faber and Faber, 2007); and David Greig, *Dunsinane* (London: Faber and Faber, 2010).

73 Alan Sinfield, "*Macbeth*: History, Ideology and Intellectuals," *Critical Quarterly*, 28 (1986), pp. 63–77.

74 Fulke Greville, *The Life of the Renowned Sr Philip Sidney* (London: Henry Seile, 1651), pp. 143, 161.

75 Greville, *The Life of the Renowned Sr Philip Sidney*, pp. 145–46.

76 Greville, *The Life of the Renowned Sr Philip Sidney*, p. 148.

77 Greville, *The Life of the Renowned Sr Philip Sidney*, pp. 149–50.

78 Rebecca Lemon, "Scaffolds of Treason in *Macbeth*," *Theatre Journal*, 54 (2002), pp. 25–43, 26.

79 Lemon, "Scaffolds of Treason in *Macbeth*," pp. 27, 29.

80 Sir Philip Sidney, *The Defence of Poesie* (London: William Ponsonby, 1595), sig. E4$^v$.

81 Edward Bowles, *The Mysterie of Iniquity Yet Working in the Kingdomes of England, Scotland, and Ireland* (London: Samuel Gellibrand, 1643), p. 47.

82 Finnegan, "O'More, Owny."

# 15

CATHERINE M. S. ALEXANDER

## *Coriolanus* and the Use of Power

### Contexts

In the mid-nineteenth century, Robert Lemon of the State Paper Office noted the name of William Shakespeare in the 1605 muster roll of trained soldiers in the village of Rowington in the Barlichway Hundred, an historic division of the county of Warwickshire that included Stratford-upon-Avon and Henley in Arden. Lemon informed J. Payne Collier, the controversial Shakespeare editor and forger, of his find and Collier included the information, inconclusively, in his 1858 edition of Shakespeare. It resurfaced in 1865 in the work of the English antiquarian William J. Thoms as the conclusion of one of his *Three Notelets on Shakespeare* titled "Was Shakespeare Ever a Soldier? (1859)."[1] He wanted to prove that Shakespeare accompanied or followed the Earl of Leicester to the Low Countries to fight the Spanish when he sailed from Harwich on December 4, 1585, landed at Flushing on the 10th, and returned a year later on December 3, 1586. He suggested, in his only reference to *Coriolanus*, that Cominius's lines describing the leadership skills of Coriolanus "As weeds before / A vessel under sail, so men obeyed / and fell below his stem" (2.2.102–4) are evidence of the seamanship that Shakespeare experienced on his way to the Low Countries.[2] Thoms also made use of a letter from Sir Philip Sidney to his father-in-law Walsingham, dated "at Utrecht this 24th of March, 1586," which included a reference to "Will, my Lord of Lester's jesting player," but the bulk of his "evidence" was drawn from the texts of the plays: he worked through Boswell's edition of Malone's Shakespeare (1821) extracting quotations that are connected to military life and experience. Any reference to weaponry or rank, however slight, was claimed as an "image drawn from [Shakespeare's] own military experiences."[3] He stopped his trawl at the end of Malone's ninth volume and so never reached the Roman or history plays, which would certainly have given him more ammunition for his biographical conjectures, nor did he consider other contextual conditions that inform the composition of the plays. Had he examined *Coriolanus* he would, rather than extracting a single quotation, have encountered armies, soldiers, battles, sword fights, hand-to-hand combat, a triumphal march and, in addition to conflict between warring states, read a character study of an inflexible military and social situation that would now be described as class warfare and had echoes of contemporary events.

The immediate context of civil unrest was the Midland Revolt of 1607, the year before the probable composition of the play, which was described in Edmund Howes's 1615 update to John Stow's *Annals*:

> About the middle of this moneth of May, 1607 a great number of common persons, sodainly assembled themselves in Northamptonshire, and then others of like nature assembled themselves in Warwickshire, and some in Leicestershire, they violently cut and brake downe hedges, filled up ditches, and laid open all such enclosures of Commons, and other grounds as they found enclosed, which of ancient time hadde bin open and imploied to tillage.[4]

England was still largely rural with an economy based on agriculture and Stow's account reflects a series of bad harvests, grain shortages, and high prices, plus high unemployment, particularly in the cloth industry, which were all exacerbated by enclosures, the moves, sanctioned and enforced by acts of Parliament, that enclosed formerly open and common land for the benefit of wealthy landowners to extend their estates, thus disadvantaging the common people, the rural peasants, who lost their smallholdings and their grazing rights. Warwickshire-born poet Michael Drayton, writing in the voice of Arden, the area north of Stratford, saw this as a battle between grasping ("gripple") developers and the fertile land:

> My many goodly sites when first I came to show,
> Here opened I the way to mine own overthrow:
> For, when the world found out the fitness of my soil,
> The gripple wretch began immediately to spoil
> My tall and goodly woods, and did my grounds inclose:
> By which, in little time my bounds I came to lose.[5]

As Stow recorded, the rural workers organized a response to these conditions – marched, rioted, protested, cut down hedges, filled up ditches – and much of the most serious unrest took place in Warwickshire, Shakespeare's county. He himself was a landowner and had been fined for hoarding grain. In 1605, he had bought a house in Stratford from William Combe, the high sheriff of the county, and it was Combe, in that capacity, who reported the following to Lord Salisbury in June 1608:

> I am overbold to acquaint your Lordship with such grievances as the common people of this county ... are troubled with: dearth of corn, the prices rising to

some height, caused partly by some that are well stored, by refraining to bring the same to market out of covetous conceit that corn will be dearer.... The matters make the people arrogantly and seditiously to speak of the not reforming of conversion of arable land into pasture by enclosing.[6]

The conflict between rich and poor was not only a rural problem. Many in the first London audiences would remember the civil unrest of the 1590s, particularly the insurrections that broke out in 1595 in London, where at least thirteen separate incidents included riots when apprentices attempted to seize overpriced food such as butter and fish. These are exactly the sort of conflicts, in town and country, with which the play opens with the citizens planning to mutiny:

> You are all resolved rather to die than to famish?
> ...
> Let us kill him [Coriolanus] and we'll have corn at our own price.
>
> (1.1.3–4, 9–10)

The leading citizen compares their starving situation to that of their well-fed leaders:

> We are accounted poor citizens, the patricians good. What authority surfeits on would relieve us. If they would yield us but the superfluity while it were wholesome, we might guess they relieved us humanely, but they think we are too dear. The leanness that afflicts us, the object of our misery, is as an inventory to particularize their abundance; our sufferance is a gain to them. Let us revenge this with our pikes, ere we become rakes; for the gods know I speak this is hunger for bread, not in thirst for revenge. (13–21)

Few situations could be more topical and this is a perfect hook for the audience: while the groundlings might well see this scene as sympathetic to their plight, the wealthier will be reassured shortly when Menenius appears, assuring the citizens that of course the patricians have their best interests at heart and recounting the famous parable of the belly. The belly, he argues, is a part of the body that *appears* to do no work but in fact supports the rest of the body or the state. The senators of Rome are the belly generously distributing food to the rest of the body. The relevance of this debate is captured by Francis Bacon, who also uses the belly analogy, in his description of sedition written in the same period as the play:

> The causes and motives of seditions are, innovation in religion; taxes; alteration of laws and customs; breaking of privileges; general oppression; advancement of unworthy persons; strangers; dearths; disbanded soldiers; factions grown desperate; and whatsoever, in offending people, joineth and knitteth them in a common cause.[7]

While clearly reflecting contemporary social concerns, *Coriolanus* is also evidence of the widespread interest in the classical world and what was regarded as the civilized and civilizing literature of ancient Greece and Rome. Its study was integral to education in the grammar schools and universities and its literary legacy, reinforced by later Latinate writers, underpinned much drama and narrative poetry of the period. While translations of Virgil, Ovid, and Plutarch provided plots and Seneca influenced the style and structure of tragedies and history plays, classical figures and their activities offered authoritative exemplars in different sorts of writing and modes of thought, with the implicit assumption that these early texts were instructional and moral. So in addition to their literary legacy, they informed current ideas about humanism and republicanism. In issues of governance and civil and military matters particularly, it was the ancient world and the actions of its leaders that were the reference points and examples. Thus King James I, writing instructions to his son in *Basilicon Doron* (1599) while he was still King James VI of Scotland, used biblical and later Christian allusions to illustrate personal conduct, but used examples from antiquity when touching on law, justice, and military conduct. He wrote of Caesar, for example: "For I have ever been of that opinion, that of all the Ethnick Emperors, or great Captains that ever were, he hath farthest excelled, both in his practise, and in his precepts in martial affairs." He quoted Plutarch too when advocating horsemanship as the best activity for a prince, alluding to Philip speaking of his son Alexander: "especially use such games on horseback as may teach you to handle your arms thereon; such as the tilt, the ring, and low-riding for the handling of your sword."[8] William Segar employed more explicit classical examples to illustrate the first book in his *Honor Military, and Civill* of 1602, where almost all of his thirty-five short chapters concerning the conduct of soldiers employed figures and actions from antiquity to support his intention to:

> Reasonably incite all young gentlemen to employ their time in study of moral and military virtue; thereby to become serviceable to their Prince, profitable to their country, and worthy of all honourable estimation and advancement.[9]

The source of Shakespeare's plot is Thomas North's translation of Plutarch's *Lives of Noble Grecians and Romans*, first published in 1579, in which he too saw a pedagogical, moral function in accounts of the classical world, as he indicated in his preface:

> Stories are fit for every place, reach to all persons, serve for all times, teach the living, revive the dead, so far excelling all other books, as it is better to see learning in noble men's lives, than read it in Philosophers' writings.

North used a French translation for his version (Jacques Amyot), which he probably encountered when he was living in France with his brother, an ambassador at the court of Henri III. Although North is best remembered now as a translator, it is sometimes overlooked that he moved in powerful circles and had a career as a soldier, serving in Ireland and helping to put down the Essex Rebellion. This style of life and his allegiances certainly disposed him to think well of powerful figures, as is evident in the character analysis that opens his introduction to *The Life and Times of Caius Martius Coriolanus*. His knowledge of statecraft and, particularly, his military experience clearly inform his account: the weapons, armor, targets, horses, and battle plans are distinctly Elizabethan rather than Roman.

It is not difficult to see how such an intriguing character as Coriolanus – conflicted, as it might now be said, with both good and bad qualities, and both admired and hated – was immediately appealing to the playwright. Shakespeare took more than the character from Plutarch/North; the play contains the longest continuous passage that he borrowed from any source – Volumnia's plea to her son to save Rome and his response. The playwright also made some changes to create a more relevant context: in the source, the unrest is about the lack of protection from unscrupulous moneylenders, and while Shakespeare makes a passing reference to usury, his citizens are concerned with food shortages. Plutarch, too, is more sympathetic to the people of Rome, some of whom have wounds from earlier military action and are refusing to go to further wars, while Shakespeare makes his protesters noncombatants, thus exaggerating the difference between the military and the civil.

In addition to the contemporary contexts of the Midland Revolt, the source, and interest in the classical world, Elizabethan and Jacobean engagement with warfare should not be overlooked. Between 1585 and 1603, at least 105,800 men were conscripted for military service overseas in the Netherlands, at sea on the coasts of Spain and Portugal, in France, and in Ireland out of a population of about 4,000,000.[10] It is reasonable to assume, given the high proportion of adult males, that a significant number of audience members had immediate experience of warfare, military life, or its effects, and that stage representations of battles and hand-to-hand fighting had a particular resonance and relevance. The figures point as well to another contemporary source of civil unrest. A letter from Edward Hext, justice of the peace in Somerset, to Lord Burleigh, dated September 25, 1596, describes the "thieves and robbers that are abroad in this County" and the "lewd young men of England ... devoted to this wicked course of life":

> The most dangerous are the wandering soldiers and other stout rogues of England ... of these sort of wandering idle people there are three or four

hundred in a shire ... [who] do meet either at fair or market, or in some Alehouse once a week. And in a great hay house in a remote place there did resort weekly ... where they did roast all kind of good meat.[11]

He went on to describe how the soldiers evaded capture and punishment either by the intimidation of justices and court officers or "through intelligence of all things intended against them" achieved through attending court disguised as "honest husbandmen." Hext is describing a pressing problem: vagrancy and vagabondage were widespread after the armada and particularly during the summer of 1589 following the expedition to Portugal. Thousands of demobilized and unemployed soldiers wandered the countryside looting and pillaging to support themselves. Legislation in 1593 eventually provided ex-soldiers with travel licenses and pensions after 500 had threatened to loot Bartholomew Fair, but the problem remained. These further examples of civil unrest, particularly with their military connotations, add to an understanding of the original reception of the play.

But, without wishing to generalize and stereotype, where does that leave the women in the audience? That leads to Shakespeare's masterstroke in this play: the use he makes of three female characters – Volumnia, Coriolanus's mother, his wife, Virgilia, and Valeria their companion. In the source material, Volumnia is a passive and indulgent parent; in Shakespeare, she becomes ambitious, proud, and political. She wants him to become consul, delights in his martial activity, which she has encouraged since childhood, gloats over the number of his wounds, and is a bully, or at the very least an emotional manipulator, when she persuades Coriolanus to save Rome. The women become essential to the plot and not simply to characterization, although Volumnia's role in determining Coriolanus's personality is evident from the first act: she waits, with Virgilia, for news of the battle. She recalls his boyhood, encouraging him to seek danger, sending him intentionally to a cruel war, and Valeria adds an approving anecdote about him tearing the wings off butterflies. As Volumnia imagines Coriolanus's battle triumph against Aufidius, she revels that he may be returning wounded and with a bloody brow, which appalls his wife. Volumnia responds to her: "Away, you fool! It more becomes a man / Than gilt his trophy" (1.3.36–37).

The few words given to Coriolanus's son, Young Martius, "I'll run away till I am bigger, but then I'll fight" (5.3.128), reinforce the sense of nurture as well as nature that dominate the play and are reminders too that contemporary shifts in the perception, understanding, and interpretation of history were leading to different explanations of human behavior; it had less to do with divine providence or the wheel of fortune or contested theology than with character. So the fates of Shakespeare's Roman military heroes – Titus,

Antony, or Coriolanus, say – are not preordained or inevitable but determined by character and actions, and unlike other great warriors, Othello or Macbeth, the behavior of Coriolanus is explained by his upbringing.

## The Play and Its Afterlives

While warfare is a significant part of the plot or backstory in almost all of Shakespeare's tragedies, it is most prominent in the Roman plays and integral to *Coriolanus*. Here military life, its sources and effects, drives the drama and makes plot and character inseparable. Conventional warfare is confined to the first act with subsequent scenes exploring the aftermath of the actions of a military hero but a flawed human being, typifying the Aristotelian definition of a virtue concerned with honor: pride or megalopsychia, where two different qualities – resentment of injury and indifference to fortune – are combined. Class warfare and a dysfunctional family exaggerate and emphasize the conflict that drives the play.

There are no records of early seventeenth-century performances, so the only evidence of staging is the first published text in the 1623 Folio, where it is the first play of the tragedies section. It has remarkably elaborate stage directions and scholars have long argued, inconclusively, whether they are authorial. The editor of the Oxford edition (R. B. Parker), for example, suggests that when he wrote *Coriolanus* Shakespeare was already in semi-retirement in Stratford and provided particularly detailed stage directions so that the theater company back in London would know exactly what he wanted. Others argue that the stage directions were written by a scribe preparing the text for publication, for readers, and perhaps recording what he'd seen on stage. In either case, they deserve attention, potentially reflecting contemporary performances that probably first took place in the indoor theater at Blackfriars in 1609. They are frequently permissive and descriptive, as is evident from the opening conflict of the play: not simply "Enter citizens" as might be expected but the detailed "Enter a company of mutinous citizens, with staves, clubs, and other weapons." Thus dissent is immediately evident before any lines are spoken and is indicated visually by the characters' demeanor and props. Similarly, when the citizens leave the stage they "steal away" rather than simply "exit," guiding the response of actors, audience, or readers.

The second conflict, the warfare between the Romans and the Volsces, is similarly detailed:

> They all shout and wave their swords, take him up in their arms, and cast up their caps. (1.7.76 SD)

Titus Lartius, having set a guard upon Corioles, going with drum and trumpet toward Cominius and Caius Martius, enters with a Lieutenant, other soldiers and a Scout. (1.8)

A long flourish. They all cry "Martius, Martius," cast up their caps and lances. Cominius and Lartius stand bare. (1.9.40)

While these stage directions are certainly visual and indicate actions and gestures, weapons and costume, status and relationships, they are also concerned with the sounds of warfare, and *Coriolanus* has more stage directions for music than any other play in the canon. In the offstage battle scenes of the first act, for example, the sound effects of drums, trumpets, and cornets contribute to the general activity but also identify each faction: trumpets are associated with the Romans and cornets with the Volsces. The sounds are aural signals of battle success so that the scene often referred to as the "Triumphal March" in act 2, scene 1 begins with a fanfare (sennet): "A sennet. Trumpets sound. Enter Cominius the general and Titus Lartius; between them, Coriolanus, crowned with an oaken garland, with Captains and Soldiers and a Herald" (2.1.150 SD). The moment has often been expanded significantly in performance so that the advertisement for Sheridan's adaptation of the early 1750s announced "In the Military procession alone, independent of the Civil, there were an hundred and eighteen persons." While this is unlikely to reflect original staging, Elizabethan and Jacobean Londoners were familiar with celebratory processions such as the moment recorded in the portrait of the queen, attributed to Robert Peake (c. 1601), in which she is carried aloft and processes to Westminster, accompanied by noblemen, to give thanks for the defeat of the Spanish Armada.

The stage direction that concludes the play, "Exeunt, bearing the body of Martius, a dead march is sounded," indicates action and music, and in addition to indicating a formal exit to the beat of a muffled drum, reminds the audience that they have just witnessed the death of a great military man.

While this has been described as Shakespeare's noisiest play,[12] it is a remarkable moment of silence that is particularly affecting onstage. In act 5, scene 3, Coriolanus is approached by his wife, mother, young son, and Valeria to plead with him to save Rome. It's a tense scene and the stakes are high, for Cominius and Menenius have already tried and failed on the same mission. The text and the directions are very clear and their actions support their words as curtseys, bows, kneeling, kisses, and tears are all indicated. Eventually Volumnia prevails and the direction tells us that Coriolanus "holds her by the hand, silent" before crying "O mother, mother! / What have you done?" (5.3.182–83). That silence is electrifying as Coriolanus, who has always refused to compromise, realizes that "a happy victory to

Rome" is "most mortal to him" (186, 189). Conflicted between his mother's demands and his own determination not to change his mind, he has capitulated and in so doing has signed his own death warrant. It is this moment that has often dominated the afterlife of the play.

For his 1744 edition of Shakespeare, Sir Thomas Hanmer gave detailed instructions to the artist Francis Hayman of the scenes that he wanted illustrated for each play. For *Coriolanus* he specified act 5, scene 3 and described his desired composition as follows:

> A plain with the Volscian camp at a little distance backwards. Coriolanus and Aufidius two Generals in martial habits. Volumnia mother to Coriolanus, Virgilia his wife, Valeria the Wife's friend, and the boy Martius his son all kneel before Coriolanus. Volumnia being foremost holds up her hands closed together as in the action of prayer. Coriolanus stooping presses her hands between his as with relenting pity. Aufidius stands by sternly frowning with a discontented look.[13]

The result is certainly an attractive composition and the moment of domestic rather than military tension was later replicated by Gavin Hamilton, the Scottish painter of classical scenes, for Boydell's Shakespeare Gallery of 1789, but it reflects an incident in the play that Hanmer has visualized through reading rather than performance. Until David Garrick's nine show run at Drury Lane in 1754, staged largely to compete with Sheridan's popular adaptation at Covent Garden, the play as written by Shakespeare was unknown to eighteenth-century audiences. Yet even illustrations ostensibly associated with performance focused on Volumnia, suggesting that interest was less military or political than personally emotional. Thus the two *Corionalus* images from *Bell's Shakespeare* are both of Volumnia in similar poses of kneeling supplication: James Roberts's portrait of Elizabeth Hopkins (published February 12, 1776, engraved by C. Grignion) and E. F. Burney's image of Mary Ann Yates (published August 22, 1786, engraved by J. Thornwhaite).[14] In fact these pictures reflect an interpolated moment from the popular adaptations: as part of her supplications Volumnia draws a dagger from beneath her costume and threatens suicide. The role – and this moment – became the best-known features of the play and associated with the skill of great actresses even if, as is the case with Hopkins and Yates, they never played the part.

*Coriolanus* as written by Shakespeare has a checkered performance history and has never proved the easiest play to stage: until the nineteenth century it was only presented in adapted or heavily cut versions, largely because of the complexity of the title character who is neither a clear-cut hero nor villain. He is undoubtedly a great fighter, a successful soldier who can inspire love and respect and finally saves Rome, yet he treats the citizens with contempt and struggles to compromise. Some find his qualities admirable, while on the other hand, the mob, the starving populace, certainly has a good case but is fickle and ill-served by its representatives, the Tribunes. That certainly elicits some sympathy, but such ambivalence has confused and concerned those who prefer less complexity in a tragic hero. Brian Vickers has made the point that Coriolanus "exists not as a free individual but as a man with a role to play on behalf of others"[15] and manipulated for the benefit of others: for his mother as a soldier and consul; for the patricians as a consul to pursue their own desire for power; for the tribunes as a figure greedy for fame and status, and an extension of class hatred. This idea may be extended into responses to the play: Coriolanus has a role to play on behalf of theater directors, critics, and those working in other media.

So what is noticeable is that productions have tended to ignore the complexities, Shakespeare's subtleties, the ambivalence, and plump instead to support one side or the other, either Coriolanus or the democratic aspirations of the citizens, resulting in adaptations or cuts. The focus has often been on the political disturbance or conflict and reflected contemporary events. Thus Nahum Tate's adaptation *The Ingratitude of a Commonwealth; or, the Fall of Coriolanus* of 1681 was written as a protest against the anti-Catholic riots generated by the false rumors of a Popish Plot to murder Charles II. Then in 1719, John Dennis's adaptation, *The Invader of his Country; or, The Fatal Resentment* was a response to the Jacobite rebellion and attempted to generate patriotic sentiment. In 1789, John Philip Kemble's debut in the role coincided with the French Revolution and it was what Hazlitt, in the *Times* review of June 25, 1817, when the actor retired from the stage, described as his "haughty dignity of demeanour" that perfectly suited the anti-Republican interpretation of the adapted plot and established the tone that would endure into the twentieth century. It was Hazlitt, too, who drew attention to the relevance of *Coriolanus* to contemporary politics:

> Anyone who studies it may save himself the trouble of reading Burke's Reflections, or Paine's Rights of Man, or the Debates in both Houses of Parliament since the French Revolution or our own. The arguments for and against aristocracy or democracy, on the privileges of the few and the claims of the many, on liberty and slavery, power and the abuse of it, peace and war, are here very ably handled, with the spirit of a poet and the acuteness of a philosopher.[16]

Kemble's Coriolanus was clearly a military figure and his pose and facial expression in Sir Thomas Lawrence's portrait are remarkably similar to the same artist's portrait of the Duke of Wellington after his success at the Battle of Waterloo in 1815.

It was Kemble and to a lesser extent his immediate successors on the London stage, Edmund Kean and William Macready, who made the role and the play sufficiently familiar for it to form the basis of Cruikshank's 1820 cartoon "Coriolanus addressing the Plebeians," in which George IV, clearly well-fed and well-dressed in Roman attire, addresses a ragged mob of armed plebeians wearing the distinctive red caps associated with workers' revolts and with banners proclaiming "Age of Reason," "Revolution," "Parliamentary Reform," and "Blood and Plunder." The king's address, written beneath the cartoon, is Coriolanus's first scene speech demanding "What would you have, you curs / That like nor peace nor war?" (1.1.159–60). The scene is ambiguous: Cruikshank himself is part of the mob yet also reproduced, in French, is a quotation from the naturalist and evolutionist de Buffon that appears to praise nobility. Unambiguous, however, were the prevailing social conditions that were not dissimilar to those in place in the period of the play's composition: the poor were suffering again after the economic stresses of the Napoleonic Wars – from poor harvests, high food prices, unemployment, overtaxation, and further enclosures. The play was becoming associated with contemporary civil strife and unrest.

In 1972–73, John Osborne reworked *Coriolanus* as *A Place Calling Itself Rome* set in contemporary Britain at the time of labor disputes and strikes. He followed the plot closely, adding a brief preliminary scene where Coriolanus (very much an "angry young man") is unable to sleep and is jotting down rather incoherent notes about his life. The second scene opens with Osborne's version of Shakespeare's first stage direction "Enter a company of mutinous citizens with staves, clubs and other weapons":

> a cross-section mob of students, fixers, pushers, policemen, unidentifiable public, obvious trade unionists, journalists and the odd news camera team, sound men etc, shrills of police horses, linked arms on all sides, screaming girls, banners of the nineteenth century sort, banners of the modern kind – "Caius Marcius go fuck yourself"; "We want a lay not delay."... Roman troops can be in flak jackets and helmets. Patricians like MPs or high ranking officers.[17]

Further details of a flag burning, stones thrown, a pop group joining in, precede the First Citizen yelling, "Hear me! Will you listen to me!" Osborne's equivalent of Shakespeare's line, "Before we proceed any further, hear me speak" (1.1.1). Subsequently, most of the text is Osborne's prose, although key moments, including stage directions, remain Shakespearian. Aufidius taunts Coriolanus as "boy,"[18] for example, and "Coriolanus holds his mother by the hand, silent,"[19] while Aufidius's final instruction

"Take him up" becomes the moment that Coriolanus's body is lifted to a helicopter while a piper plays a lament.

Shakespeare's version, rather than such adaptations, has of course often been performed and frequently with a star actor in the demanding title role – Sir Laurence Olivier, Alan Howard, Sir Ian McKellen, Tom Hiddleston – in productions that emphasized the military skill and heroism of Coriolanus (particularly evident, from the late twentieth century onwards, in the publicity shots that focused on the bare, blood-spattered chest of the leading man), but "conflict" has been most evident in productions and responses to them that took place in the twentieth century during the rise of fascism and gave the play a renewed topicality. In France in 1934, for example, the political party Action Française persuaded the Comédie-Française to present the play in a new translation as an assault on democracy, provoking violent demonstrations between royalists and fascists, on the one hand, and government supporters, on the other. The year after this, in a version approved by Stalin, a production in Moscow treated Coriolanus as a contemptible, aristocratic enemy of the people. Shortly afterwards in Germany, the Nazis adopted *Coriolanus* as a school text to show Hitler Youth the weaknesses of democracy and promoted Coriolanus as a heroic führer leading his people, "as Adolf Hitler in our days wishes to lead our beloved German fatherland." Immediately after the war the US army of occupation banned the play until 1953.[20] At the time of his death in 1956, Bertolt Brecht was working on a version of the play, reflecting Marxist theories of the class struggle, which was performed throughout Europe and the United States in the 1960s. It came to further prominence when Günter Grass produced *The Plebeians Rehearse the Uprising*, which showed Brecht rehearsing his play while ignoring the real-life East Berlin workers' protest that was happening at the same time. Other productions, if not resembling or reflecting contemporary conflicts, have chosen an identifiable setting that will give the audience a recognizable peg to locate the action and immediately identify conflict. Thus, David Thacker's 1994 production for the RSC was clearly set during the French Revolution with a huge rear-stage copy of Delacroix's canvas of *Liberty Guiding the People*. The 2011 film directed by and starring Ralph Fiennes was shot in Serbia and has reminded many viewers of events in the former Yugoslavia.

William J. Thoms, whose conjectures about Shakespeare's soldiering opened this chapter, had little personal military experience: he owned that he was "called upon to shoulder a brown bess" in April 1848 but acknowledged his ineptitude, recognizing that "if unhappily compelled to use it, it might peradventure prove more dangerous to my Conservative friends than to the noisy Chartists against whom its fire would have been really directed."[21] There is a clear assumption that in a domestic military conflict (and here he is writing of the Chartist riots, the working class movement for parliamentary reform) he, his readers, and Shakespeare himself would have been on the same side. Unwittingly, however, he points to a further political appropriation of *Coriolanus*. He was perhaps unaware that in 1842 Thomas Cooper of Leicester had compiled a *Shakespearean Chartist Hymnbook*,[22] learned whole plays by heart, lectured on Shakespeare to his fellow Chartists, and when charged with inciting a riot in the Potteries staged a performance of *Hamlet* to raise money for his defense. At the same time, the regular column in the Yorkshire-based and best-selling weekly newspaper the *Northern Star*, called "Chartism from Shakespeare," found precursors of the People's Charter in a number of Shakespeare's plays. It quoted from *King John*, *Julius Caesar*, and *2 Henry IV*, citing passages as precedents for parliamentary reform and making particular use of some of the citizens' speeches from the opening scene of *Coriolanus*:

> Our sufferance is a gain to them. Let us revenge this with our pikes, ere we become rakes.... Suffer us to famish, and their storehouses crammed with grain ... repeal daily any wholesome act established against the rich, and provide more piercing statutes daily to chain up and restrain the poor.[23]

Such textual familiarity has not been sustained to the present day, however, and while occasionally featuring as an A Level play in the UK, *Coriolanus* has rarely provided the reference points and allusions in popular culture of Shakespeare's other tragedies. A minor exception is the rivalry between the Romans and the Volsces that, along with the enduring tensions caused by Italy's role in World War II, form an intermittent part of the background to Elly Griffiths's crime novel *The Dark Angel* (2018).[24] On the other hand, poets have often been fascinated by the politics and violence of the play. Coleridge, for example, admired what he believed to be "The wonderful philosophic impartiality in Shakespeare's politics" that he saw in the text and was intrigued by the disparity between the beauty of Aufidius's "All places yield to him" speech (4.7.28–57) and the speaker's intention.[25] T. S. Eliot, who in his 1919 article "Hamlet and His Problems" in the *Athenaeum* described *Coriolanus* as "Shakespeare's most assured artistic success," and referenced it in *The Waste Land*, used the plot as the impetus for his unfinished verse sequence *Coriolan*. Written in 1931, it clearly reflected the rise of fascism in Europe and "Triumphal March," one of two completed sections, includes a listing of armaments used in the First World War. It was in the 1930s too that Yeats, flirting with fascism, attempted to influence the performance of the play in 1936 in the Abbey Theatre, Dublin, as described by Frank O'Connor:

> It had just been produced in Paris in coloured shirts and caused a riot. Yeats demanded that we produce it in coloured shirts among our European classics, in the hope that, as in France, a Dublin audience might riot.[26]

Later the poet Geoffrey Hill became intrigued by the play and, particularly, the ambivalent responses of Eliot and Yeats to its morality, politics, violence, and attitudes to warfare.[27]

While *Coriolanus* may have little to do with Shakespeare's personal experience of warfare, it certainly reflects contemporary events and interest in the classical world and, while ostensibly a play about conflict between Rome and the Volsces with a flawed military hero, offers a commentary on the use and abuse of power, allegiances, and leadership that has engaged playwrights, directors, and poets for 350 years: it is not difficult, as I write in 2018, to see its continued relevance.

*Further Reading*

Barlow, Adrian (ed.). Special issue on the literature of the First World War, *The Use of English*, 65 (Spring 2014).

Barton, Ann. "Livy, Machiavelli, and Shakespeare's *Coriolanus*," in Catherine M. S. Alexander (ed.), *Shakespeare and Politics*, Cambridge, Cambridge University Press, 2004, pp. 67–90.

Bristol, Michael D. "Lenten Butchery: Legitimation Crisis in *Coriolanus*," in Jean E. Howard and Marion F. O'Connor (eds.), *Shakespeare Reproduced: The Text in History and Ideology*, London, Methuen, 1987, pp. 207–24.

Dessen, Alan C., and Leslie Thomson. *A Dictionary of Stage Directions in English Drama, 1580–1642*, Cambridge, Cambridge University Press, 1999.

Dobson, Michael. *The Making of the National Poet: Shakespeare, Adaptation and Authorship, 1660–1769*, Oxford, Clarendon, 1992.

Dollimore, Jonathan, and Alan Sinfield (eds.). *Political Shakespeare: New Essays in Cultural Materialism*, Manchester, Manchester University Press, 1985.

Edgar, David. *How Plays Work*, London, Nick Hern Books, 2009.

Hawkes, Terence. *Meaning by Shakespeare*, London, Routledge, 1992.

Kahn, Coppélia. *Roman Shakespeare: Warriors, Wounds, and Women*, New York, Routledge, 1997.

Kraye, Jill (ed.). *The Cambridge Companion to Renaissance Humanism*, Cambridge, Cambridge University Press, 1996.

## NOTES

1 William J. Thoms, "Was Shakespeare Ever a Soldier?," in *Three Notelets on Shakespeare* (London: John Russell Smith, 1865), pp. 115–36.

2 Thoms, "Was Shakespeare Ever a Soldier?," p. 123.

3 Thoms, "Was Shakespeare Ever a Soldier?," p. 130.

4 Edmund Howes, *The Annals, or, General Chronicle of England* [...] *vnto the Ende of This Present Yeere 1614* (London, 1615), p. 889.

5 Michael Drayton, *Poly-Olbion* (London, 1612–13), song 13, ll. 19–24.

6 *State Papers Domestic: James I*, vol. xxxiv, p. 4, quoted in R. B. Parker (ed.), *The Tragedy of Coriolanus*, by William Shakespeare, The Oxford Shakespeare (Oxford: Oxford University Press, 1994), p. 34.

7 Francis Bacon, *The Essays or Counsels Civil and Moral*, ed. Brian Vickers (Oxford: Oxford University Press, 1999), p. 34.

8 Johann P. Sommerville (ed.), *King James VI and I: Political Writings* (Cambridge: Cambridge University Press, 1994), pp. 46, 56.

9 William Segar, *Honor Military and Civill, contained in foure Bookes* (London: Robert Parker, 1602), n.p.

10 These figures are from John Morrill, *The Oxford Illustrated History of Tudor and Stuart Britain* (Oxford: Oxford University Press, 1996), p. 338. Estimates inevitably vary.

11 Edward Hext to Lord Burleigh, September 25, 1596, MS, Lansdowne 81, nos. 62, 64, British Museum.

12 Adrian Poole, *Coriolanus*, Harvester New Critical Introductions to Shakespeare (London: Harvester Wheatsheaf, 1988), p. xii.

13 Marcia Allentuck, "Sir Thomas Hanmer Instructs Francis Hayman: An Editor's Notes to His Illustrator," *Shakespeare Quarterly*, 27 (1976), pp. 288–315.

14 Kalman A. Burnim and Philip H. Highfill Jr., *John Bell, Patron of British Theatrical Portraiture: A Catalog of the Theatrical Portraits in His Editions of "Bell's Shakespeare" and "Bell's British Theatre"* (Carbondale: Southern Illinois University Press, 1998), pp. 57, 83.

15 Brian Vickers, *Shakespeare: Coriolanus* (London: Edward Arnold, 1976), p. 19.

16 William Hazlitt, *Characters of Shakespear's Plays* (London: R. Hunter et al., 1817), p. 69.

17 John Osborne, *A Place Calling Itself Rome* (London: Faber, 1973), p. 13.

18 Osborne, *A Place Calling Itself Rome*, p. 77.

19 Osborne, *A Place Calling Itself Rome*, p. 73.

20 This information is recorded and referenced in Philip Brockbank (ed.), *Coriolanus*, by William Shakespeare, The Arden Shakespeare (London: Methuen, 1976), p. 86, but is disputed by Balz Engler, "The Noise That Banish'd Martius: *Coriolanus* in Post-War Germany," in Boika Sokolova and Evgenia Pancheva (eds.), *Renaissance Refractions: Essays in Honour of Alexander Shurbanov* (Sofia: St. Kliment Ohridski University Press, 2001), pp. 179–86.

21 Thoms, "Was Shakespeare Ever a Soldier?," p. 124.

22 Thomas Cooper, *The Life of Thomas Cooper* (London: Hodder and Stoughton, 1897), esp. ch. 21, "Chartist Life Continued: Sturge Conference: Second Trial: 1842–1843."

23 Antony Taylor, "Shakespeare and Radicalism: The Uses and Abuses of Shakespeare in Nineteenth-Century Popular Politics," *The Historical Journal*, 45 (2002), pp. 357–79, 367.

24 Elly Griffiths, *The Dark Angel* (London: Quercus, 2018).

25 Samuel Taylor Coleridge, in Terence Hawkes (ed.), *Coleridge's Writings on Shakespeare* (Harmondsworth: Penguin, 1969), p. 275.

26 Frank O'Connor, *My Father's Son* (London: Macmillan, 1968), p. 152.

27 Karl O'Hanlon, "Noble in His Grandiose Confusions: Yeats and *Coriolanus* in the Poetry of Geoffrey Hill," *English*, 65 (2016), pp. 211–33; Peter Kishore Savac, *Shakespeare in Hate: Emotions, Passions, Selfhood* (London: Routledge, 2015), esp. ch. 2, "Rage in the World"; Christopher Ricks, "Hill's Unrelenting, Unreconciling Mind," in John Lyon and Peter McDonald (eds.), *Geoffrey Hill: Essays on His Later Work* (Oxford: Oxford University Press, 2012), pp. 6–31; and Geoffrey Hill, "How Not to Be a Hero" (lecture on interpretations of *Coriolanus*, October 21, 2000, BBC Radio 3).

# INDEX